ESSAYS IN LEGAL THEORY

Law and Philosophy Library

VOLUME 46

The titles published in this series are listed at the end of this volume.

ESSAYS
IN LEGAL THEORY

ROBERT S. SUMMERS

*William G. McRoberts Research Professor of Law, Cornell Law School, and
Arthur L. Goodhart Visiting Professor of Legal Science, Cambridge University, 1991-92.
B.S. 1955, U. of Oregon; LL.B. 1959, Harvard Law School; Doctor of Laws, Honoris
Causa, U. of Helsinki, 1990; Doctor of Laws, Honoris Causa, U. of Göttingen, 1994*

KLUWER ACADEMIC PUBLISHERS
DORDRECHT / BOSTON / LONDON

A C.I.P. Catalogue record for this book is available from the Library of Congress.

ISBN 0-7923-6367-1

Published by Kluwer Academic Publishers,
P.O. Box 17, 3300 AA Dordrecht, The Netherlands.

Sold and distributed in North, Central and South America
by Kluwer Academic Publishers,
101 Philip Drive, Norwell, MA 02061, U.S.A.

In all other countries, sold and distributed
by Kluwer Academic Publishers,
P.O. Box 322, 3300 AH Dordrecht, The Netherlands.

Printed on acid-free paper

Printed in the Netherlands.

DEDICATION

TO

DOROTHY KOPP SUMMERS

COPYRIGHT ACKNOWLEDGMENTS

Congress of IVR pp. 412-419, Franz Steiner Verlag, Stuttgart Germany, 1997.

TABLE OF CONTENTS

PART THREE
LEGAL REASONING

PART FOUR
CONTRACT THEORY

PART FIVE
CRITIQUE OF ECONOMIC ANALYSIS OF LAW

PREFACE

As I explain in the introduction, this is the third in a series of collections of my previously published essays in legal theory. All of the essays here but three have been revised for this volume. I now wish to record my gratitude and indebtedness to various persons. I am most indebted and grateful to my wife, Dorothy Kopp Summers, to whom I dedicate this book. I also wish to record my gratitude for his interest and patience to Hendrik-Jan van Leusen of Kluwer Academic Publishers. He strongly encouraged me to put this collection together, and without his efforts, it certainly would not have appeared in this timely fashion. I also wish to thank his successor, Sabine Wesseldijk, for assistance.

In the course of my academic career, I have benefitted greatly from the many Cornell Law School students serving as my research assistants. I have also been privileged to have the fine aid of many Cornell Law School secretaries and administrative assistants. Foremost here is Mrs. Pamela Finnigan who has so ably seen this collection put together from start to finish. Several deans and faculty colleagues have also been highly supportive, and I thank them warmly. I also wish to give special thanks to Dr. Geoffrey Marshall, Dr. Peter Hacker, and Dr. John Lucas of the University of Oxford, to Professor D. Neil MacCormick of the University of Edinburgh, to Professors Enrico Pattero and Michele Taruffo of the Universities of Bologna and Pavia respectively, to Professor Dr. Ralf Dreier of the University of Göttingen, and especially to Professor Dr. Okko Behrends also of the University of Göttingen, for many illuminating letters and discussions on various themes in the book. I also thank Prof. Dr. Aulis Aarnio of the University of Tampere for many helpful comments over the years on several of the essays here.

Robert S. Summers

Ithaca, New York
December, 1999

INTRODUCTION

The sixteen essays here, all addressed to important contemporary issues in legal theory, have except two, been previously published, but I have revised all but three for appearance in this collection. The essays originally appeared in journals published in several countries: the United States, Great Britain, Germany, and Italy. These journals are themselves diverse, some devoted to law, some to philosophy, to legal theory, and some to interdisciplinary scholarship. The earliest essay here appeared in 1981, the latest in 1999. Yet the essays all fall within the field of legal theory, and are devoted to overlapping and connected themes. It is thus appropriate as well as convenient to have them drawn together in a single volume, which will be the third in a series of volumes collecting my previously published essays. The earlier two volumes are *Essays on the Nature of Law and Legal Reasoning* published in 1991 by Duncker & Humblot of Berlin, and *The Jurisprudence of Law's Form and Substance*, published in 2000 by Dartmouth Pub. Co. in Great Britain.

The sixteen essays published here are organized under five categories the first of which is "the general theory of law." The first essay, on H.L.A. Hart's *The Concept of Law*, identifies the contributions of one of the two leading books in legal theory in the twentieth century, and includes a personal memorial. The essay in Chapter Two is concerned with the work of the great 19th Century German jurist at the University of Göttingen, Rudolf von Jhering, and focuses on the considerable influence he seems to have had on leading American legal theorists, especially Lon L. Fuller (1902-1978), Karl N. Llewellyn (1893-1962), Roscoe Pound (1870-1964), and Oliver Wendell Holmes, Jr. (1841-1935).

In Chapter Three, on "Law As A Type of Machine Technology," I offer correctives to the widespread resort in American legal theory of the twentieth century to technological metaphors in characterizations of law. These metaphors abound in the works of such leading legal realist thinkers as Karl N. Llewellyn, who even wrote that law is "an engine (a heterogeneous multitude of engines)." Chapter Four is entitled "On Identifying and Reconstructing a General Legal Theory". In this essay, I address the problem of rationally reconstructing the basic tenets of the dominant twentieth century legal theory in the United States. That theory is often called "legal realism," but I argue it is better denominated "pragmatic instrumentalism". Chapter Five, called "My Philosophy of Law" is just that, and it reflects my work to date on that cluster of themes, with emphasis on my most recent work on form, law, and legal theory.

The set of essays, in Part Two, falls under the category "form in law". I define "form" mainly as the organization of legal phenomena such as institutions, rules, methodologies of application, and other functional units in a legal system. I view this as a vast neglected field of legal theory — indeed as the most important undeveloped branch of the entire subject, one on which I am now writing a book. The three essays here (Chapters Six, Seven and Eight) represent disparate yet related treatments of the place of form in the fundamentals of law. Chapter Five in Part One is highly relevant here, too.

In the four chapters in Part Three on legal reasoning, the focus is on interpreting statutes, on applying precedents, and on the reasoning that figures in judicial fact-finding. In Chapter Nine, "Interpreting Statutes and Precedents — Two Comparative Studies", I summarize major substantive and methodological themes set forth in two books co-authored by the members of the Bielefelder Kreis, a circle of mainly European scholars from ten countries who met annually over fifteen years under the co-chairmanship of myself and Professor D. Neil MacCormick of the University of Edinburgh. The two volumes to which I refer are *Interpreting Statutes — A Comparative Study* (Dartmouth Pub. Co. 1991), and *Interpreting Precedents — A Comparative Study* (Dartmouth Pub. Co. 1997). These works are being well received, and Professor MacCormick and I feel most privileged to have had the opportunity to be a part of such a rewarding joint enterprise. I am especially indebted to Professor MacCormick for so much stimulating co-operation, his extraordinary insight, his generosity, and his friendship.

Part Three on legal reasoning includes three further chapters: "The Argument From Ordinary Meaning in Statutory Interpretation," "Interpreting Statutes — Should Courts Consider Materials of Legislative History?", and "Formal Legal Truth and Substantive Legal Truth in Judicial Fact-Finding," titles that aptly convey the subject matter. The first named essay delves into the complexities of language-oriented argumentation in the interpretation of statutes in England and the United States. This essay, at the least, demonstrates that some academic writers in some countries may be too ready to dismiss language-oriented arguments as "conclusory", "literalist", or "wooden". The essay indicates how, in a variety of ways, the resources of ordinary language argumentation are rich and deep. I co-authored the essay with Dr. Geoffrey Marshall, recently Provost of The Queen's College, Oxford University, and member of the Oxford University politics faculty, from whom I have never ceased to learn about interpretation since we first co-taught a seminar on the subject in Oxford University in 1965. The essay on the use of legislative history to interpret statutes is dedicated to Geoffrey Marshall in honor of his 70th birthday.

Part Four is on Contract Theory, an interest arising out of my teaching of the first year course in contracts mainly at the University of Oregon, and at Cornell University over a period of forty years. The first essay here, Chapter Thirteen, treats the various ways that the general obligation of good faith in the contract law of many Western countries can and should be conceptualized. The essay grows out of my earlier work on this subject which formed part of the foundation for the American Restatement of Contracts sec. 205 on good faith. The essay also draws on the writings of the Oxford analytic philosopher, J.L. Austin.

Part Four also includes Chapter Fourteen on "Substantive Justification in Contract Cases — The Primacy of Rightness Reasons." In this heretofore unpublished essay, I seek to demonstrate (1) that the justificatory force of some types of reasons for judicial decision in a contract case derives not from projected consequences of the decision which serve social goals, but rather from the way in which the decision accords with present or past regarding norms of rightness, and (2) that reasons of this latter kind appear to play a far larger role in the opinions of judges resolving basic issues in leading contract cases than consequentialist reasons.

In the final part of this book, Part Five, the two essays frontally address one of the most prominent new movements in Western legal theory — the economic analysis of law. Chapter Fifteen poses some of the obstacles to the attempts of some economics minded scholars to reduce law, legal analysis, and legal theory to economics, economic analysis, and economic theory. Chapter Sixteen, co-authored with Leigh B. Kelley, one of the two or three ablest student assistants I have ever been privileged to work with, dissects and evaluates "economist's reasons" for judicial decisions in a detailed and extended fashion.

R.S.S.

Part One

General Theory of Law

CHAPTER 1

H.L.A. HART'S *THE CONCEPT OF LAW**

I. Introduction

Herbert Lionel Adolphus Hart, the leading figure in twentieth century Anglo-American jurisprudence, was born in Harrogate, England on 18 July 1907 and died at the age of 85 in Oxford on 19 December 1992[1]. As an undergraduate at New College, Oxford he "read" Literae Humaniores (Greek and Latin language, and ancient history and philosophy), taking his degree in 1929. Thereafter, he studied law privately and then practiced in London at the Chancery bar from 1932 until 1940. During the war, he was with MI5 (British military intelligence) and made a major contribution to the "false" D-Day landing plan which more or less successfully deceived the Nazi Command thereby facilitating the Normandy landings. Immediately after the war he returned to New College as a tutor and lecturer in philosophy.

In 1952, Hart was elected (by a slim margin) Professor of Jurisprudence in the University of Oxford to succeed Arthur L. Goodhart. (Earlier holders of the chair included Sir Frederick Pollock, Sir Paul Vinogradoff, and Sir Henry Maine.) Hart had neither a Ph.D. (nor its equivalent) in philosophy, nor a law degree. By 1952 he had advanced to 45 years of age, and in jurisprudence had published only one article and one book review. By American standards, it would very likely have been said at the time that Hart's academic credentials were insufficient, that he was virtually certain never to publish much, and that his election to the chair would therefore be a mistake. But Hart had been brilliant as an undergraduate at what at that time was one of England's two leading universities, had been a success at the bar over a period of nine years, and as tutor and lecturer at New College after the war, had achieved a reputation among fellow philosophers for quite extraordinary acumen and insight. After his election to the chair of jurisprudence in 1952, Hart launched a career of publication, lecturing, and other teaching that has been more important to the progress of western jurisprudence in the twentieth century than that of any other figure (save, possibly, Hans Kelsen). The central achievement in this singular career

1

occurred in 1961 when, at the age of 54, Hart published *The Concept of Law* with Oxford University Press[2]. Professor D. Neil MacCormick has remarked that this book "will be read wherever law is studied and English spoken (or the many other languages into which it was translated)"[3].

A "second edition" of *The Concept of Law* appeared in 1994, about two years after Hart's death. "Second edition" is a misnomer, for the 1994 version is the same as the 1961 edition except for minor corrections and a posthumous "Postscript" by Hart. Hart's Postscript of 38 pages, written over several years, includes sections on the nature of jurisprudence, legal positivism, rules, legal principles, the relation of law and morals, and judicial discretion. In most of the Postscript, Hart responds to Ronald M. Dworkin's criticisms of the first edition of *The Concept of Law*. Probably of most interest is Hart's response to Dworkin's argument that Hart's theory of legal validity cannot (conceptually) account for the recognition of principles as a major form of valid law[4]. Hart's theory includes "source-oriented" criteria which determine the validity of putative law by reference to "adoption by a recognized authoritative source". (p. 264) Valid legal principles, as recognized in some Anglo-American systems, include, for example, the familiar one that "no person may profit from his own wrong". In Dworkin's view, any such principle has a dimension of "weight" and, indeed, is sometimes *outweighed* in particular cases, as when, for example, the foregoing principle is outweighed by a valid legal rule allowing a party to acquire title to real property by adverse possession. Moreover, in Dworkin's view, it is not possible to specify in Hart's source-oriented criteria of validity how much and what kind of weight a principle must have for it to prevail as law when in conflict with an otherwise valid rule or other normative phenomenon. Yet such principles often do prevail, and thus are in fact recognized as an important type of valid law, at least in some systems. In Dworkin's view, it follows that Hart's theory of legal validity fails to account (conceptually) even for all major types of valid law.

In the Postscript to the 1994 version of *The Concept of Law*, Hart responded that his theory *is* conceptually adequate to account for the validity of principles as law. Principles such as the principle that "no person may profit by his own wrong" may qualify as valid law pursuant to source-oriented criteria, at least whenever, as Hart has put it in his Postscript, such principles are "consistently invoked *by courts* in ranges of different cases as providing reasons for decision, which must be taken into account, though liable to being over-ridden by reasons pointing the other way." (p.265) (Emphasis added.) It follows that the mere fact that a principle thus "consistently invoked" may sometimes be outweighed (as in the above adverse possession example), does not, of itself, preclude its identification as generally valid law. Even a legal rule, the validity of which Dworkin concedes *can* be captured by a Hartian source-oriented criterion of validity, may be outweighed in a particular case by a competing principle (as in Dworkin's own famous example of *Riggs v. Palmer*[5]), yet the *general* validity of that rule as law remains intact. It is simply not necessary for the general validity of a principle (or of any form of law) under a Hartian source-oriented criterion that it always generate a conclusive reason for decision, i.e., that it always outweigh competing forms of law. Though Dworkin has responses available to him here, I now believe Hart has had the better of this. This is not to say there are no other possible objections to Hart's theory of legal validity.[6]

The reappearance of Hart's *The Concept of Law*, with its posthumous postscript, is an occasion to address much larger questions, even if only briefly. How did Hart conceive the subject of jurisprudence? In general terms, what were his main contributions in the first edition of *The Concept of Law*, now reprinted with only minor corrections several decades after its first appearance? How influential has the book been? Why? Of course, I cannot do full justice to these questions here. I will merely offer some estimations and reflections, and will close with a personal memorial.

II. Estimations and Reflections

Hart's main contributions in *The Concept of Law* were, admittedly, contributions to the resolution of classical jurisprudential problems, and so are doubtless of no great interest to those many contemporary professors (perhaps a majority in the United States) who now define the subject of jurisprudence in essentially political or other non-traditional terms. Thus, in what follows, I assume that the reader is one who allows for jurisprudence of a type that does not purport to advance some political movement, program, or cause in a particular country at a particular time. Although Hart himself was keenly interested in political issues, he was not on the whole politically active, and certainly did not conceive of jurisprudence in terms of political movements or current politics. The traditional mainstream jurisprudential problems which interested Hart include major ones that are *relatively* apolitical, or politically neutral. In Hart's own words, some of these problems are "descriptive and general in scope, the perspective of which is not that of a judge deciding...what the law requires in particular cases...[let alone a legislature deciding what equality, or freedom, or some other ideal requires]...but is that of an external observer of a form of social institution with a normative aspect, which in its recurrence in different societies and periods exhibits *many common features of form, structure* and *content*".[7] (Emphasis added.)

I believe many Anglo-American scholars would today agree that Hart, in *The Concept of Law*, made at least five major contributions, "descriptive and general", to our understanding of law's "common features of form, structure, and content". I will now identify these contributions in summary terms. First, though it is hardly novel to say that law's form has partly to do with rules, Hart carried the analysis and description of rules far beyond where his contemporaries and predecessors left this subject. He differentiated rules from commands, orders, and other types of normative phenomena. He differentiated, in form and function, important types of rules which he called primary (duty imposing) and secondary (power conferring). He explained the efficiencies of rules. He illuminatingly contrasted rule-observing behavior with merely habitual behavior. In this, he emphasized that those who accept and apply rules generally respond critically to deviations, and he extended this analysis, with qualifications, to legal rules. He showed how legal rules and the "normativity" of law generate authoritative reasons for decisions and actions by officials and citizens, constitute standards for criticism of decisions and actions, and provide bases for claims of right and of duty. In thus deepening our understanding of rules and their roles in social life, Hart also enabled us to see   the shortcomings of Austin's theory of law as sovereign commands, various inadequacies of Kelsen's "pure" theory, and the deficiencies of American realist predictivism. Contrary to Llewellyn, and other realists, legal rules cannot be reduced to predictions of what officials will do about disputes.[8] Here is what Llewellyn said (though he later withdrew it):

This doing of something about disputes, this doing of it reasonably, is the business of law. And the people who have the doing in charge, whether they be judges or sheriffs or clerks or jailers or lawyers, are officials of the law. *What these officials do about disputes is, to my mind, the law itself.*

. . . And rules, in all of this, are important so far as they help you see or predict what judges will do or so far as they help you get judges to do something. That is their importance. *That is all their importance, except as pretty playthings.* (Llewellyn, *The Bramble Bush* p. 12, 14 (3d ed. 1960)).

In Hart's *Concept of Law*, we find rules at the forefront, not predictions of court decisions in hypothetical or actual disputes. Contrary to Llewellyn and other rule skeptics, Hart stressed that only if we have rules can we have courts in the first place; only if we have rules can we have authoritative decisions of courts at all; and only if we have rules can there be correct judicial applications of rules not reversible on appeal. Moreover, via what Hart calls the internal point of view of those subject to the rules, citizens treat rules as providing reasons for action out on the front lines of human behavior, typically in circumstances that involve no dispute of any kind. Of course, some actions come only after the citizen seeks legal advice. Here Hart substitutes the idea that rules themselves provide citizens with reasons for action in place of the notion that rules are merely bases for predicting what courts will do about disputes. The law's primary mode of operation is not through judicial action but through citizens who apply rules to their own circumstances and thereby order their own affairs (often with legal advice). As Hart said in *The Concept of Law*:

If it were not possible [through rules] to communicate general standards of conduct, which multitudes of individuals could understand, without further direction [from judges or other officials], as requiring from them certain conduct when occasion arose, nothing that we now recognize as law could exist. (p. 124)

So, law is to a large extent an affair of rules, and it must be so. But what are rules? Hart does not give us a systematic account of the defining features of rules, though he does contrast rules with orders, and also with principles, albeit briefly. Hart stresses the differences between important types of rules. There are primary rules that impose duties, and secondary rules of various types. These types include rules for changing the rules, rules of adjudication which define courts, and rules of recognition which specify criteria for determining the validity of rules and other law. All are characteristic of law. Indeed, with the law's primary rules imposing duties in mind, Hart stressed that "The most important general feature of law is that certain kinds of human conduct are no longer optional, but in some sense obligatory." Further, through secondary rules for changing rules, through rules of adjudication, and through "the rule of recognition" specifying criteria of valid law, Hart explained another general feature of law, namely that it regulates its own creation and application.

Hart's treatment of rules has been the object of much discussion and considerable criticism. Prior to Hart, we did not have anything like the vast literature we have today addressed to the nature, functions, and limits of legal rules. Of special interest is Hart's concern with what he called the internal point of view that citizens and officials take toward rules and other forms of law. Many legal rules function in our lives as sources of reasons for action, as standards of criticism, and the like. The same is true of other major forms of law such as private contracts. Another noted American realist, the judge, Oliver Wendell Holmes, Jr. said: "The duty to keep a contract . . . *means* a prediction that you [will] pay damages if you do not keep it and nothing else." One who has digested Hart could not agree with this. The duty to keep a given contract *means* that the circumstances in question fall under a rule requiring one to keep a contract. Moreover, the terms of a contract, like rules, give rise to reasons for contracting parties to act, constitute bases for claims of right, and serve as grounds for criticizing actual or proposed action.

A second major theme in *The Concept of Law* is Hart's rejection of the common view in legal theory that rules and other forms of law typically achieve their ends through coercion and force or threats thereof. Hart acknowledged that rules may require enforcement through coercion or the threat thereof, but he did not think coercion or its prospect to be, as he put it, "the normal motive for compliance." Here is how he put matters, and I quote:

> No doubt the advantages of mutual forbearance are so palpable that
> the number and strength of those who would co-operate voluntarily

in a coercive system will normally be greater than any likely combination of malefactors. Yet, except in very small closely-knit societies, submission to the system of restraints would be folly if there were no organization for the coercion of those who would then try to obtain the advantages of the system without submitting to its obligations. 'Sanctions' are therefore required not as the normal motive for obedience, but as a *guarantee* that those who would voluntarily obey shall not be sacrificed to those who would not. To obey, without this, would be to risk going to the wall. Given this standing danger, what reason demands is *voluntary* co-operation in a *coercive* system. (p. 198)

At the same time, Hart pointed out that the authoritativeness of the rules, and the normative attitudes of officials and of citizens in light of this authoritativeness — attitudes manifest in the internal point of view of those subject to the rules, are also among the major factors that account, in part, for general compliance.

Third, Hart's book advanced our understanding of the common structures of legal systems existing in different societies. These common structures include basic institutions and facilities for the making of valid law by legislatures, courts, and other official bodies, and by private citizens. The criteria accepted within a system for identifying valid law at the least presuppose institutional and other sources of valid law, and provide a unified and coordinated scheme of priorities for determining validity when conflicts arise between laws emanating from different sources. Here, Hart deployed his distinction between rules that confer power to make valid law (one category of "secondary" rules) and valid law so made in the form of duty imposing rules ("primary" rules). He analyzed the formal structure of legal systems mainly in terms of what he called a "union" of these two types of rule. Much of this contribution is encapsulated in *The Concept of Law* in "rule of recognition" terminology. Foremost here are the sources and criteria of valid law which serve as foundational elements of system structure. In the standard case of a legal system, the judges themselves accept the criteria of validity as common public standards of validity. Without this "internal point of view" of judges toward criteria of validity, a legal system could not exist.

Hart's contribution to our understanding of system structure was not alone seminal. Probably Kelsen made an equally seminal contribution to this topic. But Hart's overall analysis is a major improvement on Kelsen. In his analysis, ultimate criteria of validity are not themselves valid or invalid but are merely accepted, at least by the courts. Thus, contrary to Kelsen, Hart explained that issues of validity can arise only *within* a system, and must be resolved by reference to the criteria accepted there. Also, such acceptance is a complex question of fact, not, as Kelsen suggested, a "hypothesis" or the like. Moreover, Hart's analysis is more fully developed than Kelsen's. For example, Hart demonstrates how his theory of validity applies despite changes within a legal system, thereby accounting for the continuity and persistence of valid law. Hart's theory also displaces John Austin's theory of sovereignty. Valid law does not consist of commands of a sovereign who happens to be "habitually obeyed". Rather, it consists of rules and other normative phenomena valid by reference to criteria of validity, themselves accepted within the system, at least by the judges. Similarly, Hart's account bears up better than the accounts of those many American theorists who subscribed to the view that valid law is merely whatever the highest courts say it is, a view that confuses finality with infallibility and leaves little room for the concept of legal error or mistake. (Even in America, and even at the Supreme Court level, appellate judges occasionally err.)[9]

Fourth, Hart's work deepened our understanding of law's essential content in modern societies. He showed that because of basic features of human nature and of the human condition, a viable legal system requires rules with content protecting persons, property, and promises. The existence of such protections is necessary to induce the majority voluntarily to forebear from harming others, and to induce them to co-operate in forming a system that can bring organized state coercion to bear on the minority of malefactors. Without these protections -- without this *content* -- the majority in a society would not be likely to cooperate and thus would not be able to organize effective legal means of coercing malefactors. Here, Hart rejected one familiar positivist thesis, namely that a system of law may have just any content, and still be viable. As he pointed out, any conceptualization of law "in purely formal terms, without reference to any specific content... [is] ... inadequate." (p.199)

In thus protecting persons, property, and promises, law and morals overlap. Indeed, Hart referred to this "common content" as the "minimum content of natural law". (p. 193) Despite the overlap, Hart stressed important differences between a system of law and one of morals. Thus, for example, while both law and morals have rules protecting persons, property and promises, only law has an elaborate scheme of power conferring rules providing for public law-making and administration, and for explicit change in the existing rules. Hart also illuminatingly treated various other relations between law and morals, besides their overlapping content, and he ultimately adhered to the much misunderstood positivist thesis that the content of any valid law is not necessarily morally right and good. On this particular point, Hart aligned himself with John Austin and a whole tradition of English and continental legal positivism, but his articulation and grounding of the necessary minimum content of a viable legal system is relatively original as well as faithful to social realities.

Fifth, Hart's treatment of the foregoing matters of form, structure, and content common to law in modern societies also casts light on legal authority and the concept of legal authority. Here his contribution is merely suggestive rather than fully articulated. Legal rules and other forms of law differentiate, constitute, institutionalize, regulate and coordinate legal offices: legislative, administrative, and judicial. In these ways, law defines and confers authority. Further, officials and private citizens exercise this authority whenever they act in accord with formal legal reasons duly generated by valid law and lawful modes of applicational legal reasoning. The law recognizes private law-making power as well. By reference to accepted criteria of validity, to the rules and other forms of law valid thereunder, and to lawful modes of applicational reasoning, one may determine whether official or private action is ultimately authoritative. It follows that the concept of action by the state is not to be analyzed essentially in terms of official execution of orders backed by threats of force or coercion, as many jurisprudential theorists have assumed. Rather, lawful force and coercion presuppose state authority. And ultimately, authorized force and coercion serve, as Hart stressed, "not as the normal motive for obedience but as a guarantee that those who would voluntarily obey shall not be sacrificed to those who would not." (p. 198) Moreover, without voluntary and organized cooperation of the majority, there could be no authority, and the authoritative use of force and coercion would simply not be possible. (p. 201)

Before concluding these general and summary remarks on Hart's major contributions in *The Concept of Law* to our grasp of the "common features of form, structure, and content" to be found in the law of any modern society, perhaps I may be permitted to remark that Hart could have pursued his interest in form and structure well beyond the considerable distance he carried it. A legal order may be analyzed in terms of a number of types of basic legal phenomena. Rules, for example, comprise one type. Rules have a number of formal attributes such as prescriptiveness, generality, definiteness, and completeness. These formal attributes are configurative, and can be designed to serve not only problem-specific policy but also "rule of law" values such as predictability, freedom from official arbitrariness, equality before the law, dispute avoidance, and even legitimacy. A rule may not have problem-specific policy content. Instead, its subject-matter may be entirely formal, as with a rule that prescribes configuration, structure, methodology, or procedure. Other basic types of legal phenomena such as legislatures, elections, source-oriented criteria of validity, methodologies of interpretation, the principle of stare decisis, and adjudicative processes also have formal attributes, and some of these also have formal subject-matter. Indeed, formalness is itself one of law's basic characteristics, along with its normativity, its legitimized coerciveness, and its core of essential content[10].

I would estimate, then, that Hart's major contributions, "descriptive and general", to our understanding of law in *The Concept of Law* include his treatments of (1) the nature and functions of legal rules, (2) the place of coercion in law, (3) the structure of a legal order - especially its foundational institutions and criteria of validity, (4) law's essential minimum content, and (5) the concepts of legal authority and authoritative legal action. Today, three and a half decades after its initial publication, the book has become a classic, for it is a work of the highest rank in its core theses and their development, in its sweep and range, in its penetration, in its originality, and in its elegance of style. The book did not fall still-born from the press. More than 150,000 copies have been sold and it has been translated into many languages. It has generated a secondary literature far greater in volume than that of any other work of jurisprudence in the English language. As Professor Honoré recently remarked, the book is now "*the* classic work of philosophical jurisprudence" in that language.[11]

The intrinsic quality of the book is, of course, a major factor accounting for its extraordinary reception. That quality is informed by Hart's methodology. Hart and others have written extensively on this methodology elsewhere.[12] I will only observe here that Hart was a professional lawyer and a professional philosopher, and brought the sophistication and techniques of both fields to bear.

Another factor in the reception of *The Concept of Law* since 1961 is that Hart's *oeuvre* included many other books, articles and reviews, all of similarly high quality which naturally drew attention to the centerpiece of his work.[13] But in all this, we must stress that Hart not only taught thousands of undergraduates, but also numerous graduate students and young academics.[14] Many of these, inspired by the man as well as his work, became scholars and theorists themselves.

Hart was also an accomplished academic controversialist, and this, too, aroused widespread interest in his subject and in his ideas. Thus we have the Hart v. Kelsen debate,[15] the Hart v. Fuller debate,[16] the Hart v. Devlin debate,[17] the Hart v. Wooton debate,[18] the Hart v. Bodenheimer debate,[19] numerous Hart v. Dworkin debates,[20] and still other debates, all of which were published in some form. Still another factor affecting the reception of *The Concept of Law* is simply that Hart traveled and lectured widely in Britain, in Europe, in Israel, in the United States, and elsewhere. In the United States alone, he lectured at U.C.L.A., at Berkeley, at Stanford, at Oregon, at Harvard, at Yale, at Georgia, at Cornell, at Columbia, at Chicago, at Northwestern, and at many other universities.

III. Some Influences on Hart

Now, I would like to offer some thoughts on the following question: Which thinkers seemed to have had significant immediate influence on Hart's main ideas in *The Concept of Law* and on his development of those ideas? If we at least go by Hart's own explicit acknowledgments in the text, footnotes, and end notes, we find important references to various classical philosophers including Plato, Aristotle, Aquinas, Bentham, Hobbes, Hume, and Mill. Hart is quite explicit, for example, that Hobbes and Hume shaped his empirical version of what he called the minimum content of natural law.

Among twentieth century philosophers, we find Hart thanking Peter Strawson for advice, criticism, and for reading the proofs, too. We also find Hart referring to J.L. Austin, Hare, Paul, Ryle, Urmson, Waismann, Winch,

Wisdom and Wittgenstein. It is evident that J.L. Austin was a major contemporary influence. We know that Hart was a founding member of Austin's Saturday mornings, that the two did some joint teaching, and that they were friends. In the Preface to *The Concept of Law*, Hart stressed Austin's formulation that we are to use a "sharpened awareness of words to sharpen our perception of, though not as the final arbiter of, the phenomena."

Further, given Hart's emphasis on rules, it is difficult to think Wittgenstein was not a significant influence. At one point in *The Concept of Law* (p. 297) Hart strongly suggests as much. And I might add this anecdote. One evening during his year at Harvard, in my presence, Hart pulled the *Philosophical Investigations* off his shelf and said with a smile: "This is our Bible."

Of course, there are influences of various philosophers and other theorists of the twentieth century who wrote specifically on problems of legal philosophy. Hart had read widely in British, American, Scandinavian, and Continental legal philosophy. Here I believe the strongest influence was probably Hans Kelsen. Importantly similar notions about how law regulates its own creation, about the rule of recognition or something like it, and about how law may be viewed as a system of rules all find expression in both Kelsen and Hart. However, Hart was not uncritical of Kelsen.

Members of the Oxford law faculty who evidently had some hand in the book include Tony Honoré and Rupert Cross. Have there been any significant American influences on Hart? Hart does mention Pound, Dickinson, Fuller, Gray, Holmes, Llewellyn, and also Rawls. I know he much admired Holmes, Dickinson, and Rawls, but no American theorist seems to have had any real influence on his thinking about the concept of law except insofar as they may have set forth exaggerations of truths about law which Hart then reformulated, or insofar as they advanced untenable theories to which Hart reacted (as in the case of Llewellyn).

Hart was in the positivist tradition as was Kelsen and also many of Hart's predecessors in England, including the first John Austin who is so much discussed in the first half of *The Concept of Law*. Thus, Hart took a positivist approach to providing a general account of the nature of law. This approach is both general and descriptive. As he put it, the approach is *general* in the sense that it is not tied to any particular legal system or culture, but seeks to give an explanatory and clarifying account of law as a complex social and

political institution with a rule-governed (and in that sense 'normative') aspect
. . . . [The] account is *descriptive* in that it is morally neutral and has no
justificatory aims . . . . (p. 239-40)

Hart was also a positivist in several more specific senses. Thus, he
generally held that law is something posited — is an act of authoritative will
of legislators and other law givers rather than a revelation of reason in the
spirit of Natural Law. He was a positivist in still another more specific sense.
He held that it is not "a [logically] necessary truth that laws reproduce or
satisfy certain demands of morality, though in fact they have often done so."
[185-86] In turn, he held that although morality often influences laws, it does
not follow "that the criteria of legal validity [in any particular system] must
include, tacitly if not explicitly, a reference to morality or justice." (p. 184)
Even morally iniquitous rules could, in some systems, still be valid law. (212)
In his view, it all depends on the criteria of legal validity accepted in the
system and these criteria may or may not rule out morally iniquitous rules. He
held that these criteria could turn on "values, not only plain facts." (248) That
is, these criteria *could* but need not incorporate moral values that rule out as
invalid putative laws having iniquitous content. (In my view, he should have
stressed that iniquitous laws do strain the *concept* of law, however valid they
may be by the criteria of validity accepted in a particular system.)

There were also some senses in which Hart was not a positivist. He did
not hold that a system could have just any substantive content and still be a
system of law. He thought it naturally, though not logically, necessary that a
system have a minimum substantive content protecting persons and property,
and enforcing promises. Nor did Hart, as have many positivists, tend to view
coercion as the essence of law.

IV. Critique of Hart's Methodology

How are basic legal institutions to be analyzed? Courts, legislatures, official
bureaucracies, sanctioning institutions, all figure directly and indirectly in
Hart's *The Concept of Law*. Hart seems to want to reduce basic legal
institutions to rules. For example, courts are reduced to various "rules of
adjudication." Yet Hart himself says that courts comprise a "salient feature
of a legal system" (p. 3) and are a "typical element of a legal system." (p. 5)
Now, a system of law is not merely a system of rules. It is also a system of

institutions. There is something unsatisfactory about Hart's rule-oriented approach to basic legal institutions. I said in a review of the first edition of *The Concept of Law* in 1964 that I found his approach unduly reductionist and rule-oriented. Hart then told me he agreed, but said "you must develop your point." I now propose a "form-oriented" analysis in place of Hart's "rule-oriented one".

What is a basic legal institution? I can offer only a sketch of how things might go, using Anglo-American courts as illustrations. Such an institution might be thought of as an organized union of formal features with non-formal elements. Consider the important institution of a trial court. An account of the organized formal features of a trial court — features to be found in the standard case — would include an independent and impartial judge, opposing parties preparing and presenting their cases, dialogic procedures governing the pre-trial stages and the public trial stage, decision based on the evidence and argument presented by the parties, machinery for enforcement, and various types of rules regulating much of this from start to finish.

These organized features are all formal in that they pertain to the constitutive form of a trial court, its essence, if you like. Most of these organized features are formal in further specific senses *all* recognized in our language. Thus some of these organized features are structural. That is, they pertain to how parts within a whole are ordered. For example, the tripartite division of functions allocates active preparatory roles to the parties with the judge assuming a passive role. Other organized features are formal in the sense that they are methodological. Judicial fact-finding is a socially constructed methodology itself parasitic upon, though far from equivalent to, an unqualifiedly empirical technique. Other features are formal in the sense that they are procedural. And so on. On a form-oriented approach, one would also identify the ends and values to be served by the various types of organizational form — constitutive, structural, methodological, procedural, and so on.

Thus, it seems to me that what is needed here is a form-oriented approach to understanding a legal institution, and not merely Hart's rule-oriented approach. If I am right, a form-oriented approach would provide concepts for the representation of important features of the institution, bearing in mind that such an institution is to be understood as a functioning union of formal features with non-formal elements which include personnel, necessary facilities, and more.

Hart's rule-oriented approach to understanding basic legal institutions is, I think, limited in several ways. First, there is far more to a court *as a whole* than can be gleaned from the rules. Hart says that without rules of jurisdiction, for example, we could not have courts. Yet if I am right, what is most fundamental here is the organized form of a functional court as a social whole — a conception to be analyzed frontally in terms of various formal features in unified relations with the non-formal elements that together comprise the whole institution. Without some such holistic conception of the form of a court we could not even know what content the rules must have in the first place. Thus, a rule-oriented approach inverts primary and ancillary.

Second, Hart's rule-oriented approach to understanding a basic legal institution such as a trial court is not only insufficiently form-oriented. A rule-oriented approach also cannot comprehend the *fullness* of certain formal features. Consider, for example, the feature of judicial impartiality and independence. Rules can have negational and exclusionary content specifically ruling out various forms of judicial partiality and lack of independence, such as personal friendship with the plaintiff, the taking of bribes, political threats of loss of job, and the like. Indeed, rules can, in these negational and exclusionary ways go far to secure judicial impartiality and independence. But there is also what might be called an affirmative side to this feature of adjudication that is even more fundamental. This more affirmative side of this basic feature is simply that the judge (or a jury) is to find facts, and to apply law to the facts, in an *objective spirit*. Obviously some rules direct and constrain the judge here, too, but my thought is that these rules can go only so far. Objective judgment requires more than that the judge not be partial and the like, and requires more than that the judge be free of improper and irrelevant external and internal influences.

My view is that objectivity — this affirmative side of impartiality and independence, cannot be fully captured in rules that meaningfully prescribe means to ends. One might call this the affirmative side of the judicial frame of mind. If the spirit of objectivity cannot be, or at least cannot be fully captured in rules, then this would be an important deficiency of a merely rule-oriented approach to understanding what a trial judge and so the institution of a trial court is.

I have not yet tried to describe in detail what activities constitute the exercise of judicial judgment in a spirit of objectivity. Where the judge finds facts, one such activity, for example, would be the weighing and balancing of conflicting evidence in a fashion that gives due weight to each item of evidence. It is possible to state rules at least of a negative kind here. Thus, for example, there could be a general rule: Discount hearsay evidence except in those circumstances where its credibility is established. But can there be a meaningful rule stating *how much* weight the judge is to give good hearsay evidence in relation to all the conflicting evidence? If not, and I doubt if there can be such a rule, then we could say that the judge is simply to treat this and the other items of evidence in an objective spirit — or perhaps as a wise judge would, when deciding on the overall weight of the evidence. If I am right, we have here an important facet of adjudication that cannot be fully captured in rules prescribing the activities of judging, and this illustrates the limits of a rule-oriented approach to the institution itself.

Third, even if a rule-oriented approach *could* capture the fullness of all formal features, it still might fail to do so. Many functioning institutions are simply not fully "prescribed for" or accurately "prescribed for" at least in the official set of rules for the institution. For example, the judges appointed to a court in some countries may be so appointed on the basis of political party affiliation, an important facet of compositional form not "prescribed for" in the rules. Likewise, the actual organizational form of a legislature may be based entirely on political party dominance, itself not provided for at all in the content of the official rules.

V. A Personal Memorial

I now turn to certain special qualities of Professor Hart as a person. These qualities are, of course, worthy of comment in their own right, but they also provide further explanations for his role in the revival of jurisprudence during the second half of the twentieth century. I will first provide some background, for I must base my remarks on "knowledge by acquaintance" as well as "knowledge by description".[21] Thus, what follows is of necessity partly autobiographical. Nearly forty years ago, in April of 1956, I was introduced to Hart while I was in Britain for the 1955-56 academic year as a "junior" Fulbright Scholar at the University of Southampton studying politics and law. This was five years prior to publication of *The Concept of Law*.

Hart had come to Southampton to give a lecture on strict liability in the criminal law. At that time I was planning to enter Harvard Law School the following September, a fact known to S. N. Grant-Bailey, then Dean of the Law Faculty, and Hart was scheduled to be a visiting professor for a year at Harvard beginning in September, a fact also known to Grant-Bailey who kindly organized a tea after Hart's lecture for the three of us. As a result of this introduction, Hart invited me to contact him in the fall at Harvard, and I saw him regularly while in my first year of law school (1956-7). For reasons of his own, he sat in on the classes in criminal law I attended (taught by Henry M. Hart) and we discussed some of those. Occasionally, I visited his own course of lectures on the concept of law. (I still have the multi-lithed reading materials he assigned the students in that course.) He lent me several books, and we discussed them. Then there was his famous Holmes Lecture,[22] which we discussed both before and after its delivery. He was then also lecturing and writing on causation in the law, and we occasionally discussed aspects of that subject. From time to time, he would invite me to dine with him, and after my wife and son arrived from Oregon at mid year, he dined with us several times in our apartment where we discussed not only law and philosophy at Harvard and at Oxford, but also much else. By mid year, I had begun half time employment at The Phillips Books Store in Harvard Square, and he would also stop in there from time to time for a book, for a brief chat, or both. After the end of the academic year came, I said goodbye. I thought it likely my own path would not cross his again.

But after Hart's return to Oxford, I stayed in touch by post. I received my law degree, practiced a while, and then in the fall of 1960 I became an assistant professor at the University of Oregon School of Law. In 1962, while Hart was a visiting professor at U.C.L.A., he came at my invitation to lecture at the University of Oregon. He arrived in Eugene full of interesting reflections, having debated Hans Kelsen at Berkeley the evening before. While in Eugene, he presented two extraordinarily stimulating lectures on issues in the jurisprudence of the criminal law. These lectures were well attended by students and faculty both in philosophy and in law. At this time, Hart discussed with me the possibility that I might spend a year at Oxford, doing research and studying under his guidance. He also kindly offered to support my applications for funds to finance such a year. As a result, for the year 1964-65, I received a fellowship from the Rockefeller Foundation. I

resided with my family in Oxford in a separate flat in the house owned by
Mrs. John Langshaw Austin (which Hart had arranged for us). During the
year, I attended lectures and studied under Hart on an informal yet regular
basis, (working at what had been Austin's desk!). After that, there were
numerous further occasions when I saw Hart, mainly while on several
sabbatical leaves in Oxford, but also from time to time in the United States.

My most vivid impressions of Hart as a person and as a teacher, derive
from the Harvard year (1955-56) and from my first sabbatical leave in Oxford
(1964-65), almost ten years later (a year during which I kept a rather full diary
on a daily basis). At Harvard, I had attended some of his lectures on what
was to become *The Concept of Law*. At Oxford during the 1964-65 year, I
attended all of his course of lectures on Kelsen, and all of his course of
lectures on rights and duties. He was a superb lecturer though he said to me
on several occasions that he really did not enjoy lecturing. On his
recommendation, I also attended his joint seminar with Professor Rupert
Cross and Nigel Walker on the mental element in the criminal law, as well
as his seminar on modern theories of law. He encouraged me to attend
certain other lectures and seminars, and I did. I was most fortunate to meet
with him regularly to discuss topics in jurisprudence. He introduced me to
his graduate students, and to various Oxford tutors and professors in law and
in philosophy. He also invited me to London to a "private debate" he had
with Lord Devlin on morals and the criminal law. But there was a personal
and social side, too. He took a generous interest in what else my family and
I might do in Oxford and environs. On numerous occasions he had me to
lunch or dinner at University College. In December, after our daughter was
born, he appeared on our doorstep with a large bouquet of flowers for my
wife, and an armful of books for our three small boys.

In the private sessions that Hart arranged during the 1964-65 year, he
always seemed ready to grapple with whatever interested the other person.
I would often leave a paper or a detailed outline with him in advance of our
meeting, and he would read and mark it up extensively (though it was not
easy to read his handwriting). His style, however, was oral. We would
discuss nearly every main point from the ground up, with our sessions
sometimes lasting two hours. He frequently had suggestions for further
reading. While quick and penetrating, and disposed to be critical, he rarely
failed to provide encouragement. One special source of encouragement was

also frequently in play -- his own modesty. He did not hesitate to share his own uncertainties. He often introduced methodological issues, including issues about the standards of criticism he considered appropriate to the subject. Sometimes there was lawyer-like emphasis on detailed examples, and their relevant features. In argument, he was direct, incisive, and clear. Beyond the humanism, and the clarity and the rigor, he displayed a passionate interest in ideas, and an extraordinary intellectual vitality. We sometimes discussed his own views, and he invited criticism. Understanding was his aim, not discipleship. My impression is that, over the years, he reached out in these ways to many of his students, including, especially those who became academics in Britain, the United States, and elsewhere. The person and the oral medium, together far more powerful than the written word, aroused interest and inspired life-long commitment to the subject. It is my belief that in these ways, as much as, if not more than through his pen, Hart revived the subject of jurisprudence in the twentieth century Anglo-American legal world.[23]

Notes

* References in parentheses are to pages in THE CONCEPT OF LAW (2nd ed. 1994 O.U.P.).

1. A.M. Honoré, *Herbert Lionel Adolphus Hart*, 84 PROC. OF THE BRIT. ACAD. 295-321 (1994). See also the Speeches Delivered at Memorial Ceremony on 6 February 1993 by Sir Isaiah Berlin, Lord Jay, Professor Ronald Dworkin, Mrs. Jean Flood, Professor Joseph Raz, Dr. Bernard Richards, and Professor Alan Ryan, with an addendum by Lord Wilberforce. See also the following obituary notices: The Independent, Dec. 23, 1992; The Daily Telegraph, Dec. 23, 1992; The Times, Dec. 24, 1992; The Frankfurter Allgemeine Zeitung, Jan. 15, 1993.

2. A full bibliography of Hart's writings, carefully put together by Professor Stanley Paulson, appeared in 8 Ratio Juris 397-406 (1995).

3. D.N. MacCormick, *H.L.A. Hart: In Memoriam*, 6 RATIO JURIS 337 (1993).

4. Ronald Dworkin, *The Model of Rules*, 35 U.CHI.L. REV. 14 (1967), *reprinted in* ESSAYS IN LEGAL PHILOSOPHY (R. Summers ed., London 1968).

5. 115 N.Y. 506, 22 N.E. 188 (1889).

6. See, e.g., L. Fuller, THE MORALITY OF LAW 133-44 (2nd ed. New Haven 1964). See also R. Summers, *H.L.A. Hart's Concept of Law*, 1963 DUKE L.J. 629, and R. Summers, *Toward a Better General Theory of Legal Validity*, 15 RECHTSTHEORIE 65 (1984).

7. ISSUES IN CONTEMPORARY LEGAL PHILOSOPHY 36 (R. Gavison ed., Oxford 1987)

8. For more detail on the limits of predictivism, see R. Summers, INSTRUMENTALISM AND AMERICAN LEGAL THEORY ch. 5 (Ithaca, 1982).

9. For a remarkably illuminating analysis of the possible applicability of Hart's "rule of recognition" to the complexities of the American system, see Greenawalt, *The Rule of Recognition and the Constitution*, 85 MICH.L.REV. 621 (1987).

10. See R. Summers, *The Formal Character of Law*, 51 CAMBRIDGE L.J. 242 (1992); R. Summers, *Der Formale Charakter Des Rechts II*, 80 ARCHIV FÜR RECHTS-UND SOZIALPHILOSOPHIE 60 (1994); R. Summers, *The Formal Character of Law III*, 25 RECHTSTHEORIE 125 (1994); R. Summers, *The Juristic Study of Law's Formal Character*, 8 RATIO JURIS 237 (1995).

11. Honoré, *supra* note 1, at 312.

12. See, e.g., *P.M.S. Hacker, Hart's Philosophy of Law in* LAW, MORALITY AND SOCIETY -- ESSAYS IN HONOR OF H.L.A. HART   (P.M.S. Hacker & J. Raz eds. Oxford 1977); R. Summers, *The New Analytical Jurists*, 41 NYU L. REV. 861 (1966); and R. Summers, *supra* notes 4 and 6.

13. *See supra* note 2.

14. Honoré, *supra* note 1, at 309, lists among the graduate students and young academics: "A.E. Gottlieb, H. Morris, I. Tammelo, B.M. Barry, V.N. Haksar, W.L. Weinstien, G.D. MacCormick, J.M. Finnis, D.H. Hodgson, R.S. Summers, P.M.S. Hacker, J. Raz, V.B. Bogdanor, G. Gilason, G.R. Carrio, R.E. Gavison, and W.J. Waluchow." To this list a number may be added including A.M. Honoré, J.R. Lucas, R.M. Dworkin, R. Kent Greenawalt, Philip M. Soper, and Lee D. Irish.

15. H.L.A. Hart, *Kelsen Visited*, 10 UCLA L.REV. 709 (1962-63).

16. H.L.A. Hart, *Positivism and the Separation of Law and Morals*, 71 HARV.L.REV. 593 (1958).

17. H.L.A. Hart, LAW, LIBERTY, AND MORALITY (Stanford 1963).

18. See, e.g., H.L.A. Hart, *Barbara Wooton, Crime and the Criminal Law,* 74 YALE L.J. 1325 (1965) (book review).

19. H.L.A. Hart, *Analytical Jurisprudence in Mid-Twentieth Century: A Reply to Professor Bodenheimer*, 105 U. PA. L. REV. 953 (1957).

20. *See, e.g.*, H.L.A. Hart, *American Jurisprudence through English Eyes: The Nightmare and the Noble Dream,* 11 GA.L.REV. 969 (1977).

21. Cf. H.L.A. Hart, *Is There Knowledge by Acquaintance?* Supp. Vol. 23 Proc. Arist. Soc. 69 (1949).

22. *See supra* note 16.

23. I am pleased to be able to record that in Ithaca in 1976, I suggested to Dr. Peter Hacker that there be a Festschrift for Hart in celebration of his work on the occasion of his 70th birthday. The Festschrift appeared the next year, thoughtfully edited by two of his former students, Dr. Hacker and Dr. Joseph Raz: LAW, MORALITY AND SOCIETY -- ESSAYS IN HONOR OF H.L.A. HART (Oxford, 1977).

CHAPTER 2

RUDOLF VON JHERING'S INFLUENCE ON AMERICAN LEGAL THEORY

I. Introduction

A number of leading American legal theorists of the 19th and 20th Centuries read major works of the great jurist, Rudolf von Jhering[1] (1818-1892). The most notable of these American theorists were Oliver Wendell Holmes, Jr. (1841-1935), Roscoe Pound (1870-1964), Karl N. Llewellyn (1893-1962), and Lon L. Fuller (1902-1978). Holmes was first a practicing lawyer, then for a brief period a professor of law at Harvard, then a judge of the highest court of Massachusetts, and finally a justice of the United States Supreme Court for many years. He substantially influenced American legal thought. Roscoe Pound, however, was probably America's most influential legal theorist, at least at the level of general directions of thought. He profoundly influenced the dominant theory of law in America during this century, a theory I call "pragmatic instrumentalism". Pound was a professor and dean at Harvard Law School. Karl N. Llewellyn was a professor at Columbia and Chicago, and a leader of the realist wing of the American pragmatic instrumentalists. Lon L. Fuller, a professor at Harvard, was a brilliant critic of positivist elements in American and European legal theory, but he developed a distinctive jurisprudential theory of his own, and also, like Llewellyn, contributed importantly to the theory of American private law.

But, of course, to have read the work of an earlier thinker is not necessarily to be influenced by that thinker. I will now consider whether Jhering influenced Holmes, Pound, Llewellyn and Fuller.[2] I have found this a difficult inquiry. I have also had to be very selective, and I have concluded that, in some major respects, Jhering probably did not have significant influence on these thinkers. I have also concluded that, in other major respects, Jhering probably did have real influence.

Jhering knew he was being widely read in America. In 1881, he wrote to a friend as follows:

. . . my writings are widely read even in the United States, and a review of my book, *The Ends of Law*, is the most brilliant which has ever appeared about any of my works.[3]

One of Jhering's earliest readers in America was Oliver Wendell Holmes, Jr. Just as Holmes was about to become a professor at Harvard Law School, he published a famous book in 1881 called *The Common Law* in which he referred to Jhering as "a man of genius."[4]

II. The Possible Influence of Jhering's Criticisms of Legal Method

It is well known that the later Jhering made distinctively vigorous and colorful criticisms of various methodological assumptions and approaches to the study of law, especially those of certain German Professors of Roman Law[5]. Some of Jhering's criticisms here could also be readily applied to the thinking of certain leading American professors, and to the reasoning of certain American judges of this era.[6] Given this dual relevance of Jhering's criticisms to the American scene, and given Jhering's fame as a major scholar in Western law, it is hardly surprising that his criticisms were read in America by leading theorists.

The nature of Jhering's criticisms is well known. He criticized the pursuit of abstractness and symmetry in legal concepts and legal doctrines for their own sake, criticized the mere deductive unpacking of legal propositions in disregard of their practical consequences, criticized the willingness to dismiss some lines of reasoning from existing doctrines as logically impossible, criticized formalistic hair splitting in legal analysis, and criticized the notion that the law is a closed system that must be taken to provide for all cases.[7] For example, in *Der Geist des römischen Rechts*, Jhering made these critical observations:

> That particular cult of the logical, which tries to twist jurisprudence into a mathematics of law, is an aberration and rests on ignorance about the nature of law. Life is not here to be a servant of concepts, but concepts are here to serve life. What will come to pass in the future is not postulated by logic but by life, by trade and commerce,

and by the human instinct for justice, be it deducible through logic or unlikely to happen at all.[8]

Now, various American thinkers who had read Jhering also made similar criticisms of certain academics, of judges, or both. Thus, the American jurist, Oliver Wendell Holmes, Jr., who had read *Der Geist* in French translation in 1879,[9] wrote two years later that "the life of the law has not been logic, it has been experience."[10] In 1897, in his most famous article, The Path of the Law, Holmes added: "[It is a] . . . fallacy . . . [to believe] that a given system, ours, for instance, can be worked out like mathematics from some general axioms of conduct."[11] Holmes expressed many such Jhering-eske criticisms not only of judges but of law professors as well.[12] Other American theorists who had read Jhering, including Roscoe Pound, Karl Llewellyn, and many so called legal realists, expressed similar criticisms.[13]

Can we be reasonably certain that Jhering's criticisms of the "cult of the logical" in fact influenced these American theorists? It is difficult to know. Given the conceptualistic and formalistic nature of the reasoning of many American judges and some American professors of this same period, such criticisms were certainly natural ones for perceptive critics to make. It therefore seems rather likely that Holmes, Pound, and Llewellyn would have made such criticisms even if they had never read Jhering. Still, even if Jhering's criticisms merely reinforced the disposition of Holmes, Pound, and Llewellyn themselves to make such criticisms, this would be important, especially given that criticisms of this nature were a major factor leading to the revolution in American legal method that occurred during the early decades of the 20th century. Even a relatively minor influence on such a major revolution would be significant. This is all the more true since Jhering's criticisms of legal method also reflected his instrumentalist theory of the nature of law, a type of theory which came to dominate American legal thought by the middle of this century.[14]

III. The Possible Influence of Jhering's Instrumentalist Conception of Law

Jhering was known to many American legal theorists through his book *Der Zweck im Recht*, the first volume of which was published in German in 1877 and the second in 1883. In 1913, the first volume was translated into English, but before that Roscoe Pound and various other American theorists had already read it in German.[15] In its English translation, the book was given the title "Law As a Means to an End". This title, though itself something of a mistranslation of the German title, nevertheless reflects Jhering's instrumentalist concept of law set forth in the book. In key passages of the preface, Jhering said:

> ... [T]he object of the present book ... [is] Law as a means to an end. ... The fundamental idea of the present work consists in the thought that Purpose is the creator of the entire law; that there is no legal rule which does not owe its origin to a purpose, i.e., to a practical motive.[16]

Holmes, Pound, and Llewellyn, all of whom had read Jhering, similarly came to embrace an instrumentalist concept of law. Thus, in 1897, Holmes stressed that when analyzing rules of law one should first and foremost "consider the ends which the ... rules seek to accomplish, the reasons why those ends are desired, what is given up to gain them, and whether they are worth the price."[17] In 1907, Pound emphasized that "Law is a means, not an end".[18] Later, Llewellyn summarized his own general position and that of many other American thinkers as follows: "[We view] ... law as a means to social ends and not as an end in itself. ..."[19]

Jhering's concept of law as a means to ends cannot be dismissed merely as an abstract generality with no concrete meaning or differentiating power of its own. In my view, Jhering's conception serves to negate or exclude at least four general views about law. By way of contrast with these views, Jhering's theory also takes on more concrete and distinct significance.

(1) First, Jhering's instrumentalist concept of law negates or excludes the view that law is some kind of an end in itself. In particular, Jhering's instrumentalism is incompatible with the view that law consists essentially

of general concepts which scholars and judges should mold into some kind of formal and symmetrical perfection merely for the sake of such perfection.

(2) Second, Jhering's instrumentalist theory of law negates or excludes the view that a system should adhere to legal rules having highly formal attributes merely in order to serve the general rationales or values behind such attributes, even when the problem-specific policy content of those rules becomes outdated or is otherwise objectionable. Jhering acknowledged that the general rationales or values behind such formal attributes include predictability, protection against arbitrariness, ease of administration, and more. He also recognized that such values generally justify legislative and judicial adoption of rules having highly formal attributes such as completeness, definitiveness, and generality. But when such formal rules are applied, their problem-specific policy content may be seen to be outdated, or objectionable in unforeseen ways that call for legal reform.   Jhering's instrumentalism took account of this need for reform of the problem-specific policy content of rules.

(3) Third, Jhering's instrumentalism negates or excludes the view that law is merely an expression of the organic customs and spirit of a people--a reflection of essentially slow moving processes of historical evolution. Jhering did not agree with this conception of law and its implication that law can have only very limited potential as an instrument for transforming society in any given time period.

(4) Fourth, Jhering's theory negates or excludes the view that rules of law should be studied in accord with a narrow scientific positivism. He rejected the notion that rules should merely be analyzed, described, and classified as social data, without consideration of the quality of their ends or of their suitability to those ends.

I cannot expand and develop Jhering's instrumentalist theory here, but the fact that it negates and excludes such basic ideas as the four I have identified also goes far to demonstrate its significance. Nor can I explore here the ways in which Jhering's own salutary instrumentalism may itself be criticized. I will merely observe that the American jurist, Lon L. Fuller, who was, I think, much influenced by Jhering, wrote a number of essays on law's means and ends and their interactions. Fuller's essays develop a more sophisticated instrumentalism.[20]

I have observed that Holmes, Pound, Llewellyn and other leading American theorists conceived of law essentially as a means to ends, and had also read Jhering. But again, these facts do not necessarily signify that Jhering influenced the rise of American instrumentalism in a major way. When Holmes, Pound and Llewellyn wrote, other theorists in the Anglo-American tradition had already articulated a robustly instrumentalist theory of law. Among the most notable of these other theorists were Jeremy Bentham in Britain,[21] and the American philosophical pragmatists, especially William James[22] and John Dewey.[23] In 1932, Professor Herman Oliphant, an American legal theorist, proclaimed that:

> A century ago, Jeremy Bentham saw law not as an ultimate but merely as a means to an end and argued that it should be scientifically exploited as such. . . . Then came the pragmatism of James and the instrumental logic of Dewey, with the result that we are beginning to catch up with Bentham. Liberals now venture to talk of law as a means to an end. . . Many are eager to stop talking and begin studying law as a means to present ends.[24]

Perhaps still another reason to doubt whether Jhering's own instrumentalism as such significantly influenced Holmes, Pound, and Llewellyn is that an instrumentalist theory of law readily applies (within limits) to the actual phenomena of law anyway. Indeed, legal phenomena affirmatively invite instrumentalist conceptualizations in obvious and not so obvious ways. An instrumentalist theory was a type of theory that it was natural for Holmes and Pound and Llewellyn to adopt, especially in the late 19th century, when technology of all kinds was being rapidly introduced into every walk of life, and Western civilization had entered what Jhering might well have called the "Age of Instruments".

IV. The Possible Influence of Jhering's General Ideas about Law's Means

I now turn to some of Jhering's more specific ideas about the nature of law as an instrumentality to serve social ends. Jhering devoted many pages of the first volume of *Der Zweck im Recht* to a discussion of law's essential means.

For him, these include the state, a legislature, rules, organized coercion, an independent judiciary, and appropriate procedure. Jhering emphasizes the importance of state coercion. In his vigorous and colorful style, he asserted that:

> Coercion put in execution by the state forms the absolute criterion of law; a legal rule without legal coercion is a contradiction in terms, a fire which does not burn, a light that does not shine.[25]

Earlier in *Der Zweck*, Jhering had claimed that "the social organization of coercion is synonymous with State and Law" and that the "state is society as the bearer of the regulated and disciplined coercive force."[26] According to Jhering, the "sum total of principles according to which . . . [the state] functions by a discipline of coercion, is Law."[27] He stressed that state force must be superior to all other force in the society, the State must have a monopoly on force, and the use of state force must be organized and regulated by law.[28]

Leading American instrumentalist theorists were similarly emphatic about the role of coercion and direct official action in a system of law. Thus, Holmes frequently stressed law's coercive element.[29] Pound asserted that "the life of the law is in its enforcement"[30]. Llewellyn said that "what . . . officials do about disputes is . . . the law itself".[31] Another prominent American theorist, Felix Cohen, added that in matters of law "whatever cannot be translated into acts of state force is functionally meaningless".[32]

Here, too, it may be that Jhering had no original influence on the American theorists, though as I have said, many of them had read *Der Zweck*, with its many pages devoted to coercion and force. After all, this theme, too, is a natural one in regard to law. It is also an ancient theme, one stressed by Thomas Hobbes, John Austin and many other English theorists known in America. Of course, on reading Jhering, American theorists might have been reinforced somewhat in their disposition to embrace law's coercive character rather unqualifiedly.

I find it surprising that Jhering, with all his sensitivity to the role of social forces in law, with his emphasis on notions of what is just and right and fitting in matters related to law, and with his remarkable grasp of the complexities of social ordering through law, gave so much emphasis to the roles of coercion, force, and direct official action. The American jurist, Lon L. Fuller, though influenced by Jhering in other ways, did not follow him here. On the contrary, Fuller made what I consider to be telling criticisms of the many legal theorists, in the American and the Continental traditions, who seemed to identify law with coercion.[33]

V. The Possible Influence of Jhering's Theory of Interests

I now turn to the question of basic law-making technique. Of course, any such technique should be designed to create law good in content. Jhering's writings, especially *Der Geist* and *Der Zweck*, include the *rudiments* of a general theory about this. As we know, that theory has come to be called the "theory of interests",[34] a theory sometimes associated with "sociological jurisprudence." Later German thinkers such as Philipp Heck and Heinrich Stoll,[35] and American thinkers such as Roscoe Pound[36] and his followers developed the so called "theory of interests" well beyond the rudimentary state in which Jhering left it. Yet Pound frequently acknowledged an indebtedness to Jhering here,[37] and the theory of interests, as developed by Pound and others, became a common mode of thought in America. Many law professors and judges used it. The Restatements promulgated by the American Law Institute reflected it. And more.

Again, I would add a caveat. Recent scholarship indicates that Jhering's own contribution here may have been rather limited and somewhat derivative. It now appears more likely that the idea of interests and the idea of balancing interests derive mainly from Jeremy Bentham, and also from Dr. F. E. Beneke of Berlin and Göttingen, who also drew on Bentham.[38] Jhering had certainly read Bentham and Beneke.[39]

This is not to say that Jhering adopted a Benthamite approach to the definition and measurement of what is socially valuable. He did not. Indeed, in the second volume of *Der Zweck*, Jhering criticizes Bentham's utilitarianism as too subjective. Jhering says that Bentham wrongly embraces the mere subjective utility to individuals as the criterion and measure of the objectively and socially useful.[40] But what, for Jhering is the objectively and socially useful? He does not explicitly provide an ultimate criterion or measure of value, but in my opinion he does reveal at various points a deep faith in the power of contextual practical reason to justify choices in lawmaking. This faith is perhaps reminiscent more of natural law theory than of utilitarianism and Interressenjurisprudenz.[41] Jhering does not seek to work all this out in any detail, but asserts that law should be made to conform to the "real purposes of man in society"--objective notions of right and wrong, not merely the subjective purposes of individuals. And, of course, Jhering also wanted to bring to bear on problems of lawmaking any available scientific knowledge and any relevant truths distilled from historical experience.

VI. The Possible Influence of Jhering's Ideas about Purpose in Law

I will now turn to how law's content is to be determined by considering some of Jhering's general ideas about law's ends. When in *Der Zweck*, Jhering turned from the law's means to the law's ends, he said: "From the form of the law we now proceed to its content; or, since the content is determined solely by its object, to its purpose."[42] According to Jhering, the:

> formal elements . . . [such as the state, rules, the judicial process, and coercion] tell us nothing about the content of law. By means of these we know only that society compels its members to certain things, but we know not why or for what purpose. It is the external *form* of the law, remaining always alike and capable of receiving the most varied content. It is through content that we learn the purpose which law serves in society. . . .[43]

Jhering emphasized that "Everything found on the ground of the law was called into life by a purpose and exists to realize some purpose".[44] And, in similar terms, he asserts that "All legal measures . . . have man as their purpose. But social life, in joining mankind into higher groups through the community of permanent purposes, extends thereby the forms of human existence."[45] In sum: "The fundamental idea of [*Der Zweck im Recht*] consists in the thought that Purpose is the creator of the entire law; that there is no legal rule which does not owe its origin to a purpose, i.e., to a practical motive."[46]

In the last third of the first volume of *Der Zweck im Recht*, and also in the second volume, Jhering treated various general purposes of law. Ideally, the law for him is to be a coherent purposive system based on the whole range of "permanent" human values. He recognizes that formal law itself has some purposes more or less of its own, such as order, predictability, freedom from arbitrariness, legal equality, legal security, and legitimacy.[47] (In my own scheme of thinking, these are general rationales for legal formality--values behind form in law.) Jhering perceived that such general purposes of law itself, combined with immediate "practical motives", i.e. problem-specific policies, ultimately determine the content of the rules. Moreover, most of the law to be made by legislative law makers and by constitution makers transcends time and place. At an important level of generality, and in regard to some basic issues of lawmaking, no serious conflicts of purpose and legislative choice arise. Thus, he says that: "Certain legal principles are found among all peoples; murder and robbery are everywhere forbidden; state and property, family and contract are met everywhere."[48] Other matters are more relative to time and place, and pose difficult problems of choice between conflicting purposes, including general purposes of law as well as problem-specific policies, i.e., "practical" motives or purposes. These choices are mainly for legislatures, rather than for judges.[49]

Did the leading American legal theorists in the first half of this century follow Jhering on the role of purpose in the creation of law? In two major respects, most of them did not. First, and as I have noted, most of them, at the level of theory, embraced some version of Benthamite utilitarianism, with its *quantitative* notion of maximizing the *subjective* utilities of the parties affected by laws or court decisions. As Holmes put it, law makers should examine conflicting desires, "make a quantitative comparison," and choose that form of law which will bring the "greater" satisfaction of desires.[50] In my view, Jhering would have strongly disagreed with Holmes' famous dictum: "The first requirement of a sound body of law is, that it should correspond with the actual feelings and demands of the community, whether right or wrong."[51] Nor would Jhering have endorsed Pound's general idea that law makers should strive merely to secure the most "interests with the least friction".[52] As I have already indicated, Jhering advocated a far more *qualitative* and *objective* approach to value in his theory of law making.

Secondly, unlike Jhering, most leading American theorists did not think and write about law in the idiom of purposes--purposes attributed to rules, to legal processes, to institutions, to the state, and to society. Indeed, most of these theorists would not have endorsed Jhering's extensive teleological attributions to inanimate phenomena.

But one major American theorist was, I think, greatly influenced by Jhering here. He was Lon L. Fuller (1902-1978). Fuller, like Jhering, rejected subjectivist utilitarianism. Fuller, like Jhering, embraced more qualitative and objective theories of value. Fuller, like Jhering, often wrote about law in the idiom of purpose, and stressed the primacy of purpose. Lon L. Fuller is one of the two or three most important figures in American legal theory in the second half of the Twentieth century.

VII. Jhering's Possible Influences on Fuller's Legal Theory

Fuller studied law in the mid-1920's and then became successively a professor at the University of Oregon, the University of Illinois, Duke Law School, and finally at the Harvard Law School where he was a member of the faculty from 1939 until 1972. Fuller read *Der Geist*, probably in the late 1920's, and from citations in his published writings seems to have read most of Jhering's books, including, of course, *Der Zweck*. (I have seen what was Fuller's own personal copy of *Der Zweck*, and it includes many marginal notes.) Fuller also read some of Jhering's articles. There is evidence that Jhering influenced Fuller on several major jurisprudential topics.

I will first indicate how far Fuller went in subscribing to what Jhering might have called the purposive character of law. Fuller himself frequently equated purpose in law with value, and claimed that the very existence of a law is bound up with purpose. For Fuller, the statement that "L is a law" implied that "L has a purpose". A purposeless law cannot exist as a law. As Fuller put it, in the field of "purposive human activity . . . value and being are not two different things, but two aspects of an integral reality."[53] Fuller was also emphatic that the meaning of a law cannot be divorced from its purpose. As he phrased it, "the essential meaning of a legal rule lies in a purpose, or more commonly, in a congeries of purposes."[54] Similarly, for Fuller, legal processes such as adjudication are "purposive human arrangements," and participants in such processes must give due attention to the relevant purposes.[55] At the highest level, Fuller conceived of the legal system as a whole as the "purposive enterprise of subjecting human conduct to the guidance of rules", an enterprise with distinctive procedural purposes of its own.[56]

Although teleological approaches to law are at least as old as Aristotle, the nature and extent of the emphasis on purpose in Fuller and in Jhering's *Der Zweck*, combined with the considerable evidence of Fuller's admiration for Jhering, have led me to conclude that Fuller probably drew heavily on Jhering here rather than on the teleological tradition as such, or merely on his own thought. I cannot now evaluate the views of Jhering and Fuller on the purposive character of law. I note only that the matter is very complex, and add that I no longer unqualifiedly admire Fuller's own highly purposive approach to statutory interpretation, an approach that downplays language-oriented argumentation.[57]

VIII. Jhering's Influence on Fuller's Contract Jurisprudence

Fuller also wrote two major articles on the theory of contract law, and in the American legal literature these articles rank among the very best of the Twentieth Century. In both articles, Fuller appears to have drawn heavily on the theoretical work of Jhering. The first of Fuller's articles on the theory of contract appeared in the Yale Law Journal in 1936 and was called "The Reliance Interest in Contract Damages".[58] Fuller opened this article with two sentences very much in the spirit of Jhering's *Der Zweck*:

> The proposition that legal rules can be understood only with reference to the purposes they serve would today scarcely be regarded as an exciting truth. The notion that law exists as a means to an end has been commonplace for at least half a century.[59]

Fuller went on to say that in American contract law, however, scholars and theorists had failed to articulate the purposes which underlie or may underlie the enforcement of promises generally. He then differentiated three principal purposes which courts may pursue in awarding contract damages.[60] First, where a plaintiff has conferred some benefit on the defendant, in anticipation of a return performance, and the defendant then fails to perform, the court may force the defendant to return the benefit. The obvious purpose of the law here is to prevent unjust enrichment by the defaulting promisor at the expense of the plaintiff. Fuller called the interest protected here the "restitution" interest.

Second, the plaintiff may rely on the defendant's promise as by making expenditures, without conferring any benefit on the defendant. Here, if the court reimburses such expenditures, it protects what Fuller called the "reliance" interest, another basic purpose in awarding contract damages. The award of reliance damages places the plaintiff in as good a position as the plaintiff was in before the promise was made.

The third basic purpose is, of course, protection of the plaintiff's "expectation" interest. Here, the court awards damages for a broken promise in an amount that would put the plaintiff in the position that the plaintiff would have been in had the contract been performed.

Fuller believed that, in general, damages for breach of contract should be measured by lost expectancy rather than reliance losses or the extent of any unjust enrichment. But Fuller showed in his article that American scholarship, the first Restatement of Contracts, and some of the case law had unduly neglected the reliance interest in awarding contract damages. The first Restatement of Contracts, published in 1931, did not even acknowledge the reliance interest as such, and allowed reimbursement for out-of-pocket costs in only very limited circumstances, as where there were difficulties of proving lost expectancy. Also, reliance damages were not recoverable under the Restatement when the contract was not in writing as required by the Statute of Frauds, for example. Such damages were also not recoverable when not incurred in performance or in preparation for performance, as where a business lessee in reliance on the lease bought a stock of goods. And they were not recognized as recoverable in still other important categories of cases. Fuller argued that reliance expenditures should be more widely recoverable, and he found some American cases supporting his position.

But Fuller not only thought that the reliance interest had been under-emphasized in American law. He also thought that in some important types of cases it would be more appropriate for the court to grant *only* reliance damages. For example, in some of these cases the parties had "not quite" made a contract.[61] Or they might have made a contract involving a non-market transaction in which the expectation interest was not truly firm or readily measurable. Fuller argued that in such cases the party at fault should only be required to compensate the aggrieved party for any change of position, that is, pay reliance damages, not lost expectancy damages.

In 1982, an American contracts scholar expressed the opinion that: "No scholarly work during the period between the first and second Restatement of Contracts [1931-1981] had more impact on the law of contracts than . . . [Fuller's article]."[62] Did Fuller draw on Jhering's work here? Fuller is quite explicit. In the text of his article, Fuller states:

> In his pioneering article on culpa in contrahendo, Jhering suggested
> that the reliance interest (in his terminology, the negative interest)
> ought to be the proper measure of recovery in a series of situations
> which we may call 'not quite' contracts.[63]

Here, it is not so much that Jhering is calling attention to neglect of the reliance interest as such, but rather that Jhering is suggesting the distinctive appropriateness of the reliance measure for certain kinds of cases where a court might otherwise refuse any recovery because there is 'not quite' a contract. Fuller himself stressed this as one of the main points of his own article, too. In his article he said that in granting reliance recovery in such cases, "We stop halfway between full contract liability (expectation interest) and a denial of liability altogether."[64] And he added that cases granting such reliance recovery "represent a kind of midway station between no contract and a 'complete' contract."[65] Two years later, in a letter to Karl Llewellyn, Fuller wrote as follows:

> To me it seems clear that no analysis of contract law can be realistic
> or adequate which does not recognize that there exists a hierarchy
> of contract interests, which may be sloganized by saying that they
> extend from restitution through the reliance interest to the
> expectation interest, with a number of little midstations, disturbing
> to elegantia juris, along the way. . . . I feel, incidentally, that your
> failure to employ this approach is attributable in part to your

preoccupation with businessmen's business agreements, especially sales. . . . I consider the contribution made in my article on the reliance interest to lie, not in calling attention to the reliance interest itself, but in an analysis which breaks down the contract-no-contract dichotomy, and substitutes an ascending scale of enforceability.[66]

Fuller also wrote another pioneering article on the theory of contract law. This article was on the Anglo-American doctrine of consideration, and it appeared in 1941 in the Columbia Law Review.[67] In this article, Fuller addressed what he called the substantive and formal bases of contract liability. In regard to the formal bases, Fuller treated among other things, the rationales behind the American requirement of consideration for a valid contract. The requirement of consideration in our law of contract is formal in the sense that it is content-independent. It does not require that, to be valid, an agreement must have any particular content. Rather, it generally requires only that an agreement take the form of a bargained for exchange.[68] When discussing the rationales for this requirement, Fuller explicitly drew on Jhering's treatment of the general rationales for legal formalities appearing in Der Geist.[69] Thus Fuller discusses what he calls the evidentiary, cautionary, and channeling functions of legal formalities, and points out, for example, that the requirement of consideration--of a bargain--serves both the cautionary and channeling functions.[70] In regard to the cautionary function, Fuller endorses the view that in a bargain transaction, as opposed to a gift transaction, each party is likely to exercise caution. That is, each party, thinking of the quid pro quo he or she is to receive, is likely to adopt a circumspective frame of mind. In regard to the channeling function, Fuller suggests that the bargain form itself provides a distinct mode of thought and expression which, when the parties resort to it, enables them reasonably to assume that they are entering into a binding relationship.

Here, Fuller draws heavily on Jhering's Der Geist and acknowledges Jhering's insights with respect to legal formalities.[71] In Der Geist, Jhering provides a comprehensive analysis of the "advantages of form", and these include the very evidentiary, cautionary, and channeling functions that Fuller mentions.[72] Indeed, in my view, Jhering's discussion is better than Fuller's, especially in regard to the cautionary and channeling functions.

IX. Jhering and the Formal Character of Law

I will now conclude with comments on the formal character of law, and Jhering's possible influence on my own much more modest efforts. In *Der Zweck*, Jhering indicates in several places that in his view law has several fundamental characteristics. One characteristic of law is that it has distinctive substantive content which includes prohibitions against violence and protection of personal property from theft. Another characteristic is that law is basically purposive in nature. Still another characteristic is that law is coercive. But Jhering emphasizes that law is formal in character, too, and by this he meant far more than that the law of contract includes formal requirements. Jhering, however, did not develop this thesis. The thesis that law is formal in character has not yet been frontally and systematically developed by any Anglo-American legal theorist, either. I am currently at work on a book on the subject.[73] I regret that Jhering did not himself frontally address the subject. There can be no doubt that he was far more qualified to provide a full account of form in the law than am I, given his classical training, his great knowledge of legal history including that of the Roman law, his language abilities, his extraordinary perceptiveness, and his theoretical sophistication.

Though Jhering did not attempt a general theory of law's formal character, he did point out that such implementive devices of the law as its embodiment in published rules and the existence of adjudicative procedures for their coercive application are *formal*, in contrast to the substantive *content* of the rules to be applied. I will elaborate Jhering's general point here only by remarking that, in varying degrees, rules have formal attributes such as prescriptiveness, definiteness, generality, and simplicity. In my book on formality that I am working on, the first branch of my thesis will be not only that legal rules, but *all* basic types of legal phenomena are significantly formal in character. This is not a mere tautology, for it is an important and difficult question just in what ways and how far legal phenomena are formal. In my own system of thought, legal phenomena include, in addition to rules, legislatures, source-oriented criteria of legal validity, the methodology for statutory interpretation, the basic principle of stare decisis, general limits on the power of judges and other officials to modify rules at point of application, adjudicative processes, the phenomena of legal personality, and more. I believe Jhering's writings indicate that he would have agreed with the first branch of my thesis.

It is a second branch of my thesis that a functioning legal system viewed as a whole has, in some degree, major formal features. These include a unified institutional structure, coherence of the substantive law, and adherence to principles of legality when implementing the law. The formalness of these systemic features can be elaborately analyzed, and our legal literature includes some fine essays on these topics, though not conceived as part of a theory of form in law. I believe Jhering would have been interested in seeing the second branch of my thesis developed in detail, too.

The formal character of law is a function of the *necessities* of legal ordering, a function of general *rationales* (values) special to law's formalness, a function of *institutional* and *processual* considerations, and a function of the demands of problem-specific *policy*. Let us consider briefly what I call the general rationales special to formalness. A distinct class of varied general *rationales* specially justifies and informs, as appropriate, the formal character of basic types of legal phenomena, and the formal character of the legal system viewed as a whole. If we consider only legal rules, as one basic type of legal phenomenon, we can readily see that they, like all basic types of legal phenomena, are complex fusions of form and content. In the case of rules, the fusions are, as it were, informed by special rationales for formalness and by various institutional and processual values on the one hand, and by the problem-specific policies that call law into play in the first place, on the other hand. These special rationales include predictability, uniformity of application, constraint of official arbitrariness, and more. Rules, then, are not just a means to the end of serving problem-specific policies or purposes, as Jhering himself observed. Rules are also a means of serving or fulfilling special rationales for formalness and also institutional and processual values. Though Jhering did not so name these rationales, he acknowledged their role.

Depending on the problem, the rationales for formalness may conflict with problem-specific policy. In the event of such conflict, at the law-making stage, the rationales for formalness may even justifiably modify or over-ride problem-specific policy to a significant extent in the final fusion of form and content in a legal rule. When so, form leaves an especially deep imprint on content. Moreover, what I have just said about form and content in relation to rules applies to all types of legal phenomena, *mutatis mutandis*, and also to form in the legal system as a whole, *mutatis mutandis*.

The formal character of law, then has its own distinctive normative claims in social ordering through law, and its own special bearing on law's overall content. Today this is not very well understood in some quarters. The complex interactions between form and content are also not very well understood, and are studied even less. One consequence of this is that some branches of American law are relatively formless and almost infinitely pliable. Many American theorists are unduly impatient with form. Indeed, to some American theorists, the law, when it errs, always errs on the side of being formalistic and never on the side of being substantivistic. Some theorists regularly collapse the distinction between the formal and the formalistic in law, and even treat the formal in law as *ipso facto* bad, or as little more than a kind of unavoidable excrescence.

But Rudolf von Jhering had profound respect for legal form and its normative claims. Though he was critical of conceptualism and of the excesses of logic in legal reasoning, this did not lead him to denigrate the role of form in law. Rather, he stressed the role of form in private law and in public law, and even emphasized that legal form can be a safeguard of liberty. Indeed he claimed that form is the twin sister of liberty and the sworn enemy of the arbitrary. If Jhering were here today, I believe he would encourage us in the pursuit of nothing less than a general theory that law is formal in character.

Notes

1. Unfortunately, several major works of Jhering have not been translated into English. In particular, DER GEIST DES RÖMISCHEN RECHTS, and the second volume of DER ZWECK im Recht have not been translated. I will sometimes refer to these as Der Geist and Der Zweck, although when I cite to the first volume of Der Zweck, this will usually be to the English

translation of the 4th German edition of that volume: Rudolf von Jhering, LAW AS A MEANS TO AN END (1914, MacMillan, New York). Der Geist was published in its first edition in several volumes in 1865. The first edition of the first volume of Der Zweck appeared in 1877; the second in 1883. See generally, Okko Behrends, Rudolph von Jhering (1818-1832) *Der Durchbruck zum Zweck des Rechts,* in RECHTS- WISSENSCHAFT IN GÖTTINGEN-- GÖTTINGER JURISTEN aus 250 Jahren 229-269 (Fritz Loos, ed. Göttingen 1987). See also, Franz Wieacker, *Rudolph von Jhering* in GRÜNDER UND BEWAHRER pp. 197-212 (1959).

2. An intellectual influence may itself not be original. Also, an influence does not have to shape the actual content of the views of a later thinker. It may also take the form of reinforcing an idea already held, or the form of articulating an idea better so it stands more of a chance of survival, or the form of merely contributing to an intellectual climate in which an idea can take root and flourish. And more.

3. Zweigert and Siehr, *Jhering's Influence on the Development of Comparative Legal Method,* 19 AMER. J. OF COMP. LAW 215, 225 (1971).

4. O.W. Holmes, Jr., THE COMMON LAW 208 (Boston 1881).

5. Notably in SCHERZ UND ERNST IN DER JURISPRUDENZ (9th ed., Leipzig 1900), translated in part into English in M. Cohen and F. Cohen, Readings in JURISPRUDENCE AND LEGAL PHILOSOPHY 678-689 (Boston 1951).

6. In regard to the professors, see, e.g., C.C. Langdell, A SUMMARY OF THE LAW OF CONTRACTS (2nd ed., Boston 1880); *Teaching Law as a Science,* 3 LAW Q. REV. 124 (1887). On March 16, 1937, Professor Lon L. Fuller, then of Duke Law School, wrote Professor Phillip Heck of Tübingen a most interesting letter (in response to a letter from Heck) in which Fuller, in the spirit of Jhering, remarked that "the Begriffskultus" was not a "peculiarly German disease" and that "we had here in America a veritable juristischen Begriffshimmel on earth." Fuller went on to single out as examples Dean Langdell of Harvard, and various others. Fuller stressed that this "Begriffskultus is by no means dead today." The letter is in the Lon L. Fuller Papers at Harvard Law School. For discussion of "conceptualist" and "formalistic" judging in this era, see Robert S. Summers, INSTRUMENTALISM AND AMERICAN LEGAL THEORY Ch. 6 (Ithaca 1982).

7. See supra, note 5.

8. III DER GEIST DES RÖMISCHEN RECHTS, 321 (Breitkopf and Härtel, Leipzig 7th ed. 1923).

9. Mark D. Howe, JUSTICE OLIVER WENDELL HOLMES, JR.: THE PROVING YEARS 152 (Cambridge, Mass. 1957).

10. Holmes, supra note 4, at 1.

11. Holmes, *The Path of the Law,* 10 HARV. L. REV. 457, 465 (1897).

12. Holmes, *Law in Science and Science in Law,* 12 HARV. L. REV. 443, 460 (1899).

13. See, e.g., Pound, *Mechanical Jurisprudence,* 8 COLUM. L. REV. 605 (1903), and Karl N. Llewellyn THE BRAMBLE BUSH, esp. at 67-72 (New York 1930). See also H.L.A. Hart, *Jhering's Heaven of Concepts and Modern Analytical Jurisprudence* in ESSAYS IN

JURISPRUDENCE AND PHILOSOPHY 265 (Oxford 1983).

14. See Robert S. Summers, INSTRUMENTALISM AND AMERICAN LEGAL THEORY ch. 6 (Ithaca 1982) and Robert S. Summers, PRAGMATISCHER INSTRUMENTALISMUS UND AMERIKANISCHE RECHTSTHEORIE--DARSTELLUNG UND KRITIK (Freiburg 1983)(a very general summary of the book in English in the preceding reference).

15. See, e.g., Pound, *Enforcement of Law*, 20 GREEN BAG 401, 403 (1908).

16. I LAW AS A MEANS TO AN END, Author's Preface liii-liv (Eng. trans. of 4th German edition, New York 1914).

17. Holmes, supra note 11, at 476.

18. Pound, "The Need of a Sociological Jurisprudence", 19 Green Bag 607, 612 (1907).

19. Karl N. Llewellyn, "Some Realism About Realism--Responding to Dean Pound", 44 Harv. L. Rev. 1222, 1236 (1931).

20. Fuller's best writings on law's means and ends and on the means-end relation in law are MEANS AND ENDS in Lon L. Fuller, THE PRINCIPLES OF SOCIAL ORDER 47-64 (K. Winston ed., Durham 1981); L. Fuller, ANATOMY OF THE LAW 36-39 (London 1968); Fuller, *An Afterword: Science and the Judicial Process,* 79 HARV. L. REV. 1604, 1626-28 (1966); Fuller, *American Legal Philosophy at MidCentury*, 6 J. LEGAL ED. 457, 473-81 (1954); and Fuller, *Memorandum in On The Teaching of Law in the Liberal Arts Curriculum* 37-43 (H. Berman ed. Mineola, N.Y. 1956). See also R.S. Summers, INSTRUMENTALISM AND AMERICAN LEGAL THEORY Ch. 2 (Ithaca 1982).

21. J. Bentham, THE PRINCIPLES OF MORALS AND LEGISLATION IN I WORKS (J. Bowring ed., London 1838-43).

22. See, e.g., William James, *The Moral Philosopher and the Moral Life*, in THE WRITINGS OF WILLIAM JAMES 623 (J. McDermott ed., New York 1967)

23. See, e.g., John Dewey, THEORY OF THE MORAL LIFE 98-101 (New York 1932).

24. Oliphant, *The New Legal Education*, 131 THE NATION 495 (1930).

25. Supra note 16, at 241.

26. Id. at 231.

27. Id.

28. Id. at 233-39.

29. See, e.g., supra note 11.

30. Pound, *The Scope and Purpose of Sociological Jurisprudence*, 25 HARV. L. REV. 489, 514 (1912).

31. Karl N. Llewellyn, THE BRAMBLE BUSH 3 (New York 1930).

32. F. Cohen, *The Problem of a Functional Jurisprudence*, 1 MOD. L. REV. 5, 21 (1937).

33. Summers, *Professor Fuller's Jurisprudence and America's Dominant Philosophy of Law*, 92 HARV. L. REV. 433, 445-47 (1978).

34. THE JURISPRUDENCE OF INTERESTS (trans. and ed. Magdalena Schoch, Cambridge 1948)(including translations of Rümelin, Heck, Oertmann, Stoll, Binder and Isay).

35. Id.

36. Pound's main writings on this theme are collected in R. Pound, III JURISPRUDENCE 3-376 (St. Paul 1959).

37. Id., at 15 (Pound says he has "preferred to build on Jhering's idea of interests.").

38. See generally, Coing, *Bentham's Importance in the Development of Interessenjurisprudenz and General Jurisprudence*, 2 IRISH JURIST 336 (1967).

39. Coing points out that Jhering refers to Beneke's translation of Bentham. See Coing, supra note 38, at 342 n. 30.

40. Rudolph von Jhering, II DER ZWECK IM RECHT pp. 132-213 (Breitkopf and Härtel, Leipzig 1883).

41. See also Jenkins, *Rudolf von Jhering*, 14 VAND. L. REV. 169, 173-74 (1960).

42. Jhering, supra note 16, at 325.

43. Id.

44. Id. at 330.

45. Id. at 345.

46. Id. at Author's Preface liv.

47. Id. at 267-294.

48. Id. at 328-329.

49. Id. at 246, 322.

50. Holmes, *Law in Science and Science in Law*, 12 HARV. L. REV. 443, 456 (1899).

51. Holmes, supra note 4, at 41.

52. Pound, supra note 36, at 331.

53. Lon L. Fuller, THE LAW IN QUEST OF ITSELF 11 (Evanston 1940).

54. Fuller, *American Legal Philosophy at Mid-Century*, 6 J. LEGAL ED. 457, 470 (1954).

55. Fuller, *The Forms and Limits of Adjudication*, 92 HARV. L. REV. 353 (1978).

56. Lon L. Fuller, THE MORALITY OF LAW (2nd. ed., New Haven 1969). See generally, Robert S. Summers, LON L. FULLER ch. 2 (Stanford 1984).

57. Summers and Marshall, *The Argument From Ordinary Meaning in Statutory Interpretation*, 43 NO. IRELAND LAW QUARTERLY 213 (1992).

58. Fuller & Perdue, *The Reliance Interest in Contract Damages,* 46 YALE L. J. 52 (1936).

59. Id. at 52.

60. Id. at 53-54.

61. Id. at 86.

62. Hudec, *Restating the Reliance Interest*, 67 CORNELL L. REV. 704 (1982).

63. Fuller, supra note 58, at 86.

64. Id. at 87.

65. Id.

66. Lon L. Fuller Papers, Harvard Law School Library.

67. Fuller, *Consideration and Form*, 41 COLUM. L. REV. 799 (1941).

68. Thus, in logical terms, two agreements could have the same content in the sense that in each there could be a transfer of the same objects from one party to the other, but only one agreement be a valid contract because only in it were the objects reciprocally bargained for. Or two agreements could be very different in content in the sense that the objects being transferred are very different, yet both could be valid because the objects were reciprocally bargained for.

69. Fuller, supra note 67, at 800-801.

70. Id. at 816.

71. Id.

72. II DER GEIST DES RÖMISCHEN RECHTS 493 et.seq. (Breitkopf and Härtel, Leipzig 8th ed. 1923).

73. For a preliminary and tentative sketch, see Summers, *The Formal Character of Law*, 51 CAMBRIDGE L.J. 242 (1991).

CHAPTER 3

LAW AS A TYPE OF "MACHINE" TECHNOLOGY

1. Introduction

In the United States during the first half of the last century, a great instrumentalist revolution in the general theory of law occurred. The leaders of this revolution were Oliver Wendell Holmes, Jr. (1841 - 1935), John Dewey (1859 - 1952), Roscoe Pound (1870 - 1964) and Karl N. Llewellyn (1893 - 1962). In an earlier article, I summarized the general tenets of this highly influential body of instrumentalist thought.[1]

One important overall theme in the writings of many instrumentalists is that law may be conceived of as if it were a type of "machine technology". In this article, I will use the phrase "machine technology" to mean either the body of knowledge governing the design of a type of machine, or to refer to the actual machines themselves. Perhaps the most significant machine technology of the past 100 years is the internal combustion engine. It is therefore not surprising that a leading American instrumentalist, Karl N. Llewellyn, referred to law as "an engine (a heterogeneous multitude of engines)" and proclaimed that theorists must develop an "effective legal technology".[2] Llewellyn and most other leaders of the American instrumentalist movement, including even Roscoe Pound, frequently used this and other technological metaphors when thinking and writing about law. Thus, for example, they wrote of law as "machinery" and referred to the design and implementation of law as "social engineering".[3] This style of thought continues to be influential in America today. It may become increasingly influential as we move into another great era of technological advance.

Obviously, law is itself not a type of machine technology. As the philosopher-theologian Bishop Butler would have said, "Law is what it is, and not another thing".[4] It would be absurd to *reduce* law to machine technology. Yet there are certain general similarities between some machine technologies and the law, and it is largely because of these similarities that many American instrumentalists came to think of law as if it were a kind of machine technology. In this article I will identify several such similarities. In regard to each, I will explore how an emphasis on it might contribute to a better understanding of law or to wiser uses of law. In this way I will attempt to bring out some possible virtues of conceiving of law itself as if it were a type of machine technology. But I will explore, as well, how an emphasis on each similarity might impair our understanding of law or possibly lead to its unwise use. In this way I will underscore possible vices of thinking about law as if it were a kind of machine technology. My topic is general and vast. In an article, it will only be possible to suggest some of the general directions in which a book-length study of my subject might proceed. A full scale study would also carry us well beyond this article into a number of disciplines besides law, and into various branches of technology, including literary theory and the general study of metaphor, the history of science, the sociology of knowledge, and the philosophy of technology.[5]

II. Machine Technologies, Law, and Human Inventiveness

Machines are the products of deliberate creative efforts taking place at specific, datable, points in time. Machines are systematically designed for anticipated uses in light of existing scientific, technological, and practical knowledge. When made, they are, as such "finished products". Much law is similarly invented by law makers at particular points in time. Statutes are good examples. For instance, a statute may provide that "No vehicles are to be taken into the park". This statute is designed in light of community goals, general knowledge, and perhaps specific empirical research, to keep the park safe and quiet. Once made, it may also be a relatively "finished product".

An emphasis on the general similarity between machine technology and the law (at least statutes) as "products" of human inventiveness may be salutary in a number of ways. For one thing, it is easy to lose sight of the fact that law, like machine technology, is a major and fertile field for the play of human inventiveness. In the course of history, many ingenious legal devices have been invented, often in light of existing scientific and other knowledge. There is much scope in the law for the play of something analogous to technological rationalism. It is even possible to invent whole new techniques for the deployment of law.[6] When making a statute to secure quiet and safety in a park, a lawmaking body should gather facts about vehicles (and other sources of noise) in the park, should identify alternative feasible prohibitions and enforcement devices, and determine which will serve the most goals at least cost.

Also, given the vast and seemingly impersonal character of our law, much of which was made long ago by people dead for many years, it is easy to lose sight of the fact that every law inherited from the past was at one time the product of the heads and hands of a responsible person or persons. As a result of having lost sight of this elemental fact, citizens today may not be so ready to assume their proper democratic responsibility for the quality of law that continues in force now. Instead, some citizens tend to assume that the nature and content of our inherited law just is a "given", or part of "the nature of things", rather than the product of individual human creativity and therefore something that can be remade or even unmade by citizens acting today through their lawmakers. Yet if law is analogized to technology, it is possible to see immediately that this picture of law is false. Existing machines are constantly being improved. Obsolete machines are constantly being abandoned. Similarly, it follows that laws can be reformed. Obsolete laws can be repealed, too. For example, speed limits in parks for horse carts became obsolete when autos were invented (a form of legal obsolescence caused by technological change itself).

But this emphasis on the similarity between machines and law as products of human inventiveness can also be misleading or dangerous in important ways. Not all significant forms of law are like statutes in how they are made, or in their ultimate form. They are thus much less like machines. For example, customary law is not deliberately created at specific, datable moments in time. It just grows up and evolves over time. Nor are such general moral principles as that "no person shall be allowed to profit from his own wrong" created in the fashion of a statute, yet such principles play important roles inside the law. Nor can all judge-made rules of law be traced to specific instances of judicial inventiveness. Rather, some have simply accumulated and become more than the sum of their parts.

Actually, even statutes are rather more different from machines than I have so far assumed. Many statutes are partly inchoate, fragmentary and nascent even when initially enacted, so that they must take on further content and meaning over time. And very often statutes are over-inclusive or under-inclusive and require some corrective interpretation. Suppose, for example, that a park attendant drives a truck into the park to empty the trash bins. A statute that reads: "No vehicles shall be taken into the park" would be over-inclusive if applied to this truck driver. Although a truck might be a "vehicle taken into the park", on a sound interpretation, the park attendant should be not guilty of violating this statute. Such problems of interpretation are unavoidable. It is rare that a statute, or any other form of law, is truly a "finished product" in the fashion of the usual machine. A statute always needs some further interpretation.

Scientific empiricism and technological rationalism can be carried too far. These "isms" led some American instrumentalist jurists to think of lawmaking as solely empirical and technological in the following general ways. Lawmakers begin with the facts of a problem. They determine facts about the wants and interests of affected parties, and facts about any conflicts between those wants and interests. (Democratic processes and sometimes rough administrative and judicial judgment help in this.) Wants and interests thus factually ascertained are then translated into possible goals of laws that might be pursued to resolve or alleviate the problem. Available legal means are identified. What these are is essentially a factual question, as are differences between those means and the degree of "fit" between means and goals. Factual estimates — predictions, about the efficacy of different means-goal hypotheses have to be made. Predictions are also made about likely further consequences and side effects. Comparative estimates about which alternative means-goal hypotheses will fulfill what wants or interests, and how effectively, are made. Finally, the lawmakers adopt the most effective means-goal hypothesis, overall. Thus, in the foregoing ways, essentially factual considerations cumulate to "dictate" all decisions.

But this is a false picture, however much it may appeal to the empirically minded technological rationalist. Not all important questions are questions of fact. Wants and interests have to be debated and evaluated, especially in a democracy. And even when a question is one of fact we need not necessarily turn to scientific empiricism or technological rationalism for the answer. We also have a great humanistic tradition from which to derive knowledge when making law. For example, we know that children love to play in parks and even to make some noise there. How important is such play? Should children be allowed to use motor scooters in the park? Motor driven toy airplanes? These are not, as such, questions of fact. And if the answers to these questions are "yes", then the statute should not prohibit all vehicles in the park.

The technological analogy is perhaps most dangerous when it leads law makers to treat questions of law making as technical in their entirety, with decision-making power then assigned solely to experts. For example, experts who have devices for measuring noise levels may, *in effect,* be given the authority to decide whether a proposed statute to control noise in the park should prohibit toy airplanes with motors. When this occurs, other affected persons, including those who have special concerns for the children, may have no effective voice in the decision. Only the experts are called upon to decide, because they are masters of the "relevant technology". Their primacy is reinforced because they can measure noise levels in the park, whereas it is not possible to measure the joy to children of playing there. Thus, quantifiability and expertise triumph. Here again the scientific and technological tradition displaces the more humanistic one.

III. Machine Technologies, Law, and the Instrumentalist Ethos

Machine technologies are designed and created to serve human ends. They are practical means to practical goals and thus essentially instrumental phenomena. Similarly, law has its instrumental facets. It, too, consists of practical means to practical goals.[7] An emphasis on this general similarity between technology and law can be a virtue. For example, a society may be one in which lawmakers or lawmaking bodies are overly ready to turn to law to solve problems.[8] It would then be especially important to stress the nature of the grounds upon which legal intervention can be justified. It is immediately obvious that a technology cannot be self-justifying. A technology must be justified as instrumental to a goal. Those who fully understand this general truth about technology might also be more readily persuaded that any given use of law can only be justified on instrumentalist grounds (defined suitably broadly). That is, proponents of a law, actual or proposed, must show that it appropriately serves or would serve some goal (or goals) external to that law. For example, proponents of a statute providing that "No vehicles shall be taken into the park" must justify it on some such ground as that it would secure justified levels of quiet and safety (external goals).

Yet there is some risk of serious distortion in thus presenting law as if it were *merely a means* to external goals in the way that, for example, an electric cow milking machine is merely a means to the external goal of saving labor costs. In regard to such a machine we do say, or can say that it is *merely a means.* The case of law is somewhat different. In regard to any potential use of law of any real degree of complexity, several possible goals to be secured are usually involved, and usually there are several alternative means. One means will serve one set of goals at varying levels, and at the same time disserve certain other goals. Another means will serve another set of goals at varying levels and disserve certain other goals. For example, proposed Statute A prohibiting all motor vehicles in the park will greatly improve quiet and safety in the park but at the cost of interfering with children playing with motorized toy airplanes, or with motorized scooters. But proposed Statute B which prohibits *only* "trucks, automobiles, and motorcycles" will not secure as much quiet and safety in the park, yet will allow much more play. (We are assuming that play is a major park goal, too.) But it is somewhat misleading to say that each of these statutes is *merely a means.* Rather, each is a means to one set of goals, with accompanying sacrifice of other goals. Thus, it is better to say each is an *integrated means-goal complex* that promises a form of total, overall, goal realization different in kind from any alternative means goal complex. (The external goals of each means-goal complex are somehow *integral* to their means.) In sum, laws should not be characterized merely as means.

There is a further and equally fundamental reason why law should not be characterized *merely as means* to external goals of social policy. When law is made, lawmakers frequently take into account certain considerations special to law besides the dictates of external goals of social policy. These desiderata include having the law appropriately intelligible, in the form of a rule, factually administrable, generally prospective, and the like. Such internal desiderata, as well as the law's external goals determine its content. Law is not "all means" and "no goals". Law has goals (non-technical values) of its own.[9]

Distortion is possible, too, if it is assumed, in instrumentalist fashion, that goals of law are always realized only after a law is put to successful use and that use has somehow come to an end. Actually, the goals of some kinds of law are processual, and are realized only in the course of a law's use.

Consider, for example, a law requiring a fair hearing for a person accused of an offense. For example, a person accused of taking a motor cycle into the park contrary to the "no vehicle" statute should be allowed a fair opportunity to prove he or she was not riding, but only pushing, it in the park, and that the motor was shut off (if this was the claimed defense). This fair opportunity is realized in *the course* of the trial process, not after it is over.[10]

It is true that machines are usually mere tools in the hands of their operators to be wielded or deployed more or less at will. But if law is viewed technologically as a mere *instrument of* political power, this distorts its nature in another fundamental way. Law is not essentially an instrument of political power with no autonomy of its own. It can even have a kind of autonomy of its own in relation to political power. Of course, in a particular society, law may not actually have such autonomy. It may be totally subservient to political power. But there are societies in which law is not thus subservient, and this shows it can be autonomous. In such societies, the law itself defines what constitutes a lawful exercise of political power in three ways: Law specifies who may exercise political power, how, and *within what* limits. One important type of exercise of power is that of making a political decision without laying down a general rule applicable to a class of cases of which the case at hand is one instance. Another type of exercise of political power is that of punishing people. The law itself may limit the extent to which holders of political power may do such things. For example, it may adopt the principle nulla *poena sine* lege. According to this principle, police and prosecutors alone would be without power to punish persons who drive noisy trucks through a park. A law would also have to be passed such as the one providing that "No vehicles may be taken into the park", before such truck drivers could be stopped, convicted and punished. Furthermore, when lawmakers do purport to make law in the form of general rules, the law may prescribe how and within what bounds this may be done. In these ways, law constitutes and constrains political power, and thus has a kind of autonomy of its own, at least in relation to political power.

Similarly, when putative law is being identified as law (as "valid"), the law itself may specify the standards by which particular instances of putative law are to be identified as law. The law itself may also specify that such law is to be objectively interpreted in accord with a specified general technique, and that disputed issues of fact are to be objectively resolved in accord with a process designed to that end. Indeed, these law-identifying, law-interpreting, and fact-finding functions may themselves be assigned in the first place, or at least by way of appeal, to an independent judiciary that is institutionally isolated from, and not directly amenable, to the wishes and decisions of current holders of political power. Thus, for example, a truck driver who is unpopular with the government because of his political views and who also happens to be charged with unlawfully driving his truck in the park would have to be convicted, if at all, by a court that is institutionally isolated from the political process. In these obvious ways, too, law may constitute and constrain political power and thus have autonomy of its own.

Of course, an emphasis on the similarity between law and technology as instrumentalist phenomena might lead to improvements in the use of law, as well. This type of emphasis tends to give efficiency its due. The probability becomes higher that due regard will be paid in the design of the law to determining the most efficient "fit" between means and goals. An instrumentalist orientation probably also fosters a purposive approach to interpretation in which the law's purposes infuse its literal language with authoritative meaning. The purposes of a law (its goals) are frequently not expressly stated in its language. For example, the purposes of securing quiet and safety are not stated in the statute that provides: "No vehicles shall be taken into the park." Moreover, the complex implementive verbiage of a law may actually serve to obscure its underlying purposes. Thus an instrumentalist orientation which conceptualizes law as a means to goals fosters a general consciousness of purposes when solving problems of interpretation. A judge alert to the importance of purposes would, for example, not interpret the above statute to exclude battery-driven wheelchairs even though they are vehicles, if they do not interfere with the statute's purposes of securing quiet and safety.[11]

But again, there is another side to this story. A technologically inspired emphasis on law's instrumental character can also foster a means-mindedness — an undue concern with efficiency when making and administering law, and an insufficient concern for the substantive quality of the law's means and the substantive quality of its goals. Lawyers may be specially subject to these risks. Many of them already tend to be willing to devise means of furthering the goals of any public bodies whom they advise, and the goals of their private clients, without subjecting those goals themselves to careful evaluative scrutiny, when appropriate.

The adoption of an instrumentalist perspective on law born of technological analogies can, in a special way, not only distort our understanding of the workings of law but also help explain why citizens sometimes fail to subject the official administration of law to the vigilant scrutiny it requires. Such a perspective may lead some lay citizens and even lawyers to view the workings of law as technical, ministerial, and even mechanical. Yet this view of law as an essentially automated phenomenon is false. Law's effective and sound administration, day by day, is regularly dependent on acts of thoughtful human judgment in finding facts and in interpreting and applying law. Officials themselves must remain conscious of this. Lawyers and informed citizens must not take their eyes off official administration, for it is not a mechanically self-executing affair. The administration of law must be carefully scrutinized, especially in its discretionary aspects. The policing of parks should not be left solely up to the police!

IV. Machine Technologies, Law, and Complexity

Most machine technologies are complex and some are exceedingly complex. When embodied in actual machines, this complexity takes the form of various component parts that interact in various ways, often intricate. Similarly, much law is complex. A statute, for example, may consist of various densely packed paragraphs that interact in various ways, often intricate.[12] Not only are much technology and much law similar in the nature and degree of their complexity, they can be brought together in a kind of interlocking complexity. Indeed, many complex laws and their administration presuppose, incorporate, or otherwise involve complex technology. Even a simple scheme of legal regulation such as that applicable in our public park example may bring technology into play in a variety of ways: park attendants may carry radios to call for help when offenses occur in the park, carry clocks to determine when to close the park at night, use intricate locks to lock park gates, and so on.

A stress upon the similarity between technology and law in terms of their complexity may likewise prove salutary. Just as machines can often be improved by making them more complex, so, too, can legal rules or bodies of law often be improved by making them more complex, as by drawing more distinctions, or by adding preconditions, coordinating provisos, and so forth. Where these truths are generally understood, the populace may also be led to see that increased complexity may be one avenue of improvement in our law.

Moreover, complex technology requires the recruitment and training of specialists to improve and to maintain this very technology. Advanced societies even adopt general social policies that facilitate the education and functioning of such specialists. Similarly, societies must recruit and provide for the training of specialists to improve, maintain and help carry out the law. The law is too complex to be left solely to the custodianship of lay citizens. Citizens in a highly technological social order who understand the need for trained technologists and support for technology may be more easy to convince of the need to provide support for the training of lawyers and for general improvements and maintenance of the legal order. (At the same time, it is not surprising that general social movements of an anti-technological kind have tended to be skeptical of specialists generally - including lawyers.)

On the other hand, in a modern industrial society with all of its technological complexity, general attitudes of mind may emerge which lead lawmakers to create increasingly technical and complex law, and induce citizens to accept such law as more or less inevitable, or even as a part of the natural order of things. In this way technological complexity may foster excessive legal complexity. At the very least, citizens may become more tolerant of high levels of legal complexity. If they cannot understand the workings of all the numerous machines and gadgets in their midst, why should they expect to understand the numerous laws in their midst? It is undeniable that in many western technological societies, law is becoming, in many of its branches, highly complex. Instead of simple signs at the entrances to parks that read: "No vehicles shall be taken into the park", we not infrequently today encounter very large signs at park entrances which set forth lengthy regulations on quiet and safety, sometimes even with definitions of key terms in the regulations set out separately!

Excessive legal complexity can take many forms, and is not without important costs. I can here only pause to identify the main costs. First, the average citizen may not be able to tell what his or her rights are, even when going to a lawyer, for the complexity of the law may be beyond the grasp of the average lawyer. This is true today, in varying degrees, of many tax laws, environmental regulations, and local zoning laws in America, for instance.

Second, excessive legal complexity can give rise to serious inequalities in the exercise of legal rights. Only those who have money to pay extraordinarily competent lawyers will be able to realize the advantages of highly complex laws. This is a major criticism of certain American laws governing tax liability.

Third, when laws become unduly complex, it is much more difficult for informed lawyers and citizens to serve as watchdogs over the official administration of such laws. If only the highly specialized administrators of the law can know what the law really means, no one else can check on whether these administrators are properly interpreting and applying the law. Yet we know that all administrators make mistakes, or err in judgment.

Fourth, the excessive complexity of laws that depend for their effectiveness on general citizen observance helps to explain why such laws are not very effective. Complexity is a major factor operating to limit the efficacy of law. An ineffective law can itself be costly in many ways.

Fifth, just as highly complex technology leaves citizens with a sense of powerlessness, overly complex laws can undermine the sense of autonomous self-governance within a democracy. Thus the very health of that democracy may be at risk.

Other factors help to explain the increasing complexity of much of our law besides the force of examples of complex technologies ever present in our midst. But the general force of these examples is reinforced by the very fact that law itself may be conceived in technological terms, so that it is thought of, discussed, and treated as if it were a type of machinery with more or less inevitable tendencies to complexity.

V. Conclusion

There are many other important similarities between technology and law besides the three I have been able to identify here. There are also some major differences between technology and law which I have not alluded to at all. But if I were to consider these other similarities and differences, I am certain I would also conclude in the end that the virtues of conceiving of law as if it were a type of machine technology (or indeed any kind of technology) are not as great as the vices.

Notes

1. R. S. Summers, *Pragmatic Instrumentalism and American Legal Theory*, in: Rechtstheorie 13 (1982) p. 257. See also R. S. Summers, PRAGMATISCHER INSTRUMENTALISMUS UND AMERIKANISCHE RECHTSTHEORIE, Freiburg - Munchen 1983, and Summers, INSTRUMENTALISM AND AMERICAN LEGAL THEORY, Ithaca, New York 1982.

2. The "engine" quote is in: K. N. Llewellyn, *A Realistic Jurisprudence: The Next Step*, 30 Columbia L. Rev. 432, 464 (1930): the "technology" quote is from: W. Twining, KARL LLEWELLYN AND THE REALIST MOVEMENT, Birkenhead, 1973, p.522.

3. R. Pound, AN INTRODUCTION TO THE PHILOSOPHY OF LAW, New Haven, 1922, p. 47.

4. See the preface to G. E. Moore, PRINCIPIA ETHICA, Cambridge, 1956.

5. On the philosophy of technology as such, see F. Rapp, ANALYTICAL PHILOSOPHY OF TECHNOLOGY, DORDRECHT, 1981.

6. Over the last two hundred years, we have even seen the invention of two new large-scale legal techniques: the administrative-regulatory, and the benefit-distributive. See R. S. Summers, *The Technique Element in Law*, 59 CALIF. L. REV. 733 (1971). For discussion of other legal inventions, and references thereto, see Summers, INSTRUMENTALISM AND AMERICAN LEGAL THEORY, Ithaca, New York, 1982, ch. 8.

7. Indeed, Llewellyn wrote of the American instrumentalist legal theorists that: "They view rules, they view law, as means to ends. ... " K. N. Llewellyn, Some Realism About Realism, 44 HARV. L. REV. 1222 (1931).

8. It is often stated that American society is such a society. See B. Manning, Hyperlexis: Our National Disease, 71 NORTHWESTERN L. REV. 767 (1977).

9. For more extended discussion, see R. S. Summers, *Some Considerations Which May Lead Lawmakers to Modify a Policy When Adopting It As Law*, in: ZEITSCHRIFT FÜR DIE GESAMTE STAATSWISSENSCHAFT 41 (1985), p. 141.

10. For further discussion of such "process values", see R. S. Summers, Evaluating and Improving Legal Processes - A Plea for Process Values, 60 CORNELL L. REV. 1 (1974).

11. See further, R. S. Summers, LON L. FULLER, Stanford U. Press, Palo Alto, 1984, p. 118 - 122.

12. This is most especially true of tax laws in some Western countries, particularly the United States. See generally, W. L. Cary, *Reflections on the American Law Institute Tax Project*, 60 COLUMBIA L. REV. 259 (1960).

CHAPTER 4

ON IDENTIFYING AND RECONSTRUCTING A GENERAL LEGAL THEORY

I. Introduction

My purposes in this article are dual: to discuss some relatively neglected issues about the scope, aims, and methods of legal theory that arise out of, yet transcend, the differences between Professor Moore and myself, and to comment on some of Professor Moore's criticisms of my book, *Instrumentalism and American Legal Theory*.[1]

What counts as a general legal theory? How does the subject of legal theory differ from legal sociology? What role should rational reconstruction play when interpreting the writings of a group of theorists? These important issues have been relatively neglected in the history of legal thought. Though they may not be susceptible of definitive resolution in general terms, they certainly merit more discussion than they have received.

Professor Moore's criticisms of my book are comprehensive. He even doubts that there is much of value for legal theory in the entire tradition I have chosen to call "pragmatic intrumentalism" — a tradition that includes certain works of Holmes, Pound, Dewey, Gray, Llewellyn, and Felix Cohen. In the course of discussing the above general issues about the scope, aims, and methods of legal theory, I will comment on some of Professor Moore's criticisms. We do agree on several points. He finds my description of the views of particular theorists to be accurate.[2] He concludes that my reconstruction of their views is legitimate and informative.[3] He concedes that this body of thought has "heavily influenced our contemporary legal theory."[4] But on certain points Professor Moore has not fully understood what I was trying to say. I will single out three of the most important. First, on the opening page of his critique he inaccurately formulates my central thesis. My central thesis is not that pragmatic instrumentalism forms America's only indigenous legal theory, but the nonhistorical thesis that the pragmatic and instrumentalist facets of law are a fertile subject matter for a distinctive type

55

of legal theory on which American and other theorists did some important work, with much still remaining to be done. Second, Professor Moore mischaracterizes my overall assessment of the American contribution to this type of theory. I did not claim that American pragmatic instrumentalism was unqualifiedly a good legal theory, or the "right" legal theory.[5] Nor did I even claim that it was as good as each of the other major legal theories, present as well as past.[6] I did dwell on what I took to be its virtues,[7] but I stressed its deficiencies as well, and it can hardly be said that I accorded it an "exalted position," overall.[8] (Also, when I did compare it with other theories, I compared it mainly with theoretical work already done in other traditions before the instrumentalists came on the scene, not with the most recent work of today, as Professor Moore would have me do.) Third, and contrary to what Professor Moore says, I did set forth in my book several criteria for identifying a body of thought as a general legal theory, and I did defend my judgment that in light of these criteria, American pragmatic instrumentalism qualifies. In so doing, I did not take the position that ordinary empirical sociology of law is, as such, a branch of legal theory.

II. American Pragmatic Instrumentalism

I will first summarize briefly the central tenets of American pragmatic instrumentalism as I reconstructed them in my book. This summary will not only provide important background for my own arguments in subsequent sections of this article, but should also help readers understand more fully the methodological and other issues Professor Moore raises.[9]

First, in this body of thought, one encounters a broadly utilitarian theory of value.[10] The law exists to serve "wants" or "interests" external to law. ("Interest" is defined as the object of any desire.) As Holmes said, "The first requirement of a sound body of law is, that it should correspond with the actual feelings and demands of the community, whether right or wrong."[11] Wants or interests may conflict, and the law should resolve these conflicts so as to maximize the realization of all the wants or interests involved. This overall approach to value may be characterized as pragmatic, rather than ideological.

The second fundamental element is an instrumental conception of legal rules and other forms of law.[12] The law is essentially a body of social means — instruments to serve goals derived from underlying wants and interests. The law is thus a kind of elaborate technology. This technology, in Llewellyn's words, is a "heterogeneous multitude of engines": It is vast and sophisticated and may be broken down into a variety of component parts.[13] Law's technology is a man-made set of tools that may be deployed to serve goals as needed. The officials who make and apply law are viewed as "social engineers," in whose hands the instrumentalities of the law have great potential for social improvement through "social engineering." Officials thus play a large role in instrumentalist theory and generally exercise vastly more discretion than the formalist doctrines of Langdell, Beale, and others allowed.

Third, the instrumentalists espoused a prescriptive theory of law-making in which judges as well as legislators participate fully. Lawmakers are to draw on social scientific knowledge extensively and to take full account of substantive, future-regarding considerations.[14] Formalistic notions, including ideas about the separation of powers, had obscured the true and proper role of judges. Judges can and should join with legislators in making the law. All lawmakers should draw heavily on the findings of the social sciences because the issues in lawmaking can ultimately be reduced to questions of fact. Lawmakers must also draw on democratic processes and on rough and ready judicial judgment, in determining actual wants and interests, and in formulating means-goal hypotheses to maximize them. Social phenomena, including legal precepts, processes, and structures are relatively plastic or malleable and can thus be readily adapted as legal means. The key ends of legal formalism — harmony, coherence and consistency with the rest of the system are relatively unimportant when making new law. In lawmaking, choices should be made in light of the probable substantive effects of alternative means and the extent to which these effects fulfill wants and interests. The entire lawmaking process must be essentially scientific and, of course, consistent with the instrumentalist theory of value. Forms of law are experiments which require constant monitoring and evaluation. The general theory of lawmaking requires an empirical science of law.

The influence of legal positivism is evident in the instrumentalists' official-oriented and source-based theory of legal validity.[15] According to this fourth tenet, a putative rule qualifies as valid law only if an appropriate court or other body has acted upon it or laid it down as law. The content of a putative precept (including its reasonableness and its moral quality) is largely irrelevant to whether the precept is valid. Moreover, the "law in action" prevails over the "law in books."[16] Therefore the behavioral regularities of officials must be scientifically catalogued and described, for law is far more than mere words on paper. Lawyers, when identifying valid law, must *predict* the behavioral regularities of officials, particularly judges. Some instrumentalists also held that legal rules and other forms of law are essentially indeterminate, at least when compared to true rules.

Fifth, judges and other administrators are to follow goal-oriented methods when interpreting and applying valid law.[17] Judges should not follow literalistic "plain meaning" methods, nor should they resort to conceptualist "logic" or other essentially formalistic methods. Forms of law are to be interpreted in light of authoritative goals and other purposes attributable to the law in question. Policy considerations should inform interpretation and application. In deciding on the meaning of judicial precedents, lawyers should consider not only what judges say they are doing, but also what the judges are actually doing. Lawyers should categorize holdings narrowly in terms of patterns of fact. Otherwise, they will overgeneralize and misapply the law. Judges and other officials should not pretend that the law is always determinate. Instead, they should frankly confront the necessity of choice and come to grips with extralegal considerations in the decisional process.

A sixth tenet, also positivistic, is that law and nonlaw (particularly morals) are to be sharply separated.[18] In particular, law and morals must be sharply distinguished. Otherwise, there will be confusion and uncertainty about what the law is. Thus the validity of putative law should be determined solely by whether it was authoritatively laid down or acted upon, and not by reference to its content. If the content of law is made relevant to its validity, this would invite confusion between law and morals and thus undermine predictability. A sharp separation of law and morals also facilitates the pointed criticism of law.

That coercion, force and direct official action are characteristic of law is another leading tenet.[19] The daily effectiveness of law ultimately derives largely from the state's monopoly on coercion, force, and direct action. As

Felix Cohen said, "Whatever cannot be . . . translated [into acts of state force] is functionally meaningless."[20]

Finally, the success of uses of law is to be judged by the effects of those uses.[21] Put roughly, if the desired effects have occurred, then a use of law has been successful. Determinations of the effectiveness of uses of law are factual rather than evaluative, and thus relatively straightforward. In the face of social change, the uses of law must be constantly monitored so that appropriate reforms and adjustments can be made.

The central tenets and corollaries of American pragmatic instrumentalism call for further elaboration, and much of my book is devoted to this.[22] The foregoing is only the barest summary. The tenets are hardly above criticism, and much of my book is devoted to critical evaluation.[23]

I have chosen the name "pragmatic instrumentalism" mainly because of its descriptive accuracy — various elements of this type of theory are instrumentalist and pragmatic. The main task of legal theory is conceived to be that of providing an understanding of law that will make it more valuable as a practical tool in the hands of legal personnel. The varied instrumental facets of legal phenomena including law's goals, law's means, and their interactions are the primary focus of study. Rules of law are viewed essentially as social instruments rather than as mere authoritative norms, expressions of reason, historical data or the like.

This type of theory is also pragmatic in ways not necessarily implied in the term "instrumentalist." For example, these thinkers concentrate on the law *in use* — the "law in action" as well as the "law in books." This focus extends beyond law's external effects and includes the internal workings of its processes. Such theories are also pragmatic in their conception of the relative malleability, for human use, of social and legal phenomena, including legal processes and institutional structures. Further, the law's means and goals are held to derive significantly from functional interrelations emergent in discrete social contexts, also a pragmatic notion.

I concede that the name, "legal realism," is already *sometimes* used to refer to the American version of the type of theory under study. In my judgment, there are many good reasons to cease the use of "legal realism" and to adopt "pragmatic instrumentalism." The expression "legal realism," as often used, is both underinclusive and overinclusive. On the one hand, as often used, it does not include Holmes, Pound, Dewey, and Gray, but refers rather, to a group of younger thinkers writing mainly in the 1920s and 1930s such as Llewellyn, Frank, and Cook. So used, the term is underinclusive. If I am right, it is justified to group Holmes, Pound, Dewey, and Gray together with Llewellyn, Frank, Cook et al., for these thinkers were all participants in the same general directions of thought I have called pragmatic instrumentalism. Indeed, Holmes, Pound, Dewey, and Gray were not mere precursors. Their work was seminal, and highly influential on the younger thinkers who followed. (Nothing is proved by the fact that Llewellyn, Frank, and Cook seem closest to us in time. The past is not a mere backward extension of the present.[24])

On the other hand, the expression "legal realism," as often used, is overinclusive in an important way. Insofar as it is taken to refer to certain views of leading realists of the 1930s (Llewellyn, Frank, Cook, and a number of others), the expression may encompass several extreme tenets that did not, in my view, become part of our dominant instrumentalist philosophy of law, e.g., a cynical conception of the factors that influence judicial decisions (gastronomic jurisprudence), a radical moral skepticism, a notion that the reality of law resides in the behavior patterns of judges, and a view of legal theory as essentially an empirical science. Despite the stridency with which such views were expressed in the 1930s, as I read the historical record they did not become widely influential in the world of law. Yet the expression "legal realism" is frequently taken today to encompass some or all of these views, whereas "pragmatic intrumentalism" does not. Of course, one might legitimately refer to an "extreme realist wing" of pragmatic instrumentalism. But even this formulation is misleading insofar as it signifies that this wing was as influential as instrumentalist theory generally.

In addition, to some thinkers, the term "legal realism" has misleading philosophical connotations. Most instrumentalists were not realists in traditional philosophical usage. They did not share the realist doctrine that abstract words name entities that "exist" outside the mind.[25] Nor did they generally subscribe to a version of scientific realism (in which, roughly speaking, all objects of knowledge are taken to exist independently of the knower).[26]

"Pragmatic instrumentalism" then is a descriptively accurate name for the type of legal theory involved, whereas "legal realism" is not.[27] (Nor is "sociological jurisprudence.") "Pragmatic instrumentalism" is the name I have given not only to the American version, but also to a general type of legal theory originating in the eighteenth century. Bentham led an instrumentalist revolution in legal thought in Great Britain in the late eighteenth and early nineteenth centuries.[28] Rudolf von Ihering led an instrumentalist revolution in the second half of the nineteenth and in the early twentieth century in Germany and Austria.[29] A common name for both the general type of theory and the American version is desirable. The idiosyncratic American term, legal realism, is inadequate for this purpose.[30]

Notwithstanding the growth of instrumentalism throughout the West, the American version of this general theory was the most sustained and prominent instrumentalist movement in the history of Western legal theory. In my opinion, the substance and range of instrumentalist theory qualify it as a fourth great tradition in Western legal theory, alongside analytical positivism, natural law philosophy, and historical jurisprudence.[31]

III. Criteria for Identifying a General Legal Theory

In this section I will undertake three tasks. I will first set forth my own criteria for identifying a body of thought as a general legal theory and, in light of those criteria, argue that American pragmatic instrumentalist thought qualifies as general theory. Thereafter, I will summarize Professor Moore's criteria for identifying a body of thought as a general legal theory and will argue that these criteria, as he formulates them, are inappropriate. Finally, I will try to show that even if Professor Moore's criteria are appropriate, American pragmatic instrumentalism goes rather farther than he acknowledges to satisfy those criteria.

A.   When Evaluated by Appropriate Criteria, Instrumentalism Qualifies as a General Legal Theory

I set forth several criteria in my book for identifying a body of thought as a general legal theory. One of those is largely historical, namely: What is the traditional subject matter of legal theory?—a criterion Professor Moore himself at times accepts.[32] The family of traditional topics includes: the nature of law and legal systems, values and the law, the theory of lawmaking, criteria for determining valid law, the character of basic legal processes such as adjudication and legislation, general issues of legal method (including the theory of interpretation), and the separation of law and morals. By this historical criterion, American pragmatic instrumentalism qualifies as a general legal theory, for most of the questions that occupied these thinkers fall within, overlap substantially with, or can be readily related to these traditional topics of legal theory. Indeed, at one point Professor Moore goes rather far to concede precisely this.[33]

In my book, I also pointed out that instrumentalist theory focused on facets of law of broad theoretical interest, thus satisfying another basic criterion. I characterized these as "instrumentalist and pragmatic" facets of law, and I summarized most of the key theoretical questions addressed to these facets: To what extent, and in what ways is law instrumental to social goals? What are the varieties and complexities of the goals law may serve? What are the basic techniques and modes of operation of law? How may uses of law be justified in terms of their effects? What tasks must be performed to create law and translate it into effective use? What counts as valid law when the law that has been laid down — "the law in books," differs from the "law in action"? How should the success of uses of law be judged? What of theoretical interest can be said about the effectiveness of law in human affairs?

Another criterion I articulated in my book is that a significant proportion of the tenets of the body of thought in question must be sufficiently developed for it to qualify as a legal theory.[34] This criterion is difficult to apply. What constitutes a "significant proportion"? When is a tenet "sufficiently developed"? There can be no formulae for resolving such questions. Although I acknowledged in my book that American instrumentalist theory was seriously underdeveloped,[35] I continue to believe that it nonetheless qualifies as a general legal theory. Instrumentalist thinkers, together and in many cases individually, sufficiently developed a significant proportion of tenets. This position could be defended at length along the following lines. Instrumentalism was sufficiently developed to be a source of considerable influence on subsequent thought, a fact Professor Moore concedes.[36] It was sufficiently developed to be a meaningful object of extensive criticism at the hands of sophisticated critics including H.L.A. Hart, Hans Kelsen, Morris Cohen, John Dickinson, and Lon L. Fuller.[37] And if I am right, it was sufficiently developed to enable me to elaborate several of its tenets in my book in ways that can be readily seen to be consistent with their evident purport.[38]

To qualify as a legal theory, a body of thought must also be unified or integrated, or at least subject to reconstruction in ways that sufficiently display this feature.[39] I identified several general integrating ideas in instrumentalist thought, including the instrumentalist concept of law, the notion of legal tasks and personnel, and the ideas of law as something for use, and in use, in daily life.[40] I now think that the concept of law as a social instrument is a more powerful integrating conception than I had earlier assumed. This conception alone may even integrate the various aspects of instrumentalist theory more fully than any single integrating notion within any other general legal theory.[41] It immediately invites analysis of the general nature and variety of legal means, and of legal goals and goal structures. It is but a short way from these related ideas to the notion of forms of law as means-goal hypotheses that are not self-justifying but which must be justified in light of independent values, particularly values reflected in projected effects of the law involved. The relevance of and necessity for a general theory of value thus becomes immediately apparent. So, too, do general issues about how law is to be created and used, issues that call forth theories of lawmaking, of implementive legal tasks, and of legal method. The instrumentalist conception of law therefore naturally suggests a general concern with the place of official personnel, and with the general division of legal labor in the creation and use of law. Finally, methods of judging the effectiveness of law become a natural concern of a theory that conceives of law as an instrument for social improvement. In my book I devoted a chapter to each of the foregoing topics.

Another important criterion for judging whether a body of thought can qualify as a legal theory at all is whether the theory incorporates concepts and terminology adequate to the faithful representation of the phenomena of law.[42] The instrumentalists adopted such concepts as instrument, means, goals (or purposes), wants and interests, scientific lawmaking, social engineering, judicial legislation, prediction, the law-in-action, efficacy, and scientific fact finding. This conceptual equipment, with its accompanying terminology, was not in all respects felicitous. For example, I do not believe that the concept of prediction[43] or of law-in-action [44] can be used, without distortion, in the ways most instrumentalists used them. But neither can it be said that all the concepts of Hartian or Kelsenian theory are felicitous. To disqualify American instrumentalist theory here, it would be necessary to show that an undue proportion of its key notions are conceptually inadequate. In my view, this simply cannot be done.

I do not here propose to treat all plausible criteria for characterizing a body of thought as a general legal theory. I will comment only on one further criterion: Did instrumentalist theory fulfill the kinds of functions or purposes characteristically associated with general legal theories? Two widely acknowledged general functions or purposes of legal theory are these: to contribute to the better use of law within particular societies, and to advance our general understanding of the nature of law and its use. Instrumentalist theory has contributed to the *better use of law* in the United States. Among other things, instrumentalist thinkers overthrew formalism,[45] introduced empiricism and technological rationalism into the law,[46] and focused attention on the need to justify uses of law partly in light of their effects.[47]

The instrumentalist revolution in American legal theory also advanced our *general understanding of the nature of law and its use* in a number of important ways. For example, rules and other forms of law are much more than formal, authoritative norms to be obeyed or carried out — they are also instruments which incorporate specific adjustments of means and goals.[48] And the "law-in-action" is often a distinctive admixture of official action and antecedent norms.[49] Further, most forms of law are inevitably dependent to some extent for their content and justification on social facts and values external to law.[50] Also the law must be applied to changing social circumstances and thus is constantly in need of some modification or readjustment.[51] The legal system as a whole is a complex form of social organization with many interacting elements, elements that must themselves be studied as general social facts rather than as "timeless givens."[52] That such truths as these are now widely understood in the American system is a tribute to the instrumentalists. One can today point to whole societies in which such truths are not widely understood.

I have little to add beyond what I said in my book about whether pragmatic instrumentalism qualifies not only as a general theory, but also as a distinct type of general legal theory.[53] I continue to believe that its questions, its focus, its scope, and its frequent resort to general social facts do mark it off as a distinct type of legal theory.

B. The Inappropriateness of Professor Moore's Criteria

As I understand Professor Moore, a body of thought about law can qualify as a general legal theory only if addressed (at least after any necessary reconstruction) to roughly the same set of questions as other established general types of legal theory.[54] Moore seems to assume that the other established traditions in legal theory — analytical positivism, natural law thought, and historical jurisprudence — are all addressed to "the same thing,"[55] and he claims that this enables us to see these theories as "genuine competitor[s]" of each other.[56] In light of this criterion, Moore registers serious doubt that instrumentalist theory can qualify as a general legal theory, because it does not address enough questions in common with the other traditions.[57]

In my view, Professor Moore misconceives the nature of much that falls within the established traditions. The various established traditions in legal theory differ significantly from each other in orientation, method, and scope.[58] Moore's "common focus" criterion is therefore too stringent. It forces us to question whether any traditional legal theory really qualifies. In broad terms, analytical positivism addresses the nature of law, the varieties of legal norms, their status as law, their hierarchical ordering, the analytic relations within and between them and other fundamental legal notions, and certain relations between law and morals and law and coercion;[59] Most traditional natural law theory focuses on the implications for legal ordering of the nature of human beings and the human condition, on the appropriate content of law and on standards for criticizing that content, on the role of reason in law, and on the limits of the duty to obey law;[60] historical jurisprudence is mainly concerned with law as a historical phenomenon, including its organic, evolutionary, and customary elements, and with the general modes, forms, and sources of legal change over time and in different places.[61]

If my characterizations are even roughly accurate, there is much less common focus in the history of legal theory than Moore's criterion can tolerate. Yet presumably he does not want to deny that the other established traditions qualify as general types of theory on the ground that they cannot be construed to compete with each other "about the same thing."[62] If so, he must then concede that commonality of focus cannot be one of the essential requirements of legal theories. It follows also that some tenets of traditional theories can be true or sound in important respects without casting the slightest doubt on certain tenets of other legal theories.

According to Professor Moore, not just any focus on any common set of general questions will qualify a body of thought as a legal theory. He also requires that the theory have a certain core of content:

> The core issues of legal theory concern theories of adjudication, legislation, and citizenship. These theories are both descriptive and normative, telling us how judges, legislators, and citizens do and should perform their roles. Whether describing or prescribing, such theories focus on the legitimacy of the conduct and decisions of occupants of legal roles. For example, a legal theorist focusing on the legislative role either may prescribe the correct limits to which a legislator should seek to legislate conventional morals or may describe the limits thought by legislators in certain systems to be legitimate.[63]

Professor Moore's "content" criterion goes far to disqualify some major traditions of legal theory he wishes to acknowledge as established. Traditional *analytical* positivism does not reveal much concern for the normative issues of legitimacy that Moore says must be the focus. Analytical positivists such as Austin[64] and Kelsen[65] rarely addressed such matters, and one finds relatively little about legitimacy in the work of H.L.A. Hart,[66] the leading contemporary analytical postivist. With respect to the historical jurists the story is much the same.[67] Yet Professor Moore says legitimacy as such must be the focus, and he seems to equate this conception of required content with what has traditionally been characterized as legal theory.

Professor Moore goes on to suggest that if a purported general legal theory incorporates an adequate theory of adjudication, then this alone goes far to qualify it as a general legal theory, even though it remains silent or says little about legislation and citizenship. In his view, "the theory of adjudication (of any type) is a large part of any general legal theory . . . . "[68] He also claims that it is a test case of a legal theory.[69] Indeed, according to Moore, the theory of adjudication just is "jurisprudence."[70] Moore's criteria lead him to conclude that both natural law theory and analytical positivism qualify as "major types of legal theory."[71] To understand Moore's conception of adjudicative theory as a kind of "test" for identifying a body of thought as a legal theory, one must explore his notion of what the right questions are in a "theory of adjudication":

> A theory of adjudication . . . should contain a number of subtheories within it: (1) a theory of law proper that tells judges what standards their office obligates them to consider when they decide cases; (2) a theory about facts and about descriptions of facts that legitimates the use of some descriptions, but not others, of "what happened" within the legal decisional process; (3) a theory of interpretation legitimating only some interpretive premises in a judge's attempt to apply the law to the facts; and (4) a theory about logic and the place of logic in legal reasoning.
>
> A theory of adjudication should contain each of these subtheories, at a minimum, because every judicial decision necessarily requires a judge to ascertain the relevant law, to find the facts of the case, to connect the law to the facts via the meanings of the terms employed in the law, and to use logic to justify deductively the result reached.[72]

Later, Moore adds a fifth subtheory: a "theory of value."[73] In sum, if I interpret him correctly, a body of thought goes far to qualify in his world as *a general legal theory* if it merely consists of no more than a theory of adjudication that is addressed to the ("right") questions, is sufficiently detailed, developed, or complete, and is philosophically sophisticated. Indeed, Moore may hold that such a theory of adjudication alone qualifies as a general legal theory.

Contrary to what Professor Moore seems to assume, the other traditions in legal theory go far here to flunk any such adjudicational test for determining whether a body of thought qualifies as a legal theory. With rare exceptions, the major analytical positivists of the past set forth no theories of value (or only highly anemic ones) and little or no theory about facts or descriptions of facts.[74] A few analytical positivists did address "the nature of logic and its place in legal reasoning,"[75] but natural law theorists rarely treated the topic. Natural law theorists addressed matters of value, but none had what Moore would call a detailed or complete theory of value.[76] Moreover, neither the major analytical positivists nor the leading natural law theorists of the past worked out a full-fledged theory of interpretation of the kind Moore requires. And the historical jurists did not set forth theories of adjudication of the kind he requires.

Professor Moore seems to hold that whatever else a general legal theory addresses, it must address the sorts of issues he treats in the form of a theory of adjudication.[77] This is a dubious position. If we return to the list of questions I posed earlier[78] as inquiries addressed to basic instrumental and pragmatic facets of law, we can well imagine a theory robustly treating most of those questions and at least certain aspects of others without developing *a theory of adjudication.* Yet it would not follow that the resulting body of thought would necessarily lack sufficient substance and range to qualify as a general legal theory, devoid though it be of a Moorean theory of adjudication. Natural law theory and analytical positivist theory do not address all fundamental facets of law. Historical jurisprudence neglects important issues treated by analytical positivists and natural law theorists. By our traditional standards, a body of theory need not be comprehensive to qualify as a general legal theory.

Moore's concentration on adjudication as the core of legal theory is somewhat curious. If any single general topic has been most central in the long history of Western legal theory, it is not the theory of adjudication, but the general theory of the nature of law and of legal systems.[79] Indeed, this latter topic has been the dominant preoccupation of one entire tradition — analytical positivism. Leading analytical positivists such as Kelsen and Hart actually wrote relatively little about adjudication. The same is true of most continental natural law theorists. At the least, Moore should defend his assumption that adjudication should be more central than the general nature of law and legal systems.

In my view, the omission of a systematic theory of adjudication, would not necessarily be fatal to a general legal theory; this kind of theory can encompass much besides a theory of adjudication. One way to see this is by noting the nonadjudicative significance of Moore's "subtheories of adjudication." A good case can be made that theories of legal validity, interpretation, and value, have most significance outside adjudication. Theories of value inform legislation and administrative rulemaking in our age of statutes and regulations. And theories of legal validity and interpretation are relevant far more often out of court when lay people and their lawyers identify, interpret, and apply law than in court during the workings of adjudicative processes.

C. Assuming the Appropriateness of Professor Moore's Criteria, Instrumentalism Goes Far to Satisfy Them

The instrumentalists had as much of a theory of adjudication, even in Professor Moore's terms, as did most analytical positivists or natural law theorists. Moore fails to acknowledge that the instrumentalists had more of a theory of value than many participants in other traditions.[80] The instrumentalists did not have a full-fledged theory of statutory interpretation, but what they did propound was generally purposive in orientation and at least the equivalent of that of most major figures in the other traditions.[81] They did little with the affirmative place of logic, but that too is true of other major thinkers except for a few analytical positivists.[82] The instrumentalists had a general source-based theory of legal validity that purports to tell "judges what standards their office obligates them to consider when they decide cases."[83] That theory requires judges to treat as law whatever has been laid down or acted upon as law by authorized officials.[84] As I stressed in my book, the instrumentalists were ambivalent here, and they did not develop their own source based theory as elaborately as Kelsen[85] and Hart[86] tried to do. Moore concedes that the instrumentalists "asked exactly the questions [about a theory of facts] that needed to be asked."[87]

We need not accept Professor Moore's particular adjudicative model as a test for qualifying a body of thought as a general legal theory. I know of no one else who has set forth just such a model of a genuine theory of adjudication. It is therefore not surprising that theories do not conform to it. Moreover, the model is not uncontroversial. For example, some theorists would reject the proposition that a judicial decision must be "deductively" justified.[88] Also, Moore makes no specific place in his model for the play of substantive reasons, including institutional reasons dealing with the appropriate court-legislature relationship — a facet of adjudication frontally concerned with issues of legitimacy.[89] Any minimally adequate general theory of adjudication should address these matters.

Moore says that his test case of adjudication is a fair one because:

> ...these issues in adjudication greatly concern both Summers and the instrumentalists; if the instrumentalists failed to propound much of a theory here, they have failed where Summers must claim they have succeeded if he is to support his thesis that pragmatic instrumentalism represents a major type of legal theory worthy of our respect.[90]

But the instrumentalists had at least as much of an affirmative theory of adjudication as the other traditions. Even if they did not, Moore neglects their most important critical contribution, which was to demolish the formalistic theory of adjudication that had been so influential in the United States.[91] A virtue of the instrumentalist contribution was that it drew so much attention to adjudication. One is prompted to wonder whether Professor Moore, and others today would accord so much significance to adjudication if there had been no instrumentalist revolution in American legal thought. The instrumentalists also made many specific contributions to legal method (including adjudicative method), which I summarized in chapter 6 of my book. Most of these have commanded widespread respect.

Professor Moore sees little of value in the legal theory of the instrumentalists mainly because of deficiencies he sees in their positive theory of adjudication.[92] He is, however, decidedly ungenerous in his own reconstruction of that theory. I will cite only three examples. First, Moore says any theory of adjudication must include a theory "that tells judges what standards their office obligates them to consider when they decide cases."[93] Thus, the theory must include a subtheory about criteria of valid law which judges are to apply. Moore considers here only the instrumentalists' famous predictivist theory that valid law is whatever we may predict the courts will do. He rightly condemns this as an inadequate theory of validity (as did I) and he says instrumentalists were "wrong because they never even saw the right question to ask."[94] Moore could have more charitably attributed a different theory of validity to the instrumentalists, namely, their source-based theory which posits that valid law is whatever has been laid down or acted upon by an authorized official. In failing to do this, Moore neglects the whole fourth chapter of my book which is devoted to this instrumentalist tenet. Of course, Moore could criticize this theory too, for it is subject to certain well known objections. Still, it remains a far more respectable theory of legal validity than predictivism (which cannot, logically, serve as such a theory at all). Indeed, one of Moore's paradigm legal theorists, H.L.A. Hart, seems to have subscribed in large measure to a version of this source-based theory.[95]

Second, Moore attributes to the instrumentalists a theory of precedent that only very few held, namely that "a deciding judge should attach precedential significance to what the preceding court did on the facts before it, and no significance to what it said."[96] This theory is subject to powerful objections. But not even Oliphant, whom Moore cites, held this theory. Nor did Holmes, Pound, Dewey, Gray, Llewellyn, or Cohen, to name the leading theorists of American instrumentalism. In three different places in my book, I discuss the views they did hold.[97] Those views are more respectable than any view that ignores all of the language in a judicial opinion.

Moore also finds instrumentalist interpretational theory highly deficient. He suggests that the instrumentalists were rule-skeptics and functionalists, and thus could not devise an adequate theory for giving content to written language in which law is authoritatively expressed.[98] Most of these theorists, including such leading progenitors as Holmes, Pound, and Dewey were not rule-skeptics. Although a number of them seem to have adopted what might be called a functionalist theory of meaning, this did not, as Moore claims, translate into the idea that judges may ignore "any pre-existing meaning (ordinary or otherwise) of legal standards."[99] If it is wrong to attribute to instrumentalism any such view of the meaning of language in which precedents are expressed, it is bizarre to do the same with respect to statutory language.

Again, Moore neglects my claim that one of the greatest contributions of the instrumentalists was their demolition of various facets of the formalist theory of adjudication. This was a considerable achievement. The instrumentalists' antiformalist strictures are forever relevant, because the very nature of law itself, and especially the complex technical law of modern industrial societies, is inherently subject to formalistic tendencies.

IV. Legal Theory and Sociology of Law

One reason American pragmatic instrumentalism is sometimes not recognized as a general theory about the nature of law and its use is that people mistake it for sociology of law. Various theorists of instrumentalism have themselves been partly to blame for this confusion. Pound often used terminology suggesting that in legal theorizing he might be concerned with sociology of law as such.[100] Some of Llewellyn's early theoretical writing was similar in this respect.[101]

Professor Moore has been led to think that instrumentalist theory was to a large extent mere sociology, and he suggests that such work does not qualify as legal theory.[102] He also says that to conjoin legal theory and legal sociology in the fashion of the instrumentalists is to produce something "rather lumpy." And he complains that there is "no common question to which the legal theory and the legal sociology provide the links of a unified answer."[103] What is at stake here? Moore correctly suggests that one thing at stake is having the right people do the right jobs: legal theory is for the theorists, but sociology is for social scientists.[104] I believe, however, that truth and soundness in legal theory are ultimately at stake. If theorists were to act on the spirit of Moore's criticism, they would impoverish legal theory.

Moore does not stop to sort out the different uses of "sociological." At least four uses must be differentiated: (1) empirical field research on particular social facts, or gathering of particular social facts from existing published sources, (2) the devising of conceptual frameworks in the preliminary stages of projects of empirical research on particular social facts, (3) the assembling of reminders of general social facts and/or the description of general social facts, based on a variety of sources, and (4) the analysis of concepts and terminology we use to represent general social facts, including concepts that figure in legal or sociological theories about the nature of general social facts or about causal and other relationships between social events and states of affairs.

A close reading of Professor Moore's critique reveals that when he uses the word "sociological" to characterize what he objects to as merely sociological in American instrumentalist legal theory, he frequently seems to intend one or both of the first two senses of "sociological" differentiated above. Thus he seems to claim that the instrumentalists treated empirical research on particular social facts as legal theory. Many instrumentalists did advocate more research on particular social facts, and some of these thinkers in fact did empirical research on particular social facts.[105] But very few of them seriously viewed this work as "legal theory," or "jurisprudence," or "legal philosophy," as such. Nor did I, in my book, use these words to refer to empirical research on particular social facts. Rather, insofar as they (or I) used "legal theory" (or its equivalent) to designate anything characterizable as sociological, they (and I) usually had in mind the third and fourth senses of "sociological," above.[106] These theorists (and I) were interested in general social facts of and about law, and in the concepts adequate to understanding and representing them. Indeed these theorists had far more interest in these matters than was usual for legal theorists, a respect in which their tradition is distinctive. In the "mix" of the conceptual and the sociological, in the third and fourth senses of sociological that one inevitably finds in a general legal theory, the instrumentalists did stress the sociological far more than other theorists. But it is highly misleading for Professor Moore to characterize chapters 2, 8, 9, 10, 11, and 12 of my book dealing with American instrumentalist themes as if these chapters were sociological in senses one and two. They are not. With one exception, they are sociological in senses three and four.

Professor Moore apparently does not perceive the relevance of the distinction between senses one and two of "sociological" on the one hand and senses three and four on the other. Yet even participants in other established traditions of legal theory have recognized the legitimacy of a "sociological" focus, in senses three and four, for *legal theory*. Professor H.L.A. Hart, whom

Moore regards as a model legal theorist, considers much of his own work in legal theory to be "descriptive sociology."[107] One could demonstrate in detail that most (if not all) of Hart's descriptive sociology is "sociological" only in senses three and four above. Instrumentalist legal theory is criticizable by Moore as "merely sociological" if, but only if, Hart's work is too.

Hart,[108] Peter Hacker,[109] and other leading philosophers have suggested that legal theory necessarily includes a distinctively large sociological element in senses three and four above. After all, a legal system is a complex, multifaceted, and interrelated set of social phenomena. An important job for legal theorists is to develop adequate accounts of certain general social facts of and about law, not just as a preliminary to doing legal theory, but also as legal theory itself. Such facts must figure directly in descriptive accounts of various general facets of law. In addition, we could not do a lot of the normative and conceptual work in legal theory that we now do without such facts (or such facts fairly assumed). Because Professor Moore is not alone in appearing to fail to appreciate these points fully, it is especially important to cite a range of examples of legal theorizing in which the theorist appeals directly to general social facts in criticizing or constructing (or both) some element of a general theory. I will draw my examples solely from the work of a theorist whom Moore would immediately concede to be a true legal theorist, H.L.A. Hart:

(1) In response to a criticism that citizens generally do not know enough about the workings of a legal system — a general social fact — to justify attributing to them a conscious awareness and acceptance of the various standards for the identification of valid law in their system, Hart revised his theory to require only that the officials of the system have this conscious awareness and acceptance, or "internal point of view."[110]

(2) Hart criticized Kelsen for holding that rules of law are addressed to officials in the first instance, and that these rules specify the conditions under which officials may impose sanctions. This view, according to Hart, obscures the "characteristic way law functions in the first instance," namely through private self-application — another general social fact.[111]

(3) In developing a taxonomy of the important varieties of legal rules found in modern systems of law —general social facts—Hart went beyond Austin's focus on duty-imposing rules backed by sanctions. Hart identified another major category, those rules which confer power to make contracts and wills, and to exercise official jurisdiction. Noncompliance with such rules results in nullity, instead of the imposition of a sanction.[112]

(4) Contrary to much positivistic legal theory holding that the validity of putative law is to be determined by discovering whether officials in power have duly laid it down, Hart recognized that customary law arising from the interaction of private parties does not satisfy this criterion.[113] Yet many forms of customary law are widely recognized in modern systems — a general social fact.

(5) Kelsen and others had held that the law of a legal system is a formal receptical which can have any substantive content and still be a legal system. Hart constructed an elaborate opposing argument that a legal system must have a certain minimum substantive content in the form of rules against the free use of violence and simple forms of theft, given the nature of humans and the human condition—further general social facts.[114]

The foregoing are but a selection from many possible instances in which Hart appeals to general social facts in his general theory of law. It is not surprising that he characterized this work as "descriptive sociology." I do not claim, incidentally, that the facts to which Hart appeals are of one single variety. Some are intimately legal (3), some psychological (1), some biological (5), some behavioral (4), and so on. But in all instances, Hart can hardly be said, to be appealing to the particular findings of empirical sociological research projects (senses one and two above). Instead his theorizing, insofar as it is sociological, involves appeals to widely recognized general social facts (senses three and four).

Modern legal theorists regularly presuppose, draw on, or address general social facts of and about the phenomena of law, in the fashion of Hart. We have had vast experience with law and thus already have an accumulated stock of general social facts dealing with law as we think we know it. Professor Moore takes much of this for granted, and emphasizes the conceptual and the normative at the expense of the sociological (senses three and four). Perhaps I may suggest the following scenario. Let us imagine that Ms. Theorist is assigned the task of developing a general theory about the nature and use of law in Society A, a relatively new society. She knows nothing at all about Society A, except that it is said to be very different from our own, and that it has a system of law. How would Ms. Theorist begin? Would she simply sit down and start theorizing? Or would she first try to find out some general social facts about law and its use in this society? Surely the latter. Of course, I do not deny that Ms. Theorist would bring her own general working conceptions of law to bear in deciding what general social facts to look for. In a legal theory, such notions and the general social facts must "inform" each other in complex ways that I cannot go into here.[115] In some fields, for example, set theory, the conceptual element overwhelmingly dominates any factual element. Legal theory, however, is not one of these fields. And for theorists in the instrumentalist tradition the factual element was especially large.

It is possible that the legal theorists in a given society might, over time, fail to take sufficient account of general social facts (senses three and four), so that such facts about the nature and use of law in that society do not appropriately inform legal theory. This was true during the formalist era at the turn of the century when the American instrumentalists came on the scene. It is, therefore, not surprising that a significant part of their contribution should take the form of calling attention to general social facts — sociological work in senses three and four. (I do not claim that they finished all that they addressed, or that they always got the general social facts right.)

There is another method by which skeptics might be brought to see these matters more clearly. Some theorists downplay sociology, in senses three and four, and tend to subscribe to what might be called the "timeless concept of law." According to these theorists, once this concept is worked out, we need no more knowledge of general social facts (if we ever did), for we have put matters straight, once and for all.[116] At one point Moore himself writes of basic ideas of and about law in the sense of "timeless propositions."[117]

One presupposition of the "timeless concept" approach is that no changes in the general social facts of law and its use in a society could possibly alter an initially correct analysis of the nature and use of law. This is an objectionable form of apriorism. Consider this example. One important facet of law is what I have called its "technique element." By what basic techniques does law operate in a society?[118] Hart,[119] Raz,[120] and other paradigm legal theorists have acknowledged this as an important problem of legal theory. If Bentham and Austin (also paradigm legal theorists) had this matter straight in 1800, would it stand up for all time at least for Great Britain? Or would changing social facts about law and its use make a difference to latter theorists? I submit they could make a major difference. In 1990, a Bentham or an Austin would have to say that at least two relatively new basic techniques of law had come into use, the regulatory and the distributive, so that a prior account in 1800 of only three techniques (the penal, the grievance remedial, and the private-arranging) would have to be supplemented.[121] There is no timeless concept of law immune in all basic respects to future changes in general social facts about the nature and use of law. To be an adequate general theory about law and its use, many of the concepts in the theory must be subject to revision as needed to take account of new manifestations of the social reality of law.[122]

In this section, I have stressed the roles of general social facts (the sociological, in senses three and four) when constructing and evaluating legal theories. In so doing I have concentrated mainly on the truth that, among other things, general social facts inform the *conceptual* components of legal theories. I have neglected the ways in which general social facts also bear upon the normative components of legal theories. Yet such facts must inform normative legal theory too, a matter I cannot go into here.

If Hart, Hacker, and others (including myself) are correct about the large element of descriptive sociology in legal theory, then Moore and others of like mind may wish to reconsider their overall position. Moore's examples of illegitimate "sociological" elements in instrumentalist legal theory include: the instrumentalist conception of law as essentially a means to some social goals, my own effort to map some of the means-goal structures in our legal system, structural questions about the legal means available to implement goals, the nature of legal personnel involved in the implementation of goals, theories about why people obey the law when they do, and what it means to judge the efficacy of forms of law and how one goes about measuring this.[123] Yet if I am right, in all of these examples, with perhaps one exception, the theorist *must* appeal to general social facts much in the same way that Hart did in the various examples I cited earlier.[124] If Hartian theory is legal theory, then so too is this.

Professor Moore has two further general complaints. He says, in effect, that even if sociology of law is in some sense legal theory or a branch of legal theory, the way I carry on this work in my book is both relatively purposeless and excessively taxonomic. Thus he suggests that my "sociological" efforts to revise and develop instrumentalist theory often leave one "the impression of being an answer to a question that is not asked by any properly focused legal theory."[125] I will not here recite chapter and verse to the contrary from my book. Instead I will take up only the examples Moore cites. He suggests that my inventory of the main types of goals and goal structures has no clear relationship to legal theory.[126] As I point out in my book, these theorists conceived of forms of law essentially as instruments to goals. Thus goals are of natural instrumentalist concern. Professor Fuller (no mean legal theorist) even argued that some intelligible goal is required before law can exist at all.[127] Distinctions of diverse potential significance can be drawn between types of goals that may figure in or lie behind forms of law. Also, these goals may conflict with each other in diverse ways calling for sensitively formulated syntheses of various sorts.

More is at stake than an advance in theory that may increase general understanding of immediate interest mainly to theoreticians. As I noted in my book, the United States Supreme Court has unwisely invalidated certain state statutes under the equal protection clause because the Court failed to see how these statutes must inevitably reflect the efforts of lawmakers to reconcile complex conflicts of goals in pursuit of some optimal state of affairs.[128] Moore acknowledges this possible practical bearing of my theoretical efforts but dismisses it as superfluous: "such knowledge of values is part of our cultural heritage. Our ability to apply that cultural heritage in understanding particular laws probably exceeds our ability to develop an explicit taxonomy of all such values."[129] The issues in these cases did not deal primarily with the intelligibility of the values involved. They dealt with the typical structural interrelations between goals, interrelations the Court misunderstood. But even if intelligibility were the issue, we would not be warranted in concluding, with Moore, that relevant values are always satisfactorily intelligible for the law's purposes because they are "part of our cultural heritage". Judges and lawyers not infrequently fail to appreciate the worth of important values. Are these failures *never* because the values involved are to some extent unintelligible to them? Surely not. In order to render certain values intelligible it is essential to grasp the variety and complexity of their manifestations in concrete phenomena. Values manifest themselves in the variety and complexity of law's goals (though not exclusively there). The realization of a value usually will depend on how concrete means-goal hypotheses work out. One may add that a deeper understanding of the complex goal structures that figure in and lie behind forms of law may enhance our capacity to interpret statutes and other forms of written law, a matter of immense theoretical and practical import.[130]

Despite Professor Moore's allegation that "too often throughout" my book I failed to link up my sociology with legal theory, Moore cites only one further example of "sociological" work — my preliminary inventory of implementive legal tasks. He finds it is possible to relate this inventory to other more general concerns of theoretical interest.[131] But then, without going into any other examples, he rests with this concluding statement: "Too often throughout the book Summers presents his taxonomies in the same way as did Bentham (whom Summers greatly admires); he presents these taxonomies without indicating their intended uses."[132] This statement is false.

Moore's other general complaint is that many of my sociological efforts to revise and develop instrumentalist theory often reduce to the formulation of mere "taxonomies," and at one point he ridicules my efforts by offering a lengthy "taxonomy" of what he calls my "taxonomies."[133] He purports to gather ten such "taxonomies" in his list. On inspection, one can see that virtually any itemization or any type of scheme of distinctions or concepts qualifies as a taxonomy in Moore's world. He not only so classifies my inventory of basic types of implementive legal resources, but also my three-fold conceptual differentiation of "external," "constitutive," and "intrinsic" relations between goals and the means of their realization through law, and the various tasks in my theory of implementive legal tasks. According to Moore, almost any time one differentiates between varieties that number three or more, one is creating a taxonomy. On this view, his five-fold typology of "subtheories" in the general theory of adjudication is a taxonomy, as well as his differentiation between the "philosophical," "historical," and "evaluative" theses of my book, and his differentiation between "modest," "imperial," and intermediate forms of reconstruction in the history of ideas. Presumably the standard trichotomy of descriptive, normative, and conceptual also qualifies as a taxonomy. Thus in Moore's world taxonomies proliferate. If all or nearly all forms of differentiating analysis yield taxonomies, how can it be a criticism that a theorist sometimes resorts to taxonomies?

The concept of taxonomy is problematic and has been the subject of much controversy in the social sciences. In truth, various concepts of taxonomy are recognized. One of these is concerned with the classification of phenomena to explain and predict events, processes, structures, etc.[134] This scientific concept of taxonomy is probably the most common, and Professor Moore appears to be under the influence of this concept, given his remarks about "empirical data,"[135] causal "variables,"[136] and "fruitful generalizations."[137] Yet many of the schemes of distinctions appearing in my book that he classifies as taxonomies are not taxonomies in this sense. My inventory of implementive legal tasks is not. Nor is my account of the basic relations between means and goals. Nor is my differentiation of basic legal techniques. Indeed, only *one* of the ten items Moore lists plainly fits the foregoing scientific conception of taxonomy — the one relating to factors of law's effectiveness.

I do not wish to be counted among those who deny the value of certain taxonomies of the nonscientific variety. As H.L.A. Hart has demonstrated, they can be used to display the range of legal phenomena under study, such as the variety of types of rules, "free from the prejudice that all must be reducible to a single simple type."[138] Taxonomies can also be used fruitfully to order and classify phenomena under study, calling attention to essential similarities and differences in ways that deepen understanding. Taxonomies can themselves be manifestations of theory. Sometimes their use indicates that the theorist is only at an early or intermediate stage in evolving his overall scheme of thought. It is not surprising that my reconstruction of instrumentalist theory includes some taxonomies, for as I have stressed in my book, this body of theory was admittedly undeveloped. In short, just as genuine zoology is far from disreputable, "legal zoology," *properly understood,* is hardly disreputable. Of course, I do not claim (contrary to Professor Moore's allegation) that "taxonomies inevitably generate worthwhile understanding."[139]

V. The Reconstruction of a General Legal Theory

A number of American instrumentalists did not write as if they were constructing a general legal theory. Many wrote rather unsystematically about theoretical issues. And only one of those I included in my study made much of an effort to identify and formulate the various theoretical tenets that participants in their movement shared in common.[140] For these and still other reasons, I chose not to content myself with eleven reports on the specific views of eleven selected thinkers. Instead, I chose to perform a version of what is today frequently called a *reconstruction,* and not just of individual views, but of the whole American instrumentalist movement (as manifested in the work of these thinkers).[141]

After studying the works of individual thinkers, I sought to devise a comprehensive framework which revealed the theorizing of these thinkers as an intelligible and coherent body of thought.[142] The main feature of my framework was a set of widely shared leading tenets, some descriptively sociological, some conceptual, and some normative. In devising my framework, I certainly did some weeding out and selecting among alternatives; not all of what these thinkers wrote was theory, let alone instrumentalist theory.[143] I also had to cope with inconsistencies within a given thinker's work and between thinkers. I accepted some matters as more in keeping with instrumentalist theory and rejected others. Sometimes I was called upon to judge whether a given thinker could readily be said to subscribe to a particular tenet. I did not require that every thinker subscribe to every tenet. I concluded, however, that no tenet failed to command numerous adherents, and that each thinker adhered to a large majority of the tenets.

Although these tenets represent meaningful and suggestive general directions of thought about law, a number of them were seriously under-developed. Consequently, I tried to flesh out instrumentalist theory in a number of places. In some instances I merely filled obvious gaps; in others, the result was more my own making, though still instrumentalist in spirit. I selected the name "pragmatic instrumentalism" for this general legal theory, a name that has the virtue of descriptive accuracy, as general names go.[144]

My reconstruction yielded some rather radical or at least heretofore relatively unnoticed results. Some of the thinkers involved had never viewed themselves as subscribers to a general theory. Yet my reconstruction legitimated this characterization. Law professors, judges, and lawyers not uncommonly deny that they subscribe to or are influenced by any general theory of law. The instrumentalists were no exception, and it is important to see this. If I am right, general theory profoundly influences the law, something of which those in the law should be more conscious. My reconstruction also exposed similarities of view that justify (for my purposes) grouping such otherwise different thinkers together as Dewey and Gray, and Pound and Frank. At the same time, this reconstruction exposed what I believe to be an important truth, namely, that the instrumentalist movement can (and in my view should be) bifurcated into a "mainstream" in which certain views of Holmes, Pound, Dewey, and Gray were widely influential, and an extremist wing characterized by certain realist views expressed stridently in the 1930s but which were not widely influential and therefore did not become part of our dominant general theory of law.[145] In addition, my approach revealed the *constructive* general directions of thought in instrumentalist theorizing, a corrective to the common view that most of these theorists were merely "destructive trashers." I was also able to demonstrate the considerable extent to which various tenets of instrumentalism are technological and scientific in spirit. Finally, my reconstruction brought out the distinctively progressive and optimistic tenor of this body of thought as a whole.

Professor Moore acknowledges the legitimacy of reconstructive en-terprises[146] but thinks I did not go far enough. He distinguishes between "modest" reconstruction and "imperial" reconstruction.[147] He suggests that the intellectual historian doing a modest reconstruction would accept the questions that the earlier thinkers addressed and content himself with reordering or developing in some way the answers those thinkers gave to the questions. The historian doing an imperial reconstruction, however, would "reorganize" the views of the earlier thinkers involved as answers to contemporary questions in legal theory.[148]

According to Professor Moore, I should have presented pragmatic instrumentalist theory as an imperial reconstruction in order to avoid relegating these ideas to a "scrapbook of historical curiosities;"[149] to enable others to judge the correctness of my historical thesis that these thinkers actually shared a legal theory;[150] and to allow others to see how their theory competes with contemporary ideas so that we can judge whether they had a "good legal theory."[151]

I do not believe I needed to do much "imperial" reconstruction, even if I were so inclined. Moreover, many questions that occupied pragmatic instrumentalists continue to be "our questions today," at least in abstract terms. Moore concedes much of this when he acknowledges that more than half of my book is addressed to "core issues in contemporary legal theory."[152] Nevertheless, he offers an elaborate demonstration designed to show that I failed to perform necessary "imperial reconstruction." He identifies five questions that he says figure in our contemporary theory of adjudication: What standards must judges apply to identify the law when deciding cases? What facts and descriptions of facts may legitimately figure in judicial decisions? What theories of interpretation and precedent are appropriate in applying law to facts? What is the nature and role of logic in legal reasoning? And what theory of value is appropriate for the adjudication of cases? He then concedes that the American instrumentalists addressed adjudication (in truth, they were preoccupied with it) but implies that they failed to address or did not directly address the foregoing five questions. Thus, according to Moore, I should have "imposed" his five questions from "contemporary theory" on the instrumentalists, thereby "forcing them to answer our questions."[153] This reconstruction, he says, would have been "preferable" to my "more modest" approach. An analysis of these questions demonstrates, however, that I had no need to "force" these thinkers to answer "our questions" via an imperial reconstruction. With one exception, "our questions" about adjudication substantially overlap their questions![154] If it had been necessary for me to force our questions on them, however, I would have declined to do so. It would be wrong to reconstruct "answers" to our present day questions out of answers to quite distinct questions.[155] (At bottom, I suspect Moore's dissatisfaction here is with the instrumentalists' answers, not their questions.)

Professor Moore believes that without imperial reconstruction of instrumentalist views, we cannot avoid relegating their ideas to a "scrapbook of historical curiosities."[156] Without relating the views of instrumentalists to any present concerns as such, we could keep them out of the scrapbook merely by noting how they improved on the formalistic views of adjudication prevalent in many quarters when they came on the scene.

Professor Moore states that imperial reconstruction is necessary in order to "judge the correctness of [my] historical thesis that these influential people had a legal theory."[157] Adopting Professor Moore's own premises about what can count as a legal theory, premises which accord central place to adjudicative theory, we can see (with or without reconstruction) that the instrumentalists were vitally concerned with issues of adjudicative theory. Even if this were not so, other theorists could still bring their own views to bear as to what a legal theory is and judge whether these thinkers had a legal theory.

Moore asserts that without imperial reconstruction, we cannot see how instrumentalist ideas compete with contemporary ideas and thus cannot assess my alleged thesis that American pragmatic instrumentalism was a "good legal theory."[158] This is a nonsequitur; one need not see an idea in competition with another idea (present or past) to discern whether it is valuable.

Imperial reconstruction, if carried out consistently, might actually obscure or neglect important truths of American instrumentalist theory. For example, many contemporary legal theorists are relatively uninterested in questions of descriptive sociology that occupied many instrumentalists. If we are to take contemporary questions as our polestars, then presumably we are to ignore prior theory that cannot be channeled into those questions. Thus, we might ignore the implications of conceiving of law as a social instrument. And we would inevitably obscure the historical dialectic between instrumentalists and formalists over basic issues of legal method. Yet it was the common formalist "enemy" which brought forth many instrumentalist ideas in the first place. The instrumentalists won this battle so convincingly that it might be thought that the issues involved are no longer contemporary questions. By Professor Moore's polestar, the issues would, therefore, no longer be relevant to legal theory, a conclusion to which I could not subscribe. As I remarked earlier, the formalistic tendencies of a system of law run deep, and we must remain forever on guard against them.

I believe that a version of "presentism" may motivate some of Professor Moore's emphasis on the desirability of more "imperial reconstruction."[159] He even sometimes appears to believe that whatever is most recent is right. Of course, no such belief, in a humanistic discipline, can be at all tenable. Consider only one example from the discipline of philosophy: the epidemic of moral nihilism or radical moral skepticism which afflicted many philosophers until well into mid-century, and from which we still suffer to some extent, both in the law and out. Moore's "presentism" is also manifest in his relative neglect of historical perspective. One cannot fully understand the meaning of certain tenets of a given legal theory, such as instrumentalism, without first grasping the historical context out of which these tenets arose. And some of these tenets can only be understood in relation to historical sequences, for they address facets of law as played out in historical sequences. What Professor Moore himself calls a theory of "change in law" is illustrative.[160] Similarly illustrative are the interactions between means and goals. Only in historical perspective can one grasp the potency of legal theories for social influence. And only in that perspective can one fully understand the distinctive elements of such theories, or see how major movements can occur in legal theory when no movements of similar magnitude are occurring at the same time in other branches of social and political thought. Only in historical perspective can one see how the general social facts of law may change in fundamental ways over time, calling for fundamental revisions in legal theory. Then, too, there is the history of legal theorizing as such. By seeing how instrumentalists went wrong and why, we better understand their theoretical enterprise, and ours.

VI. Conclusion

I have taken this occasion mainly to focus on various aspects of the scope, aims, and methods of legal theory. Perhaps others better equipped than I will be led to carry these matters farther. I hope, in particular, to see more effort devoted to the complex interrelations between descriptive sociology and the conceptual element in legal theory.

Although I wish to acknowledge an indebtedness to Professor Moore for challenging me to revisit issues of scope, aims, and method in legal theory, I would be less than honest if I did not also say that I was a little surprised to find that so many features of his critique are rather uncharitable towards instrumentalist theory (and to my treatment of it). I believe there is a growing tendency for legal theorists to denigrate American instrumentalist legal theory in general, though some current fire is more narrowly aimed at the extreme "realist" wing of this tradition. Perhaps this general denigratory tendency is in part attributable to the fact that many American practitioners of instrumentalism were "philosophically unsophisticated" (an explanation that may account for Professor Moore's own skepticism).[161] Today many legal theorists do look to the philosophers as exemplars, and not merely in matters of idiom and style. Yet it is not inherent in the nature of things that instrumentalist theorizing must be philosophically unsophisticated. Whatever the explanation for the general denigratory tendency, I believe it will be unfortunate if this tendency diminishes the number of theorists who try to build on the work of the American instrumentalists. I believe this general type of legal theory has a real future, a view I continue to find confirmed in a variety of forms, not least in some important work by American social scientists that appeared after my book.[162]

Notes
1. R. Summers, INSTRUMENTALISM AND AMERICAN LEGAL THEORY (1982).
2. Moore, *The Need for a Theory of Legal Theories: Assessing Pragmatic Instrumentalism. A Review Essay of Instrumentalism and American Legal Theory by Robert S. Summers*, 69 CORNELL L. REV. 988 (1984).
3. *Id.* at 1000, 1011
4. *Id.* at 1011.

5. *Id.* at 1000. Among the other significant misunderstandings are these: (1) Professor Moore says I merely organized my book around themes that interested the American pragmatic instrumentalists. I organized the book around themes *of legal theoretic interest* that concerned these thinkers. (2) Professor Moore calls my reconstructed version of instrumentalist theory a *Weltanschauung* — a "world view." But the tenets of instrumentalist theory are not, in the usual sense of the word a *Weltanschauung.* (3) Professor Moore suggests that extreme rule skepticism was widespread among the instrumentalists. It was not widespread among those theorists I selected for study in my book. *See generally* R. SUMMERS, *supra* note 1, at ch. 6, 161-62. (4) Professor Moore says that a theory of change in the law is the nominal topic of my chapter 3. This is not so. The nominal as well as the substantial topic of that chapter is the general theory of law making. (5) Professor Moore remarks that in my book I do not recognize the weaknesses of the "what was done" theory of precedent. This is untrue. The reader should see my chapters 4, 5, and 6, especially pages 102-05, 112-15. (6) Professor Moore says that I omit entirely any treatment of instrumentalist writings on facts and factual analysis in the law. Parts of chapters 1, 3, and 6 are devoted to this, and I remark at pages 279-80 of my book that this is an important area of further inquiry that these thinkers opened up. (7) Professor Moore complains that I did not give enough emphasis to instrumentalist theories of interpretation. He adds, however, that these thinkers largely failed to articulate a theory of interpretation, a point I also make in my book at pages 153-54. (8) Professor Moore says I am unable to state "precisely" how values enter a theory of adjudication. On page 173, I do treat an important aspect of this, and I go into it more fully in an earlier article. *See* Summers, *Two Types of Substantive Reasons: The Core of a Theory of Common-Law Justification*, 63 CORNELL L. REV. 707 (1978).

6. Moore, *supra* note 2, at 1011.

7. In the book I stated that:

> The virtues are impressive. Many of these theorists saw the importance of formulating a general theory of value. As instrumentalists they naturally saw how law is itself an expression of value. It might even be said that they reconceptualized law's nature. They saw it as a set of practical social tools with specific uses and identifiable effects, rather than as an authoritative and formal body of preexisting precepts. Surely these alone were gigantic steps.
>
> Those who had gone before had drastically overstated the necessary limits of law's efficacy. The instrumentalists corrected this, and at the same time introduced technological rationalism and an empiricist mentality into legal thought. They brought to the fore the element of personnel in the law and provided a devastating critique of formalism, especially as it afflicted judges.
>
> It is appropriate to say that the instrumentalists *opened up* several relatively new branches of legal theory (including some that even the percipient Bentham had missed). Among these were the nature and variety of the means at law's disposal, the law's varied and complex goals and goal structures, the element of personnel in law, and the limits of law's efficacy.

R. Summers, *supra* note 1, at 279 (emphasis in original).

8. In the book I stated that:

> Beginning with the vices, we can conclude that these theorists dwelled far too much, in their theorizing about values, on the merely quantitative maximizing of wants and interests (as conventionally given). They thus failed to give qualitative notions of the just, the right, and the good their due. In stressing the practical and "technological" aspects of law, they neglected its normative character. It is true that they unmasked judicial lawmaking, but they devoted too little attention to the norms that should govern it. They were also unduly change-minded and experimentalist. They did not work out a general theory of justification for common law cases or for cases involving written law. They were excessively means-minded, and failed to grasp fully how law can be understood in terms of a continuum of means and goals. They adopted restrictive models of law's goals and means — models essentially behavioral in nature. They generally misdescribed the nature of the criteria of validity at work in our system, and insisted on a misleading and, in my view, unhealthy version of the doctrine that law and morals are separate. They espoused an untenable predictivism. They failed to see major differences between legal and machine technologies. They overstated the roles of coercion and force. And they were naive about the complexities and difficulties of determining law's effects and social facts generally. These are not small failures. Yet many are failures of overemphasis or of neglect and can thus be remedied.

Id. at 278-79.

9. It is a defect of my book that it does not include a summary of the leading tenets. For a more extended summary than the one I now offer, see Summers, *Pragmatic Instrumentalism and American Legal Theory,* 13 RECHTSTHEORIE 257 (1982).

10. R. SUMMERS, *supra* note 1, ch. 1.

11. O.W. Holmes, THE COMMON LAW 41 (1881).

12. R. SUMMERS, *supra* note 1, ch. 2.

13. Llewellyn, *A Realistic Jurisprudence — The Next Step,* 30 COLUM. L. REV. 431, 464 (1930).

14. R. SUMMERS, *supra* note 1, ch. 3.

15. *Id.* ch. 4.

16. *Id.* at 112-15.

17. *Id.* ch. 6.

18. *Id.* ch. 7.

19. *Id.* ch. 10.

20. F. Cohen, *The Problems of a Functional Jurisprudence*, 1 MOD. L. REV. 5, 8 (1937) (footnote omitted).

21. R. Summers, *supra* note 1, ch. 11.

22. Id. at 62-66, 69-70, 74-78, 105-12, 161-74, 182-89, 193-201, 212-22, 227-35, 258-67.

23. *See, e.g., id.* at 49-59, 66-69, 70-74, 78-79, 92-99, 105-15, 121-33, 161-75, 179-89, 201-08, 215-22, 225-30, 250-52.

24. *Cf.* text accompanying *infra* note 159 (on "presentism").

25. *See, e.g.*, A.G.N. Flew, A DICTIONARY OF PHILOSOPHY 228 (1979).

26. *See generally* Boyd, *On the Current Status of the Issue of Scientific Realism*, 19 ERKENNTNIS 45 (1983).

27. The so-called legal realists might be called "realists" in literary parlance, for they were concerned with fidelity to real life and with the accurate representation of life.

28. *See generally* J. Bentham, THE WORKS OF JEREMY BENTHAM (J. Bowring ed. 1843).

29. *See generally* R. Ihering, LAW AS A MEANS TO AN END (I. Husik trans. 1913). On Bentham's possible influence on Ihering, see Coing, *Bentham's Bedeutung für die Entwicklung der Interessenjurisprudenz und der allgemeinen Rechtslehre*, 54 ARCHIV FÜR RECHTS- UND SOZIALPHILOSOHIE 69 (1968).

30. There was also a rather different movement in Scandinavia called "legal realism". *See* Hart, *Scandinavian Realism*, 17 CAMBRIDGE L.J. 233 (1959).

31. Professor Moore writes as if I referred only to the American theorists when I made this claim. The European instrumentalists also qualify as part of this tradition.

32. Moore, *supra* note 2, at 993.

33. *Id.* at 988-89.

34. R. Summers, *supra* note 1, at 273, 279-80.

35. *Id.* at 38 ("Sometimes the American theorists carried the analysis rather far. More often, they merely gestured suggestively (yet unmistakably) in certain directions."). *See id.* at 279-80.

36. Moore, *supra* note 2, at 1011.

37. *See, e.g.,* works cited in R. Summers, *supra* note 1, at 288-90.

38. *See supra* note 22.

39. R. Summers, *supra* note 1, at 22-26, 269-70.

40. *Id.* at 269-70.

41. In fact, I know of no single notion in any other theory with similarly wide-ranging integrating properties. Some such properties are logical, some functional, and some otherwise.

42. I did not discuss this criterion in my book. *See generally* Nowell-Smith, *Philosophical Theories,* 48 ARISTOT. SOC. PROC. 165 (1948); Summers, *Notes on Criticism in Legal Philosophy,* in MORE ESSAYS IN LEGAL PHILOSOPHY 9-10 (R. Summers ed. 1971).

43. R. SUMMERS, *supra* note 1, at ch. 5.

44. *Id.* at 112-15.

45. *Id.* ch. 6.

46. *Id.* chs. 3, 8, 9, 11.

47. *Id.* chs. 11, 12.

48. *Id.* chs. 1, 2.

49. *Id.* at 143-44.

50. *Id.* ch. 1.

51. *Id.* ch. 3

52. *Id.* chs. 2, 3, 8, 9, 10, 11, 12.

53. *Id.* at 272.

54. The question of what properly qualifies as a general legal theory merits more extensive treatment than either Professor Moore or I have been able to give it here. The question is exceedingly complex and requires a book of its own.

55. Moore, *supra* note 2, at 1013.

56. *Id.* at 1012.

57. *Id.* at 1013.

58. I am indebted to my colleague Professor David Lyons for discussion of this point.

59. *See, e.g.*, J. Austin, THE PROVINCE OF JURISPRUDENCE DETERMINED (1832); H.L.A. Hart, THE CONCEPT OF LAW (1961); H. Kelsen, GENERAL THEORY OF LAW AND STATE (1945).

60. *See, e.g.*, T. Aquinas, *Summa Theologica*, in SELECTED POLITICAL WRITINGS 52 (A.P. d'Entreves ed. 1959); 1 W. Blackstone, COMMENTARIES ON THE LAW OF ENGLAND (W.C. Jones ed. 1976); H. Grotius, PROLEGOMENA TO THE LAW OF WAR AND PEACE (F. Kelsey tr.1957); S. PUFENDORF, DE JURE NATURAE ET GENTIUM LIBRI OCTO (H. Milford ed. 1934); Locke, *An Essay Concerning the True Original, Extent and End of Civil Government*, in THE ENGLISH PHILOSOPHERS FROM BACON TO MILL 403, 503 (E. Burtt ed. 1939).

61. *See, e.g.*, J.C. Carter, LAW, ITS ORIGIN, GROWTH AND FUNCTION (1907); H. Maine, ANCIENT LAW (F. Pollock ed. 1906); F. von Savigny, OF THE VOCATION OF OUR AGE FOR LEGISLATION AND JURISPRUDENCE ch. 2 (A. Hayward ed. 1975).

62. Moore, *supra* note 2, at 1011.

63. *Id.* at 993. It is not difficult to trace the origins of Moore's conception. Professor Ronald M. Dworkin has written that a general theory of law, in its normative part, "must have a theory of legislation, of adjudication, and of compliance." R. Dworkin, TAKING RIGHTS SERIOUSLY VII (1978). Professor Dworkin goes on, however, to indicate that a general theory of law may also treat many other matters.

64. *See, e.g.*, J. Austin, *supra* note 59.

65. *See, e.g.*, H. Kelsen, *supra* note 59.

66. *See* H.L.A.Hart, *supra* note 59.

67. See works cited *supra* note 61.

68. Moore, *supra* note 2, at 1013.

69. *Id.* at 1002-10.

70. *Id.* at 1010.

71. *Id.* at 1013.

72. *Id.* at 1003.

73. *Id.* at 1008.

74. An important exception is Jeremy Bentham. For his views on value, see J. Bentham, AN INTRODUCTION TO THE PRINCIPLES OF MORALS AND LEGISLATION (Burns & Hart eds. 1970). For his general views on adjudication and fact finding, see Postema, *The Principle of Utility and the Law of Procedure: Bentham's Theory of Adjudication*, 11 GA. L. REV. 1393 (1977).

75. Kelsen may be something of an exception. *See* R. Moore, LEGAL NORMS AND LEGAL SCIENCE ch. 4 (1978).

76. *See generally* A.P. d'Entreves, NATURAL LAW (2d ed. 1979).

77. Moore, *supra* note 2, at 1010.

78. *See supra* p. 1022.

79. *See, e.g.*, works cited *supra* notes 59-60.

80. R. Summers, *supra* note 1, ch. 1.

81. Compare, for example, Pound, *Common Law and Legislation*, 21 HARV. L. REV. 383 (1908) with H. Kelsen, PURE THEORY OF LAW 348-56 (1967).

82. *See supra* note 75.

83. Moore, *supra* note 2, at 1003.

84. R. Summers, *supra* note 1, ch. 4.

85. H. Kelsen, *supra* note 59, chs. X, XI.

86. H.L.A. Hart, *supra* note 59, chs. V, VI (1961).

87. Moore, *supra* note 2, at 1005. *See also* R. Summers, *supra* note 1, at 54-56, 87-89, 146-47.

88. R. Summers, *supra* note 1, at 154-57; *see also* D. Lyons, ETHICS AND THE RULE OF LAW 92-95 (1984); Wilson, *The Nature of Legal Reasoning: A Commentary with Special Reference to Professor MacCormick's Theory*, 2 LEGAL STUD. 269 (1982).

89. *See* Summers, *supra* note 5.

90. Moore, *supra* note 2, at 1010.

91. R. Summers, *supra* note 1, chs. 3, 6, 11.

92. Moore, *supra* note 2, at 1002-13.

93. *Id.* at 1003.

94. *Id.* at 1004.

95. H.L.A. Hart, *supra* note 59, chs. V, VI.

96. Moore, *supra* note 2, at 1005 (footnote omitted).

97. R. Summers, *supra* note 1, at 57, 112-15, 148-50.

98. Moore, *supra* note 2, at 1006-07.

99. *Id.* at 1007.

100. *See, e.g.,* Pound, *The Scope and Purpose of Sociological Jurisprudence* (pts. 1-3), 24 HARV. L. REV. 591 (1911), 25 HARV. L. REV. 140 (1911), 25 HARV. L. REV. 489 (1912).

101. *See, e.g.*, Llewellyn, *supra* note 13, at 431.

102. Moore, *supra* note 2, at 993.

103. *Id.* at 1011.

104. *Id.* at 993-96.

105. *See, e.g.*, Moore & Sussman, *Legal and Institutional Methods Applied to the Debiting of Direct Discounts,* 40 YALE L.J. 381 (1931).

106. *See, e.g.*, Pound, *supra* note 100.

107. *See* H.L.A. HART, *supra* note 59, at vii.

108. *Id.*

109. Hacker, *Hart's Philosophy of Law*, in LAW, MORALITY AND SOCIETY: ESSAYS IN HONOUR OF H.L.A. HART 1, 8 (P. Hacker & J. Raz eds. 1977).

110. H.L.A. HART, *supra* note 59, ch. IV.

111. *Id.* at 35-38.

112. *Id.* at 27-33.

113. *Id.* at 43-48.

114. *Id.* at 189-95.

115. This complex cluster of problems requires a separate essay.

116. *See generally* Hexner, *The Timeless Concept of Law*, 52 J. POLITICS 48 (1943).

117. Moore, *supra* note 2, at 998.

118. *See generally* Summers, *The Technique Element in Law*, 59 CALIF. L. REV. 733 (1971).

119. Hart has stated this in conversation on several occasions.

120. Raz, *On the Functions of Law,* in OXFORD ESSAYS IN JURISPRUDENCE 278 (A. Simpson ed. 1973).

121. *See* R. Summers, *supra* note 1, at 198-200.

122. *See generally* Hall, *Conceptual Reform — One Task of Philosophy*, 61 ARISTOT. SOC. PROC. 169 (1961).

123. Moore, *supra* note 2, at 990.

124. *See supra* text accompanying notes 110-14.

125. Moore, *supra* note 2, at 994.

126. *Id.* at 997. It is interesting to contrast Moore's view with that of Arnold Brecht: "Far greater efforts. . . should be diverted to the critical examination of goals and goal-values than have been in the past several decades. . . ." Brecht, *Political Theory: Approaches*, in 12 INTERNATIONAL ENCYCLOPEDIA OF THE SOCIAL SCIENCES 307, 313 (1968).

127. *See* R. Summers, LON L. FULLER ch. 2 (1984).

128. R. Summers, *supra* note 1, at 66.

129. Moore, *supra* note 2, at 997 (footnote omitted).

130. For precisely this point, see Radin, *Statutory Interpretation*, 43 HARV. L. REV. 863, 876-78 (1930).

131. Moore, *supra* note 2, at 997.

132. *Id.*

133. *Id.* at 996.

134. *Id.* at 996-97. For a more elaborate account of this conception of taxonomy, see Tiryakian, *Typologies*, in 16 INTERNATIONAL ENCYCLOPEDIA OF THE SOCIAL SCIENCES 177, 177-80 (1968).

135. Moore, *supra* note 2, at 996.

136. *Id.*

137. *Id.* at 997.

138. H.L.A. Hart, *supra* note 59, at 32 (emphasis in original).

139. Moore, *supra* note 2, at 997.

140. *See* Llewellyn, *Some Realism About Realism — Responding to Dean Pound*, 44 HARV. L. REV. 1222 (1931).

141. There is a rapidly growing literature on the methodology and the pros and cons of reconstruction. *See, e.g.,* THE HISTORY OF IDEAS (P. King ed. 1983).

142. As I pointed out in my book, my ultimate interest was "aggregative." The book concentrated on theorists as members of a collectivity sharing certain tenets. *See* R. Summers, *supra* note 1, at 13.

143. I frequently pieced together the positions of individual theorists from different sources, as manyof those thinkers were not very systematic. *See* R. SUMMERS, *supra* note 1, at 25.

144. *See supra* pp. 1019-21.

145. For a listing of these extreme views, see *supra* p. 1020.

146. Moore, *supra* note 2, at 999-1000.

147. *Id.* at 1001.

148. *Id.*

149. *Id.*

150. *Id.* at 1001-02.

151. *Id.* at 1002.

152. *Id.* at 989.

153. *Id.* at 1003.

154. The instrumentalists were interested in standards of validity, *see* R. SUMMERS, *supra* note 1, ch. 4, in facts and descriptions of facts, *see id.* ch. 6, in theories of interpretation and precedent, *see id.* ch. 6, and in the theory of value, *see id.* ch. 1. They were not much concerned with the role of formal logic in legal reasoning. It cannot be said, though, that these theorists synthesized the foregoing interests into what Moore might call a "unified" theory of adjudication.

155. Quentin Skinner has explained better than could I why it would be wrong to "reconstruct" such answers. *See* Skinner, *Meaning and Understanding in the History of Ideas*, 8 HIST. & THEORY 3 (1969).

156. Moore, *supra* note 2, at 1001.

157. *Id.* at 1002.

158. *Id.*

159. "Presentism" has now become something of a name for a diverse cluster of views emphasizing currency as the criterion of relevance. *See, e.g.*, Hall, *In Defense of Presentism*, 18 HIST. & THEORY 1 (1979).

160. Moore, *supra* note 2, at 989.

161. Moore, *supra* note 2, at 1010.

162. *See, e.g.*, S. Nagel, PUBLIC POLICY: GOALS, MEANS, AND METHODS (1984); D. Mazmanian & P. Sabatier, IMPLEMENTATION AND PUBLIC POLICY (1983).

CHAPTER 5

MY PHILOSOPHY OF LAW

I. Introduction

I have not yet worked out a complete philosophy of law, and the partial philosophy I do have is addressed merely to law in developed western societies, especially in the United States and Great Britain. I am ultimately striving for an overall synthesis that takes due account of the major contributions of the four great branches of legal theory: natural law thought, positivism, instrumentalist theory, and historical jurisprudence. I do not classify the totality of my own work as representative of any one of these branches, though I have published books and articles in which I attempt to contribute to various aspects of the first three.[1]

Most of my current thinking and my academic writings of a theoretical nature have, for about ten years now, been devoted to what I call the formal character of law.[2] (I also publish on American commercial law and contract law.) I do not offer my theoretical work on formality as itself a comprehensive general theory of law, let alone as an attempt to synthesize the major truths in all four of the great branches of legal theory. Rather, in my work I treat formality as only one of the major characteristics of law. Among all such characteristics, I would not even rank this characteristic -- the law's formality -- as the single most important. I would reserve that status for the law's characteristic general purposes and essential content. Those purposes and that content include the humanistic values of liberty, dignity of the individual, justice, and other basic rights secured or securable through law.

An emphasis on the humanistic values to be realized through the law's content has traditionally been a primary focus of natural law theory, and of much instrumentalist thought. Positivists, too, from Bentham onward, have stressed humanistic values. At the same time, traditional positivists and even some instrumentalists have also focused to some extent on the nature and importance of appropriate form in the law. Even some natural law theorists have dwelled on the importance of form.[3] However, compared to the overall emphasis that natural law theorists and instrumentalist theorists have given

95

to the value content of law, and compared to the overall emphasis that many positivists have given to such non-formal factors in law as state power, coercion and force, and direct official action, form itself has had rather less attention. I also believe that the systematic study of the major varieties of form in law can be taken far beyond where all prior and contemporary theorists have left it.[4] Moreover, formality is one of law's most important characteristics. Indeed, it may be that form is law's most foundational characteristic, for without form there can be no law at all, even when such non-formal ingredients of law as trained personnel, required material resources, and knowledge of effective legal technique happen to be readily available in abundance.

What is a general theory of form in the law, as I conceive it, and what are its central topics? First, it is necessary to explain what I mean here by "law". I refer to (1) rules and other types of legal precepts or norms, (2) basic functional elements of a legal system that are institutional in character such as legislatures, courts and the processes for creating such private law as contract, wills, and property arrangements, and (3) the legal system as a whole. Second, in the general theory I offer here, I introduce various concepts of form already rooted in basic English usage and I introduce what I hope is a perspicuous and stable terminology for designating these concepts. I then apply these to the foregoing types of legal phenomena.[5] Third, in the theory, I treat systematically how form in law and the formal features of law serve as means to ends. Finally, in the theory I seek in a preliminary and not yet fully developed fashion to give due credit to form. Here, I explore the general importance of form for traditional legal theory, and for practical affairs. These are topics and questions that have not yet been treated together in a systematic way in the history of legal philosophy. Thus, it is simply not possible to say how the treatment I offer here differs from standard answers in the subject. There is simply no such standard treatment that is at all systematic.

Before turning to the various ways in which the phenomena of law are "formal", and to how the formal in law contributes to its efficacy, I will explain how I became interested in this subject. There are two main origins of this interest. In the 1980's, I co-authored a book on the "form and substance" of Anglo-American law with Professor Patrick Atiyah of Oxford University.[6] In that book, my co-author and I considered how a broad range of legal phenomena can be characterized as formal, defended the thesis that the English system is more formal than the American, and considered what differences it can make that one legal system is more formal than another. While I no longer work within exactly the same conceptual framework of form and formality adopted for that book, that framework was useful for the purposes then at hand, and it has stimulated me to reflect further, as here, on how law is formal and why it matters.

One other major origin of my interest in form in the law should be stressed. This origin is at least equal in importance to the factor I have just identified. Over the past fifteen years, I have been re-reading the major classics of political and legal theory. In doing this I have kept the nature and role of form in the law at the forefront of my consciousness. In so doing, I have encountered numerous isolated remarks that I have found worthy of extended reflection. For example, Plato emphasized that a society should "proceed to legislate with a view to perfecting the form and outline of our state."[7] Plato went on to stress the role of the rule of law -- itself a largely formal concept.[8] He especially emphasized the importance of formal features of rules such as generality[9] and definiteness.[10] Plato also dwelled on the importance of the role of writing in formally expressed law.[11] Aristotle, too, emphasized formal features of law,[12] and from Plato and Aristotle forward to modern times, one encounters in the works of classical theorists many profound and insightful remarks on the nature and significance of various types of form in the law. Yet such remarks are usually brief, en passant, and almost entirely undeveloped. Among more recent scholars, the most suggestive of all for me has been the great nineteenth century German jurist who was a professor at the University of Göttingen, Rudolf von Jhering. While he, like his classical predecessors, did not work out anything like a general theory of the formal character of law, von Jhering, too, offered many brief and fruitful thoughts on the nature and place of form in the law. For example, he said that "form is rooted in the innermost essence of law", and that "form is the sworn enemy of the arbitrary and the twin sister of liberty."[13]

Upon reflecting on these classical writings, I concluded that the formal character of law is a major void in the history of western legal theory. One of my own teachers and one of the two leading positivist theorists of the twentieth century, H.L.A. Hart of Oxford, did not give form in the law its due.[14] Nor did Kelsen, the other leading positivist.[15] Nor has any other theorist. It cannot even be said that the systematic study of legal form somehow came to a premature standstill. It really never began.

My motivations in pursuit of a general theory of form in the law have not, however, been confined to the solely intellectual and theoretical. The American legal culture, especially on the academic side, includes powerful anti-formal strains.[16] Thus my own country has special needs for a theory that seeks to give due credit to form in the law. So, too, the English and German legal cultures, but for a very different reason. In England and Germany, form tends to be taken for granted, and so in those countries it has not been the subject of much systematic reflection.

Before turning to the rudiments of my own general theory of form in the law, I wish to enter two important disclaimers or qualifications. First, in offering my theory, I do not purport to present any discoveries or new facts about law. Rather, I attempt mainly to call attention to neglected aspects of the familiar. I do not apologize for this. As Wittgenstein said: "The aspects of things that are most important for us are hidden because of their simplicity and familiarity."[17] Moreover, as the great American jurist and philosopher of law, Oliver Wendell Holmes, Jr., once said, what we often most need is not more "investigation of the obscure," but rather "education in the obvious."[18] Though I do think that much of what I offer here is in the end obvious, it may not be, at the outset for most readers, all that obvious. Thus the variety of recognized senses of the word formal that I present here may not be quite so obvious, at least at the outset. Precisely how one or more of these senses applies to rules, institutions, and other legal phenomena may not be quite so obvious. Also, the overall cumulative application of these various senses of formal to the phenomena of law -- the overall pervasiveness of form in law -- may not be quite so obvious. Further, the extent of credit to be given appropriate form in legal theory may not be quite so obvious. Just how each major variety of form can contribute to the realization of ends through law may not be quite so obvious. Furthermore, the types of interplay -- functional and conceptual -- between the formal and the non-formal in law may not be quite so obvious.

At the outset, I will identify and isolate what is formal about law. To do this, I introduce conceptualizations of the varieties of form and formal features in legal phenomena, and then introduce for these varieties a terminology that I believe to be felicitous, that marks the relevant distinctions and connections, and that provides consistency of reference and economy of expression. With these conceptualizations and terminology, it then becomes possible at least to see a whole set of related questions: What in the law is formal? How pervasive is formality in the law? What are its main varieties? How are they related, if at all? What ends and values do these varieties serve? What is the overall practical importance of form, in all its varieties, in the law? What is relevant to the design of appropriate form in each variety? What are the major types of flaws of form? What would a comprehensive pathology of form in the law look like? How does the study of form cast light on traditional problems of legal theory and jurisprudence?

Some of these questions have received relatively little or no treatment in the history of legal theory and jurisprudence. Nevertheless, I have a second disclaimer. I do not wish to claim that what I offer here is wholly novel. Others have emphasized and continue to emphasize form in the law in one or more major respects. What I do claim here is that a general theory of law's formal character, as I conceive it, has yet to be developed at all systematically. Obviously, in the space of the pages that follow, I can merely suggest how this might be done, and I can do so only in relation to a few of the questions about form that I have just posed. The main questions in the theory I will sketch here, in necessarily abbreviated fashion, are these: What is the nature and general importance of form and formal features in legal phenomena, and how does the formal character of law cast light on traditional problems of legal theory?

II. How Form and Formal Features Serve Ends and Values

To serve ends and values, law must be validly created either by officials or by private citizens, and then implemented either through citizen action, through official action, or through some combination of these. In modern circumstances, these creative and implementive actions presuppose institutions such as legislatures, court systems, administrative officials and bodies, institutions of private law and more. These actions also presuppose accepted criteria for the identification of validly created law. And much more.

But let us concentrate, for now, merely on such institutions and on such criteria of validity. When these institutions and criteria exist and are operational, they can serve such important ends and values as the constitution of legitimate authority, rationality in law-making and administration, procedural justice, the realization of democratic self-governance, limited government, and the rule of law.

Now, what are some of the varieties of form and of formal features in such institutions that play roles at least as partial means to such ends and values? Such institutions are formal in the sense that they have minimal defining features that are formal. A court cannot be a court without, for example, the feature of judicial independence, a feature to be secured partly through rules prescribing a certain content. This defining feature pertains to the minimal constitutive form of a court, and so is formal in perhaps the most fundamental sense of the word recognized in our language.[19] This formal feature also contributes to the legitimacy of judicial authority, and to the legitimacy of exercises of this authority. This is merely one major type of contribution of the formal in only one sense of that word, namely, that which pertains to the minimal constitutive form of one type of institution.

Another major contribution of still another variety of formal feature in a court is this. A duly designed judicial procedure allows each side to the dispute a fair opportunity for a hearing and affords an opportunity for rational determination of relevant facts and applicable law. This feature is formal in the sense that it is procedural. "Of or pertaining to procedure" is simply another well established meaning of the word formal.[20] And here formality in this sense serves procedural justice and adjudicative rationality.

Similarly, an electoral process to constitute the membership of a legislature is procedurally formal. And when a democratically elected legislature, with an upper house and lower house, is duly constituted and in operation, it, too, is formal in its defining features and in its procedures. It is formal in its dual chambers, and in its committee system which brings division and specialization of labor. The specified relations between chambers, and within the committee system, are structural, in that they pertain to relations between parts within a whole. "Of or pertaining to structural form," is another well recognized meaning of formal in our language.[21] Features of structural form contribute to the realization of such important ends and values as democracy, legitimacy of authority, rationality in law-making, and procedural justice, e.g., through provisions for hearings on bills, through debate, and through requirements of passage in both houses.

At the same time, the nature of the generally accepted criteria for the identification of valid law within a system can also serve such values as legitimacy of authority and democracy. One such accepted criterion will be "duly enacted and promulgated" by the properly constituted, duly authorized, and procedurally licit legislature. Such criteria of validity as these are formal because one established meaning of formal in our language is: "that which pertains to the forms that assure validity."[22] Moreover, such criteria are formal in the further sense that they are "source-oriented", another recognized meaning of formal. Without acceptance of such criteria, for example, statutes could not be valid, nor democracy served.

To this point, I have indicated how several major varieties of the formal in legal institutions and in criteria for identifying valid law in a system may operate to contribute to basic social ends and values. I have not yet even introduced the subject of the creation and implementation of the ordinary garden-variety types of social policies that may be thought of as the very raison d'etre of so many legal institutions. Here, too, it is similarly demonstrable that appropriately formal features of legal phenomena, features themselves of major significance, contribute to the realization of important policy ends and values. But here I can only consider one major example. Let us consider the problem-specific policy of securing safe and efficient highway travel. Here it will be fruitful to imagine a projected linear sequence that begins with a democratically adopted, legitimate, procedurally proper, and validly promulgated rule that, say, specifies a 70 mph speed limit on all major highways, and usually ends with all private citizens who are drivers learning of this rule, and voluntarily applying it to themselves out on the highways with success in almost all instances of its applicability. (In this example, I assume a high correlation between speeds above 70 and unsafe driving, an assumption that might not hold in respect to some highways, e.g., German autobahns.)

I have already indicated how in the very existence and operation of institutions and of criteria of validity, major formal features, contribute to such fundamental ends and values as democracy, legitimacy, rationality, and procedural propriety and fairness. What about the valid rules of law that emerge from a law making process? Are these in any major ways formal, and how do these varieties of formality in the rules so created contribute to the realization of the ends and values such as safety and efficiency of highway travel? Just what are the major choices of form?

One choice, albeit an easy one here, is whether to leave the form of the rule to customary practice, adopt it as a matter of common law, incorporate it in a statute, put it in a constitution, or something else. Certainly the subject of a highway speed limit does not rise to a constitutional level. Nor can it be left to the diversity and informality of customary practices. The best choice of what might be called "encapsulatory" form here is the fixed verbal form of a statute. Among other things, this will represent an expression of popular will through votes of elected legislators, will then in turn be promulgated widely, will appear in fixed verbal form that can be readily learned, and will promise certainty. (The various types of encapsulatory form are likewise recognized in our language as formal.)[23]

Another major choice at the outset will be whether the legislature should put such a policy in a rule at all. Other alternatives might include simply the adoption of a general principle, or a broad grant of discretion to traffic officials, or the like. The choice here is a choice between alternative types of "preceptive" form, another recognized variety of form in our language.[24] A general principle or a broad grant of discretion to officials simply could not provide enough guidance, here. The preceptive form of a rule would, however, promise more guidance to citizens out on the roadways (albeit less guidance than particular orders, which themselves would be inefficient). Let us assume that a choice of the preceptive form of a rule is adopted, and that it is made on the ground I have indicated, namely, its superior policy efficacy. This, then, must be counted as another contribution of appropriate form to the ultimate realization of the ends and values sought, namely safe and efficient highway travel.

But this is far from all that may be credited to appropriate form here. I have so far implicitly taken for granted an important, though obvious, choice of what may be called expressional form,[25] namely that the relevant rule should be in writing, and should be cast in lay vocabulary. Statutes are always written, and having a rule prescribing a speed limit in such *written* form best serves the relevant policy ends, as well as legitimacy, certainty, and still other values. Many other types of choices of form arise in the course of creating the written statutory rule itself. Thus, a rule has defining features that are formal: its degrees of prescriptiveness, generality, definiteness, completeness in its various parts, and its structure -- its specification of relations between the parts of the rule. All of these features pertain to the minimal constitutive form of rules, and so are formal.[26] They also contribute to the ends and values to be served by the rule. Again, these ends and values are not confined to the problem-specific policy of the rule, here safety and efficiency on the highways. Consider generality, for example. While this formal feature of the rule under consideration must be tailored to the policy objective of highway safety and efficiency, and so be of such generality as to apply to virtually all highway users, this is not all that is at stake in choosing degrees of generality. Also to be served is the immense social value of substituting general rules to be applied by citizens on their own to their own special circumstances in place of particular commands issued to particular individuals by particular officials on particular occasions. This social value is not to be measured solely in terms of cost savings and efficiency. It includes, as well, the dignity and the autonomy of citizen-self-direction under law (in contrast to being ordered around by officials).

That the formal feature of definiteness in a rule poses important choices of degree is also evident, and the appropriate resolution of such issues serves not merely the determinateness and guidance required for discrete levels of safety and efficiency in highway travel. It also serves "learnability" of the law, the efficacy and dignity of citizen self-direction, ease of determining the law's factual applicability, dispute avoidance, fair advance notice of the law's behavioral standards, delimitation of scope for police intervention and police arbitrariness, and more.

The specification of the relationships between parts of a rule is another major variety of form in rules, namely, structural form.[27] The appropriate design of structural form likewise poses major choices. For example, a speed limit rule may include a part that specifies a minimum fine for exceeding it. This is a choice of part in the name of completeness, a formal feature. But the further choice of whether to make the fine automatic, or to make it discretionary, is a structural choice in the sense that it is a choice about the relation within a rule between the part that specifies the speed limit and the part that provides for a fine for exceeding it. Such a choice pertains to the relation between parts of a whole. What ends and values are at stake in such a structural choice? Not merely policy efficacy. Some further ends and values that may be served by an appropriate choice here are the minimization of scope for official arbitrariness, equality before the law, fair notice of possible adverse legal consequences, dispute avoidance, and ease of administration.

We are still at the legislative stage in the linear projection of the sequences of events from law creation to law implementation. Of the further stages along any such projection, several major ones will be familiar. Beyond due enactment pursuant to appropriate powers and procedures to assure validity, other steps include due promulgation, a formal act, and official dissemination of rule content among the rule's addressees (also a formal act). Moreover, the principles of legality and the rule of law operative in many systems not only presumptively favor the adoption of general rules, themselves formal in the foregoing ways, but also generally require not only due promulgation, and official dissemination, but also prospectivity of rule. These principles of legality are broadly procedural and so in a straightforward and familiar sense formal.[28]

Let us suppose that the legislature adopts, promulgates and disseminates a 70 mph speed limit (for general conditions on all major highways). It would be possible to imagine here a variety of "scope" and other interpretive issues that might arise with respect to such a statute. For example, does the rule apply to drivers of emergency vehicles? If the rule applies only in day time driving, with a slower speed for darkness, when does darkness occur? And so on. This introduces the relevance of an interpretive methodology. *How* is such a rule to be interpreted? A general interpretive methodology might exist on which rule-interpreters could rely to determine answers to such questions. Indeed, such methodologies do exist in developed legal systems, and may, for judges at least, be more or less elaborate and refined.[29] Because these are methodological, they are formal, for this just is another important sense of the word formal in our language.[30] A formal methodology that accurately and efficiently yields determinate answers to interpretive questions serves important values, too. It generally (in regard to the usual statute) serves the policies of predictability, certainty, equality before the law, dispute avoidance, ease of administration, and other related values.

A written statutory rule, validly adopted, promulgated, and disseminated, when duly interpreted and applied to circumstances, may be said to generate, in particular sets of circumstances, what I will call a *legal reason for action*. Here, that reason would be a reason for the citizen to act on voluntarily, and would take the general form of: "Drive no faster than 70 mph." This very reason, through which various policy and other ends and values may be served, is itself formal in a number of ways. It is derivatively formal in that it derives from a formal law-making process in accord with authoritative forms assuring validity. This reason is formal also in its degree of determinateness, which is also derivative, for the various formal features of the rule itself, such as generality and definiteness, contribute to this determinateness. So, too does the very preceptive form of the rule. So, too, does its fixed verbal form in writing in a statute. Furthermore, such a reason is formal not only in its authoritativeness, and its determinateness, but also in its peremptoriness. The reason generally pre-empts competing substantive reasons emergent in the circumstances. For example, the driver is not free to drive above 70 mph merely to visit a mortally ill relative in a hospital. Such peremptoriness is formal in the sense that it generally operates independently of the variable content of competing reasons.[31]

Thus, at the end of the various stages in our linear projections from rule creation to rule implementation through voluntary citizen self-application, we see how appropriate form in many varieties contributes specifically to the realization of policies and other ends and values. And were we to subtract any of these varieties of form, or significantly reduce their degrees or levels, we could easily imagine how the ends and values at stake would be affected.

In the type of example I have posed, the rule so created would be effectively implemented without incident by citizen self-application on the front-lines of human interaction in, say, 99% of the cases. The life of such a rule of law, and of the many laws like it in many systems, is almost entirely a life led outside of court. There would, however, be some "trouble cases", only a few of which would end up in court. In one kind of trouble case, a non-judicial official responsible for administering or enforcing the law intervenes upon observing a failure of compliance. A simple illustration in the 70 mph speed limit example would involve a citizen who exceeded the limit by, say, 20 mph. By electronic means, an arresting police officer might determine the fact of non-compliance, arrest the speeder, and issue a summons directing that the speeder either pay a stipulated fine by mail or appear in court on an appointed day. In some western countries, the speeder would in nearly all cases simply pay the fine by mail. In this type of example, the arrest itself terminates an instance of unsafe driving and so serves the policy of safety. The arrest and the fine also lend credibility to the entire enforcement process and thus contribute to general deterrence of speeding, thereby also serving the policy of safety. Similarly, the very presence of patrol cars on the highway deters speeding and so furthers the policy. Important formal features of the law itself here are that it is embodied in a written statutory rule which all drivers and police are taken to know, and which can be readily learned by virtue of its simplicity and definiteness, themselves formal features. All these formal features converge to limit drastically the scope for disputes over non-compliance, and the availability of accurate electronic devices for determining non-compliance with precision delimits the scope for disputes over the fact of non-compliance even more drastically. Here, too, the appropriate formality of the law contributes in various ways to its policy efficacy.

Moreover, safety and efficiency of traffic flow in this example are not the only values to be served by such formality in cases of official intervention and coercive enforcement. The contribution of form to ease of administration and to avoidance of disputes is valuable too. So are the contributions of form to the realization of still other values. A determinate law enforceable by an official in a highly objective fashion lends legitimacy to the entire enforcement process. It also delimits scope for official arbitrariness in determining the existence of any violation in particular cases.

The contributions of appropriate formality are to be seen not only in the conditions for voluntary citizen-self-application and in the efficacy of coercive enforcement. Appropriate formality here contributes to securing the freedom and dignity of citizen self application of the law as well. For a highly determinate and readily applyable rule forbidding driving <u>above</u> 70 mph also at the same time limits the power of officials to arrest or otherwise interfere with the freedom of those who drive <u>below</u> 70 mph, too. Here, as the great Rudolph von Jhering might have put it, form is the "twin sister of liberty" and the "sworn enemy of the arbitrary."[32]

In some small proportion of cases, the alleged speeder will dispute that he or she was speeding, and will demand a judicial hearing in court to determine the fact of a violation if that be the fact, prior to imposition of penalty. Here, the minimal constitutive form of a court, its structural form, its procedural form, and its further formal features contribute to impartial, objective, rational, and fair determination of the fact of any violation, and to the similar resolution of any issue or issues of statutory interpretation that may have arisen. For example, a court just is formally organized to secure that the judge (and any jury) will be independent and so impartial.

Furthermore, the provision for, on the choice of the accused, of such a judicial proceeding implements a fundamental principle of legality and the rule of law that no person shall be subjected to penalty against his or her will without a fair opportunity to challenge the facts or the law on which such penalty is premised before an independent and impartial tribunal. This requirement of the rule of law is, like all such requirements, formal too, at least in the sense that it is broadly procedural.

In the foregoing linear progression from the creation of a speed limit law to its promulgation, its dissemination, its voluntary citizen self-application in over 99% of the instances, and its disposition of the relatively few trouble cases, we also see a relatively distinctive combination of formal and non-formal elements within an overall functional unit that we may call *the penal technique*. In this technique (which is only one of five major techniques or modalities whereby law creates and implements policy), it is typical that the legislature prohibits anti-social behavior, officials promulgate and disseminate this prohibition, citizens self-administer it, police and prosecutorial officials also administer it, and penal and correctional officials stand ready to enforce sanctions as ordered. It should be plain that any such overall modus operandi of the law -- any such general operational technique, is formal both in the sense that it is broadly procedural and also in the sense that it is structural. It is structural precisely in the respect that it connects, integrates, and co-ordinates various parts within an operational whole.[33] It specifies general relations between parts consisting of institutions and other functional elements within the system, elements that function along a linear projection from creation of law to its ultimate implementation to serve policy and other goals.

At the same time, the penal technique is not the only basic modality for the effectuation of legal goals within a legal system. As I have suggested, there are other major ones, including the private grievance-remedial technique, the administrative-regulatory technique, the public-benefit conferral technique, and the private-ordering technique (which includes the great socio-legal institution of contract). Moreover, even within these techniques there are important variations on the standard linear sequences from law creation to implementation, important variations in the roles of personnel, and important variations in the contributions of form to the realization of the relevant ends and values through law. Indeed, in some typical linear sequences, officials have vast discretion at point of application, and there is little or no scope for citizen self-application. This is true, for example, of judicial awards of child custody as between divorced parents.

Again, it is important to stress that form and formal features hardly make up the whole of the law. Much in the effective functioning of law is not formal at all: rule content consisting of social policy or moral principle, various trained personnel, material resources, communicative devices, social acceptance, coercive capacity, and more. Perhaps the most important non formal social asset of all is simply an alert, informed, legally sensitive, and co-operative citizenry. The most successful legal systems seek to capitalize at every opportunity on this vital social asset.

III. Some Implications for Legal Theory

I have so far tried to demonstrate, in quite practical terms, which, and how many, major varieties of form and formal features pervade law and contribute in various ways as means to the realization of ends and values through uses of law. I now turn to some illustrative implications of this that are somewhat more theoretical in nature.

A. Form and Formal Features in Law as Means to Ends

While there is much more to law than form and formal features, I hope to have demonstrated in the preceding section how form and formal features contribute to the capacity of law to serve as means to ends. This also bears on two staple topics of legal theory. One of these is the very nature of law itself. The other is the relation between law and morals. All agree that law is instrumental in nature. And all would also agree that the instrumental efficacy of law is traceable partly to non-formal factors such as the general social acceptance of law's content, the internal point of view of officials toward the law they apply, and also the law's general coercive capacity. But I have tried to show in the preceding section that numerous varieties of form and of features of form contribute in their own ways to the law's instrumental efficacy and so to its very nature. I have sought to identify and isolate many of the numerous and specific types of contributions of a wide variety of forms and formal features of law to the ultimate efficacy of an illustrative authoritative policy as projected linearly from initial embodiment in a rule, on through various implementive stages to citizen self-application of rule in the human interactions of daily life. In my effort to demonstrate by way of example the general truth that form and formal features are indispensable to law's instrumental efficacy, and so cast light on the very nature of law, I did not stop to explore the many issues of alternative design of form and formal features, nor did I stop to explore the growing scholarship on how such issues may be best resolved (scholarship, incidentally, in which the relevant legal phenomena are often not seen to be formal in any respect). For my present purposes, such efforts are not necessary.

My present legal theoretic aim has been only to offer a perspicuous, albeit brief, representation of form and formal features as important elements of the law as social means, and thereby contribute in a modest way to our general understanding of the nature of law itself. It is possible to under-estimate the contributions of form and formal features of law to its instrumental efficacy, and many scholars in the social sciences and in philosophy have in fact been guilty of this.[34] It is not merely that numerous varieties of formality figure importantly in the creation and implementation of numerous policies such as the safety and efficiency of highway travel.

It can be said with justification that law extends and enriches the general menu of possible ends and means of social life, and that the law's form and formal features are indispensable to this. For example, without law, and appropriate form in the law, we could not have contractual relationships that are as satisfactory as those we do have. Bargain consideration, or its equivalent, as required by the law of contract, is itself formal, and is applicable to highly varied content. It provides some evidence that the relevant promise was actually made. It also tends to put negotiating parties in a cautionary and circumspective frame of mind, so that by their own lights, they make better choices. It is also partly through form that we have the very institution of money which itself greatly facilitates contractual agreements and exchanges. Indeed, it is through agreements and the exchanges pursuant thereto that, in developed liberal societies, we not only realize many of our personal ends but at the same time experience free, autonomous, self-direction and self-governance.

As further examples of how form in law contributes to the enrichment and extension of the means and ends of social life, consider the disposition of our property by will or through trusts. These devices, like contract and property, are creatures of the law, and without appropriate form defining and validating their very existence, we simply could not "leave property by will", or "transfer property in trust". Countless further examples could be cited. I will cite merely one further, more collective, example. Without appropriate legal form we would not have the very social phenomenon of "electing legislators". This phenomenon, of course, requires actual elections, and elections are highly formal, not merely in terms of their minimal constitutive form, but also structurally, and procedurally. In these and in many other ways, then, form and formal features in law and legal phenomena are indispensable to the vast enrichment of the means and ends of social life that we today enjoy.

When theorists have treated the law as a means to ends, they have also often viewed themselves as addressing one or more facets of that other staple topic of legal theory that addresses the relations between law and morals. And in this, theorists have often emphasized only those ends that may be characterized as substantively moral. The protection of life and limb is an obvious illustration, as in my highway speed limit example. But the values at stake in a truly comprehensive general treatment of the relations between law and morals are not confined to the substantively moral, and only if we specifically address the end-serving contributions of the varieties of form and formal features in the law, especially relatively high degrees of certain formal features, can we see fully how this is so. In my demonstration in Part II of this essay, I reminded the reader how, at various stages in a linear projection of the sequences involved in creating and implementing law, law's form and its formal features help to serve many important social values *beyond* those that, in ordinary terms, qualify as substantively moral. These values include political legitimacy, democracy, procedural justice, instrumental rationality (in designing means-end relations), certainty and predictability, objectivity in application of laws, the dignity of autonomous self-direction, equality before the law, minimization of scope for official arbitrariness, dispute avoidance, ease of administration, and more. Many such values might be called fundamental political values, and others general legal values. Some of these values have been studied extensively in the history of legal theory, but others have not yet had their due.[35] Although such values, most of them, are not substantively moral, they are not without moral significance.

Fundamental political values and general legal values may be served through law, including its appropriate forms and formal features, even when the social policy content or the substantive moral content is not appropriately incorporated in the law or is otherwise not well served. Often, these various values require for their realization relatively high degrees of formality in the features of implementive rules and other legal phenomena. Moreover, even when policy or other substantive moral content _is_ duly incorporated in the law and the law can be highly effective in implementing it, the law-makers may sometimes make the further choice when drafting the law's final form and content to sacrifice some level of substantive value realization in exchange for a higher level of realization of fundamental political values or of such general legal values as predictability, objectivity in application of law, delimitation of scope for official arbitrariness, dispute avoidance, and the like, (a matter to which I return in D. below).

Then, too, the law must cope with types of social problems wherein no social policies or other substantive moral ends strongly dictate the law's immediate content. Whether to require highway users generally to drive right or to drive left is one of the most familiar examples. Here, general legal values, many of which, again, cannot be served without high degrees of formal features in rules and other legal phenomena, can receive special emphasis. Rules can be firm and determinate here, whatever their content. Yet, general legal values are, most of them, at one or two removes from substantive moral notions. General legal values are in one sense internal to law itself. This does not, of course, mean they are all devoid of moral significance. Among other things, many of these values implicate a variety of issues of fairness in the relationship between citizen and state, and such fairness is itself a matter of morality.

B. The Organizational Functions of Form and Formal Features in Law and Legal Phenomena

I return here to that staple of legal theory, the nature of law. Another fundamental facet of law's basic nature is that it is a distinctive and complex mode of social organization. The institutions and processes of law in developed societies are highly organized. Rules, principles, maxims, rulings, orders, etc. are similarly highly organized phenomena of law. The creations of private citizens as law-makers are organized, often highly so: corporations, partnerships, contractual relations, bundles of property rights, wills, trusts, and other property arrangements, and still more. And, of course, the system as a whole is highly organized. The formal character of law is one important and neglected key to understanding law as a complex mode of social organization.

There are several different senses in which such phenomena of law may be said to be organized. Each basic functional element of the system, e.g., the legislature and the court system is itself internally organized, i.e., internally constituted. Then, the relations between such elements are organized so to be functionally connected, integrated, and co-ordinated, as required. So, too, the system as a whole is organized so that it operates systematically, methodically, and in accord with the dictates and constraints of the principles of legality and the rule of law. Then the various bodies of law are also themselves organized to be generally coherent and free of contradictions. Bodies of law are organized so that their specific content is readily accessible, too.

Without concepts of the minimal constitutive forms of the institutions, rules, principles, and other precepts, and of the system as a whole, no phenomena of law and no system of law could exist. As a sagacious American judge once put matters:

> Those who are impatient with the forms of law ought to reflect that it is through form that all organization is reached. Matter without form is chaos; power without form is anarchy. The state, were it to disregard forms, would not be a government, but a mob. Its action would not be administration but violence.[36]

Even if the prospective creators of a legal system had available to them in abundance all of the *non-formal* requisites of effective law ranging from the ready potential for social acceptance of law once created, to trained administrative and other personnel, to knowledge of desired policy, to knowledge of means-end relations, to all required material resources, and more, it still would not be possible to create a functional system of law.

Without conceptions of the minimal constitutive form of a legislature, of a court, of a rule, and so on, the creators of a system would simply not know where to begin. Those who would create the system must have concepts of form, including the very "formative principle which holds together the several elements" of each institution, of each type of legal phenomena, and of the system as a whole.[37] Of course, those various concepts of minimal constitutive forms are each themselves further analyzable into various formal features, as we have seen. Many of these concepts of minimal constitutive form are internally quite complex. It should now be plain that all such concepts of minimal constitutive form in institutions, rules, and so forth are essentially organizational in nature. These concepts specify how parts of the system are themselves to be constituted on their own, and also how the whole system is to be put together organizationally, i.e., constituted.

Minimal constitutive form is not the only concept of form that is essentially organizational. All varieties of form are organizational or contribute to the organized character of law and its organized activities. Concepts of structure -- of how parts are put together, are concepts that are often elaborated beyond their constitutive minima, and are independently significant to the extent that they are so elaborated. Concepts of legislative structure and judicial structure are illustrative. For example, a legislature need not have more than one chamber to be a legislature, yet it often has two. A legislature need not even subdivide itself into a set of committees, yet this is typical. Once these elaborate steps are taken, relations between parts must be specified, and this generates structure. Then, too, ideas of procedural design are formal. And so are ideas of accommodative form for institutions -- ideas of how far the scope of operation of an institution is to apply to varied subject-matter content.[38] Concepts of appropriately definitive form in institutions are likewise formal. For example, on one view of appropriate legislative definitiveness, the composition, structure, procedure, and accommodative scope of the legislature are tightly organized and operate in highly regularized fashion. On another conception, the legislature is less tightly organized, and less regularized in operation. But whatever the degree of the governing concept of definitiveness, this idea is itself a formal organizing idea.[39]

So far, I have merely suggested (and without attempting to be comprehensive) how the creation of legal phenomena and of a system of law are necessarily dependent upon *prior* notions or concepts of form: at least minimal constitutive form, structural form, procedural form, accommodative form (applicability to variable content), and definitive form. But the concepts or ideas of appropriate form, in all their varieties, required for the design of an organized system of law is one thing, the availability of actual social means of organizing and so implementing this design, something else. What are the functional phenomena of law including institutions, processes and the systems as a whole organized out of? They are, as I have indicated, organized in light of relevant concepts of minimal constitutive form, and thus not only out of non-formal social means such as knowledge of social cause and effect, trained personnel, and material resources, but also out of other social resources including most importantly, but not exclusively, out of prescriptive rules, principles, orders, and other preceptive phenomena.

Here, let us briefly consider only rules. Form and the formal features of rules have a double role. At the very outset, we must at least have ideas of the minimal constitutive form of a rule, the elaborated structural form of a rule, the expressional form of a rule, and the encapsulatory form of a rule. All these forms are required for the internal organization and existence of rules. And if valid legal rules are to exist, then they must conform as well to the criteria for the validity of such rules in the legal system, and I have already indicated the extent to which the criteria assuring validity are formal.

Valid formal phenomena, rules, are required for, and play large roles in, organizing the creation of the institutions, the processes, the implementive devices, and the system of law as a whole. Such rules prescribe organizational content and so prescribe the form and formal features of institutions and of the system, all in accord with concepts of their minimal constitutive forms, concepts of structural form, concepts of procedural form, concepts of accommodative form (applicability to variable content), concepts of definitive form, and so on. Of course, in some systems, the rules prescribing some organizational features must be prescribed in constitutional encapsulatory form.

A valid legal rule prescribing some variety of form or formal feature of some incipient legal phenomenon such as a legislature, all in accord with an appropriate concept of minimal constitutive form may be said to be in the nature of an "atomic legal particle" -- one of the small units out of which legal institutions and other phenomena of law are put together. But it does not follow that the basic legal phenomena, duly constituted, can be reduced to rules or even reduced to something essentially like rules. A legislature is an institution, not a rule or set of rules. A court system is a complex institutional organization, not a rule or set of rules. An administrative bureaucracy is just that, not a rule or a set of rules. Nor are these and other basic legal phenomena reducible to something like a union of primary and secondary rules. Rules, themselves formal in many ways, do, however figure prominently in the construction of legal phenomena and of the system as a whole. The content of many rules prescribes much of the organization of these phenomena and of the system as a whole. (Of course, the content of other types of rules prescribes social policies and moral principles, too.)

And, important though they are, rules are not the only "atomic" particles out of which organized legal phenomena and legal systems as a whole are constructed. As I have stressed throughout, functional law requires the incorporation and integration of non-formal resources too. But the "atomic particles" out of which a functioning legal order is made also go well beyond non-formal resources, too. The constitutive form, the structural form, the procedural form, the accommodative form, and the overall definitive form of, say, a legislature is itself not merely a function of the precision of basic rules prescribing these forms. Some of the rules themselves may even have large gaps in them. (For example, the organizationally prescriptive rules of the American constitution say nothing of political parties.) Other major factors besides prescriptive rules that may contribute to the definitiveness of institutions and other legal phenomena in their actual operation include social agreement on desired institutional features; public perception that the forms and formal features in place are fitting, right, and good; the stability and continuity of actual customary practices in conformity with those features; the readiness of officials, judges, and affected parties to criticize departures from prescribed or accepted organizational forms, and the readiness of affected persons to take remedial or other related action in the face of departures from prescribed or accepted organizational forms.

Law, then, is a complex mode of social organization. Moreover, the very organizational contours of institutions and other legal phenomena, including the system as a whole, can be analyzed in relatively comprehensive fashion in terms of the major varieties of form and formal features at work. Indeed, the very existence of law, as we know it, is dependent upon the creation and maintenance of legal phenomena in accord with concepts of organizational form appropriate to those very phenomena. And the formal "atomic particles" out of which these phenomena are created include another highly formal type of phenomenon, namely, rules prescribing the form and formal features of such phenomena. Form, then is an essential key to understanding the highly organized character of law itself, and an essential key to understanding what figures in that highly organized character.

The formal character of law, then, may be said to be internally organizational. At the same time, the formal character of law also provides the "formative principle[s]... which hold together the several elements of functional law."[40] That is, it is through form and formal features in all their varieties that the non-formal as well as the formal are integrated into working law. Thus, the formal in law provides stable channels and foci for the expression of social acceptance, acquiescence, and assent with respect to the law's content and its requirements. It is through the formal in law that institutional and other roles for trained personnel are defined. It is through the formal in law that the necessary deployment of material resources, and the mobilization of coercive capacity is organized and authorized. Without due form, these and other non-formal social assets could not be appropriately brought into play.

It is also true that law, as a complex aggregation of organizational forms (in part) duly integrated and duly co-ordinated, is, in virtue of this very formal character, also relatively distinctive as a type of social phenomenon, a truth that casts further light on law's very nature. Here, law as a whole may be said to be "characterized by, or regarded according to its form."[41] That is, law's formal character, itself an aggregation of minimal constitutive forms and of varied formal features, can, in virtue of such features (though not only in virtue of) be readily differentiated in illuminating ways from other social phenomena that, in the history of legal theory and the study of society, have been associated with law as cognate means of social control and social facilitation. Consider, again, the relation between law and morality. The forms and formal features of law and of morality are really quite different. It is enough to cite two major examples. First, law is indisputably in major part an affair of rules, and rules are, in major respects, formal. But there is a persuasive body of thought to the effect that morality is not truly a matter of rules at all. Second, and on the institutional plane, it can be said that social morality lacks anything like a legislature, which, as we have seen, is formal in major respects. Moreover, social morality lacks anything like a judiciary, and a judicial system is highly formal, as we have seen.

C. Form, Formal Features and Legitimate Civic Authority

Without legitimate civic authority, nothing we now recognize as law could exist. I will now focus more narrowly and frontally, than I have heretofore, on the various types of appropriate form in the creation and functioning of legitimate civic authority as such. It is only through these that the conditions for the existence of authority, including the very sources of valid law that figure in source-oriented criteria of validity, can be realized.

Appropriate form, in several major varieties, is required to localize civic authority in determinate institutional roles. Thus, the relevant institutions must be brought into being in the first place. As I have explained, we must, therefore, have a conception of a legislature with power to make general written law -- a conception of the relevant minimal constitutive form for a legislature. Compositional, structural, and procedural form, and form accommodating variable content, must all be specified, and this may be done initially through the preceptive form of rules prescribing these formal features. At the same time, the non-formal social assets required for the effective functioning of such a determinate locus of civic law-making authority must be duly organized within the overall formal framework. These include elected legislators, other trained personnel, material resources, and more.

But far more is required for the existence of legitimate civic authority to create general written law than a determinate locus for personnel within institutional roles. Further formal organization is required not only to secure quality in law making, but also to specify what is to count as the exercise of authority. In the case of a legislature, there must be some agreement, duly specified, on what is to count as the making of a law. This calls for organization with respect to what persons are legally qualified to participate as legislators, what powers they are to have, by what procedures they are to act, in what mode they are to express their legislation, how such action is to be promulgated, and how disseminated. Again, specification of these normally requires the use of rules having the requisite organizational content, itself formal in the major ways already specified: constitutively, structurally, procedurally, definitively, and so on.

Without a determinate locus of authority in determinate institutional roles, and without determinate specification of how this authority is to be exercised, legitimate civic authority could not exist, no matter how many persons around there may be who are willing to claim authority, and have access to required material resources, etc. For one thing, the institutional locus of authority could not be sufficiently identifiable and could not be sufficiently constant in time to enable it to become a social object of genuine acceptance, acquiescence, or assent. Thus, at least for a liberal society, such a locus could not survive as legitimately authoritative. And appropriate form, in most of the major varieties I have just identified, would be required for this very identifiability and constancy. Indeed, even unanimous consent of all in the society to some presumed objective authority could not legitimize such a "locus" if devoid of the determinateness and constancy that only appropriate form can provide. There is, therefore, far more to the constitution of legitimate civic authority than merely the social acceptance of a rule that confers power to make or apply law. In this, all the major varieties of form and formal features ordinarily identifiable in institutional legal phenomena must figure in significant ways. This is not to say that functional and legitimate authority is merely formal. Nor is it to say that the only sources of legitimacy are acceptance, acquiescence, and assent over time.

Matters are still more complex than I have so far indicated, having limited my focus to a single illustrative type of civic authority, namely that of a legislative body with general power to make written law. In developed western systems of law, authority is divided, partly to take advantage of the values of specialization of legal labor, and, in some systems, partly to provide internal checks and balances. Thus, a full analysis here would address not only the requirements of appropriate form in the constitution of legitimate legislative authority. The analysis would also address the requirements of appropriate form in the constitution of legitimate executive, judicial, and other authority, including the authority of private persons to create and implement law in the form of contracts, wills, property arrangements, and the like.

D. Some Priorities of Form and Formal Features in Rules and Rule-Application

In the very course of creating law, many situations arise in which it may be justified to formulate the law so that it takes a form that more fully serves what I call general legal values even at the price of some sacrifice of the basic policy at stake. I will cite one example to render my meaning more concrete. A legislature may choose to adopt a law retiring all police officers at age 60, even though this may not maximally serve the policy of having a fit police force, given that some officers are still quite fit at 60, and some no longer fit prior to 60. Yet such a formally firm and definite rule secures a fit force to a considerable degree (let us assume), and would also be better than a vague rule (retire when no longer fit), given that the formally firm and definite rule better serves such general legal values as predictability, minimization of scope for arbitrariness, dispute avoidance, the saving of the costs of case by case inquiries into fitness, and more. However, it is not correct to say merely that appropriate form in a rule has a special priority here. Instead, it is better to say that the form more appropriate to serving general legal values may take priority at some level over the form more appropriate to serving problem-specific policy. Thus, the priority is of one type of form over another.

I now turn to another type of priority of appropriate form. In general, officials, judges, and citizens are not free to depart from, or to rewrite, formal rules of law once validly created and still in force. In this, they are generally required to honor the form and the formal features of established rules, except insofar as the "rules of change" recognized in a system authorize such departures. If this were not so, society could hardly be said to be governed in accord with the rule of law. A presidential or other high administrative official generally has no power to depart from or rewrite a statute or binding precedent, let alone a constitution. Further, a highest appellate court is generally required to adhere to a constitutional provision, and also to a formal statute even if the constitution or statute might even be readily improved in its content or in its form, and by that very court, then and there. It is true that in common law countries, the highest appellate courts do have some power to over-rule or modify valid precedent. Most such courts seldom do so, however, merely on the basis that the court would have decided the precedent differently if the case were now before it for the first time.

Nor can a citizen change the law or avoid its reach merely because of some truly exigent circumstance. A motorist is not allowed to exceed the speed limit merely to say farewell to a dying relative at a hospital, even if there is no evident risk to the safety of others.

Likewise, a judge is generally not free to rewrite a contract or a security agreement such as a mortgage, or indeed, any other privately created instrument. For example, a court is not free to block a mortgagee bank from foreclosing against a debtor no matter how inequitable or unjust this may be, as where, for example, the delinquent debtor is an unemployed widow with five children and no place to go.

In all the foregoing instances, the law is in part paying homage to appropriate form and the values this serves. The conflict is not a conflict between "the formalistic" or "mere form," on the one hand, and genuine values on the other. In all the foregoing instances, the claims of form are backed at least by general legal values and rule of law values. And commonly the claims of form are also backed by social policies, moral principles, and even justice itself, at least in what John Rawls would call a "tolerably" well ordered society.[42] It is true that sometimes it is, in an especially compelling case, necessary and even justified to disregard the claims of form and the values form serves in order to "do justice in the particular case." This might be thought of as a reversal of the general priorities of form, and such rule departures comprise a general subject requiring fuller study than legal theorists have so far given it. But at least in a tolerably well ordered society, it remains generally true that it is adherence to, not departure from, antecedent law with all of its formality, that normally serves justice, even in particular cases.

Let us return to the our highway speed limit illustration. Here, form serves justice at almost every turn. When drivers self-administer a determinate speed limit, and conform to it, they thereby accord other drivers their due, and thus act justly toward them. These other drivers will have formed justified expectations of general compliance and will be seeking to co-ordinate their own behavior accordingly. Every such instance may be thought of as a particular case in which, among other things, justice is done when drivers comply.

At the same time, when police fail to enforce the speed limit against serious violations, this is unjust to other drivers then and there abiding by the law. It frustrates their own justified expectations, and imposes an unfair burden on them. When police do arrest speeders, and they are duly penalized, the police and the judges thereby see to it that the speeders receive their own just deserts. That is, justice is done in these particular cases. To the extent that fines or penalties are proportionate to the degree of the offence, such punishment itself is just. Also, to the extent that disputant speeders go on to receive a fair trial, they also realize procedural justice in the particular case. Now, in all of these ways in which justice may be done, appropriate form plays major roles. Form in the law is not fundamentally at war with justice in the particular case. On the contrary. The general priorities of appropriate form, in a tolerably well ordered society, normally secure justice in the particular case.

Notes

1. Among the books, see INSTRUMENTALISM AND AMERICAN LEGAL THEORY (Cornell U. Press 1982); LON L. FULLER (Stanford U. Press 1984); FORM AND SUBSTANCE IN ANGLO-AMERICAN LAW (with P.S. Atiyah) (Oxford U. Press 1987); ESSAYS ON THE NATURE OF LAW AND LEGAL REASONING (Duncker and Humblot 1992).

2. My thought is in the course of evolution, and I now reject some of the views I earlier espoused. My major prior writings in article form on formality are, in reverse historical order: *How Law Is Formal and Why It Matters*, 82 CORNELL L. REV. 101 (1997), *The Juristic Study of Law's Formal Character,* 8 RATIO JURIS 237 (1995); *The Formal Character of Law III*, 25 RECHTSTHEORIE 125 (1994) (Ch. 6 of the present book); *Der Formale Charakter des Rechts II*, 80 ARCHIV FÜR RECHTS UND SOZIALPHILOSOPHIE 66 (1994); *A Formal Theory of the Rule of Law*, 6 RATIO JURIS 127 (1993); *The Formal Character of Law*, 51 CAMBRIDGE L. J. (1992).

3. J. Finnis, NATURAL LAW AND NATURAL RIGHTS (Oxford U. Press 1982).

4. For earlier works devoted in significant part to form in the law, see G. del Vecchio, THE FORMAL BASES OF LAW (The Boston Book Co. John Lisle trans. 1914), Rudolf von Jhering, 2 GEIST DES RÖMISCHEN RECHTS (Scienta Verlag Galen, Darnstadt 1993), and Rudolf von Jhering, LAW AS A MEANS TO AN END (The Boston Book Co. Isaac Husik trans. 1913); Max Weber, ON LAW IN ECONOMY AND SOCIETY (2 vols. Univ. of Calif. Press, 1978).

5. I draw on the Oxford English Dictionary here for the relevant general usages of formal and form, though not for definitions of concepts of basic legal phenomena such as legislatures, courts, legal rule, etc.

6. This book was published in hard back by Oxford University Press in 1987, and in paperback with minor revisions in 1991.

7. 2 THE DIALOGUES OF PLATO 504 (Random House, B. Jowett trans. 1937).

8. Id. at 487.

9. Id. at 486.

10. Id. at 491.

11. Id. at 530, 576, 632, 603.

12. THE BASIC WORKS OF ARISTOTLE 1326 (Random House, R. McKeon trans. 1941).

13. Jhering, GEIST, op. cit. supra n. 4 at 479, and 471.

14. H.L.A. Hart, THE CONCEPT OF LAW (Oxford U. Press 1961).

15. See, e.g., H. Kelsen, GENERAL THEORY OF LAW AND STATE (Harvard U. Press 1945).

16. See, e.g., R.A. Posner, THE PROBLEMS OF JURISPRUDENCE, passim (Harvard U. Press 1990), and D. Kennedy, *Legal Formality*, 2 J. LEGAL STUDIES, 2 J. LEGAL STUD. 351, passim (1975).

17. L. Wittgenstein, PHILOSOPHICAL INVESTIGATIONS ¶ 129, at 50 (MacMillan, G.E.M. Anscombe trans. 1953).

18. Oliver Wendell Holmes, Jr., COLLECTED LEGAL PAPERS 292 (1921).

19. The Oxford English Dictionary (hereinafter OED) (2nd ed. 1989) includes as its first standard meaning of "formal," "pertaining to the form or constitutive essence of a thing." In using the expression, minimal constitutive form, I do not mean to take sides in the ancient norminalist - realist debate, nor do I mean to commit to any one model for the analysis of concepts.

20. OED entry for "form": "A set, customary, or prescribed way of doing anything; a set method of procedure according to rule (e.g., at law); formal procedure" (entries no. I.11 a. & b.)

21. OED entry for "form" no. I.5.a.

22. OED entry for "formal" no. A.5.

23. OED entry for "formal" no. A.1.c.

24. The preceptive is formal in that it always involves minimal constitutive forms of rules and the like.

25. OED entry for "form" no. I.9.

26. Op. cit. supra n. 19.

27. Op. cit. supra n. 21.

28. Op. cit. supra n. 20.

29. D. N. MacCormick and R. S. Summers, eds., INTERPRETING STATUTES -- A COMPARATIVE STUDY (Dartmouth Pub. Co. 1991).

30. OED entry for "form" no. I.10.

31. On peremptoriness, see also H.L.A. Hart, ESSAYS ON BENTHAM, ch. 10 (Oxford U. Press, 1982).

32. Op. cit. supra n. 13.

33. Op. cit. supra n. 21.

34. See, e.g., J. Searle, THE CONSTRUCTION OF SOCIAL REALITY PASSIM (Penguin, 1995).

35. Among the important questions that arise here, especially in regard to each general legal values, are these: (a) How is it to be defined?, (b) Why is it prizeable?, (c) Is it intrinsically valuable or only instrumentally so?, (d) Can it be served even when the social policy or moral principle embodied in the content of the rule is not?, (e) Does its implementation generally require high degrees or levels of formality?, (f) How is it to be weighed against

other values?

36. Judge Bleckley in Cochran v. State, 62 Ga. 731, 732 (1879).

37. This usage is recognized in OED as a special usage. See OED entry under form at I.4.d.

38. See the special usage for formal in OED at A.1.d. "free from the descriptive content that would restrict it to any particular subject-matter." See also the OED entry for form at II.18.a. ("a mould").

39. OED entry for form, no. I.8.

40. Op. cit. supra n. 37.

41. OED entry for formal, no. A.2.

42. J. Rawls, A THEORY OF JUSTICE (Harvard U. Press 1971).

Part Two

Form in Law

CHAPTER 6

THE FORMAL CHARACTER OF LAW

I. Introduction

In this paper, I will (1) state and clarify my main theses about the formal character of law, (2) sketch out and briefly illustrate how I am developing and defending these theses, (3) differentiate in a very general way my theses from the concerns of other theorists, and (4) explain how the truth or soundness of my theses may be important. But this is only a preliminary account. A book will eventually follow.[1]

II. Main Theses

A legal system consists of various basic types of legal phenomena, including a constitution; law making and law applying institutions and entities such as legislatures, courts, administrative agencies, and also private entities, corporate and noncorporate; rules and other precepts used to set forth substantive law; authoritative methodologies of interpretation; a principle of stare-decisis (at least in common-law systems); and more.

Each of the foregoing is what I call a basic type of legal phenomenon. One way to deepen or otherwise improve our understanding of law is to identify and differentiate all of the basic types of legal phenomena within modern legal systems, and then describe and analyze the leading characteristics of each type. In fact, each basic type of phenomenon has several characteristics. Thus, for example, a legal rule characteristically has a distinctive external form: it may be encapsulated in a constitution, or in a statute, or in common law. A legal rule also has formal characteristics that may be called internal: its degree of completeness, of definiteness, of generality, of cohesion, of complexity, and its mode of expression. But a legal rule has non-formal characteristics as well. Thus many legal rules have substantive content, too.

The characteristics of basic types of legal phenomena, including their formal characteristics, vary from one type of phenomenon to another. Thus, the characteristics of a constitution necessarily differ from those of ordinary legal rules used to set forth substantive law, from those of an accepted methodology of statutory interpretation, and so on.

The first of my main theses is that one or more of the characteristics of each basic type of legal phenomenon is formal.[2] In what ways such phenomena are formal (and there are several major varieties of formality), and what the significance of the formalness of law may be, comprise a major branch of jurisprudence heretofore relatively neglected. Indeed, it is a subject that, to my knowledge, has never been subjected to comprehensive, unitary, and systematic treatment. There are various explanations for this. One is that while we may be mindful of characteristics of law that are also formal, we tend not to recognize them as formal.

Most of my recent theoretical research has been devoted to the foregoing and related theses. In Section III below, I will sketch out and illustrate how my thesis with regard to basic types of legal phenomena typically found in advanced legal systems is to be developed and defended. My claim here is that at least one major characteristic of every basic type of legal phenomena may be appropriately classified as formal. I will not address the other significant characteristics of such phenomena. (Of course, the characteristics of basic legal phenomena may be classified not merely as formal or not, but in other important ways, too, which I will not go into.)

But my study of formality is not merely a study of it as at least one characteristic of each basic type of legal phenomenon. A corollary of my first thesis is that appropriately formal features of law are also desiderata. How and why this is so, and the further problems it poses will also be treated briefly in Section III. In particular, I will show that, a given degree of a formal feature of a basic legal phenomenon may, as a desideratum, be justified by reference to what I call general rationales for formality and often also by reference to what I call institutional and processual values. Of course, this degree of formalness might also at the same time be justified as a means of serving problem-specific policies. But I wish to stress that law is not just an instrument of problem-specific policy. Indeed just as often, if not more often, the formalness of law serves general rationales for formality and institutional and processual values.

We may also study a legal system as a whole, and not just types of legal phenomena. When a legal system is viewed as a whole, it may be described as having several major "systemic" characteristics. A systemic characteristic is not phenomena-specific in the way that a characteristic of a basic type of legal phenomenon is. A further way to achieve understanding of law is to identify and analyze the systemic characteristics of a legal system taken as a whole. One leading systemic characteristic is what Professor H.L.A. Hart called an essential "minimum substantive content" of the system, which includes rules protecting against violence and against destruction of property.[3] Another systemic characteristic consists of what Hans Kelsen called a "coercive order".[4] There are still other systemic characteristics. My second main thesis is that several of the systemic characteristics of a legal system viewed as a whole are to a significant degree formal.[5] These include the unity of the institutional framework of the system, the coherence of the substantive rules of the system, and the regularized legality of the system's modes of operation. Thus, we may also speak of the formal character of a legal system viewed as a whole. In Section IV below, I will illustrate how my systemic formality thesis is to be developed and defended.

Again, the characteristics of a system taken as a whole that are formal are not merely characteristics to be described as such. The relevant corollary thesis here is that appropriate degrees of such systemic characteristics are also desiderata backed by significant rationales, values, and policies, a matter that will also be treated briefly in Section IV below.

A related general thesis that I will advance here, albeit only suggestively, is that characteristics that are formal affect legal content, and that good form frequently begets or tends to beget good content. (Bad form begets bad content, too, though I will not explore this now.)

A further general thesis that I will argue for here is simply that my theses and their corollaries are important both jurisprudentially and in practice. Among other things, where form gets its due, law is used in a more law-like way. In Sections VI and VII I will explore this and related points.

In what follows, I generally do not purport to reveal discoveries of fact about legal phenomena. Rather, I will call attention to facts we take for granted. I will re-order, reconceptualize, and introduce a nomenclature for much that is already familiar. Yet this will sharpen our perception of formal features in diverse legal phenomena. And by using a uniform nomenclature for these formal features, I will underscore essential similarities.

III. The Formalness of Basic Types of Legal Phenomena

In this section, I will sketch out and briefly illustrate (1) how I propose to develop and defend my general thesis that each basic type of legal phenomenon displays one or more characteristics that are formal, and (2) how one might defend the corollary thesis that appropriate versions of such form are also desiderata. I must be selective, and can treat only five basic illustrative types of legal phenomena, and briefly at that.

A.   Form and Constitutional Phenomena

General constitutional provisions address the foundations and framework of a legal system. For example, a relatively comprehensive set of constitutional provisions will reflect such choices as the choice between a cabinet-form and a non-cabinet form of government in which the executive either does or does not control the legislature in its law making activity, the choice between a democratic and a non-democratic form of legislature, the choice between an independent judiciary and a judiciary subservient to the executive, to the legislature or to both, the choice between a unitary and centralized form of government on the one hand and a federal system on the other, the choice between having only source-oriented and therefore exclusively formal criteria for the validity of statutes and having such criteria plus additional content-oriented criteria of validity as well, and the choice between having judicial review of legislation for validity and no such judicial review. These are not all of the possibilities, but they suffice to illustrate the variety of choices of form commonly reflected in basic legal phenomena constitutional in nature.

The foregoing are choices of form pertaining mainly to the structure of a system's basic law-making and law-administering institutions and their inter-relations. These structural features are formal in contrast to the content of those regulative constitutional provisions which set substantive limits on governmental powers and prescribe how government must operate, as with, for example, bills of rights. The structural features of a system of government are also formal in contrast to the substantive content of the positive law validly created and administered by and through this structure.

Some features of formal constitutional structure are rather more fundamental than others. Indeed, some are, in modern western legal systems anyhow, both a conceptual and a practical necessity. Thus all modern western systems, either explicitly or implicitly, have some such criterion of valid law as: "Laws duly adopted by the duly constituted legislature and duly signed by the authorized executive officer shall be valid." Such a criterion is formal in the sense that it determines the validity of a putative law only by reference to its mode of origin.

Plainly, basic values lie behind the foregoing illustrative choices of form typically reflected in western constitutional provisions. That is, constitutional phenomena not merely display describable characteristics which are formal and go far to define what a constitution is. Characteristics which are appropriately formal are also desiderata, and the values behind such desiderata are varied and complex.[6]

As I have indicated, a constitution simply could not fulfill its functional roles in the system if it lacked appropriate formalness. For example, we have seen that in modern western systems constitutional criteria of validity make validity depend at least in part on formal mode of origin. Significant institutional or processual values argue in favor of such formal features in the first place. Thus, when such source-oriented criteria of validity are satisfied they usually validate laws adopted by a democratically elected legislature. Democracy is a premier institutional and processual value. Other general values that are not institutional and processual may also justify the formalness of constitutional features. These values lie behind most varieties of form and thus may be called "general rationales for form." For example, determination of the validity of a statute can be done more accurately and more consistently when done solely in light of a source-oriented and thus formal criterion of validity than when done also in light of a content-oriented criterion, such as "no law is valid that impairs free expression". Further, citizens to be affected by a new statute can be guided more readily from the very moment of adoption where a merely formal criterion of validity controls, whereas under some content-oriented criteria, citizens must frequently wait until the outcome of litigation to be sure of an answer as to the validity of a statute. Relatedly, because fewer disputes will arise over the application of formal criteria of validity, there will be less litigation. Such certainty and predictability also bring more efficiency. And so on. This is not to say a system should only have source-oriented criteria of validity. I am merely identifying important general rationales for source-oriented criteria, rationales that also underpin many other formal features of legal phenomena, too.

Other formal constitutional provisions reflect still further general rationales for formality. For example, some constitutional provisions provide for the existence of basic institutions and processes which are to organize and facilitate public decision-making activity. Such provisions divide and confer power to make effective and final decisions about discrete subjects. Without such public decision-making processes, duly organized, life under law would not be possible in modern society. This, then, is a further general rationale behind legal form (and an institutional and processual value as well). Of course, what I call general rationales behind formality vary to some extent from one type of phenomenon to another.

A formal characteristic of a basic type of legal phenomenon has significance as a desideratum independently of non-formal elements. For example, such a characteristic may, as a desideratum, be identified, analyzed, and evaluated independently of the substantive content of any particular law being created and applied. Thus, a given set of source-oriented criteria of validity may be identified, analyzed and evaluated as over-formal (i.e. as lacking appropriate content-oriented criteria), or as being under-formal (i.e. as insufficiently source-oriented), although the substantive content of the laws the validity of which is being determined may, by relevant standards, be judged good *in content*. (And the reverse.)

Yet, formal phenomena such as source-oriented criteria of validity in their own way leave an imprint directly or indirectly on the substantive content of the body of law being created and applied. Thus, for example, a legislature acting solely under source-oriented criteria of validity will almost certainly adopt some laws that it would not adopt if it were also subject to limiting criteria of validity that are content-oriented in nature.

Eventually, I will show not merely that form affects content but that good form, in some of its varieties, frequently begets or tends to beget good content. Thus, much good constitutional form begets or tends to beget better content than bad constitutional form. For example, it is more than plausible to suppose that the substantive content of particular judicial decisions and thus the overall content of case law will generally be far better in a system with an independent judiciary than where the judiciary is not independent. Here good form (judicial independence) tends to beget good content.

B.   Form and Private Transactional Validity

Most practicing lawyers in the United States, and some legal theorists, too, would, on hearing someone refer to "formality in law" or "the formal character of law", think immediately of how private arrangements such as contracts and wills must satisfy some formal requirements to be valid. Thus, in general, a valid contract, for example, must satisfy one or more of the following types of requirements:

(1)   That the parties be of legal age and have appropriate mental capacity,

(2)   That the contract be in writing as required by any statute of frauds,

(3)   That there be an agreement between the parties,

(4)   That any regulatory requirements as to size and placement of print in a "form" contract be met,

(5)   That the agreement consist of a bargained for exchange, and

(6)   That the agreement not be entered through fraud, duress, undue influence or mistake.

The foregoing six types of formal requirements do not exhaust all possible types of formal criteria of contractual validity. Nor are formal criteria the only criteria of contractual validity. For example, in American law a contract may be invalid, at least in part, and sometimes also in toto, if certain requirements as to *content* are not met. That is, some bodies of law actually *prescribe*, sometimes as a condition of validity, part of the substantive content of a contract. Most of these bodies of law relate to standard form contracts of insurance, of carriage of goods, of storage, of certain types of loans, and so on. More generally, still other bodies of law *proscribe* content of certain kinds. Thus, a contract must not embody illegal ends or utilize illegal means. A contract must not be contrary to public policy. A contract must not be unconscionable. And so on. The validity of contracts is not totally formal.

Requirements of age and mental capacity, writing requirements in so-called Statutes of Frauds, the requirement of an agreement, and regulatory requirements of type size are obviously formal in nature. But what about the requirement of consideration? It, too, does not prescribe subject-matter content. Rather, it only specifies that whatever the content of the contract, it must be a bargained for exchange. Thus, Justice Oliver Wendell Holmes, Jr., was right to say that the requirement of consideration is "entirely formal." It can be satisfied whatever the content of the contract. Thus, in logical terms, two agreements could have the same content in the sense that in both the parties are transferring the same objects each to the other, yet only one agreement be a valid contract because only in it are the objects reciprocally bargained for. And, two agreements could be very different in content in the sense that the objects being transferred are very different, yet both could be valid because the objects were reciprocally bargained for.

And what about the requirement that a contract not be entered through duress, fraud, undue influence or mistake? Again these bodies of law do not proscribe contractual content. They merely rule out certain untoward behavior or events in the formation of a valid contract. (Of course, such behavior or events may in a particular case affect contract content.)

The formalness of contractual validity is not a legalistic fetish or a mere historical accident or archaic anomaly. Nor is it a manifestation of some kind of cult of form for its own sake. That private contractual transactions should be, for their validity, at least in part, subject to formal criteria can be readily defended on rational grounds. Most formalities are not "just formalities". Important values justify the kinds of formal criteria that transactions must satisfy.

Many formal criteria of contractual validity serve what I have called general rationales for formality in the law, including certainty, predictability, and dispute avoidance. Thus such criteria as the minimum age requirement, the Statute of Frauds, the regulatory requirement of a given size of type, and the requirement of consideration are readily and relatively certainly administrable. Whether or not a party is of the age of majority, has utilized a writing, and has entered into a bargain are all issues that can, in and of themselves, usually be readily determined with considerable certainty and predictability. This is characteristic of formal requirements generally. Such formal requirements minimize disputes, and may also be dispute resolutive. The requirement of a signed writing tends to preserve evidence and assure authenticity, while the requirement of consideration itself may operate to provide some evidence that a contract was made.

A major policy furthered by such formal criteria as the requirement of a writing under the Statute of Frauds and the requirement that a contract take the form of a bargain is simply to channel, and thereby facilitate the consummation of, contractual agreements by providing legally recognized facilities whereby the contracting parties may effectuate their intentions. Here the formal requirement of a bargain restricts the freedom of the individual contracting party, yet this very restriction is ultimately liberating because it makes a facility available that enables the individual to implement intentions over a wide range of circumstances. It provides a "form" in which agreed content can be validly manifested.

Another major policy of contract law is to facilitate the existence of markets. Markets tend to maximize the range of choice and tend to further efficient resource allocation.

I turn now to institutional and processual values. To a large extent, the very institution of free private contract requires that the criteria for validity of contracts be largely formal. That is, if free private contract is to be truly that, then the content of private contracts must generally be something that private parties autonomously adopt, not some content imposed by the state. Formal criteria in effect grant the parties broad freedom to choose content. Formal criteria thereby facilitate citizen choice, planning, and self-direction central to the institution of free private contract in which private parties may even create elaborate structures of legally enforceable private rights and duties (including many that are long lasting). The justifications for this are familiar. Given the nature of these choices, private parties are the ones to make them. It is not only that they are more competent than state officials would be. It is also that private parties are the ones whose very desires are to be satisfied. They know best what satisfies them. It would be fundamentally inappropriate for public officials to prescribe the content of private contracts and thus substitute their will and their judgment for that of private parties. It would also be costly. These truths are implicit in the wide ranging autonomy of choice in matters of contract that highly formal criteria of validity authorize.

At the same time, many formal criteria of contractual validity, when satisfied, also tend to secure important *processual* values. This is true, for example, of law protecting against duress, fraud, undue influence, and mistake. All such requirements contribute to fullness and fairness of choice, processual values essential to the institution of private contract. Again such criteria of validity are formal and to a large extent dictated by the ultimate processual desideratum of free contract itself.

An appropriately formal characteristic of a basic type of legal phenomenon has significance as a desideratum independently of relevant contrasting content. Such a characteristic may, as a desideratum, be identified, analyzed, described, and evaluated independently of the substantive content of particular law being created and applied. Thus, a given set of formal source-oriented criteria of contractual validity may be evaluated as over-formal (i.e., as lacking appropriate content-oriented criteria), or as under-formal (i.e., as being insufficiently source-oriented), although the substantive content of contracts the validity of which are being determined is, by relevant standards, judged good in content.

Even so, formal criteria of contractual validity may, in their own way, leave an imprint directly or indirectly on the content of purported contracts entered into between two parties. For example, as already suggested, such a requirement as that of consideration is likely to make the parties more circumspect about what they agree to. More dramatically, agreements entered into may be invalidated for fraud, duress, undue influence and the like, all of which go to mode of origin rather than content as such and so are formal grounds of invalidation.

The foregoing examples indicate that form may not only affect content, but that good form, at least in some of its varieties frequently begets good content. Similarly, bad form can beget bad content.

C.   Form and the Phenomena of Legal Precepts, Especially Rules

Rules are used to set forth most of the content of the law of developed legal systems. It is also a primary function of the constitutional phenomena of the typical western legal system to provide for institutions and processes that make and apply such rules.

The rules of a legal system that are used to set forth its substantive and other content display what I will call "external" form. The external form of a rule reflects a choice between expressing the rule in a constitution, in a statute, in an administrative regulation, in an administrative ruling, in common law, or in customary law. Thus, what is so encapsulated is content, and *how* this content is encapsulated is formal. Obviously, a given encapsulatory form can accommodate highly varied content.

A choice of an external form to embody legal content is required if a rule of law is to exist at all. Such a choice necessarily implicates a choice between different law-making institutions and processes. Thus, when the law is essentially constitutional in type it is rationally justified to embody its content in constitutional form. When appropriate, the statutory form should be used. When appropriate, the common law form should be used, and so on. The choices of appropriate external form here implicate institutional and processual values such as legitimacy, democracy, and appropriate institutional competence. For example, in many systems some types of laws, e.g., a general tax, require for their legality that they be adopted by a legislature, and thus take statutory form. Indeed this choice may itself be laid down in the constitution so that it is no longer "open". The choices of external form also implicate what I have called general rationales for formality, too. For example, as Jeremy Bentham stressed, predictability and certainty, citizen autonomy, and self-direction, administrative efficiency and the avoidance of disputes, equality before the law, and so on, are generally better served if the rule is in statutory form rather than if it is in common law form.

Similarly, one external form rather than another may better serve what I call problem-specific policy. For example, it would not be appropriate to allow speed limits for cars merely to take the form of custom or common law. Among other things, the indeterminateness of these two external forms would frustrate the problem-specific policies of safety and efficient traffic flow.

An appropriate external form of a rule, then, is not merely a describable fact as manifest in the phenomena, but also a desideratum. It can serve institutional and processual values, general rationales for form, and problem-specific policies. An appropriate external form of a rule also has significance as a desideratum independently of the relevant contrasting content of the rule. That is, this external form may be identified, analyzed, and evaluated for appropriateness independently of the content of the rule. Thus, the external form can be good and the content bad, or vice versa. Yet the external form may leave its own imprint on the content, too. For example, the form of a common law doctrine--its embodiment in reasoned opinions resolving particular issues arising out of stated facts rather than in, say, statutory form, affects its scope, a matter of content.

A related but distinct and much more complex domain of the formalness of rules is internal, and I can only sketch its nature here. It is possible to identify such internally formal attributes of a rule as its completeness, its definiteness, its generality, its coherence, its style and mode of expression, including the extent of any "bright lines" (fiat) it may have, and its simplicity or complexity. Each of these attributes is formal. Each is an attribute of the structure, or configuration, or shape, or manner of formulation of the rule, in contrast to its substantive content as such. Such attributes even to a high degree are compatible with quite variable content. For example, two rules may be highly definite, yet of very different content. Each internally formal attribute is also a matter of degree. Thus, for example, a rule can be highly complete, highly definite, highly general, or the reverse of all these.

Most formal features of rules are to some extent characteristic of legal rules. Thus, for example, a "rule" without the formal attribute of some level of generality could not even count as a rule. But in the circumstances, the values to be served by a rule may require a higher degree of generality than merely that which is necessary for it, conceptually, to be a rule at all. The same is true of most other formal attributes of rules, and of many formal features of other types of legal phenomena. Thus, we should distinguish between minimum requirement and optimal level or degree. Furthermore, not all formal features of a rule (or, indeed, of various other types of phenomena) are characteristics of such phenomena. For example, it may be very important that a given class of rules be expressed in technical terminology, yet it cannot be said that such terminology, although formal, is characteristic of legal rules. Usually, though, a formal feature will also be characteristic of the type of phenomenon in question.

Most appropriate attributes of the internal form of particular rules are not merely describable characteristics of such phenomena, but also desiderata. Again, important values lie behind these formal attributes. Some of these values are institutional and processual. For example, an incomplete rule may only be half-made. It is usually difficult for a law making body to deliberate and vote on a half-made rule. Thus, the degree of completeness, a formal feature, implicates basic public law values such as rationality of deliberation, and consequently also legitimacy and democracy (assuming the legislature is elected, as it usually is in Western systems).

Still other categories of values that these internally formal attributes of rules implicate consist of what I have called general rationales for formality such as the facilitation of citizen self-direction from the very inception of the law, ease of administration, objective, uniform and consistent application, minimization of arbitrariness, avoidance of disputes, and so on. Appropriate completeness, definiteness, generality and mode of expression serve all these values.

At the same time, the internally formal attributes of rules also commonly serve a further major category of values: those reflected in what I have called problem-specific policy goals. A relatively complete, definite, and general statute such as "No vehicles in the park" will generally serve the problem-specific policy goals of park quiet and safety better than a vague statute: "The park superintendent may, in his discretion, exclude objects from the park".

The appropriate internally formal attributes of rules, then, as desiderata in their own right, may serve a wide range of values, including institutional and processual values, general rationales for formalness of law, and problem-specific policy. And these internally formal attributes of a rule have normative significance independently of the relevant contrasting content of the rule. Just as this content can be identified, analyzed, and evaluated independently of its formal attributes, so, too, may the internal attributes of form be identified, analyzed, and evaluated for appropriateness independently of the quality of the content of the law involved. Thus, the content can be good and the form bad, or vice versa.

Yet the internally formal attributes of rules also leave their own imprint on the content of rules, too. Here, form may distinctively manifest itself in complementary content. This is perhaps most clear when certain values behind form conflict with and to some extent over-ride problem-specific policy in the fusion of form and content in the final version of a rule legislatively enacted, or a rule adopted by a court. For example, the legislature or a court may ultimately opt for a rule that in its content is over- and under-inclusive in relation to problem-specific policy aims, given the offsetting gains that this will bring by way of serving general rationales for formality. Consider this example. On plausible interpretations, a "No vehicles in the park" statute would over-include as to battery-driven wheelchairs that do not interfere with quiet and safety, and would underinclude as to skateboards which do interfere. Yet despite this lack of fit with the problem-specific policies of quiet and safety, legislators at inception might still reasonably prefer the "no vehicles" version over a more open-ended alternative with better fit, such as "The park superintendent may, in his discretion, exclude objects from the park." After all, the general rationales for formalness of law strongly favor the more complete, more definite, and more general "no vehicles" version of the statute. These rationales include enhanced citizen self-direction. A more precise rule enables citizens to plan in advance just what they may take to the park. The rationales for formalness also include enhanced ease of official administration, greater protection against official arbitrariness (and thus more determinate liberty), greater minimization of disputes with attendant social harmony, and increased equality before the law. When this kind of trade-off favoring formal attributes and their values on the one hand, over problem-specific policy content on the other, occurs in legal ordering, form leaves an especially dramatic and distinctive imprint on the ultimate substantive content of the law.[7]

But form may not only leave an imprint on content when, as in the above example, it operates to generate content that is different from what it would have been if problem-specific policy alone informed content. Form can leave a less direct and more subtle yet very real imprint on content, as well. Some content is *jointly* determined by the combined force of general rationales for formality and problem-specific policy. This *combined* force might justify keeping the content as it is although a competing problem-specific policy is marginally better than the one embodied in the law. The policy embodied in the law might simply serve rationales for formality better than would the content of the marginally superior problem-specific policy.

Finally, not only does form affect content in the various ways just suggested. Good form frequently begets or tends to beget good content. Thus, for example, the very discipline of striving to create relatively complete and definite rules forces the lawmaker to face up to issues and to consider relations between issues, processes that tend to yield law that, in overall terms, is likely to be better in content. Similarly, the very discipline of striving to create rules of appropriate generality can yield and tends to yield law better in content.

The formality of rules, then, is analyzable as such in terms of descriptive attributes that are also, in turn, desiderata. I would add that the significance of the formality of rules extends beyond rules as one basic type of legal phenomenon. Insofar as other basic types of legal phenomena are partly constructed out of formal rules, these other phenomena are, in that regard formal. But my primary thesis here is that these other phenomena are formal in other respects as well.

D.   Form and the Phenomena of Method in Interpreting Statutes

A basic choice within a legal system is that between (1) adopting a generally applicable, coherent, systematic, and "statute respectful" approach to statutory interpretation, that is, a formal methodology, and (2) adopting somewhat less than this, or perhaps even much less, such as an entirely ad hoc "interpretive" approach, i.e., no formal methodology at all.

Generality of scope, coherence, systematicity, and "statute respectfulness" as attributes of interpretive method, can all be analyzed in detail, and, as formal attributes may be contrasted both with the content of the interpretive method itself, and with the content of the statutes to which the method is applied. Their presence, even to a high degree, is compatible with significant variations in the content of arguments that may figure in an interpretive method as well as with the highly varied content of statutes to be interpreted. I will now explain what I mean by the content of an interpretive method, but only in terms of the arguments that figure in it, for at this stage I must oversimplify. Thus, I will now merely introduce the simplified notion of a "central maxim of content" in a given interpretive method (and omit, among other things, prioritizations). This "central maxim" might be: "Interpret in accord with ordinary meanings of ordinary words in the statute whenever reasonably possible." Or this central maxim of content might be: "Interpret in accord with ultimate statutory purpose." Or this central maxim might be: "Interpret in accord with extrinsic evidence of subjective legislative intent," etc. Thus, an interpretive methodology might be general in scope, coherent, systematic, and "statute respectful", yet incorporate any of the foregoing quite varied content. But there are important limits here. For example: "Interpret in accord with the balance of substantive reasons in the particular case" could not figure as the central maxim of content. Among other things, it would not be sufficiently statute respectful.

At the same time, an interpretive method could display all of the foregoing attributes to a high degree, and yet be applicable to statutes that themselves have highly variable substantive content.

The foregoing formal attributes are characteristics of the phenomena of interpretive method. That is, merely to count as such a method, an interpretive approach must be to some extent general in scope, coherent, systematic, and "statute respectful". Otherwise, the approach could not be a method, and might even be only an ad hoc approach open to any and all substantive considerations emergent at point of application. But the values to be served by an interpretive method may require the presence of higher degrees of the foregoing formal attributes in the method than the minimum required to qualify as a methodology at all. (Thus, again, minimum and optimum may be different.)

Again, special and important values lie behind appropriately formal attributes of an interpretive method. Among other things, without a sufficiently formal method, statutes would very likely not be interpreted with appropriate accuracy and consistency. Also, many more disputes under statutory language would arise. This, in turn, would impair certainty, predictability, and citizen self-direction. Strong willed judges would be more likely to substitute their own personal judgment for legislative judgment. The implementation of legislative will would be undermined, and, along with it, the problem-specific policies informing the content of statutes, as well as the general rationales for formality and other values behind formal attributes in the statute. Statutes would also be more difficult to draft, for the legislature would not know what interpretive approach would be applied to them. Equality before the law would suffer. And more.

It follows that appropriate attributes of generality, of scope, coherence, systematicity, and "statute respectfulness" are not merely characteristics of an interpretive method, themselves formal in nature, but that such attributes are also desiderata backed by the various general rationales for formality and other values identified above. These values are not of the same order as the values that happen to be reflected in the content of the statutes being interpreted. Indeed, when judges give undue weight merely to implementing what they perceive to be (or prefer to be) the problem-specific policy content of a statute, they may sacrifice the values of a formal interpretive method as such, and the method might even degenerate in particular cases into an ad hoc and open-ended inquiry into which alternative decision is likely to have the best possible problem-specific policy effects overall in the circumstances. Thus, the significance of the formal attributes of an interpretive methodology, as desiderata, is independent of the content of the statutes being interpreted. These formal attributes may be identified, analyzed, and evaluated for appropriateness of level or degree quite apart from the content of the statutes being interpreted. An interpretive method may be good in terms of its formal attributes, but a statute to which the method is applied be bad in content, or vice versa.

It is even true that the formal attributes of an interpretive methodology may be to some extent identified, analyzed, and evaluated for appropriateness of level or degree independently of the very content of the methodology itself, that is, independently of the central type of argument (or arguments), and prioritizations between arguments, that figure in the general method.

Formal attributes of an interpretive methodology leave an imprint on the content of the methodology itself. That is, such formality manifests itself in complementary content of the method. Consider, for example, the formal attribute of generality of scope. This attribute must manifest itself at least by way of requiring sufficient generality in the central modes of argument that figure in the content of the methodology. Thus, some modes of argument that are highly particular or otherwise too narrow in scope would be ruled out, if the method is to qualify as a *general* method.

The formality of interpretive method also leaves an imprint on the content of the statutes being interpreted. The same statute interpreted according to a relatively formal methodology just will be given a different content over time from what it would have had if interpreted by a much less formal and more ad hoc method.

But again, it is not only that the formalness of method affects content here. It is also that good form frequently begets or tends to beget good content. Thus, for example, law makers cognizant of the interpretive method that will be applied to any statutes they create--a real possibility only where such method is sufficiently formal, can formulate the content of the laws they are creating in light of the interpretive method being applied. This may generate better problem-specific content, but even if it does not, it will certainly serve institutional and processual values and general rationales for formality. Content can be good in more ways than one.

E.   Form and the Phenomena of Stare Decisis

If a system is to have common law, then it must at least require that duly adopted precedents *generally* be binding on lower courts, and to some extent on the deciding court, regardless of their substantive content. Obviously, the formal principle of stare decisis applies to and accommodates precedents of highly varied content. It does not, as such, prescribe or proscribe content.

An appropriately formal principle of stare decisis is likewise not merely a describable characteristic of the phenomena whenever it prevails, but a desideratum, as well. Important values lie behind it, including not merely accurate and consistent implementation of problem-specific policy embodied in the content of the precedent, but also general rationales for formality, including facilitation of citizen self-direction, minimization of disputes, efficient and definitive dispute resolution, freedom from arbitrary decision and more. Stare decisis also furthers important institutional and processual values. Among the more obvious, it serves in some systems as a primary source of the very antecedent legal standards that adjudication requires if it is to be a process in which the affected parties themselves meaningfully participate in defining issues in terms of antecedent law, and in presenting legally relevant evidence and argument on the basis of which the decision is made.[8]

The formal principle of stare decisis, too, may itself be identified, analyzed and evaluated for appropriateness of general adherence to precedent quite apart from the content of any particular precedents. Indeed, the values behind the formal principle of stare decisis may come into conflict with desirable problem-specific policy requiring a departure from precedent, and yet these formal values justifiably prevail. Such values may, all things considered, even justifiably perpetuate unsound policy content for a time. In these and still other ways, the formal principle of stare-decisis leaves its own distinctive imprint on the substantive content of the law. Again, it is not merely that form affects content here. It is also that good form begets or tends to beget good content. Among other things, where judges know that the decisions they make will be precedents for future cases, they will have even more incentive to bring reason to bear, and the reasoned content of particular precedents is therefore likely to be somewhat better.

F.   Form and Other Basic Types of Legal Phenomena

I have sketched out and briefly illustrated how my thesis as to the formal character of basic types of legal phenomena may be developed and defended in regard to: (1) constitutional phenomena, especially criteria for the validity of statutes, (2) certain criteria for the validity of private transactions such as contracts and wills, (3) legal precepts used to set forth the substantive law, especially rules, (4) accepted methodology of statutory interpretation, and (5) the principle of stare decisis. Of course, there are other major types of legal phenomena, including legislative bodies and their procedures; court systems and adjudicative procedures as such; the restricted jurisdiction of judges to modify antecedent law; accepted methods for differentiating questions of fact from questions of law, a law of evidence, and a general theory of legal truth; administrative bodies and administrative procedures; existing general modes of organizing legal resources into basic techniques of legal implementation including sanctions and related implementive devices, and, law defining the state and other legal entities, public offices, and legal personality generally, including corporate personality. There are also the phenomena of legal reasoning as such which overlap with interpretive method and stare decisis.

I cannot, in the space here, treat the foregoing additional basic types of legal phenomena. But I will, in later work, attempt to demonstrate that my main theses apply to all basic types of legal phenomena (and not merely in the respect that formal rules must play significant constitutive, implementive, and regulative roles in all of the above).

IV. The Formalness of a Legal System Viewed as a Whole

My overall thesis that law is formal in character is a dual thesis. It is true not only that all basic types of legal phenomena that play prominent functional roles in a system of law display formality having an importance of its own. It is also true that a legal system, viewed as a whole, displays its own significant varieties of "systemic" formality, and that appropriate levels of these, too, are desiderata in their own right duly backed by significant values. Here, I will sketch and briefly illustrate this second branch of my general thesis.

A.   Formal Coherence and Unity of the System as a Whole

The characteristic coherence and unity of a legal system is an ancient and complex topic of legal theory. Here I will indicate how this characteristic is significantly formal, and is also a desideratum in its own right. I will do so by addressing briefly only a single illustrative facet of systemic coherence and unity, namely how advanced western legal systems generally harmonize conflicting laws originating from the different authorized sources of law in such systems.

In a complex western legal system there are many different sources of prima facie valid law, including constitutional processes, legislatures, courts, administrative agencies and officials, private contracting parties and will makers, and the various sources of customary law. Conflicts between otherwise valid laws deriving from such varied sources are inevitable, and modern systems generally resolve such conflicts by reference to relatively formal rules of priority. For example, in the United States, the general position is that constitutional law takes priority over statute law and all other conflicting types of law. Statute law takes priority over conflicting administrative regulation and other administrative law and over all other law lower in the hierarchy. Common law takes priority over contract and other private law and also over custom. Contract takes priority over custom. The foregoing general rules of priority are themselves largely formal at least in the sense that they determine priority in accord with a formal ranking of the sources themselves, rather than in accord with the comparative quality or other features of the substantive content of the conflicting laws. Thus, the valid laws that survive such prioritization cohere by formal rank, not content. The resulting overall contribution of this prioritization to the coherence and unity of the system is considerable. Not only is the method of securing coherence and unity formal, but the resulting coherence and unity is itself formal, too.

Such systemic coherence and unity are characteristic of western legal systems. Without effective prioritization, a legal system would not be a *system* for very long, given the potential for conflicts between new laws, and between old laws and new laws. Of course, some systems exhibit higher degrees of systemic coherence and unity than others, degrees that also exceed the minimum threshold required for a legal system to exist at all.

Systemic coherence and unity serve important values, especially in a complex legal system. They enable officials, legislators, judges, and private entities and parties to know which of two otherwise valid conflicting laws is controlling. This, in turn, serves many values, including such general rationales for formality as determinate official and citizen self-direction under law, uniformity and equality before the ultimately valid law, minimization of disputes, dispute resolution, and more.

It follows that appropriate systemic coherence and unity is not merely a formal characteristic of a legal system but a desideratum as well. Moreover, the values behind this desideratum are independent of the problem-specific policies implicated in the content of rules and other forms of law that happen to come into conflict with each other.

Again, formal coherence and unity leave an imprint on the content of the system. For example, the operation of formal rules of priority as between different authoritative sources of law greatly affects the ultimate resulting content of the law. New law valid in light of the scheme of priorities might even be bad in content, yet displace existing law good in content, as where a bad statute displaces good common law.

But again, good form generally begets or tends to beget good content. I will now suggest only one way in which this is so, continuing with the prioritization example. A clear and well articulated scheme of prioritization not merely secures formal coherence and unity within the content of substantive law, but exerts pressure of its own for improvement in the quality of the law's content. Thus, for example, when a proposed new statute would displace conflicting common law, or when proposed new common law would plainly invalidate contract terms in conflict therewith, the legislature and the courts have a more sharply focused responsibility to justify such changes in the name of reason. Where this responsibility is not so sharply focused for lack of a well defined scheme of prioritization, the quality of the law is, other things equal, likely to be lower.

B.   Formal Legality of the Operation of the System as a Whole

A legal system is an operational system. It carries out its operations in a variety of ways, and these may or may not accord with what I will call the canons of formal legality. One way to formulate such canons is as follows:

In general, citizens ought to be governed only by persons duly authorized by law to govern, and citizens ought to be governed only in accord with statutes, precedents, and other species of law which generally should take the form of relatively complete, definite and well expressed rules that are:

(1) applicable to official and citizen alike (as appropriate),
(2) uniform throughout the boundaries of the state,
(3) duly promulgated in advance of occasions for their application,
(4) appropriately published and so accessible to intended addressees,
(5) sufficiently constant through time so that addressees may have the opportunity to conform,
(6) susceptible of compliance, that is, not beyond the capacities of the ordinary addressee.

Frequently, the above enumerated canons are also stated to include governance through complete, definite, and well expressed general rules. In the above formulation I have stated this cluster of requirements in prefatory terms, but I have not enumerated it as one of the six, for I have already treated it earlier in this essay. A further canon might be enumerated requiring that, in certain types of dispute, the applicability of law be determined in accord with what in Anglo-American law would be called standards of judicial due process.

The foregoing enumerated canons of legality are largely formal, in one important sense. All but the sixth relate to the manner or style of modes of governance, as distinguished from the substantive content of the rules of law being applied. All western legal systems operate in accord with canons of legality to some degree, and not only in regard to criminal law, (though this is of special importance). Indeed, a legal system that completely failed to so operate could not, conceptually, qualify as a legal system. Some systems operate in relatively full accord with the canons of formal legality.

Some level of conformity to the canons of legality is a characteristic of the very phenomenon of a legal system. Such conformity is also a desideratum backed by those values that in the western tradition are most often associated with the rule of law itself: predictability of official action, freedom from official arbitrariness, protection of citizens from unfair official action, and more. Core tenets of the ideal of the rule of law that serve such values are familiar: subjection of government to law, and the exercise of state coercion only in accord with law publicly laid down in advance. Indeed, these tenets are among the greatest of all protections that law can provide against governmental terror.[9]

Again, the significance of the canons of legality as desiderata is to an extent independent of the content of the substantive law being applied. The canons neither prescribe nor proscribe content. The law could be good in content, yet its manner of implementation violate one or more canons of legality. For example, the system might fail to publish the law adequately in advance of occasions for its application. Of course, it is also true that the canons of legality might be observed, yet the content of the law be bad.

Plainly, the degree of conformity of officials to the canons of legality can greatly affect the content of the "law in action," as distinguished merely from the content of "paper law in books". Indeed, here the imprint of form upon content can be especially dramatic. If the canons of legality are not sufficiently observed, the law in action will frequently be very different from the law in books.   But more than this. Here, too, form not merely affects content. Good form begets or tends to beget good content. For example, such requirements of formal legality as public promulgation and uniformity of application exert special pressure of their own for law good in content (or at least law not bad in content).

C.   Other Systemic Formal Characteristics

There are still other systemically formal attributes of a legal system viewed as a whole. These include the formal conditions of civic life secured by what is often called the liberal state, the forms of the five basic techniques for implementing law, the formal continuity of law over time, and the degree to which the style of legal reasoning is formal. In further work, I will treat these and others in detail.

V. Some Remarks on the Concept of "Formal" as Used Here

Max Weber stressed that the word "formal" can be a problem: "As everyone knows, there is no expression more ambiguous than the word 'formal' and no dichotomy more ambiguous than the distinction between form and content. The import of the distinction must be established with complete precision in every given case of its use."[10] I will now offer some general remarks that are meant to clarify the concept of "formal" as used here. I offer these remarks at this stage after having made numerous actual uses of the word "formal" earlier in this essay. Against this background of concrete usage, the remarks I now offer should be more meaningful.

Here, I have frequently used the word "formal" in sentences referring to "characteristics of basic types of legal phenomena as formal," and in sentences referring to "the formal characteristics of a legal system taken as a whole." In both of these uses, I have expected the reader to grasp what I meant by "formal" partly by way of contrasting it with relevant content. Here is a summary of these uses to this point:

A. Basic Type of Legal Phenomena	Characteristic that is Formal	Content
1. Criteria for validity of state-made law, and putative such law, e.g., a statute	Source-oriented criterion; e.g., statute properly deriving from source	Substantive subject-matter of statute
2. Criteria for validity of private transactional law, and putative such law, e.g., a contract	Source-oriented criterion; e.g., contract deriving from source	Substantive subject-matter of contract
3. Rules (external attributes)	Type of encapsulatory "form", e.g., statute, or common law	Substantive subject-matter of rule so encapsulated
4. Rules (internal attributes)	Completeness, definiteness, generality, coherence, simplicity, mode of expression	Substantive subject-matter of rule with such attributes
5. Interpretive method and particular statutes to be interpreted	Generality of scope, coherence, systematicity, statute-respectfulness of the method	Substantive subject-matter by way of interpretive arguments specified in method; substantive subject-matter of statute to be interpreted
6. The principle of stare decisis, and particular precedents	General applicability of principle regardless of substantive quality of precedents	Substantive quality of precedents
B. Type of Systemic Dimension	Formality of Systemic Characteristic	Content
7. Varied authoritative sources of law; conflicting laws emanating therefrom	Priority of conflicting law in accord with hierarchical rank of sources	Substantive content of conflicting laws
8. How system operates to apply and implement laws	Application and implementation in accord with "canons of legality"	Substantive subject-matter of law so applied or implemented

I will now introduce three converging sources of clarification as to the meaning of "formal" as used in the middle column above. The reader can resort to them singly, or together, to clear up uncertainties about the meaning of formal when used in the analysis in this essay.

First, in each of the seven uses above, the reader can, at the outset, immediately grasp the relevant notion of content (of the legal phenomena or of the legal system as a whole). See the far right column, above. Then, by way of contrast with this content, the reader can, in the context, readily discern what feature (or features) are being marked off from this content and called "formal". See the middle column.

Secondly, what is so marked off and called formal is, in all seven of the above uses, in some way or ways independent of the content with which it is being contrasted. There are various possible senses of "independent" here. Two major senses will be stressed, one conceptual and one functional. The conceptual sense is this. In all seven uses of formal, above, that which is marked off from content and called formal can in its own way apply to or accommodate contrasting content that is highly variable. What is so marked off from contrasting content neither prescribes no proscribes any content as such. Thus, all listed characteristics of the phenomena that are formal have this in common: Each in its own way applies to or accommodates contrasting content independently of the subject-matter of that content. I now turn to what I call the functional sense of "independent". All seven uses of formal have this further in common: What is marked off from content and called formal can be to a large extent (or, in some cases, entirely) identified, analyzed, described, and evaluated on its own, that is, apart from or independently of, the content with which it is being contrasted. For example, the form can be adjudged good and the content bad or vice versa. In legal matters, this is an especially important type of independent significance. Of course, this does not mean form has no effects on content. On the contrary, one major thesis of this very essay is that form manifests itself in, and otherwise affects, content.

Third, ordinarily what is marked off from content and here designated as formal can, to some extent, be characterized *affirmatively* in terms that are formal, and not merely "negatively" as something that is somehow "opposed" to content. When so, this clarifies the contrast with substantive content still further. For example, such internal attributes of a rule as completeness, definiteness, and generality can be characterized affirmatively as features of the basic form of the rule, as distinguished from its substantive content. Moreover, features of form may frequently be further characterized as compositional, structural, procedural, and so on — all varieties of the formal recognized at least in English. When such affirmative characterizations are possible, we may also elaborate further on the nature of the variety of form involved in ways that would be inconsistent with treating the same feature or features of the phenomena as content. It is true that some varieties of formality cannot be so characterized affirmatively. For instance, the external form of a rule is encapsulatory. Even so, "encapsulatory" is itself an affirmative characterization that in its own way illuminatingly contrasts with the substantive content of a rule. Other formal characteristics may likewise be susceptible of their own affirmative characterizations. For example, the formal canons of legality can be affirmatively characterized as "implementive norms of process" as distinguished from the highly varied content to which these implementive norms apply.

However much conceptual and functional unity there may be in what is here marked off as formal and contrasted with content, and however much further light is cast by affirmative characterization of the formal, it remains true that the factual criteria for application of the word "formal", vary widely in the seven usages summarized above. They vary widely as between types of basic legal phenomena and the legal system as a whole. They vary widely as between different types of legal phenomena. They may even vary widely within a single basic type of legal phenomenon. Thus, for example, the factual criteria for applying the word "formal" to features of the basic phenomena of interpretive method vary widely from the factual criteria for applying the word formal to the feature I have called systemic coherence. In the first case, the reference is to attributes such as generality of scope and statute-respectfulness, whereas in the second the reference is to a scheme of prioritization by ranking of sources of law. And within a single basic type of legal phenomenon, such as rules, the factual criteria for applying the word, "formal" vary widely. This follows from the fact that external form and internal form differ greatly in factual terms. It also follows from the fact that internal form is itself highly varied factually, ranging as it does over such dimensions as completeness, definiteness, generality, complexity, coherence, and mode of expression. This wide variety in the criteria for factual applicability of the term formal is hardly surprising, given the highly varied nature of the phenomenological terrain: constitutions, criteria of validity, rules, methodologies of interpretation, stare decisis, reasoning practices, institutions, processes, systems, entities.

But from the fact that the factual criteria for the application of "formal" to features of the phenomena of law are highly varied, it does not follow that the underlying concept of what is formal is not unified or unifiable. I have demonstrated that what is formal pertains to the form of the phenomena and may be contrasted with and so marked off from content, that it applies to or accommodates highly variable content so marked off, that what is formal can be identified, analyzed, described, and evaluated independently of contrasting content, and that further light may usually be cast on what is formal by affirmatively characterizing it as compositional, structural, procedural, methodological, etc.

It remains to consider whether the contrast between form and content in my usage here is absolute or relative. In one very special sense, form is always relative to content. Content must first be identified, and once identified, that which is formal can then be marked off and contrasted with content. But in another sense, the distinction between form and content is generally absolute. That is, what is marked off from content, and contrasted as formal, does not generally vary in a way that is merely relative to the standpoint, perspective, or level of abstraction that the analyst happens to adopt. Sometimes, however, the contrast can be, to some extent, relativized in a fruitful way. That is, what is initially marked off from content as formal from one point of view or at one level of abstraction may sometimes from another point of view or level of abstraction become content as contrasted with some other variety of form. Here is one example. I have distinguished between the formal attributes of an interpretive method, e.g., generality of scope, coherence, systematicity, and statute respectfulness on the one hand, and the content of any given method on the other, and I have identified such content mainly in terms of the central modes of argument that figure in such content, e.g., the argument from ordinary meaning, or the argument from ultimate purpose, and so on. Plainly, this is a straightforward sense of content in a given method, and it readily contrasts with the foregoing formal attributes of method which specify no such particular content and are themselves compatible with highly varied content. But even so, this specific distinction between form and content is relative to analytical stand-point in the following way. If our primary interest shifts from the formal character of an interpretive methodology to the formal character of basic modes of argument, what has been content in the foregoing contrast, i.e., the mode or modes of argument that figure in the interpretive method, becomes form, and a new, contrasting, variety of content is introduced, i.e., the content of any particular argument of a given mode. To be more concrete, the form becomes, say, the general mode of argument here called the argument from ordinary meaning (or from ultimate purpose, etc.), and the content becomes whatever the content is of any particular such argument. In this example, then, the distinction between form and content sometimes turns out to be relative and not absolute. That is, here it turns out to be relative to analytical focus, standpoint, or level of abstraction. This does not, however, impair the utility of the distinction.

Is the concept of "formal" as used in this essay new? Although some refinements are offered here, the general contours of the concept are familiar from ordinary English usage. Many dictionaries record usage in which "formal" is contrasted with content or substance. It follows from this usage that "formal", so conceived, may also apply to or accommodate highly variable content or substance, as here. Further, dictionaries also record that a formal feature may be compositional, structural, procedural, methodological, or otherwise affirmatively characterized as formal, and so not be left formulated merely in "negative" terms as some kind of non-content. But what is relatively new here is the demonstration of the wide ranging and systematic applicability of generally familiar concepts of the formal to diverse legal phenomena and diverse features of a legal system viewed as a whole. The formal in law is hardly confined to formalities for valid contracts and wills, even though many lawyers and lay people tend to think of form in these narrow terms. Indeed, few legal theorists have applied any notion of form to law in a wide ranging and systematic way.

VI. Brief Comparison of Other Theories About Law and its Characteristics

So far, my main theses are: (1) that the characteristics of each basic type of legal phenomenon include one or more that are formal, and that these attributes, when appropriately formal, are also desiderata in their own right, and (2) that the characteristics of a legal system viewed as a whole include several that are formal, and that these attributes, when appropriately formal, are also desiderata in their own right.

It should be plain that my interest in the formal character of law is entirely different from the interest of formal logicians in the law. Also, my interest here is not akin to that of "pure theorists" of European legal positivism such as Professor Hans Kelsen.[11]   In his famous "pure theory", Kelsen was concerned with "the cognition of positive law" and he sought to exclude all "foreign elements" from positive law such as values. I am concerned with the formal character of law, and I stress that law's formalness is ultimately and intimately backed by significant categories of value. (There are other major differences between Kelsenian theory and mine.)

My thesis does overlap with the concerns of Professor Lon L. Fuller who wrote a book devoted largely to formal legality.[12] But in my terms, formal legality is but one systemic characteristic of, and one desideratum of, legal systems viewed as a whole. My thesis as to the formal character of law is therefore more wide-ranging than Fuller's. (And there are other differences.) My thesis is also more wide-ranging than the concerns of those contemporary theorists in the United States who focus mainly on the formal nature of a single major type of phenomenon such as rules, or decision making according to rules.[13]

Nor is my thesis to be classified as in the Anglo-American positivist tradition of H. I. A. Hart and his antecedents.[14] It is true that Hart stressed the coherence and unity of a legal system for example, and also stressed the role of rules, which he even discussed in the idioms of "form" and "formalism". But Professor Hart's important work is devoid of a general thesis as to the formal character of law.

Various German theorists and legal scholars have treated formality mainly in branches of substantive law, and I hope to study more of their work soon.[15]

VII. The Importance of Recognizing the Formalness of Law

I will first treat the jurisprudential importance of formality, conceptual and normative. I will then treat its importance to practitioners in understanding law and in reforming law.

A.   Jurisprudential Importance

The analysis of form in its varied legal manifestations advances jurisprudential understanding. To begin with, it advances understanding of the very legal phenomena under analysis. Thus, we see what the nature and role of formal features are in constitutional phenomena, in criteria of validity, in rules, in interpretive method, in stare decisis, in legal reasoning, and more. This in turn may yield related insights into general types of legal phenomena, for example, that rules display both external and internal form, and that internal form breaks down into a number of major dimensions. Or that an interpretive method must have certain formal features (heretofore neglected in legal theory) if it is to count as a method at all.

One accepted way to provide a jurisprudential account of the very nature of law is to provide a comprehensive account of the characteristics of basic types of legal phenomena, and of legal systems as a whole. But we do not yet have in Western legal theory an account that accords the formality of those characteristics their rightful due. Here I have explored the nature and roles of formal characteristics in quite diverse manifestations--what they are, how they affect content, and more. (Part of the interest of the theses just is that they range over such varied phenomena. I have also suggested here how such formal characteristics are as fundamental to law as its policy content.

Of course, basic legal phenomena and legal systems have other characteristics besides those that are formal. An understanding of the formalness of law is required for, or at least facilitates the analysis of, some of these other fundamental characteristics. Thus, one other basic characteristic of a legal system viewed as a whole is that it has essential content, as well. As Hart has shown, for a legal system to function as a coercive order and thus exist at all, it must have a minimum substantive content that at least includes rules prohibiting the free use of violence and protecting at least certain limited property rights.[16]

We can now readily see how this minimum content of a legal system as a whole, though itself an obvious and distinct characteristic, cannot be satisfactorily analyzed and understood apart from, or in abstraction from, law's formal character. The general relationship between form and substance in the content of a legal system as a whole, is not a bi-polar or dichotomous relationship but one of complementarity. A systemic characteristic of law that is formal generally manifests itself in some way in complementary substantive content. Thus, for example, the characteristic of formal legality in the modes of operation of the system manifests itself in the effective content of the substantive rules of the system, including the rules comprising what Hart called law's minimum content. Without at least threshold conformity to the canons of legality, the rules comprising such content would be merely "paper rules in books" and could not be said to exist as "law in action". Further, once beyond this threshold, the general degree of conformity to such canons still affects the extent to which law in books is translated into law in action.

But it is not only the content of a legal system viewed as a whole that cannot be adequately understood without resort to the relation between form and content. The same is true of the content of basic types of legal phenomena as well. The formal character of an applicable source-oriented criterion of validity manifests itself in the content of rules, content which would almost certainly not be the same if a content-oriented criterion of validity were also applicable. Formal attributes of rules such as definiteness manifest themselves in complementary substantive content of a rule. The formalness of interpretive method manifests itself in complementary types of interpretive arguments incorporated in the method, arguments of appropriate scope, appropriate generality, and so on. The formality of the principle of stare decisis manifests itself in general adherence to precedent in particular cases over time, thereby defining the very content of common law.

Of course, the content manifest in the phenomena that is complementary to formal attributes does not exhaust that content. In the case of rules, for example, problem-specific policy substantially informs that content, as well. Indeed, such policy (e.g., quiet and safety in the park in our "no vehicles" example) is the "prime mover" favoring adoption of some such law in the first place. We saw, however, that formalness, as backed by its general rationales and by other institutional and processual values, can justifiably override countervailing problem-specific policy considerations to some extent in the content of a rule in the course of its creation or modification.

The relation of form to substantive content in law is not like the relation of those containers to the things they contain in which, as with certain liquids, the containers when emptied, leave no trace on the content. In the first place, encapsulatory form is only one of the major varieties of legal form. In the second place, even container-like form in the law commonly imprints itself on substantive content. For example, the same substantive considerations, i.e., content, that is encapsulated in the external form of a common law doctrine will be transformed to some degree when encapsulated in the external form of a statute. Any general analysis of law's content must therefore take account of such an imprint. Whole essays wait to be written here on the varied and complex fusions of form with content, and on the homage that must be paid to form, in the content of a well-designed legal order.

In sum, characteristics of law that are formal must be analyzed as such, and on their own terms. But we must take account of form when analyzing other characteristics of law, too, especially given that form manifests itself in complementary content.

What is the relative conceptual importance of the formalness of law? I will now suggest how the formalness of law is central to law, and thus must figure in any general analysis of the concept of law. First, an analysis of the concept of law would be rather less illuminating if it were to leave out of account the formalness of constitutional provisions such as formal source-oriented criteria of validity applicable to state-made law, or if it were to leave out of account formal criteria for the validity of private transactional law such as contracts and wills, or if it were to leave out of account the external and internal formal attributes of legal rules, or the formalness of interpretive method, or the formality of stare-decisis in a common law system, or the formal coherence of the legal system, or the formal legality of modes of governance within the system. Indeed, without a general theory providing some account of the formal character of law, at least in its basic varieties, any analysis of the concept of law in western societies would be inaccurate and incomplete. In my opinion, if any one thing is what John Austin called the "key to the science of jurisprudence," the formal character of law qualifies for that status as fully as any.[17]

Second, some minimum threshold of formalness, as to most basic legal phenomena and as to some features of a system of law, is essential to the very existence of these phenomena and of a legal system as such. Formlessness is simply not consistent with the conception of law known in the West. If this be a tautology, then it is one worthy of explicit formulation. A totally formless "rule" -- one totally incomplete, totally indefinite, totally particular, etc. would not be rule. A totally formless "methodology" of interpretation would not be a methodology. A totally formless "system" of law which provided no ranking of conflicting laws originating in different sources could not really be a system of law, nor could a "system" entirely devoid of what I have here called formal legality. And so on. In short, it is not just that without an account of formality, an analysis of our concept of law would be rather less illuminating, inaccurate, and incomplete. It would not be an analysis of our concept of law at all.

Third, although they do not use my terminology, many theorists, comparativists, and other scholars today tend to differentiate between western legal systems much more by reference to basic formal variations than by reference to other factors. I believe this widespread practice tends to confirm my view that form is central to our concept of law. Thus, for example, theorists and other scholars describe what is special about legal systems in terms of differences in formal constitutional structures, or in terms of whether a system is a codified system or a common law system, or in terms of differences of basic interpretive method, or in terms of whether courts function adversarially or inquisitorially. According to my analysis, we can, in addition, go well beyond this and deploy a much more elaborate apparatus for describing differences between systems in terms of the varieties and levels of all the types of legal form that I identify here. In all this, significant differences of substantive content may also serve as a criterion of differentiation. Still, leading comparativists now hold that western systems are tending toward similar substantive solutions to the same general problems.

Fourth, any basic feature, or general set of features, that goes to the very *identity* of the phenomena in question has a claim to being conceptually central. In my view, a primary measure of the very identity of any particular legal system is the extent of its formal character, overall. One way to test my view is to imagine that a number of basic changes in the formalness of a given system take place over a discrete period, and then to pose the issue of whether that system might be said to have lost its very identity and to have taken on a new one. Suppose, for example, that the formal constitutional structure of the system is changed in basic ways, as from a cabinet form to a non-cabinet form, from a limited electoral franchise to a fully democratic one, from a system without judicial review of legislation to one with it, from a system without independence of the judiciary to one with it. Or suppose that the system is changed from one of commonly incomplete rules at inception to largely complete ones; that the system is also changed from one of open-ended rules to highly definite ones; that the system is changed from one in which the law consists largely of official orders issued ad hoc to one in which the law takes the form of relatively general rules; that the system is changed from one in which law is interpreted ad hoc and rather freely in light of substantive ends and means (actual or hypothesized) to one in which law is interpreted and applied more strictly in light of an interpretive methodology that is formal; that the system is changed from one in which judges have vast power to modify antecedent law at point of application to one in which they have only very restricted power to do so. Now, if even only some of these changes were cumulatively to occur, such a system, so changed solely in these *formal* respects with their complementary manifestations in content, would no longer be the *same* legal system. And yet many more such formal changes, major in nature, could be imagined.

Fifth, what is central to a concept of law must be linked to values fundamental to law. I have stressed that the formal character of law is not merely a datum to be studied solely in a scientific spirit of positive analysis and description. Appropriate formalness of law is also a desideratum, or rather various desiderata clustering about basic legal phenomena, and various systemic desiderata clustering about a legal order as a whole. As we have seen in this essay, all such formal desiderata are backed by various categories of important values, including general rationales for form which may justify even high levels of it. Here, it is especially note-worthy that the very ideal of the rule of law is, as implemented, to be analyzed as one basic variety of systemic form, namely, the formal legality of the modus operandi of the system. Governance in compliance with the rule of law is necessarily law-like. Governance in violation of formal legality, in violation of the rule of law, is less law-like, and if sufficiently extreme, not governance through law at all. Indeed, significant violations of the rule of law sacrifice fundamental values that we associate most intimately with law.

Yet formal legality, and the formalness of law in all its varieties, seems always to be under some strain in any society, and in some societies, is even at risk of failing to secure or to retain its rightful place. Much (though far from all) of this strain can be explained in terms of a persistent and frequently latent struggle between general rationales for formality and institutional and processual values on the one hand, and the problem-specific policies striving to inform the law's content directly and immediately, on the other hand. In the long history of jurisprudence, this deep, wide ranging, and inevitable struggle has not been fully exposed and understood for what it is. We need close, continuous and systematic study of the nature of formal desiderata, and of the justified bearing of general rationales and other values behind these desiderata, not merely in the abstract but also in concrete interaction with problem-specific policy in many and diverse contexts of actual legal experience. From such study, we would derive a deeper understanding of the very nature of law itself.

B.   Practical Importance

A general theory of law's formalness promises to deepen and otherwise improve understanding of it among officials and citizens concerned with the practical workings of law. Here, I can only identify some of the major avenues to improved understanding.

A developed general theory deploys concepts of form, formal attributes, and formality in positive law and legal phenomena in a faithful and consistent fashion that would enable us to see the formalness of law for what it is, and so grasp the force of its normative claims somewhat better, both in regard to its embodiment in legal phenomena and its affects on legal reasoning. It is important to increase our consciousness of form, and thereby combat the tendency to under-estimate its normative claims, a tendency borne not only of the failure to recognize it for what it is, but also of the latency of many values behind the formalness of law.

Only with an adequate and consistently deployed conception of form can those concerned with law recognize its manifestations throughout the law. Only with an adequate and consistently deployed conception of form can those concerned with law analyze where the law is in terms of levels of formality in any of its varieties, and go on to argue articulately where it ought to be. Only with an appropriate and uniform nomenclature for legal form in all of its varieties, can those concerned with law readily see essential similarities and relationships between these varieties.

A general theory of the formal character of law would also provide a systematic account of the general rationales and other values that lie behind and justify the existence of even high levels or degrees of formality in legal phenomena and in a system of law viewed as a whole, levels which may even involve some justifiable sacrifice of problem-specific policy goals. This in turn may lead those concerned with the law to be more conscious of how law's formalness may be significant independently of law's problem-specific policy content. In some countries, and particularly in the United States, there is a special need to understand this independent significance. Even the great American jurist, Karl Llewellyn, did not understand it very well when he pronounced on the justified scope of legal rules as follows: "the rule follows where its reason leads; where the reason stops, there stops the rule."[18] By "reason", Llewellyn meant only problem-specific policy. This kind of myopia sometimes led Llewellyn and others to applaud the willingness of American courts to modify rules at point of application almost any time the rules happen to over- or under-include in light of the problem-specific policy they are supposed to serve. Yet this disregards the force of general rationales for formal attributes of rules as such, which may still be served if the rule is adhered to. This illustrates only how one variety of form may come under pressure for unjustified change. Formality of all kinds is subject to such pressure. Judges and others may fruitfully fortify themselves here by means of a heightened consciousness of the values, often latent, that may lie behind a formal feature.

We may draw upon a general theory of legal form for resources that enable us to make more fruitful practical analyses of particular laws and other legal phenomena. I will cite only one example. Thus, a given statute may be analyzed for (1) its degrees of internal formality in terms of completeness, definiteness, generality, fiat, and manner of expression, (2) how these formal attributes manifest themselves in the content of the statute, and (3) any justified compromise in overall content as between problem-specific policy and the general rationales and other values behind formal attributes. Such analyses are relevant both to the drafting and interpretation of statutes.

Persons with practical concerns in the law also need to be fortified against certain fallacies about form that may be widespread in a given legal system. Among such fallacies current in the American system are the following: that legal form is <u>mere</u> form, e.g., a mere encapsulatory receptacle for problem-specific policy, with no other values behind it at all; that form in law tends strongly to be over-formal and so formalistic; that form cannot properly co-determine any of the law's substantive content; that the true "home" of form in law, if it has any, is confined merely to certain requirements for the validity of contracts and wills; and that form is conservative or politically "right wing". A general theory of formality can be deployed to expose such fallacies for what they are.

A general theory of the formal character of law would also enable us to see that there are many basic alternative forms and formal attributes--many choices of form to be made in the design and operation of a system of law, and that there is much at stake in these choices. This certainly makes form more important than if there were no choices. For example, there is the choice between statutory form and common law form. There is the recurring choice between "rule" and "discretion". There is the choice between an adversarial form and an inquisitorial form of adjudication. In each of these and in many other examples, there are still further choices about the degree or level of appropriate formality.

A deepened or otherwise improved understanding of basic types of legal phenomena and of legal systems as a whole provided by a theory of form bears on practical legal criticism and law reform, as well. Among other things, it enables the reformer to determine more effectively how far a given degree or level of formality in particular phenomena may be over-formal, i.e. "formalistic", or under-formal, i.e., "substantivistic". In some systems, law may generally tend to be overformal. In others, underformal. In the United States, for example, whole branches of law are substantivistically awash in a sea of policy.

Indeed, a general theory of formality can yield a multi-step methodology for determining the appropriate level of formality in a given rule or other legal phenomenon.[19] Such a methodology enables us to explain why, in some branches of substantive law, levels of formality can be high without being formalistic. Relatedly, appropriate standards of formality enable us to see how far the law in operation conforms to requisites of formal legality i.e., the rule of law.

VIII. Conclusion

The nature and importance of form, formal attributes, and formality in positive law, in basic types of legal phenomena, and in a legal system viewed as a whole are not sufficiently understood. There is not a single jurisprudential work that treats the subject in a systematic and unitary fashion. Moreover, the legal culture in some countries is actually anti-formal. It would be of value especially to American legal theorists to know more fully how far the nature and importance of form, formal attributes, and formality are studied as such and understood for what they are in Germany and other European countries. It would be especially interesting to learn of methodological writings (in addition to Weber's) that seek to avoid the many pitfalls of "form-content" analysis, including ambiguity and equivocation in key terms.

Notes

1. This is one of several preliminary essays on the formal character of law. The first such essay was initially presented as the Goodhart Lecture on 4 December 1991 while the author was the Arthur L. Goodhart Visiting Professor of Legal Science at Cambridge University. This first essay was published as *The Formal Character of Law*, 51 CAMBRIDGE LAW JOURNAL 242 (1992). The second essay, a further development of the first, has been published in German in ARSP and is entitled *Der formale Charakter des Rechts II*. See also other essays in this Part of the present book. The present essay is different from the first and second in significant ways. See also Chapter Five of this book.

2. The criticism might be made that this thesis is ultimately "tautologous", or the like. It is true that most objects of human creation must take some form. This is most evident in the case of many physical objects of human creation. But even if this is also generally true of non-physical objects of human creation, I hope to show that in the case of law, legal phenomena, and legal systems, form requires the kind of special attention I propose to provide here, and also more at length in my projected book. The appropriate conceptual explication and description of the form of a legal construct is often far from obvious. Moreover, particular legal embodiments of form, even when initially appropriate, are more at risk of degeneration or distortion than is true of form in physical objects of human creation. Also, the values served by form in law tend to be relatively latent. For this reason, among others, form may not get its due in actual practice, let alone in the work of theorists.

3. H.L.A. Hart, THE CONCEPT OF LAW pp. 189-195 (Oxford U. Press, Oxford, 1961).

4. Hans Kelsen, THE GENERAL THEORY OF LAW AND STATE pp. 18-50 (Harvard U. Press, Cambridge 1945).

5. It might be thought that this thesis, too, is subject to the criticism of being ultimately tautologous. But see note 1.

6. A formal feature of legal phenomena may reveal itself as a legal requirement, or part of a legal requirement. For example, that a statute be duly adopted by the duly constituted legislature and duly signed by the executive constitutes a legal requirement or requirements. Given this, it might seem superfluous to go on and assert, as in the text, that what is already a legal requirement (or part thereof) is a desideratum in its own right. After all, any legal requirement must be some kind of desideratum. There are several answers to this. First, my focus here is only on the formalness of any requirement as a desideratum. And in some legal cultures, including my own, the general desirability of formality in the law is frequently questioned. Second, not all formal features of law are legal requirements, in any straightforward way. For example, what I will call the external form of a given legal rule, that is, whether it is embodied in, say, a statute, or in common law, is not a "legal requirement".

7. For more extended discussion, see R.S. Summers, *The Formal Character of Law* 51 CAMBRIDGE LAW JOURNAL 242, 247-251 (1992).

8. Fuller, *The Forms and Limits of Adjudication*, 92 HARVARD LAW REVIEW 353 (1978).

9. Lon L. Fuller, *Positivism and Fidelity to Law; A Reply to Professor Hart*, 71 HARVARD LAW REVIEW, 630 (1958); Compare also Klaus Füßer, *Rechtspositivismus und 'gesetzliches Unrecht'*, ARSP 78 (1992), pp. 301ff., 319f.

10. Max Weber, CRITIQUE OF STAMMLER 79 (1977 Free Press ed'n.).

11. Hans Kelsen, THE PURE THEORY OF LAW, pp. 62-69 (U. of Calif. Press, Berkeley 1967).

12. Lon L. Fuller, THE MORALITY OF LAW (Yale U. Press, New Haven 2nd ed. 1969). See also, R.S. Summers, LON L. FULLER, pp. 36-40 (Stanford U. Press, Stanford 1984) and R.S. Summers, *Professor Fuller's Jurisprudence and America's Dominant Philosophy of Law,* HARV. L. REV. 92 (1978), pp 433-449.

13. See, e.g., Frederick Schauer, PLAYING BY THE RULES (Oxford U. Press, Oxford 1991).

14. See Hart supra note 1.

15. See, for example, K. Engisch, *Form und Stoff in der Jurisprudenz*, BEITRAGE ZUR RECHTSTHEORIE p. 251 (1984).

16. See Hart supra note 1.

17. I have argued elsewhere that the formalness of law also largely accounts for its relative autonomy as a social phenomenon. See R.S. Summers, *Judge Richard Posner's Jurisprudence*, 89 MICH. L. REV. 1302, 1327-1331 (1991).

18. K. Llewellyn, THE BRAMBLE BUSH pp. 157-58 (Oceana, 1951 ed.).

19. R.S. Summers, *Theory, Formality and Practical Legal Criticism* 106 LAW Q. REV. 407, 418 (1990).

CHAPTER 7

A FORMAL THEORY OF THE RULE OF LAW

I. Introduction

Since 1215 in England, and in ensuing centuries in most of the countries that England has influenced, we have witnessed more or less continuous progress toward government under the rule of law. England's own earliest major advance was King John's acquiescence in the Magna Carta in June of 1215.[1] The final revision of this great charter occurred in 1225, and it was confirmed in 1297 by Edward I and placed on the first or 'great' roll of English statutes. One of its original clauses (ch. 39) captures a major feature of the relatively formal theory of the rule of law that I conceptualize and argue for here:

> No free man shall be seized or imprisoned, or stripped of his rights
> or possessions, or outlawed or exiled, or deprived of his standing in
> any other way, nor will we proceed with force against him, or send
> others to do so, except by the lawful judgement of his equals or by
> the law of the land.[2]

Today, almost eight centuries later, many people in the world still do not live in societies in which a counterpart of even this basic clause of Magna Carta can be said to prevail. Recently, hopes have arisen for the extension of the rule of law into Eastern Europe and into the former Soviet Union itself.[3] And in many other countries, significant though uncertain progress is being made. The challenge, however, is not solely one of extending the rule of law into nation states where it has not heretofore flourished. It is also one of avoiding relapses in countries such as Great Britain and the United States where the rule of law has long prevailed. Isolated yet significant departures from the rule of law still occur in these countries. The price of liberty is eternal vigilance. It is the same with the rule of law.

A major explanation for the uncertain advance of the rule of law in the world and for relapses even where it has long prevailed, is that the requisites of its implementation and the values it serves are not sufficiently well understood. The staying power of any social ideal depends on how faithfully it is conceptualized, on the extent to which the values it serves are appreciated, on how well its essential supporting attitudes are focused, and on how far its clientele within the society are organized to support it. Two forms of such support are essential. First, the affirmative support for the ideal must be sufficient for it to be appropriately institutionalized in the society in the first place. Second, and thereafter the society must be ready to criticize departures from that ideal and to provide redress for such departures. With regard to an ideal such as the rule of law, students of the law, professional academics, legal practitioners and judges have special roles.

What I seek to offer here differs from much of the academic writing on the subject that has gone before. I will concentrate on one special type of threat to the rule of law, namely, the threat of unduly over-inflating the very concept itself, thereby weakening the quality of social discourse and criticism in its name. This is a distinct and fundamental type of threat to the viability of any social ideal. My central thesis is that the rule of law is best conceptualized as a relatively uninflated formal theory. What this means and why it is best are the special burdens of this essay.

II. A Relatively Formal Theory of the Rule of Law

We must first understand what a relatively formal theory of the rule of law is. Any normative theory of this kind has three basic components: conceptual, institutional, and axiological. Such a theory must be conceptualized and then institutionalized in rule making processes, in rules, in interpretive and applicational methodologies, and in processes of judicial and other enforcement. This institutionalization, in the course of its very workings and in its outcomes, serves the values of the rule of law.

In what follows, I will collapse the discussion of the conceptual component of the rule of law into the institutional and the axiological. The theory now to be sketched in Section II is formal in a number of ways that will be identified. After explaining what a more substantive theory of the rule of law is in Section III, I will focus frontally on how the theory advocated here is formal.

A. Institutional Component

The relatively formal theory of the rule of law that I advocate here cannot be encapsulated in anything concise enough to count as a definition, but it can be summarized partially as follows:

> The ideal of the rule of law consists of the authorized governance of at least basic social relations between citizens, and between citizens and their government, so far as feasible through published formal rules congruently interpreted and applied, with the officialdom itself subject to rules defining the manner and limits of their activity, and with sanctions or other redress against citizens and officials for departures from rules being imposed only by impartial and independent courts or by similar tribunals, after due notice and opportunity for hearing.

The rules are to have, so far as feasible, several formal attributes. That is, they are to be complete rather than fragmentary, definitive rather than vague or otherwise open-ended, general rather than particular, and formulated in accord with appropriately formal modes of expression. These rules must not only be publicly known, but also relatively constant through time, uniform across persons and other legal entities, free of conflict with other rules, and susceptible of compliance.

The relatively formal ideal of the rule of law that I advocate, then, is institutionalized in major part through rules having the foregoing formal attributes. The actual institutional embodiment of this ideal - the reality in which it is manifest - takes further essential forms. For there to be rules there must, of course, be rule-making bodies, including legislatures and administrative agencies, and accepted criteria for identifying valid rules in cases of dispute. The rule makers must also abide by norms favouring the making, promulgation, and implementation of rules having formal attributes of the foregoing general character. Thus, machinery for the advance public promulgation of rules must be in place. An accepted methodology for the interpretation and application of the rules congruently with their content is required. There must be rules governing the finding of facts. There must also be an independent, impartial, and accessible system of courts and other tribunals: (1) providing remedies and sanctions for departures from the rules by officials and others, and (2) providing authoritative procedures for resolving disputes over the validity of rules, over the interpretation and application of rules, and over the facts to which rules apply.

The institutional embodiment of the ideal of the rule of law does not end here. As the language of a further section of the Magna Carta put it, there must also be judges and other officials, legally obligated and "minded" to follow the rules. Thus, societies must take steps to see that procedures for the recruitment and retention of judges and other officials are well designed to secure personnel with the requisite attitudes to law and law-like ways. Moreover, citizens adversely affected by rule departures must be legally empowered to seek redress, to contest the application of criteria of validity, to challenge the interpretation of rules, and to litigate the factual basis for their application. Of course, citizens must be willing and prepared to take such steps. Among other things, this calls for appropriate education, and for rules that prohibit official and other retaliation against citizens who assert rights in the name of the rule of law. There must also be a recognized, organized, and independent legal profession legally empowered and willing to advocate before courts the causes of persons adversely affected by rule departures. Citizens, the legal profession, and officials must also be legally entitled and ready to criticize rule departures as appropriate, and there must be a free and vigilant press and media also duly protected by law. In addition, academic lawyers must be ready to criticize not only rule departures but also any anti-rule of law attitudes of officials and judges, in particular.[4]

Of course, the rule of law cannot be satisfactorily institutionalized without the threat and the actuality of remedies and sanctions. The nature of these varies greatly within and between systems, ranging from the simplest sanctions available to judges to keep order in a courtroom, to sanctions against police for exceeding the rules of lawful arrest and the like, to remedies against administrative officials, as well as against citizens, for rule departures.

B. Axiological Component

Institutionalization of the rule of law is one thing, the values it serves, another. A relatively formal theory of the rule of law characteristically serves certain values. Here it suffices to provide a merely suggestive listing:

- legitimate government (legislative and judicial as well as executive)
- domestic peace and order
- certainty and predictability of governmental action and of the legal effects of private law-making
- private autonomy within realms marked out by the law
- facilitation of free choice and planning
- respect for the dignity of the individual (e.g. citizens being responsible only for acts which they knew or reasonably could have known were somehow contrary to law at time of acting; citizen autonomy and choice duly effectuated)
- freedom from arbitrariness of official action
- ultimate imposition of remedies and sanctions for rule departures only by impartial and independent courts and similar tribunals after appropriate notice and opportunity to be heard
- actual equality of legal treatment at the hands of the government
- the appearance of actual equality of legal treatment
- the reinforcement of the courage of officials to take unpopular decisions required by law.

C. The Institutional And Axiological Core of a Relatively Formal Theory of The Rule of Law

First, we must exhaust the potential for creating rules. Without complete, definitive and appropriately general rules, nearly all the major values of the rule of law ideal could not be fulfilled or served. The rule of law is very largely a law of rules. Without antecedent rules, we could not even determine and identify the judges, legislators, administrators and other officials of the system. Without rules, the law could not generate sufficiently determinate reasons for citizens to act when occasions for action arise. Without rules, there could be no established procedures of dispute resolution.

While rules are of great importance, and while there is great potential for rules across all spheres of social life, those responsible for rule making in a society often shy away from their duty here, on such grounds as that the subject matter is not "ripe" for rules, or is too indefinite for rules, or that rules would unduly fetter necessary expert judgment, and so on. Commonly, these are bad excuses. This makes it all the more important to stress the need to exhaust the potential for rule making.

Without accepted and determinate criteria for identifying valid rules as law, a rule of law consisting in the main of a law of rules could not function. Disputes over the validity of rules are inevitable, and since rules cannot be applied unless valid, some means must be provided for resolving such disputes. A system that determines validity largely by reference to source-oriented criteria, i.e., merely whether the law in question was laid down by a body duly authorized, can operate far more determinately and predictably than a system that also makes validity depend on vague content-oriented criteria such as "substantive due process" and the like.

Similarly fundamental to the rule of law is the adoption and consistent application of a general methodology of interpretation that is faithful to the content of the antecedent rules. While this applies not only to statutes but also to the common law, I will focus on statutes, which make up the bulk of the law in many countries. Without a methodology of statutory interpretation faithful to the content of the rules, again, most of the values of the rule of law could not be satisfactorily served.

The two leading modes of interpretive argument most often in competition in Anglo-American systems are (1) the argument from ordinary meaning of the statutory words, and (2) the teleological argument from ultimate purpose. The former is decidedly superior on rule of law grounds. First, the former accords far less discretion to judges at point of application. The judge must strive to ascertain and follow the ordinary meaning of the words in which the statute is expressed. This mode of argument draws on various resources, and is far from simple. Yet it still greatly limits the opportunity for judges to substitute their own legislative judgments about appropriate means and ends, and thus diminishes scope for strong willed judges of the left, or of the right, to decide in disregard of the enacted language. The argument from ultimate purpose, on the other hand, requires that judges ascertain an ultimate purpose and then construe the implementing language of the statute accordingly. Since the ultimate purpose is commonly not stated on the face of the statute, this interpretive method may confer vast discretion on judges at point of application to determine ultimate purpose, and thus decide as they see fit.

Second, the argument from ordinary meaning generates reasons for action from the very date of the law's inception, and promises citizens that they can rely on that meaning in planning their conduct and in otherwise ordering their affairs. The argument from ultimate statutory purpose, on the other hand, is far less certain and predictable, and may even require, in regard to many statutes, that citizens wait until the statute is litigated before they can know its meaning. At worst, the argument may retroactively upset a course of otherwise justified reliance on the part of the addressees of the statute.

Third, the argument from ordinary meaning encourages judges to encourage legislators to legislate consistently with the rule of law. Thus, by adhering to the ordinary meaning, the judges encourage legislators to draft carefully. The judges also thereby encourage legislators to legislate explicitly rather than through "legislation" hidden in mere committee reports and the like, "legislation" that might not have gained true democratic assent and thus legitimacy if more explicit language had been used in the statutory text. The argument from ultimate purpose, on the other hand, is often rooted (in the American system, especially) in unenacted reports of legislative committees.

A further "rock bottom" institutional requirement for the rule of law is that rules and processes exist for the generally reliable and truthful resolution of disputes over facts relevant to the applicability of law. Many such issues arise, and from various sources at that. Without rules of evidence and without procedures for authoritative fact-finding, including allocation of burden of proof, disputes over facts would be far more numerous. The rule of law requires a rule over fact. Rules would be of very uncertain application without factual determinacy, and here the very presence in the background of courts capable of reliably finding facts contributes greatly to the rule of law. Many disputes are settled out of court in accord with law precisely because of this.

Thus, a further and central institutional requirement of the rule of law is an impartial and independent system of courts and similar tribunals with power, in cases of disputes, to identify valid rules, to interpret and apply these rules, and to resolve any issues of fact that arise. Disputes of all three kinds must be resolved consistently and congruently with the content of antecedent rules. An impartial and independent system of courts is indispensable not only for this function, but is also a necessity if remedies and sanctions are to be imposed ultimately only by courts and similar tribunals. A legislative body cannot ultimately perform these functions. Nor can administrative officials unless special institutional steps are taken. Officials will themselves often be parties to disputes over validity, interpretation, and fact, and over available remedies and sanctions, and thus not in an appropriate institutional position themselves to resolve such disputes, impartially, consistently and congruently.

Of course, a court system must be accessible as well as impartial, and independent. Resources are required for such a system to be appropriately accessible. And rules are required to secure impartiality as between litigants, and to secure independence of the judges from political and other irrelevant influences on their deliberations.

In addition, the core institutional requirements for a viable rule of law include effective restrictions on the power of judges at point of application to modify the content of antecedent rules in the course of applying them to the facts. The impetus to modify is perhaps strongest at point of application where original error or bad judgment in the earlier formulation of the rule can be seen most clearly and where countervailing substantive considerations emerge most compellingly. As a result, some limited power of judges to modify may be recognized. Judges must at least have power to correct an obvious error in the punctuation of a statute or in a cross reference in a scheme of statutes, just to cite two examples. But the pressure to extend and expand the power to modify is deep and incessant in any system. Unless the dispute is merely over facts, one litigant will always want the rule to be otherwise. And all judges will feel some urge to "adjust" at least some of the rules. Moreover, judges are not without ways of minimizing the likelihood that the full extent of their own "adjustment" will be seen for what it is.

Yet judges can have only a restricted power to modify antecedent rules of law if a system is to have a satisfactory rule of law. If judges at point of application are relatively free simply to change or make up the law as they go along, then rules displaying formal attributes, a congruent methodology of interpretation, reliable fact-finding, the virtues of an accessible, impartial and independent judiciary, and most of the other machinery for securing the rule of law, simply go for naught. As a result we necessarily lose many virtues of the rule of law, including: the generation of meaningful and "guidesome" legal reasons for action from the inception of the law, predictability and the fairness to affected persons that goes with this, and consistent treatment of similarly situated persons before the law.

Finally, as the Magna Carta so well teaches, the core institutional requirements of the rule of law demand that no significant sanction or remedy for rule departures be ultimately imposed upon a citizen or official other than by an independent and impartial court or similar tribunal, and then only after due notice to the affected party and fair opportunity to be heard, and preferably only after a further opportunity for appellate review of any initial process.

III. Differences Between a Formal and a Substantive Theory of the Rule of Law

The nature of a formal theory of the rule of law is best understood by way of contrast with a substantive theory. A substantive theory is characterized by the greater substantive content it incorporates. Thus it incorporates to some degree one or more of the following: rules securing minimum social welfare, i.e., the "welfare state", rules securing some variety of the market economy, rules protecting basic human rights, and rules institutionalizing democratic governance. Here, the contrast with formal theories is stark. Indeed, the most full fledged and robust substantive theories collapse into a single whole not only the rule of law, but also all other traditional ingredients of the ideal socio-legal order such as the welfare state, some variety of the market economy, protection of basic human rights, and democracy. This is the first major contrast between a substantive theory and a relatively formal theory.

A substantive theory also incorporates to some degree all or nearly all of the institutional forms of a formal theory, including rule making bodies, rules, criteria of validity, consistent and congruent interpretative method, reliable fact-finding processes, an accessible, impartial, and independent judiciary, significant restrictions on the power of courts at point of application to modify antecedent rules, and ultimate imposition of remedies and sanctions only by courts or similar tribunals after due notice and opportunity to be heard. But a formal theory, by virtue of its unified focus, accords special emphasis to the foregoing institutional forms, in ways that a substantive theory does not. This is the second major contrast between a formal theory and a substantive theory. Thus, in a formal theory there is emphasis on the preponderance of rule over discretion, on rules displaying formal attributes to a high degree, on consistent and congruent methodology of interpretation, on reliable fact finding, on judicially detached decision making free of the interests of litigants and of contemporary political influences, and on more consistent adherence by the judiciary to antecedent law at point of application despite pressures for modification emergent there. In these ways, then, a formal theory can be formal to a higher degree than a substantive theory.

In sum, there are two major contrasts between a relatively formal theory of the rule of law and a relatively substantive theory. First, a relatively formal theory incorporates far less by way of the substantive content of an ideal socio-legal order such as the welfare state, of some version of the market economy, of the essentials of democracy, of basic human rights, and the like. Second, a relatively formal theory, by virtue of its unified focus, stresses the institutional forms of the rule of law, formally conceived, including rule over discretion, consistent and congruent interpretive method, reliable fact-finding, judicial objectivity and independence, and restricted power of courts to modify law at point of application.

IV.   The Advantages of a Relatively Formal Theory

A formal theory of the rule of law, then, incorporates relatively little by way of the substantive content of a more comprehensive overall socio-legal ideal. A relatively substantive theory partakes of some or all of this content. The choice here is between two basic ways of setting up and organizing a social understanding of ideals. Though both a formal and a substantive theory are capable of figuring in legal and political discourse, and capable of finding expression in the realities of legal ordering, I believe a relatively formal and detached theory of the rule of law is preferable. The relatively formal and detached theory, by virtue of its unified focus, emphasizes formal rule of law values and their institutionalization as such — the preponderance of rules over discretion, the consistency and congruence of its interpretive methodology with the rules, the reliability of its fact finding, the independence from political influence of its judicial and similar tribunals, its procedural propriety, and its delimitation of judicial power to modify antecedent law at point of application. Each of these distinct emphases promises somewhat fuller realization of formal rule of law values as such. At least, there are strong reasons to suppose that this way of setting up and organizing a theory of the rule of law is likely to lead to a fuller realization of formal rule of law values than would be the case if a more encompassing substantive theory were adopted.

First, a relatively formal theory is itself more or less politically neutral, and because it is so confined, is more likely to command support on its own terms from the right, left, and center of the political spectrum of a society than is a substantive theory which not only incorporates the rule of law formally conceived but also incorporates elements of more controversial doctrines. This is not simply a point of rhetoric. It is in fact true that the values integral to a formal theory of the rule of law are relatively neutral in practical terms. Certainly in constitution making and in law making before a legislature, these values are relatively consistent either with a robust welfare state or a thin welfare state, with a robust catalogue of basic human rights or with a thin catalogue of human rights, with a robust market economy or with a thin market economy, with a robust democratic order or with a thin democratic order. Thus, any of these variations can be incorporated into a legal system through rules duly made and implemented.[5] Politicians and citizens of any political hue who embrace any of these variations can at the same time consistently embrace a relatively formal theory of the rule of law.

Moreover, the genuine values of the formal theory of the rule of law merit support from left, right and center in the political life of a country. The more the theory of the rule of law is "de-substantivized" to embrace only those institutional forms that as such serve values associated with a formal rule of law, the more likely it is that the rule of law will receive its due from all. On such a politically neutral conception, far more people from all segments of the political spectrum can be enlisted to argue for the rule of law and to criticize departures from it. On the other hand, if the rule of law is taken in general discourse to mean not just governance through rules (and closely related features) but also socialism or capitalism, a Bill of Rights or no Bill of Rights, populist democracy or limited democracy, etc., then the formal rule of law is not likely to command the range of neutral support that it merits (and requires), for it cannot be so readily seen to be a set of institutionalized forms and values worthy of the support of all officials and citizens.

Second, in actual practice, some theory of the rule of law must be deployed by officials, judges, lawyers, academics, and citizens generally to defend, criticize and improve upon features of the existing legal order. The more unified and coherent the theory of the rule of law, the more that argumentation and criticism in its name can itself be focused. And the more focused it is, the more likely it is to receive its due. A formal theory is relatively focused. By contrast, a substantive theory sprawls in its application, and necessarily ranges over highly diverse subject matter. On a full fledged and robustly formulated substantive theory, arguments purportedly in the name of the "rule of law" would tend to become arguments in the name of too many different things at once.

I now turn, thirdly, to a more complicated merit of a relatively formal theory of the rule of law. Although I have said that at the stage of constitution making, or of legislation, or of administrative rule making, a formal theory of the rule of law is compatible with the welfare state or its antithesis, with socialism or capitalism, with a vast catalogue of human rights or a thin one, with democracy or dictatorship (within limits), a formal theory of the rule of law incorporates institutional requirements that nevertheless conflict in particular cases with other values that these substantive doctrines express or implicate. Thus a substantive improvement in the content of the rules by which a system is governed may be highly desirable — it may consist, for example, of a right that is part of minimum social welfare, or of a right to pursue a business occupation previously closed to a minority, or of a right to vote theretofore denied to a group or class. Yet the mode of incorporating such an admittedly desirable change in the content of the system may, in a particular case, conflict with rule of law values formally conceived. Thus, for example, a court may take upon itself the task of modifying antecedent law at point of application to implement such a reform. In the circumstances, it may even be justified, all things considered, for a court to make the change rather than a legislature or a constitutional convention, or other appropriate body.

Still, we must not ignore the possible loss or sacrifice of values associated with the formal rule of law when a judicial reform takes place. Judicial reform entails a special kind of rule departure that frequently involves some sacrifice of formal rule of law values, such as predictability, justified reliance on law, equality before the law, and sometimes even judicial independence and impartiality, and judicial legitimacy. Judicial reform might even occur in quite blatant response to a rush of popular political opinion expressed in demonstrations on the steps of the court house. Indeed, judicial reform may go well beyond settled conventions restricting the power of judges at point of application to modify antecedent rules.

Judicial reform is but one of many institutional contexts in which a formal theory of the rule of law may come into conflict, in a particular case, with other dimensions of an ideal socio-legal order. And in the abstract examples I have chosen involving judicial reform of rules, I have deliberately selected ingredients that reflect basic and genuine values that press for reform. In many cases the values pressing for reform that conflict with rule of law values formally conceived will not be nearly so compelling, and rule of law values will be strongly implicated and grievously at risk.

It is important to set up and organize social thought about legal ordering in a way that secures the likelihood that there will be *ready perception of conflicts* in particular cases between formal rule of law values and other more substantive ingredients in a vision of an ideal socio-legal order. In my view, widespread espousal of a relatively formal theory is more likely to facilitate the perception of such conflicts. After all, it isolates and disentangles more clearly the very elements of such conflict than does a substantive theory in which the rule of law may even be taken to mean all, or more or less all, that goes into an ideal socio-legal order.

Moreover, and for the same reason, a relatively formal theory does not hold out a false hope that conflicts in particular cases between the ideal of the rule of law, as formally conceived, and other dimensions of the ideal socio-legal order, can be resolved without any degree of sacrifice of the rule of law ideal itself. I believe more substantive theories tend to foster this kind of false hope because they purport to portray all (or nearly all) such conflicts as somehow resolved under and within the rule of law rubric itself, so that what remains, in the end, may still be thought to partake of the rule of law, without any sacrifice *of it* whatsoever. A formal theory cannot hold out this kind of false hope. Rather, conflicts between it, as the rule of law, and still other dimensions of the ideal socio-legal order can be perspicuously displayed, and when the rule of law, formally conceived, is sacrificed, officials and others cannot escape facing up to this fact, and to the need to justify it. Judges, other officials, and affected citizens should not be allowed to obscure the reality of any such sacrifice by espousing an inflated ideal of the rule of law which may enable them to harbor the illusion that what is being done is in the end somehow justifiable in the name of that ideal as well.

V. Limits of a Formal Theory

Although a relatively formal theory of the rule of law has merits that make it preferable in my view to a substantive theory, it does not follow that a formal theory is without limitations. To begin, when one or more institutional requirements of a formal theory is met, it can hardly follow that the resulting legal state of affairs is necessarily right or good, overall. Plainly, a well defined and duly promulgated rule congruently interpreted and applied by an impartial court may still, in terms of its substantive content, be highly objectionable. Compliance with the institutional requisites of a relatively formal theory of the rule of law can be no guarantee that the resulting legal state of affairs is, as such, right and good overall. One limitation of a formal theory, then, is inherent. Such a theory does not, as such, embrace law right or good in content. How significant is this limitation? As a matter of logic, it is highly significant. It can never follow logically that we can judge a legal state of affairs, overall, as right or good merely on the basis of its satisfying the requirements of a formal theory of the rule law.

Another measure of the significance of the foregoing limitation is the extent to which history in fact yields more than isolated instances of genuinely bad, as distinguished from merely unsound law, expressed nevertheless in compliance with all the institutional forms of a formal theory of the rule of law as conceived here. In modern Western history, such instances have not been all that frequent. Yet the contrary is often assumed. It is said, for example, that in the twentieth century, a fascist Germany, a fascist Italy, and a fascist Soviet Union provide ready illustrations. But in truth, the Nazis combined utter disregard of the institutional requirements of a formal theory of the rule of law with laws bad (evil) in content. Far more often, bad law and disregard of the rule of law formally conceived go hand in hand. This is not difficult to explain. Laws bad in content are themselves often manifestations of substantive arbitrariness, and substantive arbitrariness and the arbitrariness against which a formal theory of the rule of law protects are not unrelated. The institutionalization of a formal theory not only rules out arbitrariness of a more formal kind but also inhibits substantive arbitrariness. That is, the institutional requisites of a formal theory of the rule of law and substantive arbitrariness of content are in practice to a considerable degree incompatible. Thus, rules that are complete, definitive, general, and publicly promulgated make highly uncongenial receptacles for bad, and especially for evil, content. Far better (from the tyrant's point of view) to submerge bad content in wide-ranging official discretion rather than in definitive and known general rules to be uniformly applied. Here, form curbs evil. Such rules can be a source of embarrassment to tyrants who find them inconveniently applicable. The requirement of public promulgation of rules is an especially formidable, though of course hardly failsafe, deterrent to the enactment of bad or evil content.

Impartial and independent judiciaries cannot be totally effective safeguards against bad laws, however. It is true that independent judges may invalidate such laws provided there is a written constitution or other appropriate law proscribing them. And they may exercise a limited power to modify bad laws at point of application (often in the guise of interpretation) in ways that diminish their ill effects. But beyond these, a formal theory of the rule of law cannot reach very far.

There is no escape from the ultimate conclusion that the satisfaction of the institutional requirements of a formal theory of the rule of law is logically compatible with the existence of laws that are bad or wrong or even evil in content. This does not, however, diminish the significance of a formal theory. Such a theory serves genuine values along side all the law's having good content. Moreover, such a theory can still serve genuine values even when the law's content is bad and the resulting legal states of affairs should therefore be condemned.

Moreover, there is nothing special about the foregoing "limitation" of the formal theory of the rule of law. That is, there is nothing special about the fact that the relatively discrete cluster of formal rule of law values, such as predictability, justified reliance, autonomous choice, minimization of disputes, and the like may conflict in particular cases with other values such as those implicated in the desired substantive content of law. The values associated with a formal theory of the rule of law are no worse off for that. The world just is a world of conflicting values of all kinds. Indeed, every discrete cluster of values is "limited" in that it cannot itself guarantee that when it is appropriately in play in legal ordering, no competing values will be in play, or that these other values will not prove to be over-riding. In this regard, there is no reason to be especially apologetic about the "limited" nature of formal rule of law values.

So far I have concentrated on how the presence of the formal rule of law is, like all achievements, only a limited achievement. There is a kind of corollary here. I turn to the absence of the rule of law, at least in some of its institutional forms. That we may not have rules, for example, in a given realm of legal ordering does not necessarily signify that this state of affairs is bad, overall. It may be the only really feasible state of affairs. Rules may not be feasible. Or complete and definitive rules may not be feasible. And if not feasible, congruent interpretation will not be feasible. And so on. From this it does not follow that the resulting discretionary ordering of human relations is bad from the point of view of a formal theory of the rule of law. Thus the absence of the rule of law in this regard is not even itself necessarily bad, overall. Thus, not only is its presence not a guarantee that the resulting legal state of affairs is good, overall; its absence (at least in some of its institutional forms) is not, as such, necessarily bad.

But again, this is not a limitation in the world of value and evaluation peculiar to a formal theory of the rule of law. It is familiar that values may not be fully realizable through law in particular circumstances, or even generally, and when that is so, we do not let this count against full fledged recognition of such values, so far as appropriate. For example, the legal means are simply not available to secure fully the value of family harmony within a lawful marriage, or the value of fulfillment for individuals within lawful employment, or the value of equal opportunity through a welfare state, yet it hardly follows that these values are any the less worth pursuing so far as feasible. Most (all?) values can only be limitedly realized through legal means. Thus it is simply false that when a value or cluster of values is fulfilled or served in a resulting legal state of affairs, it follows that this state of affairs is necessarily good, overall. It is also simply false that when a value or cluster of values is absent from a legal state of affairs in which it might otherwise be implicated, then it follows that this state of affairs is, in that respect, to be judged negatively, overall. In these ways, the values associated with a formal theory of the rule of law are no worse off and therefore no differently limited than other values.

VI. Conclusion

I close these remarks on a formal theory of the rule of law with some further words on the importance of this type of theory. We have seen how it fulfils or implicates values of its own such as predictability, justified reliance, autonomous choice, minimization of disputes and legitimacy. Indeed, so important are these values that, when they conflict, as they sometimes do, with first level policy, they may even over-ride such policy or at least require some accommodation.

Of course, most often there is no conflict, and the institutional forms of a formal theory of the rule of law can be deployed to fulfil and subserve values integral to that theory, and yet at the same time fully subserve (so far as feasible) the first level policy that calls law into play in the beginning.

Notes
1. The very meeting at which Magna Carta was first presented to King John occurred at Runnymede in June, 1215, less than three miles from Cumberland Lodge in Windsor Great Park.

2. Rudyard Kipling's poem "The Reeds of Runnymede" reads in part:

> At Runnymede, at Runnymede
> Your rights were won at Runnymede
> No freeman shall be fined or bound
> Or dispossessed of Freehold ground
> Except by lawful judgment found
> And passed upon him by his peers
> Forget not after all these years
> The Charter signed at Runnymede

3. Many so-called "socialist" countries in Eastern Europe have for several decades known systems of "political administration", rather than the rule of law.

4. That academics will stand ready to criticize rule departures should not be taken for granted. In those countries where most academic lawyers readily appear as advocates before courts the deficiency of healthy academic criticism is well known.

5. I am mindful that there have been theorists such as Hayek who argue that there is a fundamental inconsistency between socialism and the rule of law formally conceived.

CHAPTER 8

THE FORMAL CHARACTER OF LAW — STATUTORY RULES

I. Introduction

My general thesis is that law is formal in character.[*] Here I will suggestively develop how this thesis, applies to statutory rules, which comprise one of the basic, essential, and ubiquitous types of legal construct in all legal systems. I single out such rules because of their special importance. First, they are instruments both of problem-specific policy and values associated with the rule of law. Second, they are also used to shape and define virtually all other basic types of legal constructs. Thus, rules are used to shape and define legislatures, elections, courts, criteria of validity, methodologies of interpretation, the practice of stare decisis, official agencies, corporate bodies, other recognized legal entities, and so on.

II. How Might the Formal Attributes of Statutory Rules Be Analyzed?

The formal attributes of rules include completeness, definiteness, generality, and simplicity. These are all formal attributes because (1) they pertain to the shape or configuration of rules rather than their content as such, (2) they neither prescribe nor proscribe content as such, and may accommodate highly variable content. Also, these formal attributes may be isolated and analyzed and evaluated on their own apart from the problem-specific policy content of the rules.

I will now offer somewhat more detailed analyses of several formal attributes of rules. I will begin with completeness as a formal attribute of rules.

A. Completeness As a Distinct Formal Attribute of Rules

The Oxford English Dictionary (OED) defines "complete" as follows: "Having all its parts or elements; entire; full." Thus, in the case of law, we might think of a complete rule at inception as one in which all of its appropriate "spaces" are filled so that it can always generate (under an appropriate methodology of interpretation or application) full fledged reasons for action on the part of its addressees, assuming it is also sufficiently definite (on which, more later). Rules are of different basic types, and thus have different spaces to fill. For example, a basic rule of the criminal law requires the filling of spaces which differ from the nature and number of spaces within a basic rule of contract law. Thus, the crime of burglary requires that spaces be appropriately filled in respect of scope, addressees, conduct proscribed, mental element, and so on, but a basic rule of contract law conferring the power to enter valid contracts would have fewer and quite different spaces. It follows that completeness is relative, and varies at least with the type of rule involved (and that a comprehensive typology of laws would, at the least, be required for a complete analysis of completeness).

If we so conceptualize completeness, the next question is: How is completeness distinct from the content of the rule and thus identifiable as a separate attribute of the rule apart from the overall content of the rule as such? Completeness is not wholly distinct from that content, but it is not *identical* with that content either. It is not wholly distinct because completeness must manifest itself in complementary content of the rule. A complete legal rule just is a rule having content that fills all "spaces" in the rule. But the feature of completeness is not to be identified with content. Two rules can be complete in the same degree yet have very different content. In any given rule, the degree of completeness can be isolated and analyzed separately from the nature of the rule's overall content as such. We may analyze a rule for the degree of its completeness. And we may analyze a rule for its content.

Completeness is formal. First, the shape or configuration of a rule pertains to its basic form, and so is formal. The nature and number of spaces to be filled for a given type of rule is a matter of the shape or configuration of the rule, not its content as such. When a rule is complete, all its spaces are occupied by content, no more, no less. When incomplete, one or more such spaces is not so occupied, no more, no less.

Second, the nature and number of "spaces" that must be filled for a rule to be complete is a formal matter in another way. The attribute of completeness does not, as such prescribe (or proscribe) any particular content, and may accommodate highly varied content. On the other hand, problem-specific policy goals do prescribe or proscribe particular content. Thus, two rules could be formally complete (all appropriate "spaces" filled) yet have quite different content resolving the same problem differently.

Third, the difference between a formally complete rule at inception and an incomplete version of this same rule at inception is not merely that one has a greater quantum of content, but also that this greater quantum signifies that the rule is formally complete.

Fourth, a law that is complete at inception does not require an infusion of further substantive content at point of application, but an incomplete law at inception does. An incomplete law is thus open to infusion of further content, i.e., is to an extent open-ended, and cannot, at inception, always generate full fledged formal reasons for action, whereas a complete law at inception can do this (in combination with an interpretative or applicational methodology).

Completeness, then, is a formal attribute. Is it merely an attribute of the occasional rule, or are rules typically more or less complete, and thus in this regard generally formal? Having seen what completeness is, we can now acknowledge at once that most legal rules are more or less complete.

Again, it is not difficult to explain why most legal rules are more or less complete and thus why legal rules are in this regard formal in character. Incomplete rules simply cannot perform their functions very well. Among other things, they may not, at inception, generate full fledged reasons for action.

Completeness, like all formal attributes of rules, is not merely a descriptive attribute to be isolated and analyzed. It is also a normative desideratum. Completeness is a desideratum because it serves problem-specific policy goals. An incomplete law is ill suited to serve its policy goals. But completeness is a desideratum also because it serves "rule of law" values such as certainty, predictability, citizen self-direction, dispute avoidance, equality before the law, and freedom from official arbitrariness. Without completeness, a rule will not adequately generate formal reasons for its addressees to act on. Also, it is difficult for legislators and other creators of law to evaluate and vote on an incomplete rule. Completeness thus serves the value of deliberative rationality.

It follows that completeness in any particular rule can be isolated and subjected not only to analysis but also to evaluation as a means to ends. A given rule may display the attribute of completeness, yet this very same rule may lack other formal attributes in significant measure, and thus be deficient in these respects. Or completeness may be significantly absent and the other formal attributes appropriately present.

Similarly, a rule may be good in that it is complete, yet the very substantive content of this entirely complete rule may itself be unjust or otherwise bad. Or the rule may be bad in that it is incomplete, yet good in substantive content so far as it goes. These truths also demonstrate the distinctness of the formal attribute of completeness.

Completeness as a desideratum influences the quantum of content in a rule. When the desideratum is realized, this necessarily manifests itself in content. Completeness as a desideratum contingently influences the quality of the content of a rule, too. A proposed complete rule can be more satisfactorily evaluated by law creators. It will also not escape them that, other things equal, a complete rule is desirable because it can always generate full fledged reasons for addressees to act on from inception, and so is likely to be more efficacious as a means to problem-specific policy goals and to various rule of law values. Good form tends to beget good content, and bad form, bad content.

B. Definiteness As a Distinct Formal Attribute of Rules

Definiteness may be defined as that degree of specificity and detail for the rule to be sufficiently determinate. Indefiniteness is a lack of sufficient determinateness in what is an otherwise "occupied", i.e., "complete", space in a rule. Thus, for example, spaces in a rule can be complete, as with a rule incorporating a broad grant of discretion although more determinate content would be feasible. Yet, such a rule, though complete, might lack definiteness — lack the specificity and detail in legal content required for the rule to be sufficiently determinate for purposes of guiding behavior. For example, the rule that"the park Superintendent may reasonably exclude objects from the park" would be relevantly complete yet lack definiteness, for park users could not tell from it what vehicles to leave at home.

How is definiteness distinct from the content of the rule and thus identifiable as a separate attribute of the rule apart from that content and apart from other formal attributes of the rule? Definiteness is not wholly distinct from the content of the rule. Definiteness must manifest itself in complementary content of the rule. But the attribute of definiteness in a rule is not to be *equated* with the content of the rule. The attribute of definiteness can be isolated and analyzed not only apart from other formal attributes manifest in the content of the rule, but also apart from the overall content of the rule. Two rules can be similarly definite, yet have very different content. The degree of specificity and detail in a rule — its degree of definiteness — can be isolated and analyzed on its own terms apart from the character of the subject-matter content of the rule.

Definiteness, then, is a distinct, isolatable, attribute of a legal rule. How is it formal? First, the shape or configuration of a rule pertains to its basic form and so is formal. The definiteness of a rule - its specificity and detail - is a matter of the shape and configuration of the rule, and therefore formal.

Second, the specificity and detail required for the definiteness of a rule do not prescribe or proscribe particular content, and may apply to and accommodate varied content. Again, two rules could be definite to the same degree yet have quite different content resolving the same problem in different ways.

Third, the difference between a formally definite rule at inception and an indefinite version of this same rule at inception is not merely that the definite version has a greater quantum of content, i.e., more specificity and detail in that content, but also that the rule is formally more definite.

Definiteness, then is a second basic formal attribute of a rule. Is it only occasionally an attribute of a rule, here and there? Or are rules typically more or less definite? All rules are in some degree definite. Many are definite to a considerable degree. Of course, some rules are much less definite than others. Others are not very definite. But even rules that confer broad discretion will commonly be definite in some important respects, e.g., specification of the party who is to exercise discretion. The commonly definite character of legal rules is not difficult to explain. If rules are to fulfill their function in social life, they must be more or less determinate.

Definiteness is not merely a descriptive formal attribute to be isolated and analyzed on its own terms, as above. It, too, is a normative desideratum. This is so because definiteness serves problem-specific policy goals and serves "rule of law" values such as certainty, predictability, citizen-choice and self-direction, dispute avoidance, equality before the law, and restriction of official arbitrariness. Without definiteness, a rule cannot itself generate reasons for action that are sufficiently determinate. Also, it is hard for legislators to vote on an indefinite law. Thus definiteness, too, implicates the value of deliberative rationality.

It follows that definiteness can be isolated and subjected not only to analysis but also to evaluation. Thus a rule may be evaluated as appropriately definite, yet this very same rule may lack sufficient degrees of other formal attributes such as generality. Or definiteness may be absent and other formal attributes present.

Similarly, a rule may be evaluated as good in its definiteness, yet the very same rule may be bad in overall content. For example, we might imagine a highly definite health care regulation providing that "All certified lawyers shall be entitled to advance to the head of the eligibility queue for kidney dialysis". Or a rule could even be bad in terms of its lack of definiteness yet be otherwise good in terms of content.

Definiteness as a desideratum influences the extent of specifity and detail in the content of a rule. The realization of this desideratum necessarily manifests itself in the content of the rule. Definiteness, as a desideratum, may influence the quality of the content of the rule, too. A proposed rule that is specific and detailed is more likely to be fully thought out. It can also be more satisfactorily evaluated and amended by the law creator than a rule that is abstract or imprecise. Further, a definite rule generates more determinate reasons for action at inception, and so is more likely to be effective as a means to policy ends.

C. Generality As a Distinct Formal Attribute of Rules

Generality is another attribute of rules. By generality, I mean the extent to which a law at inception applies by its terms to more than one instance within any of its dimensions. Thus, generality requires "class" terms or other similar language. Our illustrative statute: "Park users may not take vehicles into the park" is highly general. It applies not just to one park guest and not merely to automobiles. Indeed it applies to all park guests and to all vehicles. There are numerous possible dimensions in which a law might be general or might be particular, including: (1) addressees, (2) acts, relations, things, objects, (3) mental states of the actors, (4) places, circumstances, (5) times, occasions, and (6) effects and consequences. A rule might be general in some dimensions and entirely ungeneral in others. Thus the above statute might say that a named park user may not bring vehicles into the park. In this specific context, such a rule with only one addressee would, without more, be odd. Most often, such laws are relatively general. Generality differs from completeness. A law could be highly complete, yet not general at all. Consider, for example, a law that prohibits a named circus company from ever using a given park again within a particular city. Or, a law could be incomplete in some respects yet highly general. For example, the rule could fail to specify a mental state of the actor and thus be incomplete, yet still be highly general such as: "No vehicles in the park".

Generality differs from definiteness, too. A law could be highly definite and entirely lack generality: "George may not bring his black 1989 Rover sedan license, 072-681, into the park". Or a law could be highly general and lack definiteness. Consider a statute conferring wide discretion on all park superintendents and their deputies "to preserve peace and quiet in the park in any reasonable manner."

How is the generality of a rule distinct from its content and thus identifiable as a separate attribute of the rule? Generality is not wholly distinct from the substantive content of a rule. Generality must manifest itself in complementary content of the rule. In the example, "Park users may not take vehicles into the park," the two elements of generality, "park users" and "vehicles," are class terms in the content each expressing generality. Were they extracted from the rule, and singular terms substituted, this would dramatically alter content. On the other hand, generality is not to be *equated* with the substantive content of a rule. Any given rule can be analyzed for the degree of its generality. That is, generality can be isolated and analyzed as such, apart from other formal attributes, and also apart from the content of the rule as such. Two rules dealing with the same problem can be similarly general yet have quite different contents.

In what sense is generality formal? First, the shape or configuration of a rule pertains to its basic form, and so is formal. Second, generality does not itself prescribe or proscribe subject-matter content. It also applies to and accommodates highly varied content. The degree of generality of a rule can be held constant while differing versions of its content are incorporated. Third, while the degree of generality of a particular rule or other precept is always manifest in specific complementary content, this same degree of generality may be manifest in other rules of very different content. Rules can be usefully characterized and classified according to their levels of generality as well as according to their subject matter content.

Generality can be isolated and evaluated not merely as a descriptive attribute but as a desideratum as well. Generality is desirable because it serves problem specific policy goals. Generality also serves "rule of law" values. For example, without appropriate generality, like treatment of like cases is not possible. And more.

It follows that generality can be isolated and subjected not only to analysis but also evaluation as well. Thus a rule may be evaluated as appropriately general, yet it may lack other formal attributes. Or generality may be absent and other formal attributes present. Similarly a rule may be judged good in its generality but bad in some aspect of its content or vice versa. (These truths also further demonstrate the formalness of generality.)

Generality as a desideratum influences the extent to which a law at inception applies to more than one instance within any of its dimensions — addressees, their actions, the circumstances of actions, etc. Generality necessarily manifests itself in the problem-specific policy content of the rule. Generality as a desideratum contingently influences the quality of that content of a rule, as well. The intellectual discipline that the formal desideratum of appropriate generality imposes on law creators to justify including types of instances within, and also to justify excluding types of instances from, the scope of generality of the rule exerts special pressure for the drawing of *rational* distinctions in the content of the rule. Among other things, such "generality- driven" discipline requires the law creator to think through goals and available means, to bring standards of consistency to bear in light of actual and hypothetical cases of inclusion and exclusion, and to deploy reductio ad absurdum argumentation as appropriate.

Furthermore, although a highly particular rather than a more general rule may itself generate from inception a full fledged reason for the addressee to act in the circumstances, such a law might be more in the nature of an order rather than a rule. If the problem specific policy goal to be implemented is one that requires action (or inaction) by more than one similarly situated addressee in a range of circumstances, as is usually the case, generality of rule makes the law a far more efficacious means to such a goal. Appropriate generality may also be more likely to induce voluntary self-application, for an addressee will see that the law applies to parties similarly situated, and not merely to that addressee. Appropriate generality also saves administrative costs because a general rule can be applied by addressees on their own without the need for official intervention through issuance of official orders.

Again, good form — appropriate generality — tends to beget good content and bad form - no or inappropriate generality - tends to beget bad content. Indeed, form may affect content sweepingly, as where a court has a choice of adopting one of two approaches when creating a law and adopts the one more susceptible of formulation in a rule displaying completeness, definiteness, and generality. Even though the first approach might be substantively preferable in terms of policy implementation, the court may conclude that it is best to have a more formal rule and not risk, for example, leaving the law on a slippery slope, as the first approach might.

D. Simplicity As a Distinct Formal Attribute of Rules

Degree of simplicity or complexity is another attribute of rules. Indeed, simplicity may be defined as the absence of complication. It may also be defined in terms of non-reducibility into further elements. The law includes many simple rules as well as many complex ones. A given rule may be simple in one respect and complex in another. Or it may be simple in all respects or complex in all respects.

How is simplicity distinct from the content of a rule and thus identifiable as a separate attribute of the rule apart from the content of the rule and apart from other formal attributes of the rule? Simplicity is not wholly distinct from the content of a rule in which it inheres. Simplicity must manifest itself in complementary content of the rule. But the attribute of simplicity is not to be *equated* with the overall content of the rule. The attribute of simplicity can be isolated and analyzed not only apart from other formal attributes manifest in the content of the rule, but also apart from the nature of the substantive content of the rule as such. The uncomplicated and non-reducible character of a rule — its degree of simplicity — can be isolated and analyzed on its own terms apart from the subject matter content of the rule.

The attribute of simplicity also differs from completeness, definiteness, and generality. A rule can have all of these attributes yet lack simplicity, and vice versa.

Simplicity, then, is a distinct, isolatable, attribute of a legal rule. How is it formal? First, the shape, configuration and internal structure of a rule are matters of its form rather than its subject matter content. The uncomplicated and non-reducible character of a rule - its simplicity - pertains to its shape, configuration, and internal structure, and is therefore formal. Second, the uncomplicated and non-reducible character of a rule, i.e., its simplicity, neither prescribes nor proscribes particular content but may apply to and accommodate varied content. Thus, two rules could display the same degree of simplicity yet have quite different content resolving the same problem differently.

Simplicity is not merely a descriptive formal attribute of rules to be isolated and analyzed on its own terms, as above. It, too is a normative desideratum. This is so because simplicity serves problem-specific policy goals. For example, a simple law can be readily learned and voluntarily applied by its addressees, thereby furthering the relevant problem specific goals of policy. But simplicity also serves other values. Because it is less difficult and costly to learn, it facilitates citizen self direction. It reduces mistakes in legal analysis, and it facilitates ease of administration. It serves dispute avoidance. Also, legislators and other law makers can evaluate proposed simple laws more effectively. This, in turn, serves the end of rational legislative deliberation. And more.

It follows that simplicity can be isolated and subjected not only to analysis but also to evaluation as a means to ends. Thus a rule may be evaluated as appropriately simple, yet this rule may lack sufficient degrees of one or more other formal attributes. Or simplicity may be lacking while other attributes are present. Indeed, a rule can be highly complete, highly definite, highly general, and yet lack simplicity. Similarly, a rule may be evaluated as good in terms of its simplicity, yet the very same rule may be bad in its subject matter content.

Simplicity as a desideratum influences the extent to which the rule is free of complication. Among other things, this means the rule when first proposed can be readily subjected to evaluation by legislators, administrators, and citizens. If it survives such processes of evaluation at all, it is more likely to emerge duly amended and improved.

E. Other Formal Attributes of Rules

Completeness, definiteness, generality, and simplicity are not the only formal attributes of legal rules. Justified fiat is another formal attribute, although it may be subsumed under definiteness. The "encapsulatory" form of rules, i.e., whether embodied in statute, common law, etc. is another such attribute. So, too, the expressional form of a rule. Important questions arise about the appropriate relation between the formal attributes within a given rule, and about the appropriate relation between that part of the content of the rule informed by such attributes and "rule of law" values, and that part of the content of the rule informed by problem specific policy. The optimal formality of a specific rule is also an important question, and may involve trade-offs between "rule of law" values and problem-specific policy.

Notes
*. See R.S. Summers, *The Formal Character of Law*, CAMBRIDGE LAW JOURNAL, 51, 1992, p. 242; and R.S. Summers, *Der formale Charakter des Rechts II,* ARCHIV FÜR RECHTS UND SOZIALPHILOSOPHIE, 80, 1994, p. 60. See also Chapters Five, Six and Seven of this book. See also the next chapter in this book.

Part Three

Legal Reasoning

CHAPTER 9

INTERPRETING STATUTES AND PRECEDENTS — TWO COMPARATIVE STUDIES

I. Introduction

The creation and application of law are major realms of practical reason. In the application of a statute, it is usually necessary to interpret the statute. Indeed, in most Western systems, statutory interpretation is the single most prominent form of practical legal reasoning. In several of these systems, the interpretation of precedent is also a major form of practical legal reasoning.

The Comparative Statutory Interpretation Project was established in Helsinki in 1983 during the IVR World Congress hosted by Prof. Aulis Aarnio and his Finnish colleagues. The group that gathered there for the first meeting of this Project consisted of legal theorists interested mainly in the theory of statutory interpretation as a branch of practical reasoning. After the Project existed for several years, the Center for Interdisciplinary Research at the University of Bielefeld became an official sponsor. From 1983, the group met successively in Helsinki (1983), Lund (1983), Bologna (1984), Athens (1985), Edinburgh (1986), Bielefeld (1988), Tampere (1988), Edinburgh (1989), Bielefeld (1989), and Bielefeld (1990).

The Project was chaired by Robert S. Summers, with Professor D. Neil MacCormick as co-chair. All in all, nine disparate legal systems were represented in this Project — common law, civil law, and mixed. The systems included East and West European, North and South American.

The basic method of operation of the Project was as follows. A set of common questions (with guidelines for preparation of answers) was drafted, and all members thereafter prepared drafts and redrafts of answers. Most of the main questions were addressed to interpretational practices of the higher courts of each country and set forth in the published opinions of those courts. The answers were discussed at our annual meetings, and minutes of these meetings along with agendas for future meetings were circulated. (In the later years, an Agenda Committee met and prepared a detailed agenda for each meeting.) Over the years, the common questions, guidelines for answers, and the draft answers underwent numerous revisions. At the final meeting of the statutory interpretation project in Bielefeld in 1990, draft outlines of two general papers, one comparative, and one justificatory, were discussed at length.

Various interdisciplinary advisors met with the group over the years, in Bielefeld and also in Edinburgh. One advisor, Dr. Geoffrey Marshall of the Queens College, Oxford, participated in the last four meetings of the group. Other advisors were Professor John Bell of Leeds University; Professor Konrad Cramer of the University of Gottingen, Professor James Evans, University of Auckland; Professor Hubert Rotleuthner, Free University of Berlin; and Professor Jan Van Dunné, University of Rotterdam. In addition, Professors Ulrich Drobnig, Hein Kotz, and Kurt Siehr and Dr. H. Puttfarken, of the Max Planck Institute for Comparative Law in Hamburg, provided valuable advice in 1989, as did Prof. Dr. Dieter Grimm who was then a member of the board of directors of the Center for Interdisciplinary Research at the University of Bielefeld. Much valuable support was also provided by Dr. Gerhard Sprenger of the Center.

In the summer of 1991, the fruits of the Project appeared as a book: *Interpreting Statutes A Comparative Study*, edited by D. Neil MacCormick and Robert S. Summers. The book was published by Dartmouth Pub. Co. in England in the Applied Legal Philosophy series edited by Professor Tom Campbell of the Australian National University of Canberra. Not long before the manuscript of the book was finished, one of the most active members of the group, Jerzy Wroblewski, died. The book is dedicated to his memory. The entire group met again in July 1992 at Bielefeld at a symposium launching the book. On that occasion, several distinguished scholars and judges from several countries commented on its contents. These commentators included Mr. Justice Hans Linde of the Oregon Supreme Court, and Justice Dieter Grimm of Germany.

This Project was the first of its kind on statutory interpretation in the history of the subject. Obviously there are many things the group could have done but did not do in studying the subject. For example, the group did not compare actual interpretations of similar statutes in the different countries. The group did not ask selected judges from all the different countries to write an opinion interpreting the same statute (actual or hypothetical). Further, the group is aware that its own questions and guidelines, so central to the methodology, could have been improved still further. Even so, we believe our book manifests significant progress, and even helps to redefine the subject in fruitful ways. And, despite any mistakes of method or of substance that might have been made, we believe the book can be an important stimulus for much further research, non-comparative as well as comparative. Indeed, the book includes many ideas for further research, and much data for such research. In these respects, the book is also programmatic in nature.

II. Nature of the Comparative Work on Statutory Interpretation Co-Authored by Project Members

The table of contents is as follows:

I. Introduction
 Robert S . Summers, *Ithaca*

2. On Method and Methodology
 Zenon Bankowski, *Edinburgh, D.* Neil MacCormick, *Edinburgh,* Robert S. Summers, *Ithaca*, and Jerzy Wroblewski, *Lodz*

3. Statutory Interpretation in Argentina
 Enrique Zuleta-Pucciro, *Buenos Aires*

4. Statutory Interpretation in the Federal Republic of Germany
 Robert Alexy, *Kiel,* and Ralf Dreier, *Göttingen*

5. Statutory Interpretation in Finland
 Aulis Aarnio, *Helsinki*

6. Statutory Interpretation In France
 Michel Troper, Christophe Grzegorczyk, and Jean-Louis Gardies, *Paris*

7. Statutory Interpretation in Italy
   Massimo La Torre, *Bologna,* Enrich Pattaro, *Bologna* and Michele
   Taruffo, *Pavia*

8. Statutory Interpretation in Poland
   Jerzy Wroblewski, *Lodz*

9. Statutory Interpretation in Sweden
   Alekander Peczenik and Gunnar Bergholz, *Lund*

10. Statutory Interpretation in the United Kingdom
    Zenon Bankowski and D. Neil MacCormick, *Edinburgh*

11. Statutory Interpretation in the United States
    Robert S. Summers, *Ithaca*

12. Interpretation and Comparative Analysis
    Robert S. Summers, *Ithaca,* and Michele Taruffo, *Pavia*

13. Interpretation and Justification
    D. Neil MacCormick, *Edinburgh,* and Robert S.Summers, *Ithaca*

This book should be of interest to: legal and other academics who wish
to use it as a teaching tool in courses dealing heavily with statutory
interpretation; legal scholars, research assistants, and students working on
aspects of statutory interpretation in particular statutory fields, including the
EC; scholars in jurisprudence, legal philosophy, and comparative legal
studies; scholars in satellite fields such as linguistics, semantics,
communication theory, philosophy, and political theory; and, practicing
lawyers.

III.   Theses, Conceptual Frameworks, Findings and Insights in the Statutory Interpretation Book

What follows is a limited selection of features, with some commentary. Chapter 2 on the methodology of the project explains how the theory of rational reconstruction is applied in the book, and develops the well known distinction between a logic of discovery and a logic of justification in regard to statutory interpretation. The focus of the book is not on psychological processes of higher court judges but on their justificatory practices as manifest in opinions.

The nine "country by country" chapters include much information about, and analysis of, interpretation in the higher courts of the countries involved. This information and analysis in regard to each country is presented in accord with a single, relatively novel, conceptual framework common to all such chapters. Much of the material in these chapters is, because of limitations of space and time, not discussed further either in Chapter 12 (comparative) or in Chapter 13 (theoretical), yet comprises an addition to the international comparative law "database" and should be useful to comparativists and legal theorists in many countries.

A very wide variety of sources (origins) of issues of interpretation is common to all the countries. Moreover, most are linguistic in nature. That is, many issues of interpretation arise in all countries from such linguistic sources as ambiguity, vagueness, and ellipsis.

A central thesis is that the field of statutory interpretation as a branch of practical reason must be analyzed mainly in terms of the leading types of arguments that judges of the highest courts deploy in their opinions in support of their conclusions. These arguments include, for example, the arguments from the ordinary or the technical meanings of the words, the argument from that meaning which best harmonizes with the rest of the statute, the argument from that meaning which best serves the ultimate purpose of the statute, the "subjective" argument from legislative intention based on travaux preparatoires, the argument from "objective" legislative intention (including presumptions), the argument from precedent interpreting the statute, and the argument from substantive reasoning (principle or policy). A major feature of the conceptual framework of the book is that it introduces a relatively uniform set of concepts and terminology for identifying, individuating, describing, and naming the leading types of arguments that judges invoke. A further set of basic categories (familiar in Europe) is introduced under which the leading types of arguments are subsumed: linguistic, systematic, teleological, evaluative, and intentional.

A significant corollary thesis of the project is that each leading type of interpretive argument is susceptible of a relatively comprehensive and systematic analysis in terms of two sets of key questions which go far to redefine the whole subject of statutory interpretation. Both sets of questions are also of interest for future research on all the leading types of argument. The main questions in the first set are: (1) How are particular instances of a general type of interpretive argument conceived and constructed? (2) What elements, including facts, values, coherence factors, or still other content, does an instance of this type of argument contain when it is well constructed? What conditions must be met if such an instance is to be "available"? (3) What accounts for the justificatory force of an instance of this type of argument when it has such force? What value rationales account for recognition of this type of argument as justificatory in the interpretation of statutes? (4) What features would be present in the ideal model of an instance of such an argument having greatest overall force? (5) What factors weaken the force of such an argument? (6) What are the most significant criticisms that are made of such an argument when it is subjected to criticism? (7) How far, if at all, is the scope of this type of argument tied to or dependent upon the nature of the statute being interpreted (i.e. its age, specificity, subject-matter, whether it displaces common law or other prior law, whether there is an administrative agency with responsibility for administering the statute, whether the statute has been the subject of scholarly analysis and discussion, etc.)? Can it be said that this type of argument has an ideal context of use? If so, what are the features of this context? (8) What significant variations are there between systems in the answers to the above questions? A conceptual insight of major importance here appears in Chapter 13 with regard to the leading type of argument known as the argument from legislative intention. There the "transcategorical" nature of such arguments is identified and explained. Thus, at least those arguments from "subjective" intention based on travaux preparations may incorporate, as the object of the intention, the essence of any one of the other leading types of interpretative argument, e.g., intended ordinary or intended technical meaning (linguistic category), intended harmonization with the rest of the statute, intended statutory analogy, intended use of general principle prevalent in the area to qualify the language, (systemic category); intended ultimate purpose, intended substantive reasoning (teleological-evaluative category).

Again, a major feature of the work is its formulation of key questions that help to redefine the subject. Thus, especially in Chapters 12 and 13, but also in earlier chapters, a second basic set of questions emerges which provides a relatively comprehensive and systematic approach to the analysis of individual types of interpretive arguments (and instances thereof) not in isolation, but rather in relation to other types of interpretative arguments. Again, the book by no means addresses all individual types of argument in this relational, and thus comparative perspective, but it so addresses some, and, again, the questions are important for future research. This second basic set of questions is: (1) What constitutes a type of interpretive argument? A leading type? (2) How is each leading type to be conceptually and materially differentiated from any other type that by its nature seems quite similar? (For example, just how does the argument from ordinary meaning differ from the argument from ultimate purpose? How can purpose figure appropriately in the argument from ordinary meaning, yet an independent argument from ultimate purpose still remain viable?) (3) How frequently, compared to other leading arguments, is the type of argument under study in play or available? Does the argument require more, or less, by way of "materials" than other arguments? Are these materials regularly available? (4) Does this type of argument have any distinctive uses or limits, compared to others? For example, is the argument from statutory analogy excluded where the statute is penal? What variables influence and define the contexts of use of given types of arguments? (5)Is the type of argument fully autonomous? Does the argument tend to be found side by side in opinions with any other type of argument? Why? Can this type of argument significantly reinforce any other type of argument? (6) When this argument and any other arguments mutually reinforce each other, is the sum of the force of these arguments greater than the force these arguments would have when merely added together? (7) How decisive is this type of argument when in conflict with others? (8) When it is decisive, by what manner is it so? By outweighing? Cancellation? Over-riding? Is a priorital hierarchy recognized here? If so, how strong (or weak) is this ordering? How does context affect it? (9) What is the relative overall role of the argument within the system, considering the extent of its availability and its relative decisiveness, not only when in conflict alone with another argument, but also as a kind of "tie breaker"? (10) How is this overall role to be explained? (11) What does the argument have in common with any of the other types of arguments? For example, how far does it draw on the same values as others? How far is it criticized in the same fashion as others? (12) What significant variations are there between systems in the answers to the above questions? (It may be that some of the above "comparative" questions can be fruitfully approached only *within* a particular system, and not across systems.)

The work also suggests some further general questions that range across the whole field of types of interpretational arguments: (1) What further is to be learned by sub- classifying the various types of arguments under a much more limited set of general categories, e.g., linguistic, systemic, teleological-evaluative, intentional etc.? (2) Which of the types of arguments are relatively formal? Relatively substantive? In what sense or senses? What is the importance of this? (3) Which types of arguments are most likely to produce the same decisional outcomes under the same statute at the hands of different interpreters? Which are least likely? Why? (4) How far is it possible to construct general models of the best possible overall justifications for the resolution of relatively discrete and basic interpretational problems such as ambiguity, vagueness, ellipsis, overgenerality, undergenerality, gaps, conflicts between statutes, obsolescence, and legislative mistakes? (Of course, more than one type of interpretive argument figures in such models, and their manner of cumulation is important, too.) (5) How far can law govern the nature and force of interpretive arguments and the resolution of conflicts between them? How far *does* law govern them? (6) How far is interpretation a matter of factual inquiry and how far is it a matter of evaluation?

Chapter 12 advances a major thesis of the book, namely,'that all systems in the project share a common core of a dozen or more leading types of argument: These include all the types mentioned above. What is the significance of this commonality? Chapter 12 treats this and related questions, and suggests possible explanations for the commonality. Despite this commonality, the contexts of use of a given type of argument may vary significantly from system to system.

Chapter 13 sets forth several theses, including the thesis that three basic patterns of justification appear in the opinions of the highest courts of each country. In the simplest pattern, one type of argument dominates, and this is usually the argument from ordinary, or the argument from technical meaning, or some version of the argument from harmonization with the rest of the statute supporting an ordinary, technical, or special meaning. Two other patterns are more complex. In the first, one or more arguments appears in order to add to or reinforce the argument from the ordinary, or the argument from a technical, meaning. Often, the harmonization argument appears in this role. So, too, in a few systems, does some version of the argument from "subjective" intention deriving from travaux preparatoires. In the second more complex pattern, there is no viable linguistic argument, and various other arguments appear in its place to clarify or specify an appropriate meaning. The chapter contributes an important distinction between arguments that merely coincide, and arguments that cumulate in a mutually reinforcing way so that the overall force of cumulated arguments exceeds what their sum would be considered merely "additively".

In Chapters 12 and 13, there is special focus on how conflicts between interpretive arguments are resolved. A novel and important thesis of the book is that the modes of resolution here are not all reducible to "weighing and balancing." Instead, judges also resolve some conflicts by invoking "maxims" of priority, or by invoking arguments that "cancel" or nullify or sap the force of the competing argument. This whole topic has been seriously neglected in the history of the subject, and requires much further conceptual and empirical labor. In no legal system in the study have the highest courts, in justifying their decisions, clearly articulated in general terms how they resolve conflicts between arguments. The book, in Chapter 13, argues for a reflective equilibrium with respect to the deeper values that underlie the conflicting arguments.

In Chapter 12, several of the significant variations between systems in judicial resort to forms of argument and patterns of justification are identified. Comparativists and others will be interested that very few of these variations track the traditional common law versus civil law divide. Sometimes the book hypothesizes explanations for the variations, with some supporting argument. Such explanations are usually cast in terms of further (and often major) differences of political theory, of judicial role, of institutional structure, of legal culture, and of personnel and methods of staffing courts in the various countries. The well known English position limiting (as of that time) the use of travaux preparatoires was discussed here, too, and institutional explanations offered. So, too, the relatively more common resort of American judges to the argument from substantive reasons.

Chapter 12 also reveals major differences in the justificatory logic, structure, and style of judicial opinions in the higher courts. For example, in most systems in the study, the court commonly *presents* its interpretive conclusion as a kind of deductive consequence logically following from given premises (often expressed in technical language). On the other hand, in a few of the other systems, the interpretative conclusion is generally presented as the outcome of an openly acknowledged choice made in light of openly acknowledged conflicting arguments, and the opinions are discursive, and lengthy. In most systems, the court's majority opinion frequently does not include any reference to the arguments that failed to prevail. In some of these systems there are no dissents. In other systems, the losing arguments are at least mentioned, and dissents are not uncommon in a few systems.

Further, in most systems in the study, the style of the court's opinion is magisterial and authoritative. That is, the opinion is presented as a kind of imperial, "Staatsakt." In a few other systems, the style is more personal, more argumentative, and much more dialogic. Indeed, in these systems, the opinion can often be read as attempting to answer arguments of a dissenter, or of losing counsel, or of a lower court judge, or some combination. Chapter 12 also analyzes traits of logic, structure, and style along a continuum with the brief and highly logical form prevalent in the French system at one polarity and the more discursive American system at the other. This analytical device casts light in a variety of ways, and a major finding emerges. That is, the French case appears to represent a 'pure' polarity that is today alone in the European panorama. While the other systems might be plotted as 'intermediate' cases between France and the USA, most of which are not merely 'scattered' between France and the USA. Indeed such systems as Italy, West Germany and perhaps Poland and even Finland reveal a clear *tendency* to what might be called a 'third style' or 'model', in which: (1) the evaluative and creative element in interpretation is generally not openly recognized (as it is not in France), but the judges are aware that they create law; (2) a high proportion of technical language appears (as in France); (3) complex patterns of argument appear (as in USA); (4) the opinions are extended and elaborate (as in USA); (5) a high proportion of formal reasons appears (as in France); (6) the magisterial style is adopted (as in France); and (7) substantive constitutional principles play a major role directly or indirectly, in numerous interpretation cases (as in USA).

In the systems that typify the emergent third style or model, the higher courts are relatively passive, yet heavily involved in interpretive problems. It may be that these courts are revealing a deeper sensitivity to the social and political problems involved in the administration of justice. Although creative choice is generally not openly recognized, there are major exceptions. Most of these courts confront gaps directly, and recognize that statutes and codes may, because of age, require updating. Yet these courts am not nearly so 'free-wheeling' as many American Supreme Court judges have, until quite recently, seemed to be. Rather, these courts try to solve interpretive problems by resort to legal sources rather than "policy". They use tools of classical positivistic legal culture, especially linguistic and systematic argumentation, and also appeal to deductive methods as well as authoritative purposes and legal dogmatics. This third model or style emerging in the European panorama differs significantly from both the French style and the US style, and merits further analysis and exploration. Chapter 12 also offers rational speculation by way of explanation for such differences of logic, structure, and style in opinion writing.

Chapter 13 treats some broad normative questions. It considers what values underpin and account for the justificatory force of basic categories of argument type: linguistic, systemic, teleological-evaluative, and intentional. The thesis is advanced that each basic category systematically implicates (relatively distinctively) various values generally appropriate to interpretation (as contrasted with whatever problem-specific values may be implicated in the statute itself). Throughout the book, distinctions are drawn for evaluative purposes between fundamentally different objects of critical analysis within the subject, including: (1) argument types, (2) instances of argument types, (3) categories of argument types (e.g. linguistic, systemic, teleological, etc.), (4) deployments of arguments in patterns, (5) resolution of conflicts between arguments, and (6) the logic, structure, and style of opinions. Chapters 12 and 13, and Chapter One, raise the most basic normative question: What would an ideal system of justificatory practices look like? How might one, in these terms, differentiate between a system that, overall, approximates to the ideal and one that falls short? The beginnings of an answer appear in the book: An interpretational approach may be more advanced because free of false theories about how language works, or more sophisticated about meaning and legislative intent, more subtle in regard to contextual meaning, more analytical in regard to statutory argument generally, more adroit or wide ranging with what are classified as systemic arguments, more sensitive to the need for reflective equilibrium with respect to resolution of the deeper value conflicts between arguments, more careful in handling the various types of materials relevant to the construction of reasons, more realistic and candid in recognizing issues and disclosing reasons for decision, more comprehensive in making available within the opinion itself all resources necessary for the reader to make an independent judgment about the quality of the justification for the decision.

IV. A Comparative Study of Precedent

Precedent is a major form of law recognized especially in the United States, in Great Britain, and in one way or another, in legal systems of western Europe. While there are major similarities here, there are also major differences in how these systems deal with precedent. Just what these similarities and differences are, how they might be explained, and what general jurisprudential and practical insights their systematic study might yield were the main subjects of a further five year joint research project of the group that had first studied statutory interpretation. The group came to be called the "Bielefelder Kreis" because its work was sponsored off and on over many years by the Center for Interdisciplinary Studies at the University of

Bielefeld in Germany.

As we have seen, after nine years, the group published a book in 1991 comparing the interpretation of statutes in nine countries: *Interpreting Statutes - A Comparative Study.* In May of 1997, the group published a companion volume comparing precedent in ten countries called: *Interpreting Precedents - A Comparative Study.* This volume is also published by Dartmouth Publishing Co., publisher of the first book. The second book likewise seeks to advance understanding of the fundamentals of law and its methodology through systematic comparative and theoretical analysis. Each member of the group shared the view that such analysis also contributes distinctively to one's understanding of one's own system. Indeed, it is simply not possible to understand one's own system fully unless and until one sees that system compared and contrasted in its major facets with functional equivalents in other systems.

The main modes of operation of the research group have been sixfold from the beginning: (1) the formulation of agreed sets of common questions (thus cast in common concepts and terminology) to be answered for each country, with the questions printed as appendices to the volumes, (2) the preparation by members from each country of a draft essay for that country addressing the common questions, (3) extensive discussions at annual sessions of draft answers and also of the common questions, with agreed revisions of both, (4) the assignment and preparation of draft special essays on common topics based on (1), (2) and (3), (5) extensive group discussions of the draft special essays on the common topics, and (6) thorough review and editing of the final research effort by the same co-editors of both volumes, Professors MacCormick and Summers. For each annual sessions, all of which lasted several days, a set of minutes was prepared recording essential understandings and agreed further steps. There have been some differences of emphasis in approach and methodology for the two projects, and these are identified and briefly discussed in the introduction to the second volume.

The participants met on the precedent project in June 1992 at the Center for Interdisciplinary Studies at the University of Bielefeld, in May 1993 at the Cornell Law School, in June 1994 at Bologna and Florence, in June 1995 at Bologna, and in August 1996 at Tampere, Finland. After the conference in

Tampere, the co-editors met in Ithaca, New York and edited the material for publication. The entire group met again at Bielefeld in July of 1997 at a symposium launching the book. Various scholars from other disciplines commented on the book at this symposium. The table of contents reveals the legal systems treated, and the participants:

1. Introduction, D. Neil MacCormick, *Edinburgh* and Robert S. Summers, *Ithaca*

2. Precedent in Germany. Robert Alexy, *Kiel* and Ralph Dreier, *Göttingen*

3. Precedent in Finland. Aulis Aarnio, *Tampere*

4. Precedent in France. Michel Troper, *Paris,* Christophe Grzegorczyk, *Paris*

5. Precedent in Italy. Massimo LaTorre, *Bologna* and Michele Taruffo, *Pavia*

6. Precedent in Norway. Svein Eng, *Oslo*

7. Precedent in Poland. Lech Morawski, *Torun* and Marek Zirk-Sadowski, *Lodz*

8. Precedent in Spain. Francisco J. Laporta, *Madrid* and Alfonso Ruiz Miguel, *Madrid*

9. Precedent in Sweden. Gunnar Bergholtz, *Lund* and Aleksander Peczenick, *Lund*

10. Precedent in the United Kingdom. Zenon Bankowski, *Edinburgh,* and D. Neil MacCormick, *Edinburgh*

11. Precedent in the United States. Robert S. Summers, *Ithaca*

12. Precedent in European Community Law. John J. Barcelo, *Ithaca*

13. Institutional Factors Influencing Precedents. Michele Taruffo, *Pavia*

14. The Binding Force of Precedent. Aleksander Peczenick, *Lund*

15. Rationales for Precedent. Zenon Bankowski, *Edinburgh*, D. Neil MacCormick, *Edinburgh*, Lech Morawski, *Torun*, and Alfonso Ruiz Miguel, *Madrid*

16. What is Binding in a Precedent. Geoffrey Marshall, *Oxford*

17. Departures from Precedent. Svein Eng, *Oslo* and Robert S. Summers, *Ithaca*

18. Further General Reflections and Conclusions. D. Neil MacCormack, *Edinburgh* and Robert S. Summers, *Ithaca*

The book should be of interest to (1) legal and other academics who wish to use it as a teaching tool in courses dealing heavily with precedent, (2) legal scholars, research assistants, and students working on aspects of precedent in particular fields, including the European Community, (3) scholars in jurisprudence, legal philosophy, and comparative legal studies, (4) scholars in satellite fields such as political theory, government, and philosophy, and (5) practicing lawyers.

V. Thesis, Conceptual Frameworks, Findings and Insights in the Work on Precedent

The book provides informative material about precedent in each of the ten countries. This material is presented for each country pursuant to the set of common questions, and pursuant to a common format and common framework of concepts and terminology. Thus, one may go to this book to find out about the general workings of precedent in any one of the ten countries without pursuing any of the comparative and theoretical analysis elsewhere in the book.

Those concerned with the comparative and theoretical elements of the work will be especially interested in the accounts of major similarities and differences that appear in Chapter 18. There are two major similarities. First, precedent now plays a significant part in legal decision-making and in the development of law in all the countries and legal traditions that we have studied. Of course, this has long been so in the common law countries in our study. But it is now true in the civil law countries, including the mixed systems of Scandinavia. It is true that most civil law countries, precedent is not recognized as formally binding in the common law sense that failure to follow precedent is treated as an error of law that, if prejudicial, will lead to reversal of the court below. But precedent is recognized in all countries as having general normative force of some degree, and frequently this is quite high. In most countries, departures from settled precedent are taken seriously, are subjected to criticism, and may even be reversed by a higher court in some instances. Even in France where most courts at the highest levels do not even cite precedent in their decisions, precedent in fact has normative force and often plays a crucial role. The present day law in France would be incomprehensible without reference to the precedents of higher courts. For example, nearly all of the French law of tort is judge-made. So is French administrative law. Even though the relevant precedents are not usually cited in the highest courts, the French judges are, in the usual case, attempting to follow settled precedents, and judges who fail to follow them will be subjected to criticism by other judges, by scholars, and by practitioners. In most other non-common law countries in this study, precedent is frequently accepted - even called for - in legal argumentation as essential to making a satisfactory case.

Thus the frequent caricatures of civil law judges as entirely free from the shackles of precedent while the common law judges are enslaved to their own past (or engaged in 'preserving the good old order') are not even remotely accurate today, if they ever were. There is today no sharp dichotomy here, but a continuum along which the systems are converging, though, of course, not all at the same pace. It is not merely that common law countries recognize precedent as formally binding so that departures constitute errors of law subject to reversal, whereas civil law countries generally recognize precedent as having normative force such that decisions in disregard of settled precedent are subject to stringent criticism which may in turn lead to reversals in some cases. Common law countries also recognize as fully as civil law countries that there may be gradations of normative force, from the mildly persuasive upwards. Indeed, in common law countries, among the highest degrees of normative force short of formal bindingness itself is that degree of force that the highest common law courts recognize when they follow their own precedents even though such precedents are not formally binding (by our definition) because not subject to reversal, there being no higher court of appeal.

The second major similarity between common law and civil law systems is that all these systems accommodate justified legal change and evolution through judicial, as well as legislative, action. Thus, both common law and civil law practice admit of justified departures from precedent thereby setting new precedent, though this generally tends to be conducted more openly in common law systems than in most civil law ones. In addition to departures, genuine cases of first impression arise in both types of system, with decisions therein frequently setting important precedents, though again common law courts tend to acknowledge this more openly. Despite the two major convergences just discussed, there remain several important differences between common law and civil law countries in their treatment of precedent, as revealed in our study. First, most officially published opinions of the highest courts (constitutional courts aside) in most civil law countries do not include what common law observers would consider a detailed statement of the facts of the cases being decided, although such may often be available either on request from the deciding court or from other sources. Also, robust substantive appeals to policy are much less common in civil law opinions than in certain common law systems. These factors plainly affect the materials available in future cases for arguments based on precedent.

Furthermore, in civil law systems, in most fields, precedents are generally conceived as loci of relatively abstract rules or principles interpreting a general code or a statute, whereas in common law systems precedent is often restricted to a specific ruling on a legal issue in light of the material facts of the case. Such restriction almost necessarily occurs in common law fields but even when the primary source of law may be said to be code or statute, the material facts of the case play a large role in determinations of the scope of any holding. In the civilian methodology, there is no general tradition of systematic differentiation between holding and dictum, and this is true even in fields not closely controlled by code or statute. In addition, no sophisticated methodology of distinguishing precedents on their facts has developed in any civil law country (again, constitutional cases aside), yet distinguishing has long been something of a high art in common law systems.

Another difference is that in nearly all civil law countries, a single precedent is generally not, on its own, sufficient to count as authoritatively settling a point of law (again, constitutional cases aside). A further, and from the common law perspective, quite radical difference, is that lower courts, including trial courts of general jurisdiction, in several civil law countries have power, for stated reasons, to decline to follow an upper court line of precedents. Of course, they are often reversed, but the practice in itself is accepted partly on the theory that the lower court might in fact have the better interpretation or an otherwise better justified position.

Then, too, in about half of the civil law systems in our study, the higher and highest courts consciously, and more than just occasionally, depart from precedent without even mentioning this fact. Certainly departures come more easily to judges if they need not depart overtly and need not explicitly justify departures. And departures no doubt come more easily to courts which view themselves, in the main, as concerned to interpret a code as the formal source of law, so that every case is ultimately to be referred back to an undefiled code text.

Finally, in at least half of the civil law countries precedent in the higher courts is often treated as applicable without specific citation, let alone specific argumentation to that effect. And lower courts often follow precedent without any explicit reference to the precedent.

Many of the foregoing features in civil law systems seem symptomatic of a conception of precedent that deems it something other than, or less than, a full-dress formal source of law. Even so, it is by no means clear that all the foregoing major differences between common and civil law treatment of precedent add up to major differences in the actual results concretely adjudicated. As often in comparative studies, there may here be substantial equivalence in results despite considerable differences in the forms in which law and legal reasoning are presented.

In addition to the similarities and differences between systems, and the general light these cast, the work in a series of topical chapters treats the following themes: how the use of precedent varies from system to system in accord with differences in institutional factors such as court hierarchies, number of judges in the higher courts, and style and content of reporting of decisions (ch.13); how the normative force and effects of precedent in the various systems varies along a continuum and so is a matter of degree that varies in accord with several factors (ch. 14); what rationales for reliance on precedent are recognized and the bearing these may have from system to system (ch. 15); what is treated as binding within a precedent, and how this varies from system to system (ch. 16); how departures from precedent occur from system to system and at what levels (ch. 17); various reflections on and criticism of practice in relation to precedent, with proposals for reform (part of ch. 18).

The study of precedent has also generated considerable reflection on the formal features - structural and processual, required for an effective precedent system, overall. Nearly all participants in the project agree, for example, that precedent systems work better when opinions include statements of facts, when the higher level courts have relatively few judges (rather than the dozens to be found in some systems), and when appeals are restricted to a manageable number. These and related matters of reform are treated throughout the book, and especially in chapters 1, 13, 16 and 18.

Further, the co-authors treat various implications of their study of precedent for issues of legal theory. These were considered in the final conference on precedent in Finland in 1996, and prepared in final form by the co-editors, and are discussed in chapter 18. This study has important implications for (1) what one may call voluntaristic theories of law — theories of legal validity that treat valid law merely as something laid down, (2) for the doctrine of the sources of valid law, and (3) for the construction of adequate concepts for the representation of characteristics of modern legal systems.

First, this study demonstrates and so further confirms a general truth that some would claim is already implicit in the legal cultures of the common law, namely the conceptual inadequacy of narrowly voluntarist theories of the nature of law (among these, we might include the theories of Jeremy Bentham and the later Hans Kelsen). Such theories conceive of laws merely as the contents of discrete acts of will on the part of authorized officials occurring at particular moments of time (except for the case of custom, which differs in several ways). For these voluntarist theories, the paradigmatic forms of law are statutes, administrative regulations, and official decrees.

Precedents are not like these, though they do depend on judicial decisions issued in final form at discrete moments. Decisions, even judicial decisions, in their particular, individual person-addressing character are, however, not, as such, general or universal. But when a decision is conceived as a precedent, it is general or universal because it is the justifying opinion of the judge or court, not the bare act of deciding, that really counts. Decisions can be precedents only to the extent that they are conceived to rest upon justifying grounds; for these justifying grounds, according to a model of rational and discursive justification, cannot be confined to the single case. They must be available for like application in like cases, whether by some simply intuitive leap of analogical reasoning or (more plausibly) by a more reflective process that universalizes justifying grounds and tests them against similar facts in later cases.

So even with the single case, it is those features of decision-making other than the particularly volitional, namely the rationally deliberative and discursive features, that account for the exemplary character of the case *qua* precedent. This is all the plainer when several precedents accumulate, for what they together come to mean for new cases is a matter of reasoned analysis and synthesis that is quite at odds with 'act of will' theory. Again, when we consider the precedent or line of precedents in the broader context of a legal system comprising statutes, constitution, and accumulations of interpretations of these, making sense of what lies before us on an assumption of rational legal order requires an assessment of more or less coherent ways of conceptualizing the whole matter. This is not a process of voluntaristic free choice, thus of volition; but it is by no means a process of arbitrary decision, either. Thus the law becomes something that takes on a force of its own, and over time becomes something that is not so much 'laid down' from above as something that 'grows up'. Indeed, it emerges from a great patchwork of choices articulated through many deliberations and discourses, and is rethought at each time of its application, in however partial a way.

Secondly, few distinctions have played as prominent a role in legal theory as the distinction between valid and invalid law. This distinction is at home in relation to certain kinds of procedurally formal acts — legislation, subordinate legislation, issuing court orders, and executing private deeds and instruments. That law in its contemporary forms within states and multistate unions essentially includes such acts and the norms that issue from them is both true, and a fundamentally important feature of the legal scene. The voluntaristic fallacy is that which treats such norms as characteristic and thus as the exclusive body of valid law. Systems of law in which precedent plays a considerable part, that is, all the systems here studied, and all the other like systems of the present day, reveal the fallacy. Precedents do not have validity in the all-or-nothing way characteristic of acts performed under requirements of procedural formality. The validity, it might be better to say the 'soundness', indeed, the 'bindingness', or 'force' of precedent is not an all or nothing matter. This is a truth already understood in some quarters within common law systems, but the partial convergence of civil law systems recounted here requires us to face up to it frontally.

To begin with, in mature systems in which common law is recognized as valid, there are some discrete acts by judges handing down opinions which do not ever yield anything in the way of settled law, and so never achieve any validity beyond the binding effect of the concrete decision on the parties immediately affected. To become *settled law* at all, and so valid law in general, precedents in many such common law fields must at least pass a minimum threshold test both of substantive acceptability and of reasonable coherence with the pre-established legal context. If a precedent does not do this, it is likely to sink out of sight. That is, it will be ignored, 'confined to its facts', distinguished away on formal grounds, or eventually over-ruled if not simply permitted to wither away in unsung obscurity.

It is not possible to specify in the abstract just what the required threshold of substantive acceptability and coherence that any new precedent must meet to be valid law really is, and in any event, that threshold occupies a point or a series of points on a continuum, and may vary from field to field. It is not an all-or-nothing matter. It is not sharply 'on-off', as the valid-invalid distinction normally implies, if we insist on importing it misleadingly into this context. The farther from the threshold, the less normative weight a precedent carries, the nearer to the threshold, or the farther over it, the more. (Alternatively, we may, of course, reconstruct the concept of validity to make it a matter of 'more or less'.)

The continuum of degrees of normative force discussed and applied throughout the work on precedent lies outside the all-or-nothing conception of the dichotomous valid-invalid distinction. Precedent is formally, even if sometimes defeasibly or outweighably, binding, or at least has some persuasive normative force, in all systems covered by this study. Propositions of law formulated on the authority of such precedents hence have a provisional, a tentative, and a defeasible quality, and they may have to be weighed against, or adjusted in the light of, other propositions similarly founded. If we call them valid in the wider sense, we acknowledge them as valid provisionally, only insofar as certain circumstances hold, for a time, and not if confronted with better derived or farther over-threshold propositions.

Third, H. L. A. Hart and others have described one traditional task of legal theory as that of providing adequate concepts for the representation of general features characteristic of law in modern systems. We believe that the critical points we have made here about the concepts 'act of will' and 'valid-invalid' are in this spirit. But there is more to be said in this spirit which also draws on the fruits of our common research. We believe, that, for example, the very concept of bindingness as a continuum rather than as a dichotomy that we deploy here, and in our questions, is an advance because it enables us to capture the true normative-cum-valuational reality of the practices of following precedent in the various countries. Further, by introducing and systematically deploying the concept of departures from precedent, this project has been able to focus analysis and evaluation on an important element in rational legal deliberation and discourse variously exemplified in many systems.

We have also been forced to re-think a further concept which recurs throughout this book, and in much legal thought, namely that of a 'source of law'. We have variously stated and implied that it is an important difference between legal systems whether precedent is a 'formal source of law' or not. In terms of the self-characterization of legal systems, achieved under dominant paradigms of legal thought, this is quite accurate and unobjectionable. Common law systems do differ from the systems of codified law in what they characterize as their own 'formal sources'. However, once we draw clear attention to the difference between procedurally formal norm-creating acts, which do admit of all-or-nothing validity, as with statutes, and discursive or deliberative procedures of elaborating legal justifying grounds for decisions and the like, as with precedents, and once we ascribe legal normative force to a greater or lesser degree to the importantly varying products of this process, we see that there is a hopeless ambiguity in applying the term 'source' to both these cases. At that rate, we should 'side' with the civilian approach which refuses to classify precedent as a 'formal source'; but we should also 'side' with the common law in holding that, nevertheless, the propositions that are elaborated in this process have a genuinely legal quality, though having more or less soundness, greater or less weight.

CHAPTER 10

THE ARGUMENT FROM ORDINARY MEANING IN STATUTORY INTERPRETATION

I. Introduction

The subject of statutory interpretation is as old as written law, yet it is by no means fully understood. The subject is also one in which legal theory and legal practice intersect at many points. One branch of the subject takes the form of an inventory and analysis of the nature and limits of leading types of interpretive arguments. This is the branch we will explore now. But within that branch, we will concentrate on only one leading type of argument in the field, namely, the argument from ordinary meaning. This has for a long while been the leading type of interpretive argument in Britain,[1] and there are recent signs in the United States, especially in the Supreme Court,[2] that the argument from ordinary meaning is now coming more into favour.

British judges generally deploy the argument from ordinary meaning rather well. But if that be so then what is the problem? If the argument from ordinary meaning is essentially alive and well in the United Kingdom, then why go on about it? There are several answers. First, it is possible to perform a practice well without being able to provide an adequate second-order account of that practice. For example, it is familiar that a person may be able to give good directions on how to get around in a town, but not be able to draw a map of it.[3] We believe something like this is true of statutory interpretation, and especially of the argument from ordinary meaning. Many judges, practitioners and even academics are good at the argument, yet are not notably articulate when it comes to expounding its nature, force and limits. Academics of all people should be content with achieving understanding here for its own sake. But in practical affairs, too, it is not merely important to be good at deploying an argument; it is also important to be able to give a satisfactory account of what is involved. Even if judges and practitioners often get an argument right, it does not follow that they always get it right. And even if they always get it right, it does not follow that they always deploy it efficiently. Map in hand, they might find their way better.

There is a further reason to try to deepen our understanding of the argument from ordinary meaning. Judges, practitioners, and academics in the United Kingdom have been hearing recommendations[4] from Europe and the European Community,[5] and earlier on from the United States, that they would do well to abandon the argument from ordinary meaning, and instead take up in its place as the primary mode of interpretive argument, what Europeans call "teleological interpretation"[6] and what some academics in the United States call "purposive interpretation" or what we will here call the argument from ultimate statutory purpose.[7] We think it fortunate that these recommendations have so far not been adopted. Our view is that judges in the United Kingdom should generally keep on doing what they have been doing, namely, interpreting statutes where possible primarily, in accord with their ordinary meaning. (We therefore also applaud the recent trend in this direction in the Supreme Court of the United States.) But to see precisely why Judges and lawyers should keep on doing what they have been doing rather than go in for teleology and purpose, we need a better understanding of the argument from ordinary meaning, of how it differs from the argument from ultimate purpose and of why it, rather than the argument from ultimate purpose, should have primacy.

We will proceed as follows. In the first part of this essay, we seek to advance understanding of the argument from ordinary meaning by rebutting several forms of skepticism about it. This exercise in rebuttal comprises the major part of the essay. and it will be seen that we have no new discoveries of fact or results of legal research to reveal here. Instead, we will for the most part merely assemble reminders of the familiar and suggest an approach for organizing a coherent general view. In the middle part of the essay, we take up and rebut contentions of those who advocate the primacy of teleological and ultimate purpose argumentation. In the final part, we return to the foundations of the argument from ordinary meaning and show that it is an autonomous type of argument the force of which is not derived from any concurrently applicable argument from ultimate purpose.

II. Skepticism about the Argument from Ordinary Meaning

A. Preliminary clarifications

The argument from ordinary meaning may be defined as the argument from that meaning which a competent, knowledgeable, purposeful and informed user of ordinary language would give to the ordinary words of the statute in issue on the basis of what we will call the resources of ordinary language argumentation. Thus, the argument from ordinary meaning is not equivalent to whatever argument happens to support an ordinary meaning as the interpretation of the statute. Other leading types of argument may support an ordinary meaning as the appropriate statutory meaning, yet not qualify as arguments from ordinary meaning because they do not essentially invoke the resources of ordinary language argumentation. For example, the argument from ultimate purpose or the argument from that meaning which best harmonizes with other sections of the statute may happen to support an ordinary meaning in a particular case, yet these arguments do not appeal essentially to the resources of ordinary language.

We also differentiate ordinary meaning from literal meaning. In discussing the interpretation of laws, Blackstone mentions a case put by Cicero.[8] A "salvage" law prescribed that those who in a storm forsook a ship should forfeit all property in it and the ship should belong entirely to those who "stayed" with it. One such passenger, who was by reason of illness unable to escape with the rest, claimed the ship after it by chance came safely to port. Literal usage might suggest that the sick passenger in a literal sense stayed with the ship and that he might claim the benefit of the law. But it is doubtful whether a competent and purposive user of the English language, knowing the facts of the case, would feel compelled to say that the sick man was someone who had "stayed" with the ship. Such a person would almost certainly understand from the words that any reward for salvage should go only to a person who *by choice stayed* with the ship. After all, the reward is a *reward for salvage*. A sick person who is unable to do anything other than remain on board is not deserving of a reward, and could not save the ship or its contents anyway. Thus, in this context, the ordinary or common usage of "stayed" — stayed by choice — can be seen to differ from the literal meaning

— stayed in the sense merely of remaining on board.[9] The literal sense is not necessarily a narrower meaning. In fact the literal sense in this instance embraces a wider class of persons than the ordinary sense that the informed, competent, and purposive user of English would, without more, take the word to mean.

The ordinary meaning should also be differentiated from the "plain" or "clear" meaning, as these terms are often used by judges and others. The plain or clear meaning of words is not itself a general type of meaning, as is the ordinary meaning, but rather a judgment that a particular meaning is plainly or clearly correct. Of course, in a given instance, the "plain" or "clear" meaning of the words could also be a particular ordinary meaning. But the plain or clear meaning could equally be a technical meaning, or a special meaning, rather than an ordinary meaning. Blackstone also mentions a case in which a law of Edward III forbade all ecclesiastical persons to purchase "provisions" at Rome, which he suggests might, in its ordinary meaning, seem to prohibit the buying of grain or victuals.[10] But in fact the statute was made to repress the specific practice of purchasing "papal nominations" to benefices which were called "provisions" and the restraint was laid on such provisions only. For this reason, the plain or clear meaning of "provisions" was a technical or special meaning and not its ordinary meaning.

Thus we further distinguish between the ordinary meanings as opposed to technical meanings, legal or non-legal, that the statutory words might have. Ordinary words always have one or more possible ordinary meanings. Technical words always have one or more possible technical meanings. Of course, an ordinary word may have a technical as well as one or more ordinary meanings.

So, too, ordinary meanings differ from special meanings. By a special meaning, we mean either (1) a meaning different from an ordinary meaning of an ordinary word, which is not yet an established technical meaning of that ordinary word, or (2) a meaning of a technical word that is not the technical meaning of that technical word.

B.   Skepticism about the Determinacy of the Argument from Ordinary
     Meaning

It is sometimes said or assumed that although the argument from
ordinary meaning often appears on the surface to be available under a statute,
on the kind of close analysis for which lawyers are well known, one or more
sources of doubt will almost always emerge, thereby rendering the argument
incorrigibly indeterminate for the particular case. These sources of doubt are
by no means confined to adversarial contrary-mindedness. They also include
ambiguity (both semantic and syntactical), vagueness, ellipsis, obsolescence,
evaluative openness and more. At this point, the skeptic goes on to say that
in the face of these sources of doubt, we must, if we are honest with
ourselves, turn to other types of arguments such as the argument from
ultimate purpose or the argument from the meaning which best harmonizes
with the rest of the statutory scheme. Thus, as the skeptic sees it, such doubts
simply cannot be settled by resort to the resources of ordinary language
argumentation.
     Now, how are we to respond to this? First, let us remember that, in a
great many situations to which statutes using ordinary language apply, no
really credible doubts arise, even on the surface. This is not difficult to
explain. Ordinary language works rather effectively in ordinary non-legal
affairs. Why should matters be different in the law?
     But let us concede for the moment that various sources of doubt are in
fact often at work, at least on the surface. We still contend that such doubts
can usually be settled or cleared up solely by resort to the resources of
ordinary language argumentation — the resources of our competent,
purposeful and informed user of the language. As Aristotle so often said, we
should just "look and see". If we do, we will be reminded of familiar facts —
facts largely of language as used in everyday life and in law.
     We will now look at several simple examples, all of which are based on
(though not entirely identical with) some actual cases. These examples
illustrate a wide variety of sources of doubt at work; but more important for
our purposes, they also illustrate how resources of ordinary language
argumentation can be readily deployed to settle or clear up such doubts. Each
of the examples reminds the sceptic of much that should already be entirely

familiar. We have deliberately selected very simple examples, but the analysis applies to much more complex ones as well. Ultimately, what is needed here is a wide-ranging and systematic study of many examples, but that must await another day.

(1) One perhaps all too common source of doubt derives more or less *solely* from what we call adversarial contrary-mindedness. Suppose Parliament adopted the British Army Act, applicable to British soldiers everywhere, and it is duly promulgated in Hong Kong. Assume the Act said: "Any British soldier who commits an assault on or after 1 January 1957 shall be punished by court martial". Assume the defendant was convicted for committing an assault in Hong Kong at or about 2.30 am on 1 January 1957, Hong Kong time, and he appealed, arguing that the assault actually took place the day before at 6.30 pm on 31 December 1956, Greenwich Mean Time, and therefore, on his argument, before the statute could be in force in Hong Kong. In the case that arose,[11] the appeal was dismissed, despite this argument. Indeed, counsel for the Crown was not even asked to respond to appellant's so-called "argument", presumably given the quite evident determinacy of the argument from ordinary meaning.

(2) Now, consider doubt arising from syntactical ambiguity. Suppose a statute said: "Public schools or hospitals or other public institutions for education or health care must be duly certified by the Public Health Officer as satisfying Regulations 27-30". Assume the Health Officer demanded to review and certify defendant, a *private* hospital. Here we could expect the court to clear up the surface ambiguity by concluding that the statute only applies to public hospitals, since the word "public" appears initially before the phrase "schools or hospitals" and the extension of the qualifying word "public" to hospitals is confirmed by the word "other" in the subsequent "other public institutions" clause. Here, too, it is familiar that such surface doubt can be and often is cleared up solely by reference to the resources of ordinary language.[12]

(3) Another kind of doubt arises from vagueness. Suppose a statute provided: "Any person who is driving a motor car must have a license". The defendant, who had no license, was moving a car with his shoulder along a street, with one hand on the steering wheel to control its movement. Assume the court decided he could not be guilty of "driving" a motor car.[13] The court

reasoned that there is a firm distinction in ordinary language between driving and pushing. Without more, driving does not include pushing. If it did, even a person pushing a motorcycle along the road with no intention of driving it would be guilty, which could not have been meant. Again, the resources of ordinary language are often adequate to clear up surface vagueness in this way.

(4) Then there is the kind of doubt that arises from the high abstractness or generality of words from ordinary language, as applied to very particular circumstances. Assume a statute provided: "All mining machinery and apparatus shall be kept in a safe condition". The plaintiff was injured when a rung on a ladder broke and was not repaired. The court decided the ladder was mining "apparatus" within the statute, and appealed directly to ordinary usage as set forth in a standard dictionary which provided that an apparatus is "an assemblage of appliances or materials for a particular use".[14] Here, too, though we may have wished for somewhat more, the doubt is cleared up by resort to the resources of ordinary language.

(5) A further common source of doubt is that arising from the extreme unsoundness in policy terms of the result that would follow from applying the prima facie ordinary meaning of a general term or phrase. Assume a statute directed health officers in very general and unqualified terms as follows: "The health officer in charge of birth certificates shall, on application, issue a certificate to an applicant". Petitioner, who was in prison for a two-year term, sought a birth certificate. Petitioner had, as a child, been adopted with a name change. The evidence was that Petitioner had come to loathe the idea of having been farmed out by his natural mother for adoption. Petitioner was a violent person, having committed one homicide already. Petitioner sought his birth certificate in order to determine who his true mother was. The evidence indicated that he might, after learning the identity of his natural mother, do her harm when released from prison. The court decided that the health officer was not required to issue the petitioner a birth certificate.[15] Now, this result, too, can be reconciled with ordinary language argumentation. Here, we could say, as the court itself implied, that the legislature took it for granted that a health officer need not supply information to facilitate commission of a serious crime. In the use of ordinary language in ordinary daily life, much is taken for granted. Among other

things, this requires that we read into over-general language the qualifications required by context, and we regularly do so.[16] So may courts.

Of course, it is not true that in every case in which doubt arises as to the meaning of ordinary language in a statute, the resources of ordinary language can be drawn on to a substantial degree to clear up the indeterminacy. Sometimes this mode of argumentation fails, and other types of arguments must be invoked. Or sometimes this argumentation succeeds in settling the matter only with some aid from other types of arguments. For example, many vagueness cases are ones in which the *prima facie* indeterminacy is cleared up partly by ordinary meaning argumentation and partly by appeal to another type of argument. Consider a case in which the statute said that a seller of food must not "use tobacco while selling food" and the defendant was convicted of selling tomatoes with a cigarette that had gone out in his mouth. In that case, the court concluded both that in ordinary language the defendant could still be said, with some force, to be using tobacco, and also that such an interpretation would implement the ultimate purpose of the health regulation, because even cold ashes falling on the tomatoes would be unhealthy.[17]

We have now identified a number of familiar sources of doubt that motivate skeptics to claim that the argument from ordinary meaning is by nature incorrigibly indeterminate. Yet in each of the foregoing examples we are reminded of how familiar resources of ordinary language argumentation can be drawn upon by the courts to clear up such doubts. Ultimately, much more scholarship is required here. A more detailed and wide-ranging study of examples, complex as well as simple, must be conducted so that we can classify, analyze, systematize, and determine the appropriate role of particular types of resources of ordinary language argumentation.

In addition, when judging the overall determinacy of the argument from ordinary meaning, we must consider not only the trouble cases reaching the courts under a statute, but also the many more cases that never reach the courts because the ordinary meaning of the statute is sufficiently determinate. The skeptic tends to feed off the borderline and other trouble cases that do pose difficulties for courts. Again the skeptic must be reminded that in daily life ordinary language generally works pretty well. Why should it not work similarly well when harnessed to legislative ends?

But skepticism about the determinacy of ordinary language argumentation does not stem solely from the wide range of sources of doubt that frequently give rise at least to *prima facie* or surface statutory indeterminacy. Often the skeptic also assumes or asserts that even in cases where the indeterminacy is said to be settled or cleared up, this resolution is arbitrary and thus dependent solely on *ad hoc* agreement rather than on anything that can be called a general argument from ordinary meaning. Here the skeptic will stress that we do not have an accepted general procedure or methodology for settling doubts in the name of ordinary language argumentation.

In this essay, we can only indicate suggestively how one might respond to this turn in the skeptic's position. We will begin with an explanation of what we generally mean by a competent user of ordinary language. We do not say that ordinary meaning is the meaning that the common or average or popular user of the language would give the statutory words in the general context of their use. The common or popular language user in any language is likely to use words loosely and incorrectly. Do we then mean "the standard user" in the sense given to that term in phrases such as "standard English"? But there are notoriously many levels and standards of linguistic competence even within a single community. What kind of competence would such a standard user have? Perhaps at a minimum this person would have to know how to use a dictionary and to be familiar with the rules of grammar, syntax and punctuation (but how competent and how familiar?). Certainly if a possible meaning of the statutory word can be found in a standard dictionary, this will be a step.

And, dictionary in hand, the general context to which the statute is addressed may rule out several of the alternative meanings listed in the dictionary for a given word. For example, the word "draw" will be listed with several meanings, and it will mean something in a statute regulating the use of water that is different from what it will mean in a statute regulating the use of bills of exchange.

Another general determinant will often be whether and how far a given dictionary meaning coheres with the apparent ordinary meanings of other words in the statutory phrase, or sentence, considered as a discrete linguistic unit recognized in the grammar and syntax of ordinary language.

We are mindful that "knowing how to use a dictionary" is not an unproblematic idea, though very little has been written about it in the context of statutory interpretation. It means more than knowing how to find a particular word and how to understand what the dictionary entry contains. Dictionaries do not come near to teaching anyone how to use words. What they provide is a list of *possible* meanings of words, including collections of synonyms and near synonyms. They also often contain illustrations of usage. A newly arrived Martian who was provided with the twenty volumes of the *Oxford English Dictionary* and with as many works of English grammar and syntax as he wanted would not find himself knowing how to use a dictionary, still less knowing how to use the English language correctly and appropriately.

Our competent user of ordinary language is, of course, also a purposive user, but in a qualified way. Every statute has implementive language and the implementive language of nearly every statute is expressed to a significant degree in ordinary language. This is necessarily a purposive use of ordinary language, and unless the legislature indicates otherwise, we are to assume that one of the purposes of the legislature is that ordinary words in the implementive language are to be given their appropriate ordinary meanings. This purpose may be characterised as the legislature's *immediate* purpose in using implementive language, and our notional competent language user takes on this purpose. To cite an example, the immediate purpose of the legislature in that most famous of all statutes, "No vehicles in the park", is to use the device of a regulatory statute to keep vehicles, in the ordinary sense, out of the park. Accordingly, our notional competent user of language, interpreting the statute partly in light of its immediate purpose, will, without more, attribute the appropriate ordinary meaning to the word "vehicle". Of course, the legislature will also have one or more *ultimate* purposes in enacting the statute, too, including perhaps the reduction of noise, the promotion of safety, the preservation of clean air in the park, etc. But as we will see, such ultimate purposes will often prove problematic when deployed in interpretive argument.

Thus, ordinary meaning argumentation is not purposeless. It has regard at least to the *immediate* purpose of the legislature in using ordinary language in the implementive provisions of the statute. It will therefore usually help to ask: What meaning would a competent and purposive user of these ordinary words in such circumstances mean to convey?

So in identifying the standard user of the language for purposes of explicating ordinary meaning argumentation, it seems that we must be referring not just to a common or popular talker but to a putative or notional figure who is a competent and purposive user of the language. This person will usually have grown up using the language, will have undergone various kinds of experiences and acquired certain kinds of knowledge. But then, we may wonder, how *much* knowledge and what *kinds* of knowledge? What *general* knowledge? If we consider the language of modern statutes it is possible that some of them may be understood and made sense of by a language user who knows little or nothing about, say, psychology, economics, geography, or business. But nowadays there are fewer and fewer statutes of which that would be true. So our notional ordinary language user has to be an educated user with a background of general knowledge who is capable of understanding terms of some complexity. This user must know at least the "basics" of many subjects.

Our notional figure must also be someone who can cope with conceptual complexity. Even many simple-sounding and quite ordinary words have complex ordinary meanings, *ie,* complex conceptual content. This is true of even elementary sounding notions of individual responsibility. Consider "dishonest" or "reckless", for example.

Often it is necessary to decide whether ordinary words apply or are appropriately used in circumstances that may not previously have occurred even to a competent, purposive and knowledgeable language user. This requires the ability to consider hypothetical arguments, to compare the force of rival analogies, and to deploy abstract reasoning of a not very ordinary order. But to do these things is not to leave the world of ordinary language and enter a specialized legal world governed entirely by some special tongue. Conclusions reached here about meaning can usually be reached in the name of ordinary language argumentation.

Many cases involving statutory interpretation turn on the application of a general term in a statute to novel factual situations. Is milk a "beverage"?[18] Is blackcurrant syrup a "medicine"?[19] Is nude male bathing in the presence of ladies "indecent"?[20] Is disrupting a tennis match "insulting behaviour"?[21] Is a person pushing a car and using the steering wheel "driving"?[22]

These words are all ordinary words in the English language avowedly used not in any technical or special senses, but in their ordinary senses or meanings. Now what does it mean to say that the questions posed about the uses in the cases in question can be answered by our notional language user who appeals to what we call ordinary language argumentation? Certainly we do not say that ordinary language *always dictates* an answer. What then is the point of saying that we are applying our understanding of the ordinary meaning of words to such questions? There is perhaps the obvious contrast with the idea of applying words in some secondary or clearly different technical or special sense. Resolving cases such as those in the examples we have given is not at all like taking some naturally or obviously occurring *prima facie* ordinary sense and modifying it in the light of various kinds of knowledge or expertise. The knowledge or expertise is what fixes or goes to fixing or drawing out the *ordinary* non-technical and non-special usage that the language has. For example, in one type of case, we do not take a term such as "driving" in the statute against driving without a licence and modify it in light of our knowledge of the language. Rather we settle the ordinary meaning in this set of circumstances in light of, for instance, our knowledge that the language has a much more apt word, namely "pushing", to cover the facts of the case that has arisen (pushing a car without a licence to drive), and therefore we decide, in the absence of anything further, that "driving" does not apply. In this way we are operating with the language, not *on* it. To operate with language in problematic situations requires us to bring to bear understanding of the language, general knowledge, awareness of the immediate purpose of the legislature, hypothetical case analysis and reflective capacity. As Glanville Williams has said:

> We understand the meaning of words from their context, and in ordinary life the context includes not only the other words used at the same time but the whole human or social situation in which the words are used.[23]

Now we must fill out the idea of ordinary meaning in ordinary language to include the meaning that would be attached to words not only by the competent, generally knowledgeable, purposive and reflective user, but also by the specially informed and instructed user of the language for the particular circumstances in question. Suppose a statute limits the amount of contributions to electoral expenditures by persons who "promote or favour the election of a candidate". Does a person who campaigns against a candidate at an election "promote or favour the election of a candidate"? On the face of it the phrase "opposing a candidate's election" does not mean "promoting a candidate's election" and someone who had done the first might say that he had not in the ordinary sense of the words done the second. Nonetheless, a competent, generally knowledgeable and specially informed ordinary language user who was familiar with or had the factual background of elections and electoral machinery drawn to his attention might come to agree that his doing of the one act was equivalent to his doing of the other, given the language and the immediate purpose of the statute evident on its face and inferable from the ordinary meaning of the language used.[24]

In many problematic cases no special factual instruction is necessary but the language user may need to be reminded of, or have suggested to him, factual considerations or distinctions that might not occur naturally. Consider the argument reported in a typical case of this kind. In *Newbury v Cohens (Smoked Salmon) Ltd* [25] the issue was whether a Sunday trading ban which permitted the sale on Sunday of only certain categories of articles, including "meals or refreshments", permitted the sale of raw kippers and packets of tea. It was argued for the prosecutor that kippers in a raw or uncooked state were not within the meaning of "meals or refreshments" since the bulk of people or reasonable people did not eat raw kippers or tea. Various considerations were advanced, including the following:

The Lord Chief Justice: Why is it so extraordinary that people eat kippers without cooking? We do not know what the inhabitants of Clapham like. Counsel submitted that "meals or refreshments" meant such things as a bun or a snack, such as might be got in a railway refreshment room.

Mr Justice Cassels: One cannot allow a railway refreshment room to be a standard when one reflects what cannot be got there.

The Lord Chief Justice: I do not think anyone eats a leg of mutton raw.

Mr Justice Cassels: There is a school of dieticians which advocates eating raw food. There is a common that some gentlemen are eating their way across.

Mr Justice Donovan: Does "meals or refreshments" mean for human beings only? Why shouldn't raw kipper be a meal for my cat? (Counsel for the shopkeeper submitted that the words were wide enough to include all food, cooked and uncooked, consumed by human beings.)

The Lord Chief Justice: That is the difficulty. You do not consume tea but water in which the tea has been infused together with cream, milk or lemon. But it might not mean that you could not buy cocoa on Sundays because cocoa is consumed. Children eat it out of the tin. Everybody knows that and they get smacked for it.

The Lord Chief Justice, giving judgment, said that you could sell smoked salmon, you could sell smoked trout, smoked eel or other varieties of herring and yet it was said that you could not sell smoked herring, namely a kipper. In his opinion it was impossible to say that a kipper could not be a "meal or refreshment". It could be a very good meal. But he felt some difficulty about the packet of tea.

In this case the special facts and circumstances appealed to — eating habits; routine culinary experience; the character of railway refreshment rooms; the behaviour of children — seem to be things already within the experience of the ordinary knowledgeable language user, including, of course, the experience of the statutory drafter and statutory interpreter, and their bearing on the issue in hand involves, perhaps, not only special factual instruction, but also reminding, reflecting, weighing and assessing the known facts in various hypothetical lights.

The types of general resources of ordinary language argumentation that we have identified here, and the suggestions we have made as to their general deployment, do not yet rise to the level of a general procedure, let alone one publicly acknowledged among lawyers. But we believe this account should at least fend off the most radical indeterminacy skeptics who assume that in cases of dispute, there is no general way to determine ordinary meaning at all. The various resources to be brought to bear by the ordinary language user include: general linguistic competence, dictionaries, grammar books, the bearing of a general context of usage, general knowledge of the language user, purposive analysis drawing at least on *immediate* purposes in the circumstances, the drafter's knowledge of usage in parallel circumstances in ordinary life, special factual knowledge, reminders of factual considerations already familiar, the use of hypothetical analysis, analogy, standards of consistency and systematic reflection.

The ordinariness of ordinary language when thus brought to bear is not easy to describe in general terms. What we are concerned with seem to be conclusions as to the meaning of ordinary words that are drawn or coaxed out of the use of words by our competent, purposive and knowledgeable language user after due reflection and possible argument. In this sense we may claim that ordinary language may contain a solution to an interpretive problem though it will not necessarily dictate it or bear the solution on its face.

A great many problems of statutory interpretation, then, will go away because ordinary language can be made sufficiently determinate for resolution of the case at hand. But, as we have said, a comprehensive and systematic study of a wide range of examples, complex as well as simple, is needed here, and would cast much light both on the nature and variety of the resources of ordinary language argumentation and on just how it settles doubts. In the end we might even reconceptualize and retitle our subject not as "the argument from ordinary meaning" but as a variety of language-oriented arguments for refining meaning or settling doubts about ordinary words.

Even when the process of ordinary meaning argumentation yields a determinate conclusion, the interpreter should consider other types of argument as well. Further analysis may yield an argument that lends additional support to the argument from ordinary meaning. Indeed, in those cases where ultimate purpose can be satisfactorily shown, it is entirely expectable that ordinary meaning will be found to serve some ultimate purpose, too. But a conflict may arise between ordinary meaning and some version of an ultimate purpose argument (or between an ordinary meaning argument and still another type of argument). On this, more later.

C.   Skepticism about whether the argument serves interpretive values and
      thus has justificatory force

We now turn away from indeterminacy skepticism to skepticism about
whether the argument from ordinary meaning serves interpretive values and
thus has genuine justificatory force. The skeptical position here is frequently
that the use of language in a statute is such a specialized use that an ordinary
meaning of any ordinary words appearing therein can have no essential
relevance to statutory interpretation, and therefore no essential relevance to
the values to be served by genuine interpretive argument. On one radical
version of this skeptical view, the specialized statutory use of words is a
special "socially instrumentalist" use. Thus, statutes exist not to communicate
meaning in a fashion that is generally the same as, or analogous to, the way
competent, knowledgeable, purposive and specially informed users of
ordinary language communicate meaning. Rather, statutes exist as social
instruments to advance public policies, vindicate authoritative moral
precepts, uphold social norms and the like. These socially instrumentalist
uses of words are not really analogous to, let alone the same as, ordinary uses
of language: Law is first and foremost "policy", whereas ordinary usage is
merely "linguistic", and the merely linguistic is not itself policy oriented.
Accordingly, the language of the law is almost always heavily freighted with
special or *technical* meanings, *not* ordinary meanings. It follows, or so it is
said, that ordinary meanings cannot, *as such,* serve statutory ends, and
therefore cannot serve any genuine interpretive values.

In our view, this radical form of skepticism does not call for extended
rebuttal. The language of most statutes, however "socially instrumental",
consists overwhelmingly of ordinary words used by drafters who, we may
assume, are competent, informed and purposive users of ordinary language
addressing audiences of competent, informed and purposive users of ordinary
language. Thus, when a statutory drafter uses ordinary words, we may
assume that those words are being used with appropriate ordinary meanings
unless a technical or special meaning is shown. And even when statutes are
drafted with technical or special meanings, this will almost always be in the
syntax and grammar of ordinary language, and many ordinary words with
ordinary meanings will frequently appear.

Moreover, ordinary meaning can be readily harnessed to many socially instrumental ends. We do not require two languages, a "socially instrumental" language for use in statutes, and ordinary language. Nor is it difficult to explain why this is not necessary. The kinds of communicative demands that drafters of statutes must meet regularly arise in daily social life where ordinary language is at work. We saw clearly how this was so in earlier examples, including the case from Blackstone in which a claimant who "stayed" with a ship in distress merely because of illness was denied the rights of a salvor. The competent, informed and purposive language user in ordinary life would not suppose "stayed" in a salvage law to include an immobile sailor who was in no sense a ship salvor.

We turn to a less radical form of skepticism here. The skeptic may concede that ordinary language is an indispensable resource for the drafter but question whether the argument from ordinary meaning can consistently or sufficiently serve interpretive values. On one view, ordinary language is thought to be too "acontextual" to do this. This kind of skepticism may be countered first by pointing to the elemental fact that legislatures, as collective bodies, can legitimately act only via some kind of formal assent to, and enactment of, words in fixed verbal form. Insofar as the statute is drafted in ordinary language, we must, without more, assume that the legislature voted on and adopted the statute understanding it in terms of the ordinary meanings of ordinary words in it. In this way, ordinary language is an essential vehicle for the expression of democratic will. In giving effect to ordinary meaning, the interpretive argument not only serves democratic will but also facilitates the accountability of legislators to the electorate. These are interpretive values of the highest order.

A further interpretive value that the argument from ordinary meaning serves is this. It is more susceptible of even-handed application across time and space in the hands of different and changing judicial and administrative personnel, and in the hands of lawyers advising clients, than is any other mode of argument (except the argument from technical meaning). This is a not inconsiderable value, given that predictability and equality before the law are at stake.

Further, the ordinary meaning of the statute serves to constrain wilful judges (of the left and of the right), thereby confining them not only within their sphere of competence but also within their appropriate judicial role. Courts lack institutional competence to make fully-fledged legislative judgments about ends and means, and ought not to substitute their judgment for that of the legislature anyway. This erodes the very phenomena of legislation and of legislative power itself.

Adherence to ordinary meaning also affords those who must rely on statutory language from the time it goes into effect rather more protection than interpretive arguments which take account of materials extrinsic to the statute not readily available to addressees at the time of reliance. Relatedly, adherence to ordinary meaning generates reasons for citizens to act from the effective date of the statute (which is when they have to act), rather than postponing the ascertainment of authoritative meaning to the point of application by a court (as is often so with the argument from ultimate purpose).

Finally, the argument from ordinary meaning encourages legislators to legislate consistently with the rule of law. By adhering to ordinary meaning, judges in turn encourage legislators to draft openly and carefully. They invite legislators to legislate explicitly and thus not through "legislation" hidden in mere legislative history and similar "legislation" that might well not have gained true assent if more explicit language had been used in the statutory text.

D. Skepticism about the availability or decisiveness of the argument from ordinary meaning

A further fundamental form of skepticism about the argument from ordinary meaning is that it is available only occasionally, or is not very decisive when available, and therefore cannot be a major justificatory resource in statutory interpretation.

First, the skeptic assumes that the conditions for the availability of the argument frequently do not exist. The conditions required for the availability of the argument from ordinary meaning consist of: (1) a section of statutory text which is itself at least partly cast in ordinary language; (2) relevant conventions of ordinary usage; (3) the various other resources of the hypothetical or notional ordinary language user who, as we have seen, must be a competent, knowledgeable, purposive and informed user of language with capacity for argument and reflection, and (4) the absence of irreconcilable ambiguity, vagueness, generality, ellipsis, obsolescence, evaluative openness, and the like. When these conditions are not present, no credible argument from ordinary meaning can be available at all. The skeptic assumes that unavailability of the argument is the rule rather than the exception, and thus that commonly the resources of ordinary language cannot clear up any *prima facie* indeterminacy. In turn, this general state of affairs is attributed to such factors as poor drafting, the nature and limits of language and lack of foresight.

Now, this first source of skepticism might, in principle, be assessed in light of an extremely tedious and complex factual inquiry which, needless to say, no one has ever undertaken. Indeed, to our knowledge, no one has ever tried to estimate, even in a small and discrete branch of a given field of law, the proportion of instances in which the general conditions for the ultimate availability of the argument from ordinary meaning appear to be present.

Nevertheless, it just is a fact that every year, the highest courts in the United Kingdom decide a significant number of cases in which they say that the argument from ordinary meaning is controlling or substantially controlling. The judiciary and practicing lawyers do not view such cases as oddities or aberrations. Even if it were true that such cases represent a relatively small proportion of the total number of *disputed* statutory interpretation cases in each field, it would hardly follow that the argument from ordinary meaning must only be a minor justificatory resource. That is, so long as the highest courts accord appropriate force to the argument from ordinary meaning even in the relatively few cases that do reach those courts, it is probable that the argument from ordinary meaning similarly serves as a major justificatory resource both in the many litigated cases that never reach the highest courts and in the still far greater number of disputed cases that are never litigated at all.

One should strive for comparative perspective here. Just what type of argument can count as a "major" justificatory resource? Presumably this *at the very least* includes a type of argument that is as often in play, and is as widely decisive, as each of the other leading types of arguments recognized in statutory interpretation. Compared to virtually all other major types of arguments recognized in the field of statutory interpretation, there are strong reasons to suppose that the conditions required for the argument from ordinary meaning to be available and to have decisive force exist at least as often, if not much more often, than is true of any one of the other leading types of argument.

The distinct argument from the technical meaning of ordinary, or of technical, words is the only serious rival of the argument from ordinary meaning in terms of frequency of availability. Without attempting any kind of quantitative study, we may confidently affirm that the argument from ordinary meaning is in play at least as often as the argument from technical meaning. Many statutes have no or very few technical words, and it is not uncommon that ordinary words in a statute have their ordinary meanings.

The independent argument from harmonization with the general statutory context might be thought a serious rival of the argument from ordinary meaning; but in its most powerful forms, the harmonization argument requires for its availability other sections of the same statute or sections of closely related statutes that are appropriately worded, and such materials frequently do not exist.

It might be thought that the argument from ultimate statutory purpose is also a close rival; but, again, this is not so. The conditions for the availability of this type of argument are frequently not present. Thus, authoritative evidence of ultimate statutory purpose may not exist. Or if it exists, it may point quite ambiguously to different and conflicting ultimate purposes (as is frequently true in American cases). Or an authoritatively formulated ultimate statutory purpose may be very general and thus fail as a decisive criterion for determining which of two or more interpretations best serves the ultimate purpose. Or the facts may not be clear as to which competing interpretation would more efficaciously serve the ultimate statutory purpose. Or the implementive language of the statute may not be worded in a way that truly bears the strain of a purposive argument.

Even in the American federal system, the conditions for credible arguments from subjective legislative intent (rooted in materials of legislative history such as committee reports) are not sufficiently often available for this type of argument to be a major rival of arguments from ordinary meaning. Indeed, the conflicting and indeterminate nature of the legislative history materials in the American system is notorious. In the United Kingdom, it is generally not appropriate for counsel even to put most such material before the judge. (Of course, it is true that when the argument from ordinary meaning is not available, one or the other major types of argument such as the argument from ultimate purpose may possibly be available, but this proves nothing.)

A second basic source of skepticism about the overall justificatory significance of the argument from ordinary meaning may seem more important. Even if the argument is available, it still may be:

(1) cancelled, or

(2) over-ridden under a priority rule, or

(3) outweighed.

These truths, however, do not really diminish the overall decisiveness of the argument. What is true here of the argument from ordinary meaning is true of all the other leading types of interpretive argument as well. Any of them may be cancelled or over-ridden, or outweighed. If these possibilities imply that the argument from ordinary meaning cannot be a major justificatory resource, then no interpretive argument can ever be such a resource. There is no evidence that the argument from ordinary meaning is more often cancelled, or over-ridden, or outweighed than is true of any other possibly leading type of argument.

The third basic source of skepticism about the overall justificatory significance of the argument from ordinary meaning is that this argument is not alone enough to justify the interpretive conclusion in some cases. For example, in borderline cases under a vague statute, the argument from ordinary meaning may require reinforcement from contextual harmonization or from ultimate purpose. But, again, this is true of all leading types of argument. They just are deployed in some cases in which they require reinforcement from another argument if the interpretation is to be well justified, overall. Thus, there is nothing special here about ordinary meaning argumentation.

III. Why Teleological or "Ultimate Purpose" Argumentation Should Not Take Primacy

We now take up a second basic theme of this essay, namely, why the teleological mode of argumentation (as it is often called in the European Court of Justice and in the European Community generally) or the argument from ultimate statutory purpose (as it is sometimes called by its advocates in the United States) should *not* take primacy over the argument from ordinary meaning, at least in regard to most kinds of statutes. Not many years ago, the English Law Commission received recommendations that the ultimate purpose argument should be imported from America and become the primary mode of interpretive argumentation in the United Kingdom.[26] People here were not persuaded. Today the entreaties come more from Europe. We have not yet found any significant cases in which British judges could be said plainly to have succumbed. But purposive argumentation has been mentioned in various cases.[27] It has also been put forward in a House of Lords debate on interpretive method.[28] Some British treatise writers may now be headed in this direction too.[29]

A type of argument may be said to have primacy among interpretive arguments when it is available in a significantly higher proportion of cases than any competing type of argument. The argument from ultimate purpose cannot have primacy in this sense over the argument from ordinary meaning. It is common that reliable evidence of ultimate purpose is not available to the interpreter. It is one thing to be able to read an *immediate* purpose off the implementive language of a statute. Thus, the immediate purpose of a statute stating "no vehicles in the park" is to use the device of enacting a regulatory statute to keep vehicles, in the appropriate ordinary sense, out of the park. But a statute in the United Kingdom (and in the United States) typically incorporates no explicit statement of ultimate purpose, and frequently, as with the "no vehicles" statute, we can imagine a whole range of possible ultimate purposes any one of which, if taken as authoritative, might yield different results in particular cases. Moreover, in the United Kingdom, counsel may not cite most major forms of legislative history as evidence of ultimate purpose. On the other hand, materials for reliable construction of an argument from ordinary meaning are commonly available.

We have already alluded to many other problems in applying the argument from ultimate purpose. Even if an authoritative ultimate purpose can be ascertained, it will often itself be very general, and so indeterminate. And even if it alone would be determinate, several ultimate purposes of the same statute will often appear, and some will conflict with each other. Further, it may not really be clear from the facts which of two possible interpretations of the implementive language would best serve even an authoritative and otherwise determinate ultimate purpose.

There is a further basic problem with the argument from ultimate purpose that limits its availability and force in a very large category of cases, a problem almost entirely ignored in the academic literature. Legislation, particularly of a regulatory or penal kind, may superficially have a single stated or obvious objective. The purpose of road traffic regulation is to promote road safety. The object of mine safety laws is to promote safety in mines. But these are only abbreviated statements of the statutory purpose which is not to promote the stated objectives in any and every way whatsoever, but to promote them *by the means and through the words set out in the statute and not to do so in any other way.* It is almost as much an object of a penal statute *not* to convict those who do not fall within its provisions as to convict those who do. So if the issue is whether particular persons or circumstances fall inside or outside the statute's provisions, the statute's ultimate purpose will itself not resolve such an issue and appeal to it will commonly be empty or tendentious. Thus, if a legislature enacts "No firearms in the park" with the general objective of preventing danger (rather than for example prohibiting anything likely to be dangerous), a full statement of the legislature's ultimate purpose would include the propositions that it was to permit danger in the park if not arising from the presence of a firearm and also to ignore the fact that some firearms might be brought into the park without danger (yet still violate the statute). In such circumstances, an argument from ultimate purpose will not be conclusive in determining whether a catapult or a bow and arrow is a firearm (though it might have *some* relevance), and the argument ought not to produce the conclusion that rifles carried in a ceremonial parade (without permission) are not firearms. In sum, because of the foregoing considerations, the argument from ultimate purpose, when such purpose is faithfully and fully characterized, will frequently have little, if any, independent bearing on the appropriate scope of a general or vague statutory term.

We now turn to a second and rather different sense in which a type of argument may have primacy. Thus, an argument may be said to have primacy if, in cases of conflict with other arguments, it generally should prevail. In this sense, too, the argument from ordinary meaning has primacy over the argument from ultimate purpose. At the very least, a credible argument from ordinary meaning should prevail over a conflicting argument from ultimate purpose, unless the latter happens to be exceptionally strong. Several factors justify subordinating the argument from ultimate purpose in this way. Among other things, the argument from ultimate purpose generally does not implement democratic will and secure democratic accountability as fully as the argument from ordinary meaning. Indeed, the ultimate purpose argument may even frustrate democratic will, given that it implicitly delegates to judges discretionary power to determine what the ultimate purpose is, and to determine the implications of that ultimate purpose for construal of the implementive language of the statute. In actual operation, this mode of argumentation invites strong-willed judges, in effect, to substitute their own views for the views of the legislature, an event which has occurred in the United States twice! The argument from ordinary meaning, taken seriously, allows much less scope for this.[30]

Furthermore, the argument from ultimate purpose generally does not serve what might be called "rule of law" values as well as the argument from ordinary meaning. Precisely because the argument from ultimate purpose at least implicitly confers discretion on judges to determine ultimate purposes and their interpretive implications, the authoritative meaning of the statute frequently cannot be known until the statute is interpreted at the point of application where such discretion has to be exercised. This means that instead of statutes constituting meaningful reasons on which citizens may act from the time of enactment, citizens must often wait to point of application by a court to determine what the law is, a process that undermines predictability and upsets the reliance of citizens on antecedent law rather more than where the argument from ordinary meaning has primacy.

In addition, the statutory draftsman has more difficulty drafting effectively where the legislation is to be interpreted primarily in accord with an ultimate purpose, than where the legislation is to be interpreted primarily in accord with ordinary meanings of words used. The drafter will frequently be without legislative authority to insert a given ultimate purpose unless it happens to be vague and indeterminate and thus unobjectionable to all legislators. It just is a fact of legislative life that legislators can far more readily agree on implementive language than on the reasons — the ultimate purposes — for adopting such language. Moreover, when legislators do agree on implementive language, that language itself almost always reflects compromises between competing ultimate purposes. In such circumstances, it is not faithful to the realities of the legislative process to seize upon one of these purposes as *the* basis for extending or limiting the implementive language. The argument from ordinary meaning, however, is not similarly problematic.

IV. The Autonomy of the Argument from Ordinary Meaning

We now turn to the ultimate trump card of the teleologists. This is the view, seldom set forth explicitly, that whenever the argument from ordinary meaning itself appears to have force, this is really attributable ultimately to a concurrently available argument from that interpretation which best serves the ultimate statutory purpose, even though that argument may not even be set forth in the opinion.[31] On this view, the apparently autonomous force of the argument from ordinary meaning is in the end illusory. Rather the force of any argument from ordinary meaning is always entirely parasitic on a distinct and independently significant argument from ultimate purpose that is available on the facts, even if not set forth. According to the teleologists, when ordinary meaning does happen to serve the relevant ultimate statutory purpose, an interpretation to that effect is justified, but solely for that reason. To illustrate: Assume a statute has as its *ultimate* purpose to secure quiet and safety in the park, a purpose explicit in materials of legislative history. The statute adopted says: "No vehicles in the park". Here what we call the *immediate* purpose appears in the implementive language, namely, to use the device of enacting a statute to keep vehicles out of the park. Even though the ordinary meaning argument would obviously exclude a sports car from the park, the skeptic would here attribute the apparent force of this argument *entirely* to the way this ordinary meaning serves the ultimate purpose.

We now offer three brief rebuttals to this skeptical line. First, the argument from ordinary meaning will frequently be available in a case although an argument from ultimate purpose will not be available in that case, because, for example, we cannot reliably determine a single guidesome ultimate purpose. In such a case, the force of the argument from ordinary meaning simply cannot be dependent upon the concurrent availability of the argument from ultimate purpose. In fact, judges frequently invoke the argument from ordinary meaning to justify an interpretation without at the same time invoking any argument from ultimate purpose. In many such cases it is difficult to see how an argument from ultimate purpose could be available on the facts. Consider this example. A statute (also posted on a sign) says: "No vehicles in the park". A court interprets the statute to rule out the use of battery-driven wheel chairs on park sidewalks, and invokes the argument from ordinary meaning during the course of which the court cites a dictionary definition of vehicle: "a means of conveyance provided with wheels or runners and used for the carriage of persons or goods". Assume that the court does not, however, also go on to invoke the argument from ultimate purpose of the statute, for lack of reliable evidence of ultimate purpose. Assume the court adds:

> We have reviewed all the evidence and we find no satisfactory evidence of ultimate purpose here. Internal legislative history, messages of the executive, reports of commissions, and the like are silent or quite conflicting as to ultimate purpose. Further, there is no separate ultimate purpose clause in the statute — only the above implementive language ("No vehicles in the park"). Also, the implementive language does not itself express any ultimate purpose as would, for example, a statute providing *"No noisy* vehicles in the park", and the word "park" is itself quite ambiguous as to ultimate purpose, which could be quiet, safety, health (no exhaust fumes), aesthetic concerns, etc. In addition, no ultimate purpose is inferable from other related statutory sections, for there are none. Then, too, we cannot infer an ultimate purpose by way of contrast with the wording of prior law. The statute is entirely new. Moreover, we cannot reliably infer a single ultimate purpose by (a) constructing

hypothetical instances of unquestioned application of the statute, and (b) rendering explicit the ultimate purpose implicit in those instances and then arguing by analogy to the case at hand. This is because we cannot be sure that what we consider instances of unquestioned application of the statute would be what the legislature meant, nor can we be sure we are extracting from those instances *the* ultimate statutory purpose "implicit" in those instances and so attributable to the legislature.[32] Finally, while we can imagine possible policies that different possible ultimate purposes of the legislature here might serve, we cannot assume that the ultimate purpose of the statute coincides with any one or all of those policies. As already suggested, such policies might include preservation of quiet, or securing safety, or aesthetic considerations, or health (eliminating exhaust fumes), etc. Outcomes could well vary depending on which ultimate purpose (policy) is adopted.

Secondly, even if it were true that the argument from ordinary meaning is never alone available on the facts, it still would not follow that whatever force the argument from ordinary meaning has in such cases of joint availability must be derived solely from a concurrently applicable though unstated argument from ultimate purpose. The argument from ordinary meaning qualifies on its own as an autonomous type of argument itself having genuine justificatory force. As we have seen, when appropriately in play it serves basic interpretive values such as the implementation of legislative will, accountability of the legislature to the electorate, the generation of definite and certain reasons for action from the very inception of the law, the protection of justified reliance on the language of the law, restriction of the power of wilful judges and wilful administrators, and more. Observe that the argument from ultimate purpose does not serve some of these values at all and serves others only limitedly.

This is not to say that the argument from ordinary meaning is always wholly autonomous. It may need "help" from an available argument from ultimate purpose as where a vague word ("vehicle") confronts a *borderline* case ("rollerskates"), or as where a facially ambiguous statute can, when ultimate purpose is taken into account, be rendered more determinate.

Ultimate purpose, then, has diverse roles: (1) as a full-fledged argument which may or may not reinforce the ordinary meaning argument, and (2) as a less than full-fledged argument which may plug holes in, or otherwise strengthen an ordinary meaning argument.

Thirdly, the argument from ordinary meaning and the argument from ultimate purpose may conflict. When this is so, judges in fact frequently allow the argument from ordinary meaning to prevail. In such cases of conflict, if the argument from ordinary meaning were truly parasitic on and derivative from the argument from ultimate purpose, it would always lose to that argument. But it often wins. Consider these two examples:

Example 1: Under the "no vehicles in the park" statute, assume the court refuses to exclude loud toy airplanes flown by motor through remote control by park guests, even though substantial evidence in legislative history indicates that the reduction of noise was an important ultimate purpose. Here, to exclude such toy airplanes as vehicles would strain ordinary meaning, and ordinary meaning would not be cancelled by an ultimate purpose categorically to eliminate all noise because, let us assume, the legislature chose not to implement this ultimate purpose to the fullest extent possible, given the importance of competing ultimate purposes here, such as the use of parks for recreation and play. One court has aptly remarked:

> [N]o legislation pursues its purpose at all costs. Deciding what competing values will or will not be sacrificed to the achievement of a particular objective is the very essence of legislative choice —
> and it frustrates rather than effectuates legislative intent to assume that whatever furthers the statute's primary objective must be the law.[33]

Example 2: The court decides that the ordinary meaning of "vehicle" rules out the use of skateboards in the park, and the court so holds although there is considerable evidence in the materials of legislative history *(e.g.,* a key report of a commission on park regulation or a key committee report) of an ultimate purpose only to rule out vehicles causing "noise and exhaust fumes", an ultimate purpose not served by ruling out skateboards. Among other things, the court here might think that the evidence of ultimate purpose is simply not sufficiently authoritative to control. (But even a full-fledged argument from ultimate purpose might not be sufficently strong to cancel an argument from ordinary meaning.)

In cases where the judge gives the argument from ordinary meaning priority, it necessarily follows that the argument from ordinary meaning does not draw *any* force from the defeated argument from ultimate purpose.

In the foregoing rebuttals, we have so far implicitly resisted all efforts of those who would collapse ordinary meaning argumentation into ultimate purpose argumentation. We emphasize (1) that the two are conceptually distinct; (2) the two are not rooted in identical interpretive values; (3) one may be available but the other not; and (4) the two may conflict, yet the argument from ordinary meaning triumph.

There is a temptation the other way, too, which is to regard ultimate purpose argumentation *as part of* ordinary meaning argumentation, at least when the ultimate purpose is present on the face of the statute and expressed in ordinary language. This, too, should also be resisted. In such a case, ultimate purpose argumentation can be distinctly identified and given appropriate effect as an argument that either concurrently supports, or opposes, the ordinary meaning argument. If the ultimate purpose argument and the ordinary meaning argument are somehow collapsed into one, neither of these normative effects is given its due.

V. Conclusion

Ordinary language argumentation is multifarious and complex. We still do not fully understand it, and we believe much work remains. Even so, we hope here to have put the ordinary meaning argument on somewhat better footing. To give primacy to ordinary meaning arguments in statutory interpretation is not to prefer literal meaning of words. Nor is it to rule out the possibility of effective appeals in at least some cases to ultimate statutory purpose. But appeals to ultimate purpose, or indeed to any other type of interpretive argument, will not in general be as available or as justifiably decisive as reliance upon the resources of ordinary language. In sum, the argument from ordinary meaning is sound, autonomous and deserves primacy.

Notes

1. As Lord Blackburn put it, judges should give "the words their ordinary signification": *River Wear Commissioners v Adamson* (1877) 2 App Cas 742. For a general account of interpretive practices in the United Kingdom, see MacCormick and Summers (eds), INTERPRETING STATUTES — A COMPARATIVE STUDY (1991), Ch 10.

2. See e.g., *John Doe Agency v John Doe Corp* 110 S Ct 471, 476 (1989); *Commissioner v Asphalt Products Co* 482 US 117, 120 (1987); *United States v Locke* 471 US 84, 93 (1985); *Griffen v Oceanic Contractors Inc* 458 US 564, 570 (1982). For a general account of interpretive practices in the US Supreme Court, see MacCormick and Summers (eds), INTERPRETING STATUTES — A COMPARATIVE STUDY (1991) Ch 11.

3. See Ryle, THE CONCEPT OF MIND (1949), p 49: "Excellence at surgery is not the same thing as knowledge of medical science."

4. Some of these recommendations are referred to in the Report of the Law Commission and the Scottish Law Commission, *The Interpretation of Statutes* (HC 256, 1969).

5. See, for example, *R v Registrar General, The Times*, 18 November 1990 where Lord Justice Staughton wrote that a given interpretation "was consistent with the growing tendency, perhaps encouraged by Europe, towards a purposive construction of statutes, at all events if they did not deal with penal or revenue matters."

6. See e.g., Kutscher, METHODS OF INTERPRETATION AS SEEN BY A JUDGE AT THE COURT OF JUSTICE (1976), pp 39-41.

7. For what is probably the most influential American formulation of purposive argumentation, see Hart and Sacks, THE LEGAL PROCESS: BASIC PROBLEMS IN THE MAKING AND APPLICATION OF LAW (unpublished teaching materials, 1958), pp 1148-1158 and 1410-1417.

8. 1 *Comm* 62.

9. We might also notice that the literal use does not necessarily in a linguistic sense entail a narrower usage.

10. 1 *Comm* 61.

11. *Cf R v Logan and Others* [1957] 2 QB 589.

12. There are countless examples of syntactical ambiguity in the reported cases — see generally, BENNION ON STATUTE LAW (3rd ed 1990), pp 258-259.

13. *Cf R v MacDonagh, The Times*, 20 February 1974.

14. *Cf Brebner v British Coal, The Times*, 23 July 1988.

15. *Cf R v Registrar General, The Times*, 12 November 1990.

16. See generally MacCallum, *Legislative Intent* in Summers (ed), ESSAYS IN LEGAL PHILOSOPHY (1970), pp 254-260.

17. *Cf Pitt v Locke* (1960) 125 JP 93.

18. *R v Rouse* [1936] 4 DLR 797.

19. *Customs and Excise Commissioners v Beecham Foods Ltd, The Times,* 26 January 1972.

20. *R v Stanley* [1965] 2 QB 327.

21. *Brutus v Cozens* [1971] 2 All ER 1297.

22. *R v MacDonough* [1974] 2 All ER 257.

23. *The Meaning of Literal Interpretation* (1981) 131 *New LJ* 1128, 1129.

24. *DPP v Luft* [1977] AC 962 (pamphlets urging "Don't vote National Front").

25. *The Times,* 27 April 1956.

26. See *supra* n. 4.

27. See *e.g., supra* n. 5.

28. See 503 *HL Debs*, cols 278 *et seq* (18 January 1989).

29. See *e.g.,* Bell and Engle, CROSS ON STATUTORY INTERPRETATION (2nd ed, 1987), p 95.

30. We are not unmindful that some skeptics would argue that, on the contrary, the argument from ordinary meaning is itself often deployed by judges to implement, yet hide, their own value preferences. Here we must distinguish two versions of the skeptical position. On one version, the language of the statute really does have the ordinary meanings that the court attributes to it. Here, presumably the value choices *of the legislature* are appropriately implemented in accord with the argument. The fact that values *of the judges* are also at the same time implemented, though "covertly" without the judges owning up to it, is irrelevant and can be disregarded, even though implementation of these values might well be the true motivation of the interpreting court.

The other possible version of the alleged abuse is more troublesome. We are presumably to suppose that, on appropriate analysis, the argument from ordinary meaning is not really available because the conditions of its applicability are missing, or though these conditions are present, doubt remains which the argument from ordinary meaning does not sufficiently settle, yet the court invokes the argument to further its own value choice covertly, that is, without explicit acknowledgement of that choice. Several things should be said about this. First, it will often be difficult to know whether this is really what is going on because there will be little, if any, evidence that the court is in this way seeking to vindicate its own value choices as opposed to the presumed value choices of the legislature. Secondly, just how often this occurs and the proportion of instances in which it occurs are very difficult to assess. Materials for the appropriate empirical study are not really accessible. Thirdly, we may point out that the court's unjustified invocation of the argument from ordinary meaning merely as a cover for its own value choices is, when this is publicly evident, subject to criticism by higher courts or by commentators (or both), criticism that will have some corrective effect generally, albeit not necessarily in the particular case.

31. For variants of this view, see Hart and Sacks, *supra* n. 7 at p 1157. See also Fuller, *Positivism and Fidelity to Law — A Reply to Professor Hart* (1958) 71 HARV. L. REV 630, 663.

32. See Hart and Sacks, *supra* n. 7 at pp 1151-1157 and 1413-1417.

33. *Rodrigues v United States* 107 S Ct 1391, 1393 (1987).

CHAPTER 11

INTERPRETING STATUTES — SHOULD COURTS CONSIDER MATERIALS OF LEGISLATIVE HISTORY?

I. Introduction

Among Geoffrey Marshall's many contributions are his various writings on the legislative process and statutory interpretation.[1] I have, over the years, learned much from him about statutory interpretation, beginning with that session of Hilary Term twenty-five years ago when he and I jointly taught a class on statutory interpretation at The Queen's College. It is, for me, a privilege, and a special honor, to have this opportunity to join in a tribute to him and to his work, as he becomes 70.

A legislature may keep official verbatim or other records of the evolution of a bill from its introduction until enactment as law. Materials of legislative history to be found in such records differ in different systems, and may take a variety of forms, including: preliminary drafts of parts or all of a bill, proposed clauses or amendments withdrawn before vote, statements and other materials provided at committee hearings on the bill, committee reports on the bill, records of what is said about the bill and its effects during debates, including speeches or other statements of sponsors of bills, reports on the bill of any joint committees of both chambers, and more. I will refer to these as "materials" of legislative history.

Legal systems also differ on whether, and if so, the extent to which, materials of legislative history may play roles in the interpretation of statutes. Where permitted, judges and others may use materials of legislative history for three quite different purposes in statutory interpretation: (1) to demonstrate an ambiguity or obscurity or other doubt as to the meaning of the statute that does not otherwise appear on the face of the statute, and thereby identify what may seem to be a need for interpretation, (2) to try to provide either the essential content of a specific application of the statutory words or of a general meaning of those words, as the subjective "intention of the legislature", and (3) to attempt to contribute part of the content of, or reinforce any of, several other general types of relatively autonomous

251

interpretive arguments. Some examples of this third use are as follows. The materials of legislative history might be thought to include authoritative evidence of the general purpose that the language of the statute is to serve, and so provide some of the required content for one version of the general and relatively autonomous type of argument to the effect that a given reading of the statute best serves its general purpose. Or, the materials of legislative history may, for example, be thought to indicate which of two ordinary meanings of a word in the statute at least some members of the legislature embraced, and so contribute content to, or reinforce, that general and relatively autonomous type of argument based on the resources of ordinary language argumentation. Or, materials of legislative history might indicate how at least some members of the legislature reconciled the statute with closely related and even apparently conflicting statutory provisions, and so suggest content for that general and relatively autonomous type of argument that a given reading of the statute best harmonizes with other language of the statute and any closely related statutes.

In the British and American legal systems, there has been and continues to be much debate over the use of materials of legislative history in statutory interpretation. In Britain, the courts have, for some time, generally used reports of Royal Commissions, reports of the law commissioners, and "white papers" not to determine the meaning of words in the statute as such, but to determine the mischief the statute was adopted to cure. But until the decision of the House of Lords in Pepper v. Hart on 26 November 1992,[2] the modern position in Britain had been that records in Hansard of Parliamentary debates on a bill could not be consulted when interpreting a statute. Pepper v. Hart changed this. The very decision itself continues to be controversial. Since the 1950's the United States Supreme Court and the lower federal courts have regularly consulted various materials of legislative history, including Congressional debates, when interpreting federal statutes.[3] This general practice has, however, long been controversial. In recent times, the Supreme Court has resorted to such materials far less often than earlier.[4] Among American Supreme Court justices, the leading current opponent of the use of legislative history materials to interpret statutes is Justice Antonin Scalia, but he is by no means alone, and among respected predecessors of like mind, Justice Robert Jackson stands out.[5] Some American judges have even taken legislative history rather more seriously than the statute itself! Thus, one judge once said: "The legislative history... is ambiguous . . . . Because of this ambiguity, it is clear we must look primarily to the statutes themselves to find the legislative intent."[6]

Of course, not all American statute law is federal. In fact, far more statute law is made by state legislatures, in the aggregate, than by the American federal Congress. Some American states have more than twenty million inhabitants and so are, in their own right, sizeable legal systems. The highest courts of the various states, not federal courts, are the final arbiters of the interpretation of state statutes. Unlike the U.S. Supreme Court, the state supreme courts in most states do not consult materials of legislative history at all when interpreting state statutes, if for no other reason than that the state legislature in most states does not keep usable records of the legislative history of bills as they make their way through the legislative process to final enactment.[7]

The appropriateness of using materials of legislative history in the interpretation of statutes, then, is currently disputed in Britain and in the American federal courts. The issue itself is a fundamental one of wide-ranging significance. It is one of the two or three most important issues that can arise for legislators, judges, lawyers, and scholars concerned with defining and developing a general methodology for the interpretation of statutes.

II. Relevant Considerations

The issue of whether, and if so, to what extent, interpreters ought to utilize materials of legislative history is complex, and implicates considerations ranging from the need to provide citizens with meaningful guidance from the time a statute becomes law, to the formal and other legitimacy of using such materials to interpret statutes, to the justificatory sufficiency of the recognized modes of interpretive argument that would remain if resort to such materials were not permitted, to the effects of using such materials on drafting technique, to the rule of law, and more. Analysis of the problem requires deployment of criteria for judging the overall soundness of a general interpretive methodology. And of course, there are limits to the generality of any such methodology, for the very nature of the statute involved may have some bearing. For example, no methodology should be used to extend the meaning of a criminal prohibition beyond its ordinary meaning in order to convict an alleged offender, or to impose a significant new burden (such as a tax) on citizens where the statutory language does not itself do so in clear terms, a principle that the House of Lords could easily have invoked to decide Pepper v. Hart without any resort to legislative history (as Lord Mackay noted).[8]

A. Guidance to Statutory Addressees and Their Legal Advisors Conducting Business and Other Affairs of Daily Life Far Away from Courts

A general methodology of statutory interpretation should consist mainly of authorized and relatively autonomous general types of interpretive argument. In circumstances where interpretation is required, a well formed methodology would channel reason and fact into the construction and articulation of specific instantiations of one or more of these general types of argument. It is a distinct and important task of the highest courts in any legal system to develop and refine an authoritative body of law specifying the methodology of statutory interpretation.[9] In Britain, Pepper v. Hart is one such decision. It and others have created a body of methodological common law for the interpretation of statutes. A number of landmark decisions of the U.S. Supreme Court also lay down such methodological common law.[10] Of course, courts, in devising a methodological common law for the interpretation of statutes, must address various other basic issues besides the appropriateness of using materials of legislative history in constructing interpretive arguments. In some American states, one finds that the legislature has adopted a statute on how statutes are to be interpreted.[11] Despite the passage of several hundred years, it cannot be said that the courts in either Britain or the United States have evolved a satisfactory general methodology for interpreting statutes. Nor can it be said that the American state interpretation acts carry us very far in the right direction. It may be that the methodological shortfall, overall, has been greater in the American system, but Pepper v. Hart is not in the right direction either.

It is a common error to assume, when thinking about an authoritative interpretive methodology for statutes, that the primary function of such a methodology is merely to aid courts in deciding disputes that have actually arisen between two citizens or between a citizen and the government. This is, of course, one use of such a methodology, for any statute might end up in court. Indeed, some types of statutes do lead their lives mainly in court or in disputes on their way to court. This is true of statutes dealing with the jurisdiction and procedures of courts. It is also true of statutes that confer vast discretion on judges, say, to award child custody, or to divide family assets on divorce. The main function of these statutes is to specify a rational approach to resolving certain types of disputes in courts. Something similar could be said of certain statutes to be administered mainly by administrative agencies or special tribunals.

Relatively few statutes, however, exist primarily to aid courts in resolving disputes. The primary function of most statutes is to provide guidance to citizens, to corporate and other business entities, and to still other types of statutory addressees, as they act and interact outside of, and far from, courts. This is true of statutes that define private ownership and the rights of owners of property, of statutes specifying criteria of validity for contracts and wills, of statutes providing for the creation of corporations and other business entities, statutes governing the relations of employees with employers, statutes that regulate manufacturing or other economic activities, statutes that specify speed limits on highways, statutes that provide how parties may enter into a lawful marriage, statutes that impose an income tax, statutes that define crimes, and on and on. The primary function of these statutes is to provide guidance in daily social, economic or other life. These statutes are not primarily concerned with what may happen by way of dispute resolution in a court of law. These statutes are concerned with what their addressees are to do on the front-lines of human interaction. Indeed, if such statutes could not, in the main, be "self-administered" by their addressees and advisors without going to court, these statutes simply could not serve the ends assigned to them. These statutes must be administrable in the first instance not by judges or other officials but by citizens, by corporate and other business entities, and by still other types of addressees, sometimes without the advice of lawyers. It may be said that such statutes, from their effective dates, provide their addressees with immediate reasons for action and decision in the conduct of affairs of daily life. In constructing such reasons, these addressees and their legal advisors must be mindful not only of the language of the statute, but also of the authoritative interpretive methodology to be applied in determining what the statute means. If that methodology itself fails to provide, or itself undermines, needed statutory guidance from the effective date of the statute, the methodology fails in its primary function.

Thus, when courts devise a general interpretive methodology for statutes, they must be aware that this methodology should first of all be appropriate to the needs for statutory guidance in non-litigational life out on the front lines of human interaction. The same methodology of interpretation should apply to "guidance" statutes, in court as well as out. It is not possible to interpret such statutes in disputed cases in court differently from how they are to be interpreted by their addressees and advisors out of court in daily life. The interpretive methodology that courts adopt for such statutes should be adopted with an eye to their "out of court" life, not any "in court" life they may have.

With respect to statutes addressed to affairs of business and other daily life, the courts should be *especially* mindful that the interpretive methodology they use must not require statutory addressees and their legal advisors to resort to materials and modes of interpretive argument that cannot be readily translated into meaningful guidance in daily affairs at reasonable cost. In my opinion, materials of legislative history cannot be so translated. Pepper v. Hart and its decisional counterparts in the United States Supreme Court are therefore misguided. Under those decisions, statutory addressees and their lawyers must resort to legislative history materials even when deciding what to do under statutes primarily addressed to the conduct of affairs in daily life. Even if, in some cases, such materials might provide good interpretive reasons for courts to decide particular *disputes* that have arisen, such materials do not generally serve well as a source of reasons for statutory addressees, with the aid of lawyers, to be *guided* by in daily life. There are several explanations for this.

First, most materials of legislative history are far less immediately accessible to statutory addressees and their legal advisors than is the language of statutes and the resources of various widely recognized modes of interpretive argument such as the argument from ordinary or technical meaning, and the argument from that meaning which best harmonizes with the rest of the statute, modes of argument that are not essentially dependent on materials of legislative history. As I shall demonstrate later, these and several other major modes of interpretive argument remain available for such cases even when materials of legislative history cannot be consulted. These remaining modes of argument provide quite sufficient guidance for statutory addressees and their legal advisors, as well as quite sufficient justificatory resources for judges in deciding disputes.

Second, materials of legislative history are often themselves not certain and reliable bases for citizen action. There are various explanations for this. These materials are frequently superseded by subsequent events in the very legislative process in which the statute is finally enacted. For example, an amendment in the midst of legislative deliberation may render an entire committee report irrelevant. Further, individual fragments of materials of legislative history are often unclear or conflicting, and of varying weight. The necessity of reconciling such materials not only with each other but with statutory language is still another source of uncertainty.

Third, legislative history materials are costly to gather in the first place, and it may be even more costly for legal advisors to assess them. The American experience in the federal courts is that these materials are often disparate and frequently require extended and careful assessment which can itself be very costly. (Some American federal judges and their law clerks have even been known to descend into archives upon archives of such material, not ever to be seen or heard from again!)

Fourth, judicial resort to legislative history materials in interpretive argument may even undermine and thwart the very guidance that the statute would otherwise provide. A major way in which this can occur is that a court may be led to conclude from a review of legislative history that a statute is really ambiguous or obscure when, on its face, it is not. As a result, a citizen reasonably relying on the language of the statute may later learn in court that "the law" was otherwise. When this occurs, judges utilize materials of legislative history to upset the justified reliance of citizens on the language of the statute.

Fifth, once an ambiguity or other obscurity is found in the statute, with or without aid of materials of legislative history, judges who favor the use of such materials are usually also ready to resort to such materials to resolve the ambiguity or obscurity, even though it could be readily cleared up by resort to other more reliable and more readily deployable types of interpretive argument. Simply because materials of legislative history appear to reveal an ambiguity or obscurity in the statute, it does not follow that such materials are also best suited to resolution of the issue. The other resources of interpretive argument are rich and deep, and not subject to the infirmities to which legislative history is subject. For example, the resources of ordinary language argumentation on which citizens and their lawyers can and do regularly rely are generally available, and are frequently sufficient alone to clear up ambiguity or obscurity. Merely because the nature of the interpretive issue is linguistic, for example, an issue that arises from ambiguity, vagueness, or ellipsis, it does not follow that to resolve such an issue the interpreter must go to some mode of argument other than the argument from ordinary, or technical, meaning. These modes of argument can do far more than indicate that given statutory language, after all, does have a "plain meaning". Often the argument from ordinary, or technical, meaning will include resources adequate to resolve ambiguity, vagueness, or ellipsis, too, as Geoffrey Marshall and I once demonstrated.[12]

Perhaps a rational legal system could have two interpretive methodologies — one for addressees of statutes concerned primarily with their daily business and other activities, and one addressed to statutes which lead their lives solely or almost solely in court. In resolving interpretive disputes under the former type of statute, judges could not resort to materials of legislative history. In resolving disputes under the latter type of statute, judges might consult such materials. I do not propose this, however. Even though a special "dispute resolution" methodology might be created for statutes that are or purport to be merely dispute resolutive, I would still oppose judicial resort to materials of legislative history also because such materials lack formal, democratic and other varieties of legitimacy. I now turn to these considerations of legitimacy.

B.   Considerations of Formal, Democratic, Institutional And Other Varieties of Legitimacy

Even if materials of legislative history were always accessible, clear and unconflicting, and not unduly costly to use, considerations of legitimacy would still militate strongly against their use. I do not say that such materials lack all formal legitimacy. If the courts do generally invoke such materials in the interpretation of statutes, this in itself will endow them with *some* formal legitimacy. Of course, if courts were to cease this, no formal legitimacy could derive from this source at all. The very fact that these materials come into being in the course of legislative processes also endows them with limited formal legitimacy. Even so, the general degree of such formal legitimacy from such sources is not high, and, of course, it is far lower overall than the language of a duly enacted statute.

The formal legitimacy of the language of a statutory enactment derives from its conformity to the fixed verbal form prescribed for valid statutes, from its conformity to the rule-like or other law-like form of statutes, from its adoption in accord with proper legislative procedures which includes the possibility of its formal amendment to express evolving legislative will, from its enactment within the scope of legislative jurisdiction, and from its compliance with any further criteria of validity for such statutes. Thus, a valid statutory enactment may be said to have "full fledged" formal legitimacy. In a well designed system, formal legitimacy is itself an important value and also serves important values. It signifies that the statute has been adopted in accord with the agreed or accepted general conditions for the exercise of law-making authority. Formal legitimacy also serves procedural rationality and procedural fairness. It secures that the process is deliberative, and secures that each side has a fair opportunity to participate in the process, within limits.

The materials of legislative history, however, are not required to take any fixed verbal form, and, of course, are highly variegated — often even fragmentary, diffuse and multifarious. Because such materials are rarely in the fixed verbal form of statutes, because their form is not rule-like or otherwise law-like, and because they are not susceptible of formal amendment, nearly all such materials have themselves usually not been the object of the kind of focused and intensive deliberation that can be, and frequently is, devoted to a statute proposed in due form in accord with formal procedures. Of course, legislative history materials are not at all authoritative in the way a statute is. In Britain, no piece of legislative history material has gone through the Parliamentary process to passage, and in the American federal system, no piece has gone through three readings, has passed the House and the Senate, and been signed by the President. There simply are no legal criteria for determining the *validity* of materials of legislative history. Indeed, such materials are not valid or invalid in any ordinary legal sense. In this regard, the materials of legislative history and the language of an enacted statute are fundamentally different. Valid statutes satisfy such criteria.

Legislative history materials do not satisfy any criteria of validity as such, yet some judges may even give them the effect of validly enacted statutory language!

Not only are the materials of legislative history largely devoid of all *formal* legitimacy. Such materials may have little or no *democratic* legitimacy. This is not merely because the materials, as such, always lack significant formal legitimacy, not having been authoritatively adopted in fixed verbal form by a legislative majority in accord with formal procedures pursuant to the exercise of legislative jurisdiction. It is also because even when such materials are known to both chambers of a legislative body, are known to any executive signing the bill, are clear, are consistent with other such materials, and have not been superseded by later events in the evolution of the bill prior to enactment, it still cannot be said that the materials have democratic legitimacy. The mere fact that clear, unconflicting, and unsuperseded materials are known to both chambers, and to any executive when the bill is duly adopted, does not signify majority indorsement or executive indorsement of their content. The final majority vote is a vote in favor of the wording of the bill, not the materials. Indeed, it is far from clear that there could (logically) be a genuine legislative *vote* on such materials, given their *unformed* nature.

It is true that some legislators may be moved to vote in favor of the wording of a bill because of certain materials of legislative history put before them, but we cannot know how many such legislators so voted, and so cannot know whether they comprised a majority of the body, or even a significant proportion. From the fact a majority of the body voted in favor of the wording of the bill, we cannot infer that a majority, or even a significant proportion did so because, or even partly because, of the materials of legislative history of which they were cognizant. In short, we cannot know the subjective "intention" of the majority as to the materials. The materials simply cannot have democratic legitimacy.

In reply to my argument, it might be said that many legislators voting in favor of the *wording* of a bill may not have studied that wording, and some may not even have seen the bill itself. If this be so, how can the bill itself, even though adopted, have democratic legitimacy? Yet it does have such legitimacy. This being so, then should not we say that materials of legislative history have similar democratic legitimacy, even though not known to a majority of legislators, or acted on by them, at time of voting?

A bill adopted by a majority, many of whom have not even read the bill, is still valid law, and all legislators know this. The bill has formal legitimacy, and as the object of a valid majority vote, the bill also has a significant degree of democratic legitimacy, even though a majority of voters have not read the bill. The votes being cast are still formally valid votes on a validly formulated and validly presented bill, and the votes count in favor (or against) whatever the words of the proposed bill are, despite the ignorance of some voting legislators. Each legislator who votes in ignorance nevertheless understands all this. The same procedures and the same understandings, however, simply do not exist with respect to mere materials of legislative history. These materials have little formal legitimacy, and if not known to, and acted upon by, a majority of legislators when voting on the bill itself, cannot be said to have any democratic legitimacy. As I have said, given the workings of the voting process in the modern legislature, it is not possible to know how many legislators knew of such materials, let alone whether these materials influenced their vote. Hence, typically such materials cannot be said to have *any* democratic legitimacy whatsoever.

In reply, it might be said that the rank and file legislators have *delegated* to the legislative leadership any responsibilities that the rank and file had to be aware of, and to act on, any relevant materials of legislative history. Thus, when the final vote is taken, the awareness and motivation of members of the legislative leadership deriving from their cognizance of materials of legislative history, is to be attributed to rank and file voters as well. Hence, on this delegation theory, such materials do have majoritarian democratic legitimacy. This theory fails. First, the theory rests on a fiction. There is no such generally agreed delegation to anyone. Second, the nature of the materials frequently could not allow for the play of this theory, for the materials are often unclear, or when not unclear, are conflicting. Third, the rank and file cannot lawfully delegate to the leadership their own power to vote on the bill itself. A fortiori, they cannot be said to delegate any responsibility they may be thought to have had to inform themselves of, and to act on, mere materials of legislative history.[13] The greater includes the lesser.

For the sake of argument, let us assume the judiciary adopts a general practice of reliance on materials of legislative history when interpreting statutes. Would silence of the legislative majority in the face of general judicial use of such materials endow those materials with democratic legitimacy? No. The inference from silence to acquiescence is itself invalid. There could be many explanations for such silence other than acquiescent approval.

It is true that some general interpretation statutes in American states explicitly permit courts to use materials of legislative history. (The United States Congress has not adopted any such statute.) If these state statutes are valid, they would indeed lend some legitimacy to judicial resort to materials of legislative history. But even though legitimate in the sense that these state statutes generally authorize resort to legislative history for interpretive purposes, the relevant materials in any particular case themselves still lack the formal legitimacy that derives from enactment of statutory language, and likewise lack the democratic legitimacy that such enacted language has.

Of course, when, at the time of a vote on a bill by a legislative chamber, materials of legislative history are themselves not known at all to legislators or not known to both chambers or not known to an executive participating in the process, or are unclear on their own terms, or are conflicting, or are superseded by subsequent developments in the legislative process prior to enactment, such materials also could not, on these grounds, be appropriate indicators of what any voters meant in adopting the statute, and so could not have democratic legitimacy on this basis, either.

Still another variety of legitimacy at stake here derives from considerations of institutional competency. Anglo-American systems of law do not allow legislatures authoritatively to interpret and apply their own statutes to disputed cases that arise after the statutes have been enacted. Instead, these systems separate the power of legislating from the power of interpreting, and assign the final power to interpret to courts. *One* rationale for this is that legislators would be "too political" when attempting to interpret and apply statutes to actual cases that subsequently arise. Legislators would likely focus less on the statute's objective interpretation and more on what political interests they believe their own favored "interpretations" would serve. Every "case" before them would tend to turn into another political battle. Legislators so acting would also be unlikely ever to agree even on the broad outlines of a coherent and consistent interpretive methodology. Thus, legislators, and so legislatures, are not institutionally competent to interpret their own statutes, once enacted. For this reason, too, their post-enactment interpretations would lack legitimacy.

Yet when courts resort to materials of legislative history to interpret a statute, they frequently seek to give effect to "interpretations" in these very materials by individual legislators of a bill in course of its evolution within the legislative process. If individual legislators are not institutionally competent to interpret a formally and democratically legitimate statute *after* it is enacted, why should these same legislators be any more competent, via such materials, to interpret the bill authoritatively for specific cases while it is moving through the legislative process and *before* its enactment? In truth, legislators are no more competent, and probably should be considered less competent. Pre-enactment legislative interpretation is typically a far more abstract exercise than post-enactment legislative interpretation would be. Post-enactment legislative interpretation would at least occur after the statute has been enacted as a finished product and after some kind of actual case had in fact arisen under it on which legislators might try to focus their interpretive efforts. "Pre-enactment" interpretive pronouncements of legislators, as reflected in materials of legislative history, cannot center upon a concrete case of the kind that arises after a statute is adopted. Thus, such pronouncements must lack the deliberative focus that can only be possible with respect to a genuine case or controversy. Also, "pre-enactment" interpretive pronouncements of legislators as to statutory meaning appearing in materials of legislative history frequently occur in the heat of debate or discussion without benefit of the discipline and deliberation required for truly judicious analysis of statutory language in relation to a case. Moreover, American experience tells that interested legislators, aware of a general judicial practice of resorting to materials of legislative history to interpret statutes, will *tendentiously* plant interpretive "legislative history" that, if relied on by courts, would serve the political interests of those legislators.

Then, too, there are relevant considerations of *judicial* legitimacy, as such. Judges are not to enter politics, at least not in the usual ways. Yet, at the same time, it is evident that some judges are politically strong willed: some of the right, some of the left, and some of the center. Since all statutes are meant to implement policy, even the most impartial judges may be tempted from time to time, in the guise of interpreting a statute, to "take political sides" and thus to substitute their own political judgment, at least at the margin, for that of the legislature. American experience in the federal courts indicates that the admission and full fledged use of materials of legislative history tempts some judges in just this way. A strong willed judge can often find in materials of legislative history support for that decision the judge would favor politically if sitting in the legislature. As I have indicated, some such materials are sometimes designedly "planted", and often conflict with other materials. As a result, the materials often include potential interpretive reasons for decision by judges of whatever political stripe, at least if within the mainstream. The very availability of such interpretive "reasons," tends in its own way to politicize the judiciary. As an American Supreme Court Justice, Robert Jackson, once said: "For us to undertake to reconstruct an enactment from legislative history is merely to involve the Court in political controversies which are quite proper in the enactment of a bill but should have no place in its interpretation."[14] This process can even upset hard fought legislative compromises, as where a strong willed judge overextends a statute in the name of a politically favored "general purpose" found in legislative history. This overextension may even go beyond where the legislative majority, via a compromise, agreed to go, a compromise evident from the very qualifying and limiting language of the statute.

When constructing a general interpretive methodology, then, a major factor that courts should consider in determining whether any general type of interpretive argument should be authoritatively recognized is this: Is this type of argument specially susceptible of manipulation by strong willed judges who might wish to substitute their judgment for that of the legislature, albeit in the guise of interpretation? Such "interpretation", of course, would exceed the bounds of judicial legitimacy. Yet materials of legislative history invite judges to do just this, because they appeal explicitly to political instincts and because they are often manipulable in nature. Such "interpretation" further invites legislators to play their part of the game by planting "legislative history". The American experience here has recently been recounted by a current member of the Supreme Court:[15]

> Nowadays, however, when it is universally known and expected that judges will resort to floor debates and (especially) committee reports as authoritative expressions of "legislative intent," affecting the courts rather than informing the Congress has become the primary purpose of the exercise. It is less that the courts refer to

legislative history because it exists than that legislative history exists because the courts refer to it. One of the routine tasks of the Washington lawyer-lobbyist is to draft language that sympathetic legislators can recite in a prewritten "floor debate" — or, even better, insert into a committee report.

Yet there are several other relatively autonomous general modes of interpretive argument that are not themselves so susceptible of manipulation. Not only can these be deployed to reach sound interpretive results on their own, these can also serve the important legitimizing role of curbing and checking the political inclinations of strong willed judges. This is especially true of the argument from ordinary meaning (and its variant, technical meaning). The argument from that meaning which best harmonizes the language in question with the rest of the statute and related statutes is similarly not susceptible of such manipulation, as are several other of the major remaining types of argument. It is simply not true that all modes of interpretive argument are equally malleable in the hands of strong willed judges.

Finally, the resort to materials of legislative history to interpret statutes may even diminish or undercut an important functional source of legitimacy that much legislation has. Most statutes generally resolve one or more substantive issues, more or less definitively. This resolutive effect lends special functional legitimacy to the legislative process and to the statutes that emerge from it. This is quite obviously true when there are no strong considerations on either side of a legislative issue, yet there is need for law. This is also true when there is a luxuriant array of conflicting considerations on each side of a legislative issue, and the weight of substantive reason is not clearly in favor of one side. Here, formal statutory resolution has special functional efficacy and so legitimacy. This efficacy is forfeited, and this source of legitimacy is perhaps most dramatically undermined, when a court invites the parties to introduce materials of legislative history to establish ambiguity or obscurity in a statute that does not otherwise exist, with the court then going on to use the materials to try to resolve the ambiguity or obscurity. What the legislature hath definitively resolved to resolve, the court would thus dissolve. Moreover, when such materials are themselves conflicting, as will frequently be true, the court may be drawn thereafter into a kind of "mini re-play" of the very legislative process that initially purported to resolve the issue definitively. Here the materials of legislative history are doubly disputatious and their use undercuts the functional legitimacy of the statute deriving from its resolutive effect. The use of such materials may even convert what would be relatively easy cases if resolved in accord with the usual modes of interpretive argument into contentious and difficult cases. In this way, an interpretive methodology can itself be dispute generative. Of course, this also undermines the guidance function.

C.   The Justificatory Sufficiency of Modes of Interpretive Argument That Do Not Invoke Legislative History

It might be thought that without resort to materials of legislative history, an interpretive methodology would be devoid of essential content and the whole domain of interpretive argumentation left rather barren, and so without sufficient capacity to provide guidance or resolve disputes. Some of the judges in Pepper v. Hart seem to have thought this.[16] Judges of similar view in the American federal system are not hard to find.

An interpretive methodology that does not authorize resort to materials of legislative history is still a viable interpretive methodology. After all, many statutes have been interpreted in Britain over hundreds of years without any reference to such materials. As I have said, prior to Pepper v. Hart in 1992, the general position was that records of Parliamentary debates could not be consulted, and any other materials of legislative history could only be consulted on a quite limited basis. Moreover, most state supreme courts in the United States never or only seldom resort to such materials to interpret state statutes, given that authentic records are simply not kept or are not readily usable. Yet, there is not now and never has been a general body of opinion to the effect that the interpretive reasons for decision, generated by the methodologies in use in Britain prior to Pepper v. Hart and in most American state legal systems, have been or are devoid of all justificatory force or somehow severely diminished in force, simply because they have not invoked or do not invoke materials of legislative history. Nor is it the considered general opinion that U.S. Supreme Court decisions are less well justified now than before, given that the Court less often resorts to materials of legislative history.

What, exactly, would be lost if courts were to adhere to an interpretive methodology that does not draw on materials of legislative history? It would no longer be possible for judges to use such materials to establish an ambiguity or obscurity or other doubt in the language of the statute that does not appear from an objective reading of the language itself. Such materials should not be used for this purpose anyway, given the primary aim of enacting statutes to provide their addressees with reliable guidance. If an objective reading of the language without regard to materials of legislative history does not yield ambiguity, obscurity, or other doubt, then the statute should be taken to provide reliable guidance for all addressees, including the courts.

It is also true that a methodology that does not draw on materials of legislative history would lack all possible foundation for either an argument that, in adopting the statutory words, the legislature *subjectively* intended a specific application of those words, or *subjectively* intended some general meaning of those words. But the loss of this mode of argument, the "intent" terminology of which is frequently encountered in the opinions of some judges, would not be a significant loss. Any such appeal to *subjective* legislative intent is simply misdirected. Interpretation that provides reliable guidance must be concerned with determining the reasonable and objective meaning of the statutory language, not the subjective intention of legislators, either individually or in some aggregate. Furthermore, it is unusual for the materials of legislative history to yield any evidence of actual intentions of a clear majority of legislators that bears directly on the specific issue of interpretation that has actually arisen. Usually the issue that has arisen is not one on which there is any evidence of any such subjective legislative intent. But even when such evidence exists, it typically does not, as I have explained, afford addressees of the statute a clear, certain, and reliable basis on which to act, and it is not likely to be readily accessible to statutory addressees at reasonable cost. Moreover, the subjective intentions of individual legislators or of legislative committees, as grounded in materials of legislative history, still remain grounded in materials that themselves lack formal, democratic, and institutional legitimacy, for all the reasons I have given.

What else would be lost if the interpretive methodology were to eschew all materials of legislative history? Also lost would be whatever contributions those materials might make to the construction of elements of still *other* general and relatively autonomous types of interpretive argument. In some cases, there would be loss of materials providing one source of evidence of the general purpose that might be attributed to the statute. With such evidence of general purpose, the interpreter could then select that interpretation of the implementive language which best serves this general purpose. So called purposive argumentation is, of course, one major type of interpretive argument recognized in some measure in the interpretive methodologies of many legal systems, including the European Court. Some judges in Pepper v. Hart seem to have thought that such argumentation is necessarily dependent on the materials of legislative history.[17] Again, however, such evidence of general purpose may not exist at all in the legislative history, or it may be unclear, or conflicting, or it may be tendentious or otherwise unreliable as an indicator of what the legislative majority took to be the general purpose, or it will often not be readily accessible at reasonable cost. Also, given that such materials lack legitimacy, so, too, would any purpose derived therefrom. As I will later explain, however, all this does not signify that interpreters must forego purposive interpretation altogether.

There are still other major objections here to purposive argumentation insofar as it is grounded in materials of legislative history. The type of evidence of general purpose found in such materials frequently takes the form of what I will call a detached, truncated, or abbreviated general statutory purpose, a purpose devoid of all indication of compromise, qualification or limitation. The materials of legislative history frequently yield up a general statutory purpose not itself conjoined to, but rather separated from, and so distinct from, the implementive language of the statute as finally adopted by the legislature. At the same time, in Anglo-American systems, the language of statutes typically does not contain a statement of general purpose as such. Thus, having identified an abbreviated and truncated general purpose in materials of legislative history, a judge or other interpreter will be all the more tempted to think that the separate and distinct implementive language of the statute that the legislature did adopt was adopted simply to serve the general unqualified purpose to be found in the materials. With this general purpose in detached, truncated, and abbreviated form, the interpreter may construe the implementive language of the statute *merely* as implementive, and not at all as qualifying or limiting.

But statutory language typically or at least commonly reflects compromises between general purposes:

> [N]o legislation pursues its purpose at all costs. Deciding what competing values will or will not be sacrificed to the achievement of a particular objective is the very essence of legislative choice — and it frustrates rather than effectuates legislative intent to assume that whatever furthers the statute's primary objective must be the law.[18]

> Application of 'broad purposes' of legislation at the expense of specific provisions ignores the complexity of the problems Congress is called upon to address and the dynamics of legislative action. Congress may be unanimous in its intent to stamp out some vague social or economic evil; however, because its Members may differ sharply on the means for effectuating that intent, the final language of the legislation may reflect hard-fought compromises. Invocation of the 'plain purpose' of legislation at the expense of the terms of the statute itself takes no account of the processes of compromise, and, in the end, prevents the effectuation of congressional intent.[19]

No general purpose attributable to a statute is ever meant to be implemented unqualifiedly and without limitation. The implementive language of almost any statute not only implements but also qualifies and limits any general purpose that may be attributed to it. As Geoffrey Marshall and I once put matters:[20]

> Legislation, particularly of a regulatory or penal kind, may superficially have a single stated or obvious objective. The purpose of road traffic regulation is to promote road safety. The object of mine safety laws is to promote safety in mines. But these are only abbreviated statements of the statutory purpose which is not to promote the stated objectives in any and every way whatsoever, but to promote them *by the means and through the words set out in the statute and not to do so in any other way*. It is almost as much an object of a penal statute not to convict those who do not fall within its provisions as to convict those who do. So if the issue is whether particular persons or circumstances fall inside or outside the

statute's provisions, the statute's ultimate purpose will itself not resolve such an issue and appeal to it will commonly be empty or tendentious. Thus, if a legislature enacts "No firearms in the park" with the general objective of preventing danger (rather than for example prohibiting anything likely to be dangerous), a full statement of the legislature's ultimate purpose would include the propositions that it was to permit danger in the park if not arising from the presence of a firearm and also to ignore the fact that some firearms might be brought into the park without danger (yet still violate the statute). In such circumstances, an argument from ultimate purpose will not be conclusive in determining whether a catapult or a bow and arrow is a firearm (though it might have *some* relevance), and the argument ought not to produce the conclusion that rifles carried in a ceremonial parade (without permission) are not firearms. In sum, because of the foregoing considerations, the argument from ultimate purpose, when such purpose is faithfully and fully characterized, will frequently have little, if any, independent bearing on the appropriate scope of a general or vague statutory term.

Yet, as I have indicated, the materials of legislative history tend to yield abbreviated general purposes detached from implementive language. In turn, some judges are tempted to utilize such purposes to "interpret" statutory language merely as implementive and not also as qualifying and limiting, all in disregard of the compromise nature of legislation and in disregard of the way implementive language typically qualifies and limits statutory purpose. It follows, then, that any affirmative contributions that materials of legislative history might be thought to make to the construction of a relatively autonomous argument from general statutory purpose must nevertheless be weighed against their potential for distorting the very nature of legislation itself as a compromise of conflicting notions both of ends and of means. Indeed, it is not at all salutary to use legislative history materials as a source of evidence of detached, truncated, and abbreviated general purposes that will frequently then tempt judges to construct what they consider to be general "purposive" interpretive arguments in which they "interpret" the implementive language free or relatively free of all compromise, qualification and limitation. Statutory language should never be thought of merely as means to the end of serving whatever general purpose is found in legislative history materials or otherwise.

Would judicial adoption of an interpretive methodology devoid of resort to materials of legislative history require that interpreters eschew purpose in the interpretation of statutes altogether? Indeed, would this mean that statutory interpretation simply could not be appropriately "purposive"? Some judges appear to think so. Some have even indicated their belief that without resort to such materials for evidence of legislative purpose, statutory interpretation might degenerate into an arid wasteland of literalism.[21] I will now demonstrate that these views are incorrect. I will also indicate how the overall richness of the modes of interpretive argument that remain when the materials of legislative history are put to one side is itself vast. It is this richness that explains the justificatory sufficiency of British interpretive methodology prior to Pepper v. Hart, and of American interpretive methodology with respect to state statutes in states where legislative history is simply not kept or not kept in usable form. This richness also explains the justificatory sufficiency of U.S. Supreme Court opinions that do not rely on materials of legislative history. One American Supreme Court Justice has recently remarked that he has "not used legislative history to decide a case for . . . the past nine terms" and that he has not felt his remaining justificatory resources to be at all insufficient. On the contrary, he considered himself much better off in this regard.[22]

If we identify the major types of general and relatively autonomous interpretive arguments that remain if materials of legislative history are put to one side, we can see that vast resources of interpretive argumentation remain to serve the dual ends (1) of guidance on the front lines of human interaction, and (2) of justified resolution of disputes in court. As I have indicated, it would be surprising if this were not so, given that British courts interpreted statutes for centuries without reference to materials of legislative history, that most American state supreme courts continue to do so, and that the U.S. Supreme Court is relying less and less on such materials.

The major types of argument that would remain include the following:

(1) The argument from standard ordinary meanings of the words in issue,

(2)   The argument from standard technical meanings of words in issue, i.e., a standard legal meaning the words have in the law, or a standard meaning the words have in a particular branch of knowledge or technology, or in a special trade, or the like,

(3)   The argument from the meaning indicated by contextual harmonization, i.e., how a proposed meaning fits with the rest of the statute, and harmonizes with other parts of the same statute, with related statutes, and the general fabric of the law,

(4)   The argument from the meaning that arises from contrasts with any prior law superseded by the statute,

(5)   The argument from the meaning that best implements what is considered to be the general purpose of the statute, i.e., general purpose as gleaned form sources other than legislative history,

(6)   The argument from the historically evolved meaning that the words in the statute have come to have within the system,

(7)   The argument from statutory analogy,

(8)   The argument from that interpretation which makes the statute most rule-like or otherwise law-like,

(9)   The argument from that meaning which best coheres with a general legal concept operative within the branch of law concerned,

(10)   The argument from the meaning that is most consistent or congruent with relevant and authoritative policy or principle generally operative within the field in which the statute falls.

Not one of the foregoing modes of argument is essentially dependent for its force on materials of legislative history. Foremost among these types of argument are the first two, the argument from standard ordinary meanings of the words in issue, and the cognate argument from standard technical meanings of the words in issue.

The argument from ordinary meaning may be defined more fully as the argument from that meaning or meanings which a competent, knowledgeable, purposeful, and informed user of ordinary language would give to the ordinary words in issue on the basis of the resources of ordinary language argumentation. Thus, the argument from ordinary meaning is not equivalent to whatever type of argument happens to support an ordinary meaning as the interpretation of the statute in a particular instance. Other leading types of argument may happen to support an appropriate ordinary meaning, yet not qualify as arguments from ordinary meaning because they do not essentially invoke the resources of ordinary language argumentation. For example, the argument from that meaning which best serves the general purpose of the statute (as ascertained from, for example, the face of the statute), or the argument from that meaning which best harmonizes with other sections of the same statute, may happen to support giving an appropriate ordinary meaning to the words, yet these types of arguments do not themselves appeal essentially to the resources of ordinary language argumentation. Nor is the argument from ordinary meaning to be equated merely with whatever meaning seems "plain" on the face of the statute, either. The resources of this mode of argument are not essentially literalistic in character. Such resources, rich and deep as they are, are often sufficient alone to clear up not only surface ambiguity or obscurity but also other doubts about the meaning of a statute as applied to particular circumstances.[23]

No scholars have so far canvassed and analyzed all the relevant general types of resources that may figure in the argument from ordinary meaning, but Geoffrey Marshall and I have presented a general account of the contours of these resources in an earlier essay. In that essay, we summarized those resources as including general linguistic competence, dictionaries, grammar books, the bearing of a general context of usage, general knowledge of the typical language user, purposive analysis drawing at least on immediate purposes evident from the language and the context of usage, the drafter's knowledge of usage in parallel circumstances in ordinary life, special factual knowledge fairly attributable to the language user, reminders of factual considerations already familiar, the use of hypothetical case analysis, analogy, standards of consistency, and systematic reflection.[24] Each of the foregoing is a considerable resource susceptible of extended elaboration.

The argument from ordinary meaning also has a special claim to primacy among the various major modes of argument. Its resources are extensive and deep. Most of the language of most bills is expressed in ordinary language. All of the syntax of all of the language in all bills is the syntax of ordinary language. The language of deliberation and debate is overwhelmingly ordinary language. It is more than a fair inference that legislators who studied and who voted in favor of a bill understood the bill in terms of the ordinary meanings of the ordinary words in the bill. Addressees of the new statute will understand it in similar fashion (with advice as needed). All this lends special legitimacy to this mode of interpretive argument. But this is not all. Judicial invocation of this mode of argument encourages legislative drafters to draft openly and explicitly, rather than through "legislation" hidden in materials of legislative history that might well not have gained true assent if the more explicit language required to implement the gist of such materials had been used in the text. Moreover, this mode of argument, because of its determinacy and because it is such common property, is more susceptible of even-handed application across time and space in the hands of different judicial and administrative personnel, than is any other mode of argument (except the argument from technical meaning). It thus distinctively serves predictability and equality before the law. Similarly, interpreters who invoke ordinary meaning argumentation generate reasons on which statutory addressees can reliably act from the effective date of the statute.

It is sometimes suggested that the argument from ordinary meaning is necessarily literal and wooden, and so cannot be purposive in any sense. Indeed some of the judges in Pepper v. Hart seem to have thought something like this.[25] As Geoffrey Marshall and I once emphasized, there is nothing essentially literal about the argument from ordinary meaning. An ordinary meaning of a word in the context of its use is frequently not the same as its literal meaning. In discussing the interpretation of laws, Cicero put a case of a "salvage" law which prescribed that those who in a storm forsook a ship should forfeit all property in it and the ship should belong entirely to those who "stayed" with it.[26] One such passenger, who was by reason of illness unable to escape with the rest, claimed the ship as a salvor after it by chance came safely to port. Literal usage might suggest that the sick passenger in a literal sense "stayed" with the ship and that he might claim the benefit of the law. But it is highly doubtful whether an informed, competent, and purposive user of the English language, knowing the facts of the case, would feel compelled to say the sick man was someone who had "stayed" with the ship. Such a person would almost certainly understand from the words that any reward for salvage should go only to a person who *by choice stayed* with the ship. After all, the reward is a *reward for salvage*. A sick person who is unable to do anything other than remain on board could not save the ship or its contents and so is not deserving of such a reward, anyway. Thus, in this context, the ordinary or common usage of "stayed" — stayed by choice — can be seen to differ from the literal meaning — stayed in the sense merely of remaining on board. Also, the literal sense is not necessarily a narrower meaning. In fact the literal sense in this instance embraces a wider class of persons than the ordinary sense that the informed, competent, and purposive user of English would, without more, take the word to mean.

Of course, it is possible to misuse the argument from ordinary meaning and give statutory words a literal meaning that the argument really does not support, as would be the case if the court were to hold in the foregoing example that the literal meaning of the word "stayed" should govern. Indeed, some strong willed judges impose on ordinary language. They even depart from the ordinary language of the statute in deciding the case, yet attempt to justify such "interpretation" in the guise of ordinary language argumentation. This, in turn, distorts the mode of argument itself, for it simply cannot withstand such double duty. The possibility of abuse exists with respect to any mode of interpretive argument.

As I have indicated, it is sometimes suggested that the argument from ordinary meaning is not necessarily a purposive mode of argumentation. However, this mode of argument, as appropriately defined and deployed, is inherently purposive, though it is not identical to what I call the general and relatively autonomous argument from the general purpose of the statute. Cicero's example also aptly illustrates how this is so. As already remarked, a salvor statute purposively provides a *reward for salvage*. A sick person who is unable to do anything other than remain on board is not deserving of a reward, and could not save the ship anyway. Indeed, ordinary meaning argumentation in the interpretation of statutes, properly conceived, is never purposeless. It always has regard at least to the immediate purpose of the legislature in using ordinary language in the implementive provisions of the statute. The interpreter invoking this mode of argument will ask: What meaning would an informed, competent, and purposive user of these ordinary words mean to convey in such circumstances? Such a question can be answered without looking to materials of legislative history. Of course, in daily discourse, ordinary language is typically used to convey general purposive meaning (and rarely causes trouble). In this important respect, ordinary meaning is semantically autonomous.

Contrary to the opinions of some judges in Pepper v. Hart, it is fallacious to assume that if a court invokes the argument from ordinary meaning, it must disregard the purpose of the statute.[27] The argument from ordinary meaning, faithfully conceived, is intrinsically purposive. So, too, is the argument from technical meaning, for it seeks to give effect to what an informed, competent, and purposive user of the words in a technical sense would mean to convey. Likewise, the argument from contextual harmonization is purposive. It can be said to harmonize all the relevant provisions of the statute and related statutes in light of some intelligible and coherent purpose. Of course, that general type of relatively autonomous argument from the meaning of the words that best implements the general purpose of a statute is also intrinsically purposive. It is not, however, necessary to resort to materials of legislative history even to attribute such a purpose to a statute. The statute will sometimes set forth policy or principle explicitly (though this must be consistent with the words, and not be over or under general). Even if the statute does not explicitly set forth a general purpose (as is usual), it will commonly be possible to glean the statutory policy or principle from the implementive language, from unquestioned instances of its application, from comparison of it with prior law, or from still other resources, without considering materials of legislative history at all. Two thoughtful American students of interpretive method concluded after a life long study that the best guides in constructing the *general* purpose of a statute are not legislative history materials but rather a generalization constructed from "instances of unquestioned application of the statute" in light of its implementive language and in light of comparisons with any prior law superseded.[28] At the same time, such a purpose, so derived, will *not* be truncated and abbreviated, and thus divorced from implementive language. Rather, so derived, it will necessarily take account of the qualifying and limiting effect of that language.

Indeed, each of the dozen or so aforementioned general modes of argumentation is in its own way purposive, if appropriately deployed. Thus, not only is an interpretive methodology free of references to materials of legislative history nonetheless justificatorily sufficient for the dual ends of providing guidance and of resolving disputes in court. Such a methodology, as appropriately conceived and deployed, is entirely purposive, through and through.

I do not claim that the argument from ordinary meaning, or indeed, any one general mode of argument that remains after materials of legislative history are put to one side, is universally applicable to resolve any and all issues of interpretation. Also, I know of no case that has ever arisen in which it could be said that the only interpretive resource available consisted of an argument or arguments deriving from materials of legislative history. It is true that the origins of interpretive issues are diverse, and are not confined to such linguistic ones as ambiguity or vagueness or ellipsis, sources which at least the deeper resources of the argument from ordinary meaning may still be available to deal with. The origins also include narrow gaps, obsolescence, bad drafting, uncertain fit within the fabric of the law, all ones that the argument from ordinary meaning may not go at all far to resolve. But with respect to such gaps, obsolescence, bad drafting and uncertain fit, arguments from materials of legislative history generally do not go far either. Several other major modes of interpretive argument remain, however, and one of these or two or more together will usually have quite sufficient resolutive efficacy. And in the rare case when not, then, instead of pretending to interpret the statute, the court should fall back on its general residual power to make common law supplementing the statute, and do so openly and candidly.

D. The Facilitation of Effective Legislative Drafting

If legislation is to be legitimate and effective, and if democracy is to work its will, those who draft statutes and legislators who adopt statutes must be able to do so with assurance that an appropriate and consistent general interpretive methodology will be applied to statutes as drafted and adopted. For example, a drafter can readily draft statutes to be interpreted in accord with the argument from ordinary meaning, or the argument from technical meaning, or the argument from statutory harmonization.

But how is a drafter to draft where one, or perhaps *the*, leading mode of argument recognized in the courts is the argument from an alleged specific applicational intent as found in materials of legislative history, or from an alleged general intention as found in materials of legislative history? Let us assume that at the outset of the legislative process the drafter begins on a clean slate, without any legislative history. The drafter prepares the first version of the bill. As the legislative process unfolds, is the drafter then to include a series of modifications in the text of the bill as initially drafted which negate, or affirm, as appropriate, fragments of legislative history that emerge concurrently during the process and which might be thought likely to influence a judge? How is the drafter to do this? Can the drafter do this in advance of the final vote? How is the drafter to know in advance what materials of legislative history will appear in the record? How is the drafter to know what language the majority will eventually want to adopt that might require negation or affirmation? One cure for these problems might be simply to amend the bill, seriatim, during the process. Amendment may affirm or negate or supersede some materials. Then, too, amendment may not occur. Or although it occurs, its effects in relation to materials of legislative history already in the record may be ambiguous. Perhaps after the bill is finally voted on, the statute might then undergo a series of "legislative history amendments" designed to affirm or reject fragments of legislative history in tune with, or not in tune with, the statutory language adopted by the majority? Should the majority be called on, in such a vote, only to vote on the amended statute without benefit of discussion, committee study, etc? Or at least without benefit of recorded discussion or study so that no subsequent material of legislative history is thereby created requiring negation or affirmation! The legislative process is not, however, to go on ad infinitum!

Or perhaps after preparing the initial draft of the bill, the drafter is never to re-enter the fray at all, provided at least that materials of legislative history emerge in the process and plainly indicate which of two alternative interpretations at least the leadership of the legislature intends? Instead of amending the bill to make clear which of the two is correct, it may be that the drafter and the legislative body are to assume that courts in disputes, and legal advisors of statutory addressees, will later locate the relevant legislative history and will decide cases and advise addressees as to which of the two readings is correct. One of the judges in Pepper v. Hart bordered on suggesting this.[29] Yet it would be better to amend and clarify the bill itself before it is finally adopted. Such action would provide surer guidance to statutory addressees and their legal advisors conducting business and other affairs of daily life. This would also better serve formal, democratic, and other legitimacy. It would, as well, enhance the justificatory sufficiency of the argument from ordinary meaning or technical meaning for those issues that do later arise. Yet it is noteworthy that Parliament did not have its bill redrafted to make clear in appropriate language which of the two interpretations in Pepper v. Hart was intended, even though the leadership claimed to agree on the preferred interpretation, and even though, at that time, Parliament could not count on the courts to interpret the statute in light of the materials of legislative history!

E. Values Associated With The Rule of Law

An authoritative interpretive methodology of statutory interpretation should, so far as such a methodology can feasibly do so, serve the rule of law and the values associated with it. One of the most important values here is the freedom, autonomy, and dignity of effective citizen self-direction under law, with benefit of any needed legal advice. It is, of course, preferable for citizens to apply law to themselves rather than be ordered around by officials (including judges). This serves not only freedom, autonomy, and individual dignity. It is highly efficient as well. Citizens should also be able to guide themselves about under the law without having to litigate. These desiderata require that law be general, prospective, clear, and efficiently and inexpensively "learnable". I have already identified many points of inconsistency between these desiderata and the general resort to materials of legislative history in the interpretation of statutes. What I now wish to stress is that the introduction of such materials increases the disputatiousness of statutory language, and increases the disputatiousness of interpretive methodology, and so increases the disputatiousness of the overall processes of interpretation in particular cases. This in itself can be a major independent source of uncertainty in statute law. General interpretive resort to legislative history means that there must be a reconciliation of the statutory language with whatever elements of legislative history there are. As the federal experience in America shows, this in itself can frequently be highly disputatious in a variety of ways. As I have indicated, this disputatiousness undermines efficient "learnability" of statute law, and itself increases whatever unclarity may already exist. In turn, this impairs certainty, predictability and reliability of law for all citizens seeking to exercise free, autonomous, and dignified self direction under law, the most fundamental of all "rule of law" values.

The uncertainty, unpredictability, and unreliability of statute law that derives from the increased disputatiousness of an interpretive method embracing general resort to materials of legislative history also impairs the capacity of statute law to fulfill another and related "rule of law" value, namely, *limited* government. This, too, is a fundamental value, as Locke and others emphasized. The more disputatious the law is, the less it can effectively limit and curb officials in their dealings with citizens. For example, the freedom and dignity of a citizen to choose to drive a car at lower than the legal rate of speed exists only to the extent that police may *not* intervene at the lower speed. The law setting the rate of speed generally curbs such intervention, and thus limits official power. But if the meaning of this law itself becomes more disputatious by virtue of disputatious interpretive method, the less this law can serve as an effective limit on official power. Here, too, insofar as the general availability of materials of legislative history of a speed law increases the disputatiousness of that law, the less effective that law becomes as a bastion against the exercise of official power.

The increased disputatiousness of interpretive method that derives from opening up the method to general use of materials of legislative history also disserves another fundamental "rule of law" value, namely, the legitimacy of civic governance, including, of course, the legitimacy of judicial action. I have already demonstrated how such materials themselves do not enjoy a high degree of legitimacy. This factor alone already diminishes the legitimacy of judicial interpretations based on them. Here I wish to stress that this legitimacy is diminished by a further closely related factor. The disputatiousness of materials of legislative history in many cases requires that courts exercise increased discretion in reconciling the language of the statute with materials of legislative history. In many cases, even when this discretion is exercised reasonably, the resulting judicial action will be, and will be perceived to be, more a matter of discretionary choice than of decision in accord with a rule-like statute. This, in turn, will have its own de-legitimizing effect.

In the same vein, the disputatiousness of materials of legislative history and the discretion that goes with it, make it more difficult to discern when judges at all levels are guilty of legal error or, indeed, have modified or departed from a statute, albeit in the name (or guise) of interpretation. This also impairs the efficacy of appellate review of lower court interpretation, and so the rule of law. As the American experience indicates, the materials of legislative history can be very "rich", and can appear to some judges even to authorize a repudiation of statutory language, provided that this repudiation is duly clothed in the facade of interpretive methodology and its terminology, i.e., "legislative intent" derived from materials of legislative history.

III. Conclusion

Courts in Britain and the United States, if I am right, ought not to use materials of legislative history to interpret statutes. This, among other things, conflicts with important considerations of appropriate form and formal legitimacy. Historically, the English courts have generally been more deferential to form and the values it serves than American courts.[30] Now we have the makings of an important divergence the other way, at least if we compare the House of Lords with the U.S. Supreme Court. In 1992, the House of Lords in Pepper v. Hart moved dramatically in the direction of resort to legislative history materials in disregard of form. At this very time, the U.S. Supreme Court was, and continues to be, pulling back.

Even so, there are two major respects in which the decision in Pepper v. Hart is in spirit formal, if not in the formal tradition. First, the court's reasoning is significantly grounded in analogies to positions that English courts had already taken and also grounded in analogies to positions of courts in Commonwealth countries. Second, the decision, itself is carefully hedged about in several specific rules that purport to limit its scope. If those efforts at limitation fail to work in practice, as I believe is likely, the House of Lords may pull back, too. If so, this will not only represent a triumph for form and the values it serves, but also for reliable guidance of statutory addressees in economic and other daily life, for democracy, and for the rule of law.

Notes

1. See, e.g., Geoffrey Marshall, *Hansard and the Interpretation of Statutes*, PARLIAMENT AND THE LAW ed. G. Drewry and D. Oliver (Butterworths 1998); Robert S. Summers and Geoffrey Marshall, *The Argument from Ordinary Meaning in Statutory Interpretation*, 43 NO. IRELAND L. QUARTERLY 213 (1992).
2. [1993] A.C. 593.
3. See, e.g., *Schwegmann Bros. v. Calvert Distillers Corp.* 341 U.S. 384 (1951); *United States v. Public Utilities Commn.* 345 U.S. 295 (1953).
4. See, e.g., T.W. Merrill, *Textualism and the Future of the Chevron Doctrine*, 72 WASHINGTON U. LAW QUARTERLY 351, 355 (1994).
5. For a concise summary of Justice Scalia's objections, in his own words, see A. Scalia, A MATTER OF INTERPRETATION 14-37 (Princeton, 1997). See especially Justice Jackson's opinion in Schwegmann Bros. supra note 3, at 395.
6. Citizens to Preserve Overton Park, Inc. v. Volpe, 401 U.S. 402, 412 n. 29 (1971).
7. "In most states, it is virtually impossible to collect the necessary documents for a simple legislative history outside of the state capitol or its legislative library. Debates are almost never published, bills are usually available only at the legislature and during the session itself, committee reports are published in only a few states and hearings even less often." Morris L. Cohen, Robert C. Berring, Kent C. Olson eds., HOW TO FIND THE LAW 257 (St. Paul 1995). The authors of another research book describe the process this way: "Attempting to compile a legislative history for a state law in a manner similar to . . . federal laws is often difficult and, at times, impossible. As a general rule, state legislatures do not publish their debates, committee reports, or transcripts of hearings held before legislative committees." J. Myron Jacobstein, Roy M. Mersky, Donald H. Dunn eds., FUNDAMENTALS OF LEGAL RESEARCH 244 New York (1994).

Or, as another scholar has recently said: "But in New York and likely other states as well, legislative history is relatively sparse with legislative intent evidenced primarily by the language of the statute itself. *Rarely is a committee report available.*" Judith S. Kaye, *State Courts at the Dawn of a New Century: Common Law Courts Reading Statutes and Constitutions*, 70 NEW YORK U. LAW REV. 1, 29 (1995) (emphasis added).
8. [1993] A.C. at 614.
9. Just what a general methodology should look like, overall, has not commanded much scholarly attention. In one conception, well known in scholarly circles in the U.S.A., all modes of interpretive argument are collapsed into one overall "purposive" approach. See H.M. Hart, Jr. and Albert M. Sacks, THE LEGAL PROCESS 1374-80 (Foundation Press 1994). Although on my own approach, I would accord "top-rung primacy" to what Geoffrey Marshall and I call the argument from ordinary meaning (and its variant, technical meaning), I would leave distinct places in the methodology for a number of other modes of interpretive argument, most of which are introduced later in this essay. A comprehensive methodology would include other elements, as well.

10. See, e.g., Church of the Holy Trinity v. United States, 143 U.S. 457 (1892); American Trucking Ass'n v. United States, 310 U.S. 534 (1940); Perrin v. United States, 444 U.S. 37 (1979).

11. See, e.g., IOWA CODE ANN. s 4.6 (West 1989) MINN.STAT.ANN. s 645.16 (West 1983) 1 PA.CONS.STAT.ANN. s 1921 (c) (1983).

12. Robert S. Summers and Geoffrey Marshall, *The Argument from Ordinary Meaning in Statutory Interpretation*, 43 NO. IRELAND L. QUARTERLY 217-19 (1992).

13. John F. Manning, *Textualism as a Non Delegation Doctrine*, 97 COLUMBIA L. REV. 673 (1997).

14. Schwegmann Bros., supra note 3, at 396.

15. Scalia, supra note 5, at 34.

16. Pepper, [1993] A.C., at 617 and 633.

17. Ibid.

18. Rodrigues v. United States, 480 U.S. 522 (1987).

19. Board of Governors of Fed. Reserve Sys. v. Dimension Fin. Corp., 474 U.S. 361, 373-74 (1986).

20. Summers and Marshall, supra note 12, at 230-31.

21. See, e.g., Pepper, [1993] A.C., at 617 and 633.

22. Scalia, supra note 5, at 36. A term, incidentally, is a year.

23. Summers and Marshall, supra note 12, at 217-19.

24. Id. at 224.

25. Pepper, [1993] A.C. at 617 and 633.

26. Summers and Marshall, supra note 12, at 215.

27. Pepper, [1993] A.C. at 617 and 633.

28. Hart & Sacks, supra note 9, at 1378.

29. Pepper, [1993] A.C. at 618.

30. P.S. Atiyah and Robert S. Summers, FORM AND SUBSTANCE IN ANGLO-AMERICAN LAW, *passim* (Oxford, 1991).

CHAPTER 12

FORMAL LEGAL TRUTH AND SUBSTANTIVE TRUTH IN JUDICIAL FACT-FINDING

I. Introduction

A primary function of trial court procedures (which I will also call adjudicative processes) and of rules of evidence in cases before courts in which facts are in dispute is to find the truth. Some natural scientists, some social scientists, some philosophers, and many others regularly assume that truth finding is the only important function of trial court procedures and the rules of evidence. It is true that without findings of fact that generally accord with truth, the underlying policy goals or norms of the law could not be served. For example, a rule designed to secure safety on the highways by setting a speed limit of 70 mph, and by punishing those who exceed it, cannot effectively serve its purpose if fact finders fail to find the true facts as to the speed of actual offenders and so let speeders go free of penalty. And if a party charged with speeding really did not speed, yet was found guilty and punished, this would also violate norms of justice as well as fail to implement the policy of highway safety as such.

Further, without judicial findings of fact that generally accord with truth, it would not be possible to test and improve upon the law in light of genuine experience with it in its concrete applications. If a rule of law is judicially applied to the true facts it envisions, the rule can be tested for the adequacy of its formulation and for the soundness of any means-goal hypothesis it embodies. If, in light of the true facts, the rule is found wanting, then a legislature or perhaps even a court higher in the system may modify the rule in some way.

Also, without judicial findings of fact that generally accord with truth, citizens would, over time, lose confidence in adjudicative processes as fair and reliable tribunals of justice, as effective means to policy, and as effective means of dispute resolution, both in civil and criminal cases. Interestingly, this would be undesirable also because it might lead to more litigation rather than less, for fewer parties would fear that truth adverse to their positions would emerge in court proceedings, and these would be less disposed to settle out of court. Thus, in general, and without more, a legal finding of fact in a court proceeding should accord with the actual truth. I will call actual truth "substantive truth."

I define as "formal legal truth" whatever is found as fact by the legal fact-finder (judge or lay jurors or both), whether it accords with substantive truth or not.[1] In a well designed system, judicial findings of formal legal truth generally coincide with substantive truth in particular cases, and from the foregoing we can readily see powerful reasons why the two ought to coincide.[2] But formal legal truth may, in a particular case, fail to coincide with substantive truth. There are two quite different types of possible explanations for such failure when it occurs. (And I do not mean to imply that we are always aware of, or can easily determine, the existence of any such divergence.)

First, trial court procedures and the rules of evidence, even though primarily directed at substantive truth, may, in a particular case, nevertheless lead to formal "findings of fact" that diverge from substantive truth not by design, but merely because this is the way the process happens to work, under the peculiar circumstances of the case. In such a case, any one of a host of factors may explain this divergence, including grossly unequal lawyer representation as between the parties before the court, inequality of resources available to the parties for trial preparation, prejudice or bias on the part of particular fact finders, sheer lack of competence of the fact finders in grasping and weighing evidence, fortuitous events such as the death of key witnesses prior to trial, and more. In some of these cases, when we are aware such findings are erroneous, we may be able to remedy them through appeal, reversal, a new trial, or the like. The divergence between substantive truth and formal legal truth in this first type of case cannot itself be justified on policy or related rationales. Of course, the divergence calls for explanation, and, in some particular cases, perhaps for rectification. Often the divergence simply reflects a concession to larger necessities, especially cost considerations. The law itself cannot guarantee equality of legal representation at trial, for example.

Second, there are cases where trial court procedures and rules of evidence fail to yield substantive truth for quite a different sort of reason. In these cases, substantive truth and formal legal truth diverge in a particular case because the trial court procedures and the rules of evidence, though generally directed at substantive truth, are also designed to serve other ends that actually come into play in a particular case. For example, a rule of criminal evidence law forbidding the use of even highly inculpatory evidence procured by an illegal search of a private home protects privacy. To cite a second example, a rule of evidence may forbid the court from considering a confession of guilt by the accused criminal, and also any evidentiary fruits thereof, where the police procured the confession by beating the accused. As a result of the operation of this rule excluding evidence, the court may, in the end, fail to find the true facts. Not all coerced confessions are false. But such resulting divergence between formal findings of fact and substantive truth can still be justified on policy or other grounds. It is simply not so that the exclusive business of a trial court in all disputed cases is to find the actual truth. Indeed, with respect to civil cases, a noted English jurist once wrote:[3]

> Perhaps the greatest of all the fallacies entertained by lay people about the law is one which, though seldom expressed in terms, an observant lawyer may quite commonly find lurking not far below the surface. This is that the business of a court of justice is to discover the truth. Its real business is to pronounce upon the justice of particular claims, and incidentally to test the truth of the assertions of fact made in support of the claim in law, provided that those assertions are relevant in law to the establishment of the desired conclusion; and this is by no means the same thing.

Yet given the acknowledged importance of finding the truth in the generality of cases, we have here something of a puzzle, or perhaps even a paradox. That it might be possible to justify the failure of a court to find the truth when what is at stake is something of such importance as the policy against crime, or the policy in favor of justice as between civil disputants, will at first strike many as strange, or at the very least anomalous.

Just what is going on in particular cases of this second type in which the system, partly by design, yields findings of fact that do not accord with substantive legal truth? What type of policy or other justification might at least alleviate some of our concern over the failure to achieve substantive truth in such cases? My focus here will be on these two questions, and I will draw mainly on examples from experience in Anglo-American systems of law. My general analysis applies also to leading civil law systems (though with variations).[4]

II. How Fact Findings in Court May Rationally Diverge From Substantive Truth

A variety of types of factors may operate individually or in some combination to justify excluding or at least limiting relevant evidence in a court proceeding. Yet, other things equal, deciding on the basis of all relevant evidence reasonably available should approximate actual truth better than deciding on something less than all the relevant evidence reasonably available. Thus when relevant evidence is excluded, there is often an increased risk of divergence between formal legal truth and substantive legal truth. For example, privileges of certain witnesses not to testify are recognized in the law of evidence of various countries. A husband may not be required to testify against a wife, yet this may be truth defeating in a particular case. Certainly it will be truth hostile, if not truth defeating, in the mine-run cases in which the privilege is successfully invoked. The main rationale for this privilege is simply the preservation of marital harmony.

Consider another example. Because of the limited "jurisdictional reach" of the trial court, it may not be possible to introduce before the court even evidence so highly relevant and weighty that it would be decisive if presented to the court. For example, it may not be possible to compel witnesses who are outside the jurisdictional territory of the court to appear and testify, and it may not be possible even to procure admissible written testimony from them, at least assuming the opposing party objects for lack of opportunity to test such evidence on cross examination. Yet if live or written testimony from such a party were heard, the fact-finder might well find the facts differently and truthfully so in some such cases. Here the rationales for any divergence between substantive truth and formal legal truth are partly that some concession must be made to the inevitabilities of systems in which courts have territorial jurisdiction and partly that such "extra" jurisdictional evidence, if merely written, may lack reliability.

Thus, the concept of formal legal truth is shaped partly by various exclusionary doctrines in the law of evidence. These rules relate to privileged communications, as above, exclusions for hearsay evidence, as above, exclusions where the evidence was procured through invasions of privacy, exclusions for coerced confessions, and more. Similarly, the so called parole evidence rule in the field of contracts operates in some cases to keep highly relevant evidence of the actual tenor of the parties' understanding from the fact-finder in the interest of protecting the reliance of parties on carefully drafted written agreements. In the criminal law, it is familiar that there are various specialized rules of exclusion, and these are not confined to the exclusion of coerced confessions and their fruits. Furthermore, the accused may even refuse to testify in the proceeding at all. These rules serve various policies. Some regulate police practices that coerce the accused, invade privacy or the like. There is also a concern to avoid the taint that would go with a conviction based on evidence secured by unlawful means. The procedure allowing the accused to refuse to testify is based partly on the notion that it is deeply contrary to human dignity to compel self-incrimination.

All such exclusionary and related rules have their own justifications, even though they keep relevant evidence from the fact-finder, and so may cause divergence in a particular case between substantive truth and formal legal truth. Many of the rules even have rationales that are partly or entirely truth oriented in nature. It is, of course, true that to exclude hearsay evidence in some particular case may be to defeat the truth. Yet one rationale for the general exclusion of hearsay evidence is simply that the fact-finder is likely to accord such evidence too much weight, given that the party who would merely be quoted in court is not actually present before the court and so is not available for cross examination. And another rationale, also truth serving in nature, is that exclusion of hearsay may induce the hearsay's proponent to introduce instead the live testimony of the witness who would then be subject to cross examination.[5]

Evidence may be kept from the fact-finder also because of the intrinsic requirements of the client-representational roles of lawyers in an adversarial system of trial. In some systems, the so called "attorney-client privilege" operates to exclude evidence of communications from a litigant to his or her lawyer, communications which may actually conceal the truth in a particular case. Canons of professional responsibility that impose duties on lawyers not to disclose confidential communications from clients also affect fact finding in some cases. These legal doctrines are justified partly on the ground that they facilitate the successful functioning of the lawyer as representative of the client. If the law required the lawyer to disclose such matters to the court, this would impair the effectiveness of the lawyer in a representational role. A lawyer cannot represent a client in a factual vacuum. The client must have every incentive to disclose all to the lawyer. The client will not have that incentive if the lawyer must, or is free to, divulge all confidential communications. Accordingly, many systems do not, for example, put the lawyer defending someone accused of crime on the witness stand in open court and call on this lawyer to state what the criminal defendant said to the lawyer in private interviews. While in some particular cases, such rules doubtless allow divergence between formal legal truth and substantive truth that would not otherwise occur, it may well be that, the attorney-client privilege is more truth oriented than truth defeating, overall. That is, more complete disclosure by the opposing parties to their lawyers will in the end more effectively lead to application of the relevant substantive law.

In a civil proceeding, the law in some systems generally does not require a lawyer to introduce evidence known to that lawyer but which would be adverse to that lawyer's client. Why? Among other things, it is sometimes said that this would "break the adversarial spirit" of the adjudicative process. The "adversary system of trial" itself generally serves important values, including truth finding.[6] Relatedly, some systems generally do not provide for, or encourage, the judge or jury to make any independent investigation of the facts. Instead, the fact-finder is merely to sit back and hear evidence presented by the opposing lawyers, evidence which at least in some cases would fall short of the whole truth that might be found were the court itself to make an independent investigation. Here, too, this constraint is overall more truth oriented than truth defeating. If the adversaries were to ease up their own efforts to gather evidence on the expectation that the tribunal would itself ferret out the facts, the risk of divergence between formal legal truth and substantive truth might well rise. At the same time, if the judge were to investigate the facts prior to trial, the judge might prematurely identify with one side and thus pre-judge the case.

Evidence may be kept from the fact-finder because of the time constraints operating within an adjudicative process, and because of the importance of finality. Fact finding must take place in definite time periods, and such processes cannot go on forever. Yet their conduct may not, for a variety of reasons, coincide with a time when most of the testimony of key witnesses and other evidence likely to be nearest the truth is readily available. In these terms, a trial may occur "too late" or "too soon". And when it is held, it will be necessary to get it over within a discrete time period. Disputes must be settled, and settled with finality. The law includes many doctrines which, in part, reflect such time factors. It is familiar that the doctrine of res judicata bars the relitigation of disputed issues of fact once finally resolved, even when the evidence in the new preceding would certainly be decisively different. Consider, for example, a defendant in a car accident case who has had to pay damages to an injured woman for her inability to have children, and who, in light of new evidence that the woman later had a child, could now show that the damages should therefore be reduced. The policy of finality and repose would foreclose introduction of such new evidence, after a given period of time following the trial. Of course, in the long run, general refusal to reopen a final judgment to allow new facts to be proved may tend to lead courts in some cases to arrive at the true solution in the original proceeding itself. This is because such refusal may encourage litigants to devote more effort at the beginning of trial to search for all relevant evidence then available.

Sometimes a case arising under a given substantive law may be of a type in which there is such chronic paucity of reliable evidence that the risk of divergence between formal legal truth and substantive truth is eventually seen to be intolerably high. In this type of circumstance, the legal system may take Draconian steps. It may reform the substantive law itself so that its applicability simply does not require such fact-finding at all. Consider, for example, a rule of substantive law apportioning fault between two disputants in a negligence case involving a high speed collision of two vehicles unwitnessed by third parties. Here the law may take the view that the type of fact finding task required to apportion fault between the parties is not really effectively "performable" in a sufficiently reliable way, or that while performable in some cases it would not be so in others, and the two cannot be reliably classified in advance. In sum, there are simply limits to law -- here limits to the fact-finding efficacy of law's machinery.[7] In turn, these limits may be a factor justifying a quite different alternative general legal approach to the problem: introduction of "no-fault" accident law in which auto owners, for example, all carry their own insurance against their own injuries and any other damage losses from highway accidents.

Even when all relevant evidence is available, a variety of other factors may explain and also justify, or rationally account for, the failure of a trial proceeding to find the actual truth, and so justify or rationally account for the resulting divergence between substantive truth and formal legal truth.

The necessity for a definite and immediate decision, for or against one party, may rationally account for a divergence between substantive truth and formal legal truth in a particular case. The law almost invariably calls for a definite decision, for or against one side to litigation. Among other things, this means that some facts may be formally found or not found, even though the substantive truth be otherwise. Because of any of a number of factors, one side may fail to introduce enough evidence to establish a fact, even though the evidence is available. If the party so failing has the "burden of proof" that party will lose then and there, i.e., the facts alleged will be taken to be "not proven", even though the facts alleged may in fact be true. Insofar as this factor is operative, the judicial proceeding may be characterized less as a search for substantive truth than as a search for a definite winner. It is sometimes said that in a lawsuit there can be no ties. But this search for a definite winner, too, serves distinctive ends, and so is not unjustified. There is a strong interest in the resolution of controversy as such. Controversy can be highly unproductive for the parties involved. It often interferes with what are far more fruitful pursuits. And it is also costly to the community.

The very nature of the type of legal consequences at stake may justify a divergence between formal legal truth and substantive truth. The consequences at stake may even affect what will legally count as fact--as truth--in judicial proceedings. Thus, in some systems, standards of required proof to establish facts in issue vary with what is at stake. In Anglo-American systems, it is familiar that in a criminal case the truth of facts against the accused must be established "beyond a reasonable doubt," and in certain civil cases, e.g., where punitive damages may be awarded for fraud, the truth of facts against the defendant must usually be shown by "a clear and convincing preponderance of the evidence". The more that is at stake, e.g., criminal blame, or punitive damages, the higher the standard of proof. In an ordinary civil case involving an ordinary claim for damages, the facts against the defendant need only be shown by a "balance of probabilities", a significantly lower standard of truth. Thus, depending on the relevant standard of truth, the very same evidence would warrant a finding of truth in one type of case but not in another. Thus truth varies with standards of proof, and standards of proof vary with what is at stake. Yet, as indicated, there are good reasons for these variations in standards of truth. In criminal cases for example, we accept a higher risk of erroneous acquittals in order to minimize the risk of erroneous convictions. Moreover, this may have the effect of increasing the total number of erroneous verdicts. Our tolerance for the risk of divergence, here, goes up the more that is at stake.

The so-called doctrines of "jury equity" and "jury nullification" of law may be characterized as "personnel-oriented" factors that lead to divergence between substantive truth and formal legal truth in many Anglo-American systems, and in some others, too. Some systems allow juries as lay fact-finders -- as special personnel -- to modify or nullify criminal law, and also some civil law, by refusing to find relevant facts even though the evidence is entirely sufficient to support such findings, or by finding relevant facts "differently" from the way the evidence would rationally dictate in the particular case. Professors Hart and McNaughten have had this to say about jury equity and jury nullification:[8]

> One more characteristic of legal fact-finding needs to be noted--one which enjoys clandestine respectability in the law but which in other disciplines is a hallmark of intellectual dishonesty: the facts are sometimes "bent" to serve an ulterior purpose. It is important to proper administration of the law that the public believe in the humanity and justice of decisions. This value the law seeks to serve partly through the institution of the jury trial. The jury, representing "the people", is deliberately inserted as a kind of cushion between the individual on the one hand and the coercive power of the state on the other. The jury, always in criminal cases, and within broad limits in civil cases, is allowed to thwart the law's commands--in effect to find the facts untruthfully--if it is not satisfied with the justness of the commands as applied to the case in hand.

Of course, sometimes what appears to be a divergence between formal legal truth and substantive legal truth, is really not. Thus, the very same evidence may be sufficient to justify a finding of fact for the purposes of one law or doctrine, but not for purposes of another, and not because of appropriate differences in standards of proof, but because of differences in the appropriate meanings to be attributed to the same word in different laws. Consider, for example, two rules each of which uses the word "drunk". One rule allows the police to take a drunk man off the street and have him "dried out" in a medical facility. The other rule forbids a drunk person from driving a car. Now, assume that the evidence of Edgar's drunkenness is not strong enough to justify police in finding him so drunk as lawfully to empower the police forcibly to take him off the streets to be "dried out" for several days in a local medical facility. Yet this very same evidence of Edgar's drunkenness could still be strong enough to justify a finding of fact that Edgar, if he were to get into his car and drive off, would be "driving under the influence of alcohol" and thus guilty of that offence, and this very evidentiary finding could empower the police to prohibit Edgar from driving his car. In turn, in a subsequent court proceeding, the judge could, if the issue be contested, confirm this finding and the exercise by the police of such a power to intervene. Thus, the nature of the law or legal doctrine at stake --the nature of the specific "legal difference" it makes -- can also rationally reduce what is to be taken as truth for the law's purposes.[9] It does not, however, follow that in such cases there is any divergence between formal legal truth, and substantive truth.

Similarly, many so called (by lawyers) "findings of fact" in legal proceedings are partly, and sometimes in major part, not really factual at all. Rather, they are to some extent highly evaluative determinations in which truth as such is only partly at stake. In the law, as elsewhere, the line between the merely factual and the evaluative is often not sharp. Examples include such "findings of fact" as that a defendant in a civil case was negligent, or that a defendant in a civil case induced the plaintiff reasonably to rely on the defendant's promise, or that a defendant in a criminal case was understandably provoked by the party assaulted, or that a defendant in a criminal case acted recklessly, or maliciously. In all such cases, and many of these arise in the law, it is not really accurate to say that only truth is at stake, even though the issues, in their entirety, are usually characterized as issues of fact. It follows we should recognize that, to a significant extent, scope for divergence between substantive truth and formal legal truth really does not exist in such cases. Of course, here there can still be a difference between apposite   evaluative   characterization   and   inapposite   evaluative characterization.

III. Appropriate Truth Formality

If we consider what the fact-finding would likely have been (1) in the absence of rational restrictions on availability or presentation of evidence, and (2) in the absence of the play of other types of rational factors considered here, then it is indisputable that formal legal truth diverges in some cases from substantive legal truth. And, as I have tried to show, this can, in some types of cases, even be justified.

It follows that the very nature of the law itself is correspondingly affected. Rules of law cannot have intended meaning and significance unless applied to concrete states of fact. Every legal rule or precept contemplates a state of fact. Insofar as that state of fact is taken to exist or not to exist, the law accordingly applies or does not apply, assuming that the law itself is sufficiently determinate to allow for correct application in the first place. Thus, if merely a formal, and not also a substantive, theory of truth is in play in a particular case, the law might or might not apply, or might apply very differently, from what would occur if only a substantive theory of truth were in play whereby fact-finding occurs in accord with actual truth.

A high degree of truth formality diverging from substantive truth is not necessarily appropriate in any particular case, nor is low truth formality that almost never diverges at all always appropriate. What is appropriate depends on the type of circumstances. Yet, in my view, the burden of persuasion should always be on those designers of the system who wish to justify the recognition of any factor that may lead to divergence. If such diverging factors as those treated here are not in play, or not significantly in play, high truth formality diverging from substantive truth is not appropriate. Indeed, absent diverging factors, which are by no means always significantly in play, high truth formality would be inappropriate, for, other things equal, legal fact-finding ought to approximate truthful fact-finding, i.e., ought to accord with substantive truth.

Overformality of fact-finding in a particular case occurs where the rational factors considered here are not in play or not significantly in play, yet facts are found that are contrary to the actual facts. Or such overformality may even occur with regard to an entire system of judicial procedure, one designed faultily. For example, in such a system, cases may be too readily disposed of on mere points of procedure rather than ultimately in light of their factual merits, as where a plaintiff's case is dismissed merely for a minor flaw in pleading, as occurred regularly in former times in Anglo-American systems.[10]

Underformality of fact-finding occurs in a particular case where one or more of the factors that may justify divergence of formal legal truth from actual truth is appropriately in play, yet the court disregards the force of this in pursuit of the true facts, as where, for example, a court reopens a civil case too readily because of newly discovered evidence identified long after entry of judgment, or a court admits a coerced confession. At the same time, the system could be inappropriately designed, as where a court in disputed contract cases is always to hear all parole evidence of the existence of agreed contract terms, except evidence strictly contradictory of the written terms, even though there is a written agreement that appears entirely comprehensive, and which itself recites as much.

IV. Conclusion

Formal legal truth and substantive truth may diverge in a particular case, with the court finding facts that do not represent the actual truth. While it is, for many important reasons, generally desirable that this not occur, and that substantive truth, or the closest approximation to it, generally prevail, in Anglo-American systems in some cases the divergence occurs, in effect, by design. The rationales for this can themselves be weighty, and so justify the divergence. As explained here, these rationales, some of which are themselves truth-oriented in the general run of cases, are highly varied and complex. Moreover, those that are truth hostile if not truth defeating in some particular cases, cannot be reduced to any single formula such as the "protection of individual rights" or the like.[11] It follows that the concept of "formal" legal truth, in those cases in which it diverges from substantive truth, is not necessarily something to be disparaged at all. If the system is well designed, and if, in a particular case of divergence, relevant rationales for such divergence are in play, the divergence is merely the price we pay for having a complex multi-purpose system in which actual truth, and what legally follows from it, comprise but one value among a variety of important values competing for legal realization.

Notes

1. Hans Kelsen once drew a similar distinction: "In case a fact is disputed, the judicial decision which determines that the fact has occurred... 'creates' legally the fact [formal legal truth] and consequently constitutes the applicability of the general rule of law referring to the fact. In the sphere of law the fact 'exists', even if in the sphere of nature the fact has not occurred [i.e. is not substantively true]." H. Kelsen, *Sovereign Equality of States,* 53 YALE L. J., 207, 218 (1944).

2. Edmund M. Morgan once stressed: "The trial is a proceeding not for the discovery of truth as such, but for the establishment of a basis of fact for the adjustment of a dispute between litigants. Still it must never be forgotten that its prime objective is to have that basis as close an approximation to the truth as practicable." Edmund M. Morgan, SOME PROBLEMS OF PROOF UNDER THE ANGLO-AMERICAN SYSTEM OF LITIGATION 128 (N.Y. 1956).

3. Frederick Pollock, ESSAYS IN THE LAW 275 (Oxford 1922).

4. For some confirming analysis with respect to the German system, see Benjamin Kaplan, *Civil Procedure -- Reflections on The Comparison of Systems,* 9 BUFFALO L. REV. 409 (1960).

5. Dale A. Nance, *The Best Evidence Principle,* 73 IOWA L. REV. 227 (1988).

6. For a perceptive account of some of the distinctive virtues of adversarial process, as such, see Lon L. Fuller, *Report of Joint Conference on Professional Responsibility,* 44 AMERICAN BAR ASS'N JOURNAL 1159, 1160-61 (1958).

7. Roscoe Pound, *The Limits of Effective Legal Action,* 27 ETHICS 150 (1917).

8. Henry M. Hart Jr. and John T. McNaughton, *Evidence and Inference in Law* in EVIDENCE AND INFERENCE (D. Lerner, ed. Chicago 1958), and in 87 Daedalus 40-64 (1958). See also, P.S. Atiyah and R.S. Summers, FORM AND SUBSTANCE IN ANGLO-AMERICAN LAW ch. 6 (Oxford 1987).

9. Compare Hans A. Linde, *Book Review of Harold Jacobson and Eric Stein, Diplomats, Scientists and Politicians* (U. of Michigan 1966), 81 HARV. L. REV. 922, 925 (1968): "But lawyers know the inverse relation of fact-finding to decision-making. Conclusions are needed if someone's right or power to act depends on them; they will be reached with an eye to the consequences. The legal conclusion at issue determines what 'ultimate facts', what factual inferences must be obtainable from the reconstruction of past events; the requirements of that process in turn determine the characteristics of the evidence needed." See also, John Lucas, *On Not Worshiping Facts,* 8 PHILOSOPHICAL QUARTERLY 144 (1958).

10. Roscoe Pound, *The Causes of Popular Dissatisfaction with the Administration of Justice,* 40 AMERICAN LAW REVIEW 729 (1906).

11. In a thoughtful essay, the author at one point seeks to reduce all these rationales for divergence to "...protecting the individual from possible injustice and from the coercive power of the state..." At other points, the author's formulations are more commodious. See Nicolas Rescher, *Evidence in History and in Law,* 56 JOURNAL OF PHILOSOPHY 561, 578 (1959).

Part Four

Contract Theory

CHAPTER 13

THE CONCEPTUALIZATION OF GOOD FAITH IN AMERICAN CONTRACT LAW

I. Historical Introduction

Each state of the United States has its own separate and relatively self sufficient body of general contract law. In a given state, most of this law consists of common law opinions of the highest court of that state. This means the United States has fifty bodies of general contract law. Each state legislature has also adopted the Uniform Commercial Code, a body of statute law that applies to contracts for the sale of goods, negotiable instruments, certain relations between banks, and between banks and their depositors, letters of credit, bulk sales, warehouse receipts, bills of lading, investment securities, and security interests in personal property. In addition, each state legislature has adopted various isolated statutes of its own which deal with one or more aspects of contract law. A few federal statutes also address issues of contract law.

Before the 1960s, it could not be said that the American states acknowledged any *general* obligation of good faith in their contract law. A tiny handful of states might have been viewed as exceptions to this generalization, but in none of those states was the obligation of good faith at all explicitly developed. The major contract treatises by Samuel Williston and by Arthur L. Corbin did not recognize any general obligation of good faith in the American case law, nor did any other leading scholars. But in research for an article that I published in 1968, I discovered that it was possible to identify many important types of American judicial decisions which could be construed to exemplify a general obligation of good faith in contractual relations. I also discovered that many of these decisions actually invoked not merely concepts of good faith, but also this very terminology, too.[1]

In the 1960's, the Uniform Commercial Code was being introduced in, and adopted by, the American state legislatures. That Code included section 1-203 which provides: "Every contract or duty within this Act imposes an

299

obligation of good faith in its performance or enforcement." This provision, however, was applicable only to contracts covered by the Code such as sale of goods contracts, letters of credit, and security agreements. It did not apply to contracts generally, and therefore did not apply to construction contracts, land sale contracts, real estate mortgage contracts, insurance contracts, and many other types of contracts.

Apart from UCC section 1-203, above, it was not until 1979 (with official promulgation in 1981) that there was any kind of official acknowledgment of a widespread general obligation of good faith in major types of contractual relations in American contract law, and that acknowledgment came in the form of the new Restatement of Contracts 2nd in its section 205, which provides as follows:

> 205. Duty of Good Faith and Fair Dealing. Every contract imposes upon each party a duty of good faith and fair dealing in its performance and enforcement.

The American concept of a "Restatement" is a very special type of "law". It is not statute law adopted by a state legislature or by Congress. Nor is it common law made by the highest court of any given state. It is not even an attempt to restate the actual case law of every state, state by state. Instead, a Restatement represents an attempt by The American Law Institute, a private organization of scholars, judges, and practitioners, to formulate with some precision the leading rules and principles in major fields of American law, "in the aggregate," so to speak, as if the United States consisted of only one, rather than fifty, state jurisdictions. Where the actual legal rules and principles in the various states are in conflict, or are not well developed, the Restatements frequently purport to formulate rules and principles that represent "the better view." The American Restatements began in the 1920s. The first Restatement in contract law was promulgated in 1932, and as I have said, the second Restatement officially appeared in 1981. There were several major changes between the first and second Restatements of Contracts, and the entirely new section 205, above, represents one of the three or four most significant changes. Section 205 in the second Restatement was based mainly on the accumulation of cases identified in the Article I published in 1968, on UCC section 1-203, and on an important earlier article by Professor Farnsworth in 1963.[2]

The American "Restatements" have had and continue to have substantial influence on the courts within each state of the United States. Thus, by the 1980s, not only had the Restatement of Contracts 2nd incorporated section 205, above, but the state court systems of many American states had explicitly adopted or acknowledged a general obligation of good faith applicable to contractual relations, and all the American state legislatures had adopted the Uniform Commercial Code with its section 1-203, set forth above.

One American treatise published in 1995 which deals exclusively with good faith, states that:

> In all the years before 1980, there were perhaps 350 reported cases interpreting the obligation to perform a contract in good faith. In the dozen years following 1980, there were another 600 or more.[3]

II. Some Concrete Examples of Contractual Bad Faith

Merely to lend concreteness to this article, and to provide meaningful background for the general discussion which follows, several specific examples of contractual bad faith will now be set forth. All are based on actual American case law, although it cannot be said that every American state supreme court would certainly treat each as a prohibited form of bad faith.

First, I will offer two examples of behavior in the *negotiation and formation* of contracts that would fail to satisfy a general requirement of contractual good faith, insofar as adopted and applicable, in the jurisdiction, to the negotiation and formation stage.[4]

> 1. *The withdrawing negotiator*: A negotiator tells the other party that if the other party will make certain expenditures, then the negotiator will enter a contract with the other party; but after the other party makes the expenditures, the negotiator entirely refuses to negotiate further, and there is no change of circumstances.
>
> 2. *The non-disclosing negotiator*: A prospective purchaser of real property, by trespassing on the owner' land, learns that the land contains valuable minerals unknown to the owner, but does not disclose this to the owner and contracts to buy the land from the

owner at a lower price.

Secondly, I offer two illustrative examples of behavior in the purported performance of a contract that would fail to satisfy a general requirement of contractual good faith.

3. *The diverting lessee*: Lessee who leases business premises from lessor A at a rental that is a percentage of lessee's gross sales on lessor A's premises, later leases other business premises from lessor B nearby at a rental that is a lower percentage of gross sales, and lessee then diverts customers away from lessor A's premises to the premises leased from lessor B.

4. *The uncooperative buyer*: A buyer contracts to buy land from the seller which the buyer knows the seller does not then own but plans to acquire from a third party at a public auction, yet the buyer himself also attends the auction, and outbids his seller and thus himself takes the land from the third party.

Thirdly, I present two examples of behavior in the purported enforcement of contract rights that would fail to satisfy a general requirement of contractual good faith.

5. *The opportunistic employer*: An employer in a contract terminable "at will" exercises his general legal power to terminate an employee-salesman, but this is to avoid having to pay the employee a contractually specified commission on a sale that the employee previously had made on behalf of the employer, but which was not yet payable to the employee on the date of termination.

6. *The dishonest compromiser*: A party pretends to be dissatisfied with the others' performance in order to secure a "compromise" that, in effect, reduces the contract price that the dishonest compromiser must pay.

III. The Variant Conceptualizations of Good Faith

Here, I will identify and discuss several different conceptualizations of good faith in American law and in scholarly writings. These conceptualizations appear in: (1) UCC 1-203, (2) Restatement (Second) of Contracts sec. 205, (3) writings of Professor Robert S. Summers, (4) writings of Professor E.

Allan Farnsworth, and (5) writings of Professor Steven J. Burton. Each is distinctive in some way. There are judicial decisions following each.

First, let us consider the Uniform Commercial Code conceptualization of good faith. The Uniform Commercial Code, section 1-203 does not apply to the negotiation or formation stage. The section provides that: "Every contract or duty within this Act imposes an obligation of good faith in its performance or enforcement." UCC section 1-201(11) defines good faith at least to mean "honesty in fact in the conduct or transactions concerned." This is a narrow definition. Indeed Professor Farnsworth argued that this narrow definition "enfeebled" UCC 1-203.[5] UCC section 2-103(1)(b) also includes a broader definition of good faith applicable at least within Article Two of the Code on sales of goods:

> In this article, unless the context otherwise requires. . . good faith
> in the case of a merchant means honesty in fact and the observance
> of reasonable commercial standards of fair dealing in the trade.

It may be that the Code drafters intended this broader definition to apply only when a specific provision in Article Two on the sale of goods uses the phrase "good faith". On this reading, the scope of the broader definition would be highly narrow because only thirteen sections in Article Two use the words good faith.[6] Another limiting feature of the special definition of good faith in Article Two is that it applies only "in the case of a merchant." UCC section 2-104(1) says:

> (1) "Merchant" means a person who deals in goods of the kind or
> otherwise by his occupation holds himself out as having knowledge
> or skill peculiar to the practices or goods involved in the transaction
> or to whom such knowledge or skill may be attributed by his
> employment of an agent or broker or other intermediary who by his
> occupation holds himself out as having such knowledge or skill.

The broader definition of good faith in UCC section 2-103(1)(b) can operate only insofar as there are commercial standards of fair dealing in a given trade which are reasonable. It may be difficult to determine what a trade is, and a given trade may not have any standards at all; it may be a jungle. In that event, the only forms of bad faith ruled out would be those excluded by the narrow "honesty in fact" language of UCC section 1-201(19).

Thus, for example, forms of bad faith involving carelessness or recklessness would not be ruled out. Nor would openly taking unfair advantage, openly abusing a power to specify terms, openly acting capriciously, or openly undercutting another's performance.

The Uniform Commercial Code's various sections also have accompanying "Official Comments" which the courts take seriously as guidelines to construing the Code. Numerous comments expressly require some form of contractual good faith.[7]

There is now a large body of case law interpreting and applying the Uniform Commercial Code's provisions on good faith.[8] Nearly all of these cases are consistent with the conceptualizations of good faith in the Code.

In 1994, the Permanent Editorial Board of the Uniform Commercial Code promulgated an addition to the Official Comment to UCC section 1-203 on good faith:[9]

> This section does not support an independent cause of action for failure to perform or enforce in good faith. Rather, this section means that a failure to perform or enforce, in good faith, a specific duty or obligation under the contract, constitutes a breach of that contract or makes unavailable, under the particular circumstances, a remedial right or power. This distinction makes it clear that the doctrine of good faith merely directs a court towards interpreting contracts within the commercial context in which they are created, performed, and enforced, and does not create a separate duty of fairness and reasonableness which can be independently breached.

A further proposed revision of UCC section 1-201 (19) states that good faith means "honesty in fact and the observance of reasonable standards of fair dealing in the conduct of the transaction concerned.[10]

We now turn to the second conceptualization. As we have seen, the text of section 205 of the Restatement provides:

> §205. *Duty of Good Faith and Fair Dealing*. Every contract imposes a duty of good faith and fair dealing in its performance and its enforcement.

This conceptualization is accompanied by a formal comment that, in subsections a, c, and d provides as follows (and for the full text, see the

Restatement):

  a. Meanings of "good faith". Good faith is defined in Uniform Commercial Code § 1-201(19) as "honesty in fact in the conduct or transaction concerned." "In the case of a merchant" Uniform Commercial Code § 2-103(1)(b) provides that good faith means "honesty in fact and the observance of reasonable commercial standards of fair dealing in the trade." The phrase "good faith" is used in a variety of contexts, and its meaning varies somewhat with the context. Good faith performance or enforcement of a contract emphasizes faithfulness to an agreed common purpose and consistency with the justified expectations of the other party; it excludes a variety of types of conduct characterized as involving "bad faith" because they violate community standards of decency, fairness or reasonableness. The appropriate remedy for a breach of the duty of good faith also varies with the circumstances.

  * * * * * *

  d. Good faith performance. Subterfuges and evasions violate the obligation of good faith in performance even though the actor believes his conduct to be justified. But the obligation goes further: bad faith may be overt or may consist of inaction, and fair dealing may require more than honesty. A complete catalogue of types of bad faith is impossible, but the following types are among those which have been recognized in judicial decision: evasion of the spirit of the bargain, lack of diligence and slacking off, willful rendering of imperfect performance, abuse of a power to specify terms, and interference with or failure to cooperate in the other party's performance.

  e. Good faith in enforcement. The obligation of good faith and fair dealing extends to the assertion, settlement and litigation of contract claims and defenses. See, e.g., §§ 73, 89. The obligation is violated by dishonest conduct such as conjuring up a pretended dispute, asserting an interpretation contrary to one's own understanding, or falsification of facts. It also extends to dealing which is candid but unfair, such as taking advantage of the necessitous circumstances of the other party to extort a modification of a contract for the sale of goods without legitimate commercial reason. See Uniform Commercial Code § 2-209, Comment 2. Other types of violation have been recognized in judicial decisions: harassing demands for assurances of performance, rejection of performance for unstated reasons, willful failure to mitigate damages, and abuse of a power to determine compliance or to terminate the contract. For a statutory duty of good faith in termination, see the federal Automobile Dealer's Day in Court Act, 15 U.S.C. §§ 1221-25 (1976).

Thus, Restatement section 205 does not apply to the negotiation stage, but only to the performance and enforcement of contracts actually entered. Comment a, above, sets forth three purposes of the duty of good faith and fair dealing: (1) "faithfulness to an agreed common purpose," (2) "consistency with the justified expectations of the other party," and (3) consistency with "community standards of decency, fairness, or reasonableness." Plainly all these categories overlap.

Section 205 was incorporated into the then evolving draft of the Restatement at the May 1970 meeting of the American Law Institute in Washington D.C. The transcript of the 1970 Proceedings includes the following statement by Professor Robert Braucher of the Harvard Law School who was then the chief drafter of the Restatement:[11]

Now, the trouble with this section, of course, is that it's very general, very abstract, and it needs specification the worst way, and specification is not to be had. I am indebted for its formulation here in the comments—formulations in the comments—to Professor Summers in a piece cited on page 100. He made considerable effort and collected this very large number of cases in which judicial opinions had insisted on some obligation of good faith and fair dealing in the performance and enforcement of contracts. And then he tried to categorize them, and I have borrowed heavily from his classification scheme in giving a little more detail about this.

Section 205 and its comments thus rely *partly* on what may be called an "excluder" conceptualization of good faith. That type of conceptualization is explained below.

I now turn to the third conceptualization of good faith. The article I wrote on which Professor Braucher based part of the American Law Institute's excluder conceptualization of good faith appeared in volume 54 of the Virginia Law Review at p. 195 in April of 1968. The key portion of the article follows below and appears at pages 200-206:

One of the principal theses of this article is that in cases of doubt, a lawyer will determine more accurately what the judge means by using the phrase "good faith" if he does not ask what good faith itself means, but rather asks: What, in the actual or hypothetical situation, does the judge intend to rule out by his use of this phrase? Once the relevant form of bad faith is thus identified, the lawyer can, if he wishes, assign a specific meaning to good faith by formulating an "opposite" for the species of bad faith being ruled out. For example, a judge may say: "A public authority must act in good faith in letting bids." And from the facts or the language of the opinion it may appear that the judge is, in effect, saying: "The defendant acted in bad faith because he let bids only as a pretense to conceal his purpose to award the contract to a favored bidder." It can be said that "acting in good faith" here simply means: letting bids without a preconceived design to award the contract to a favored bidder.

If good faith had a general meaning or meanings of its own—that is, if it were either univocal or ambiguous—there would seldom be occasion to derive a meaning for it from an opposite; its specific uses would almost always be readily and immediately understood. But good faith is not that kind of doctrine. In contract law, taken as a whole, good faith is an "excluder." It is a phrase without general meaning (or meanings) of its own and serves to exclude a wide range of heterogeneous forms of bad faith. In a particular context the phrase takes on specific meaning, but usually this is only by way of contrast with the specific form of bad faith actually or hypothetically ruled out. Aristotle was one of the first to recognize that the function of some words and phrases is not to convey general, "extractable" meanings of their own, but rather is to exclude one or more of a variety of things. He thought "voluntary" was such a word. And the late Professor J.L. Austin of Oxford made much of "excluders." His discussion of the term "real" is instructive:

That is, a definite sense attaches to the assertion that something is real, a real such-and-such, only in the light of a specific way in which it might be, or might have been, *not* real. "A real duck" differs from the simple "a duck" only in that it is used to exclude various ways of being not a real duck—but a dummy, a toy, a picture, a decoy, etc.; and moreover I don't know just how to take the assertion that it's a real duck unless I know just what, on that particular occasion, the speaker has it in mind to exclude. This, of course, is why the attempt to find a characteristic common to all things that are or could be called "real" is doomed to failure; the function of "real" is not to contribute positively to the characterization of anything, but to exclude possible ways of being not real—and these ways are both numerous for particular kinds of things, and liable to be quite different for things of different kinds. It is this identity of general function combined with immense diversity in specific applications which gives to the word "real" the, at first sight, baffling feature of having neither one single "meaning" nor yet ambiguity, a number of different meanings.

But it is not only because good faith is an "excluder" that the case analyst will be wise to focus on what the phrase rules out, rather than on what it means. It is also because the typical judge who uses this phrase is primarily concerned with ruling out specific conduct, and only secondarily, or not at all, with formulating the positive content of a standard.

Good faith, then, takes on specific and variant meanings by way of contrast with the specific and variant forms of bad faith which judges decide to prohibit. From the cases it would be possible to compile a list of forms of bad faith, with an opposite for each listed as the corresponding specific meaning of good faith. The beginnings of such a list might look like this:

Form of Bad Faith Conduct	Meaning of Good Faith
1. seller concealing a defect in what he is selling	fully disclosing material facts
2. builder willfully failing to perform in full, though otherwise substantially performing	substantially performing without knowingly deviating from specifications

3. contractor openly abusing bargaining power to coerce an increase in the contract price	refraining from abuse of bargaining power
4. hiring a broker and then deliberately preventing him from consummating the deal	acting cooperatively
5. conscious lack of diligence in mitigating the other party's damages	acting diligently
6. arbitrarily and capriciously exercising a power to terminate a contract	acting with some reason
7. adopting an overreaching interpretation of contract language	interpreting contract language fairly
8. harassing the other party for repeated assurances of performance	accepting adequate assurances

This list could run on and on, but it is unnecessary to extend it for present purposes. As it stands, it shows how specific meanings for good faith can be derived and shows that this phrase rules out radically heterogeneous forms of bad faith.

Given the specific meanings of good faith in the foregoing right-hand column, it may seem all the more natural to suppose, contrary to our "excluder" analysis, that there must be some single word or concise phrase which faithfully unifies all such specific meanings into one general meaning of the term. What about "honesty"? Is not acting in good faith equivalent to acting honestly? Numerous judges appear to have thought so, but this is wrong unless, of course, the definition of honesty is stretched beyond recognition. Honesty only rules out dishonesty in its various forms. But good faith, as used by many judges, excludes numerous forms of contractual bad faith besides dishonesty. For one thing, dishonesty is necessarily immoral, but in the eyes of many judges contractual bad faith is not necessarily immoral at all. A party may, for example, abuse his bargaining power, undercut the other party's efforts to perform, or act capriciously without having the "guilty mind" that would make his actions immoral—indeed, a party might even think this conduct is in the other party's own best interest. And despite this purity of mind, many judges could be counted on to say that such conduct conflicts with requirements of contractual good faith. As one judge stated, "Good faith in law . . . is not to be measured always by a man's own standard for the observance of all men in their dealings with each other."

Even if it were conceded that conduct must be subjectively immoral before it can constitute bad faith, it still would not follow that dishonesty is the only form of contractual bad faith. Thus when a man openly and straightforwardly gives another a "raw deal," he does not necessarily act dishonestly. That is, he does not undertake to mislead or deceive. Consider, for example, the conduct of a buyer who openly seizes upon trivial defects to justify his rejection of goods under a rule requiring perfect tender, admitting all along that he is rejecting the goods because the price has gone down and he wishes to buy more cheaply elsewhere. Such conduct is not dishonest. But it may well be thought immoral, and it is certainly commercial bad faith. In truth, good faith cannot be defined in terms of honesty. As numerous judges use the phrase, it excludes many forms of bad faith which a requirement of honesty alone does not.

It is submitted that any but the most vacuous general definition of good faith will similarly fail to cover all the many and varied specific meanings that it is possible to assign to the phrase in light of the many and varied forms of bad faith recognized in the cases. Of course, a particular judge might declare that for him good faith does have a general, invariant meaning which he always intends when he uses the phrase. But if such a judge should have to pass on very many of the different forms of bad faith, it is most unlikely that he could stand by his definition for long.

To summarize, general definitions of good faith either spiral into the Charybdis of vacuous generality or collide with the Scylla of restrictive specificity. Moreover, the analyst who puts general definitions aside and tries to focus on the form of bad faith which a given judge intends to exclude by his use of the term is likely to get closer to that judge's meaning, for good faith functions as an "excluder," and judges are more interested in what they are proscribing than in characterizing what is generally allowed.

In 1982, in a further article, I also added these methodological remarks:[12]

> In my view, a judge in a novel case posing an issue of good faith under section 205 with its excluder conceptualization is far from lacking meaningful guidance of the kind legitimately to be demanded in the name of the rule of law. He should start with the language of the section. Second, he should turn to the purposes of section 205 as set forth mainly in Comment a. These purposive rationales will infuse the excluder analysis with meaning in all the ways that purposive interpretation is known generally to provide guidance to judges (as in the case of statutes). Third, after completing this, he should seek guidance by the time-honored common-law method of reasoning by analogy, not only from past cases, but from the various illustrations set forth in the Comments to section 205. Such reasoning, particularly that which is done with an eye to the *reasons* given by prior judges, can provide substantial insight into how novel cases should be decided. Fourth, also in light of the purposes of section 205 and any general analogies, he can analyze the relevant facts—alleged or proven—to see what specific reasons these facts, and the values they implicate, generate for and against characterizing the action or inaction in question as bad-faith behavior. Fifth, because of the very nature of the problem, the excluder analysis is not only faithful to the reality involved, but it is itself a distinctive source of illumination. It does not focus on some presumed positive and unitary element or cluster of elements called "good faith"; instead, it focuses on whether the alleged form of bad faith behavior really is, in the context ruled out by section 205, when considered in light of its purposes and in relation to the facts of the case. The foregoing factors all the forms of guidance that section 205 provides, but they are more than sufficient to rebut the charge that a section in which good faith is conceptualized as an excluder leaves the judges at sea and the "law" merely whatever the judges say it is.

Fourth, let us consider the Burton conceptualization of good faith. In an important article in the Harvard Law Review in 1980, Professor Steven Burton offered and defended still another conceptualization of good faith performance:[13]

> "Good faith performance" occurs when a party's discretion is exercised for any purpose within the reasonable contemplation of the parties at the time of formation—to capture opportunities that were preserved upon entering the contract, interpreted objectively.

The essence of the Burton approach is as follows.[14] One of the two parties will always have what Professor Burton calls "forgone opportunities" (to that party, a "cost" of contracting). Bad-faith contractual activity is then defined as "exercising discretion" to recapture one or more of the opportunities forgone upon entering a contract. To determine whether an opportunity was in fact forgone, it is necessary to inquire into the reasonable expectations of the "dependent party" (the other party). The party with discretion to perform acts in good faith if he does not attempt to recapture a forgone opportunity. Professor Burton also argues that "whether a particular discretion-exercising party acted to recapture forgone opportunities is a question of subjective intent"—a "subjective inquiry." Moreover, the "objective inquiry" into the dependent party's reasonable expectations is not alone "dispositive." Indeed, Professor Burton stresses that instead the inquiry into state of mind is "of central importance."

We may adopt one of Professor Burton's illustrations to try to demonstrate his model at work. Assume that L and T entered into a lease providing that T was to pay rentals as a percentage of the gross receipts of T's business on the premises. T also had another store in the same town. From time to time, he diverted customers to that other store (where he owned the premises), thereby reducing the rentals otherwise payable to L. For this, L sued T, claiming that T's diversionary tactics were in bad faith. Here, according to Professor Burton, a court should presumably find (1) that a reasonable person in L's position expected to receive rentals not depleted by T's diversionary acts, and (2) that T acted with the subjective intention of recapturing a forgone opportunity.

Professor Burton, unlike many who have criticized general requirements of good faith, does believe in them and has sought to direct his efforts largely to making them more effective. Moreover, he does not ultimately seek to resolve issues of good faith through a general definition of some presumed positive content of that phrase. He also concedes that what a general good-faith requirement rules out varies to some extent depending on the context. And he generally seeks to focus on the reasons for ruling out claimed forms of bad faith. In all these respects, despite some misleading protestations to the contrary, his approach is itself generally consistent with the spirit of section 205, including its excluder conceptualization.

Professor Burton makes a number of claims on behalf of his approach, as opposed to what he calls the "traditional" approach (born not so long ago in the history of the common law and including, presumably, that of section 205). First, he says that his approach provides more analytical focus. It isolates "with greater particularity the factors that must be considered in determining good or bad-faith performance. Instead of an "amorphous totality of factual circumstances," we have an inquiry into reasonable expectations of the "dependent party" and the subjective intent of the "discretion-exercising" party—all to determine precisely whether the discretion-exercising party has acted to recapture forgone opportunities so as to constitute bad faith. Is this analysis necessarily any more focused than that of section 205 in a novel good-faith performance case? Does it focus on the right things? Does it go far enough? These are large questions, and I cannot now do full justice to them. I have already tried to show here that section 205 provides judges with considerable guidance, not merely in novel performance cases but in performance and enforcement cases generally. It is true that Professor Burton's model introduces new terminology and appears to reduce to two questions; but I do not see that anything turns on this. Why, for example, should it "advance the analysis" to inquire whether the discretion-exercising party is seeking to "recapture forgone opportunities," rather than whether his actions fall outside the reasonable expectations of the dependent party in light of the various factors in the circumstances that legitimately shape those expectations? Or why does it help (if it does) in our foregoing lease illustration to inquire whether the tenant, in diverting customers, was trying to recapture costs incurred in entering the contract, rather than whether what the tenant did was, all things considered, contrary to the spirit of the deal?

One may also question whether the Burton model really focuses on the right things. For example, does the subjective inquiry into the discretion-exercising party's state of mind really have the central importance that is claimed? Part of the claim, as I understand it, is that this inquiry is *typically* relevant, not just contingently so. This does not accord with section 205. Moreover, in a great many well-decided performance cases, courts give little or no consideration to this factor. Indeed, its independent significance in the Burton model is at least in some areas problematic. Consider, again, the lease illustration. If the court decides that the reasonable expectations of the landlord rule out the tenant's acts of diverting customers to his other store, what if anything would it add to inquire into the tenant's state of mind? It is said (a) that the "traditional analysis" focuses mainly on benefits due the promisee under the agreement and (b) that this is inadequate because the promisor may be "entitled" to withhold something in good faith. Whether or not (a) is true, (b) does not follow. If what is due the promisee really does exclude what the promisor wants to withhold, then that will be dispositive. What one is "entitled" to withhold depends on what is due the promisee. (This is not to say that an inquiry into the promisor's state of mind can never have independent significance in good-faith performance cases.)

Further, in my view the Burton model does not go far enough. That is, it does not provide as much focus as section 205 of the *Restatement Second* and the general case law now permit. I suspect that it is now possible to develop useful lists of factors generally relevant to the determination of good-faith performance in a number of different performance contexts. Professor Burton seems content, for example, to leave the general test of reasonableness of expectations relatively unanalyzed. Nothing in the excluder conceptualization embodied in section 205 is inconsistent with the articulation of such criteria. A general requirement of good faith can rule out forms of bad faith identifiable by reference to these criteria. Indeed, as I have already suggested, some such criteria in some contexts may now be ripe for formulation in rules.

Professor Burton claims that, in addition to more focus, his model provides more generality than other approaches and thus is more "lawlike." In particular, he thinks it is less a "license" for the exercise of ad hoc judicial intuition. Again, I fail to see why there is any less generality in the *Restatement Second* approach. Certainly each "context" to which Professor Braucher referred in the Comments consists of more than "the discrete case."

Indeed, he adopted a number of *general* categories for the classification of general types of bad faith—categories well populated with actual decisions. Moreover, there is no reason why the legal generalities emergent in these contexts cannot take account of factors that vary with the stage in the contracting process at which the issue of good faith arises.

Finally, Professor Burton claims that his model provides a useful new "perspective and policy framework" within which good-faith performance issues are more manageable. Close analysis suggests, however, that it is less general than Professor Burton makes it seem, and that it introduces economic ideas and terminology that may breed uncertainty or confusion. I will say something further only about the first of these observations. The model is less general because it is in truth drawn mainly from those cases in which contracting parties have in fact conferred on one of the parties some genuine discretionary power in matters of performance. Many good-faith performance cases are not of this kind; they do not confer *discretion* to perform in some way. It is not difficult to discern the likely motive here behind the Burton model. The maneuver of adopting a conceptual framework in which one party is always considered to have discretion felicitously generates the *possibility* that the "discretion-exercising" party might have failed to perform in good faith, and thus seems to give pervasive point to the "subjective-inquiry" of such central importance in the model. After all, "a party with discretion may withhold all benefits for good reasons." In many cases posing issues of good-faith performance, however, there will be no such discretion and therefore no such possibility. And even when this is not so, the subjective inquiry may lack independent significance.

Finally, consider the Farnsworth conceptualization of good faith. As I noted earlier, Professor E. Allan Farnsworth in 1963 wrote the first major article on good faith under the Uniform Commercial Code, and argued persuasively that the Code's general "honesty in fact" conceptualization "enfeebled" UCC 1-203.[15] In his influential treatise, *Farnsworth on Contracts*, published in 1990, he states: "The concept of good faith has, in a relatively few years, become one of the peculiarly American cornerstones of our common law of contracts." In his treatise, Professor Farnsworth does not offer an explicit general conceptualization of good faith. He does emphasize that:[16]

Certainly many of the uses to which the new concept of good faith is put today do not go beyond those to which the traditional techniques of interpretation and gap filling were put in yesteryear.

Professor Farnsworth includes a great many good faith cases in the section of his treatise headed "Deciding Omitted Cases." There, he offers some general remarks on the duty of good faith and fair dealing in Restatement 205. He says:[17]

> This duty is based on fundamental notions of fairness, and its scope necessarily varies according to the nature of the agreement. Some conduct, such as subterfuge and evasion, clearly violates the duty. However, the duty may not only proscribe undesirable conduct, but may require affirmative action as well. A party may thus be under a duty not only to refrain from hindering or preventing the occurrence of conditions of the party's own duty or performance of the other party's duty, but also to take some affirmative steps to co-operate in achieving these goals . . . .

IV. Scope of the Requirement of Good Faith

The Restatement and the Uniform Commercial Code limit the duty of good faith to the performance and the enforcement of a contract already made. Section 2-209(1) of the Uniform Commercial Code and some case law require that contract modifications be made in good faith. In general, the requirement of good faith in American law does not apply to contract negotiations. Of course, the parties may contract to negotiate in good faith. And there are specific instances where it might be said that the general requirement applies even at the negotiating stage. Professor Farnsworth gives the example of the "closed-mouth negotiator"—a prospective buyer of land learns that the land contains valuable minerals, unknown to the owner, but says nothing of this to the owner during negotiations prior to making a contract to buy the land. Professor Farnsworth says: "at least under the Restatement Second of Contracts, sec. 161, nondisclosure may amount to a misrepresentation unless remaining silent is consistent with good faith and reasonable standards of fair dealing."[18]

V. A Note on Remedies For Bad Faith

The appropriate remedy for bad faith in American law depends on the nature of the bad faith and the stage at, or context in which, it occurs. Bad faith may simply amount to a breach of a contractual promise or term, giving rise to damages, as where a buyer rejects non-conforming goods in bad faith in a falling market, and becomes liable for the contract-market differential. But if a seller secures a contract modification in bad faith, the appropriate remedy may only be to invalidate the modification. If a party's duty is conditioned on being satisfied with the other party's performance, and if the party is not satisfied in bad faith, the appropriate remedy may be to excuse the non-occurrence of the condition altogether, thereby rendering the party acting in bad faith liable (or whatever) as if the condition were satisfied. And there are still other possibilities that similarly reveal how the appropriate remedy depends on the stage at, or the context in which, bad faith occurs.

VI. Conclusion

In a contract world, there are still other possible forms of generally applicable law besides a requirement of good faith. These other possible forms of law include more specific rules of law such as those dealing with fraud, custom and usage, course of dealing, "implied" terms, and general principles of interpretation, as well as detailed terms of the contract. Could these other possible forms of law, alone or together, satisfy any essential need for a general requirement of contractual good faith? Is good faith redundant?

No. And there are several reasons for this. First, the world of contract law is an imperfect world inhabited by imperfect law makers and contracting parties who cannot foresee and provide in advance against all forms of contractual bad faith that may subsequently arise.

Second, it would unduly stretch the concept of contract interpretation to use it as a complete substitute for a general requirement of good faith. For instance, interpretation cannot really apply to cases of bad faith in negotiation. As my examples make clear, in many cases where a contract has been formed, interpretation as such cannot, strictly speaking, yield a genuine meaning of the parties. Among other things, the parties may not have addressed the matter at all.

Third, good faith analysis calls for a distinctive type of substantive reasoning.

The overall rational justification for the recognition in a legal system of a general requirement of contractual good faith is a two step analysis. Initially, it must be shown that other legal means are not an adequate substitute. Then, it must be shown that there are good affirmative reasons for a legal system to adopt such a requirement of good faith.

I believe there are such reasons. A general requirement of contractual good faith requires that parties not deal dishonestly or contrary to standards of fair dealing in contract negotiations. Furthermore, in regard to contracts already negotiated and formed, a general requirement of contractual good faith requires as well that parties observe the fundamental rightness norm of *pacta sunt servanda.* A specific contract, of course, brings this norm into play, and good faith (among other things) helps to particularize its meaning and thus enforce what may be the unspecified "inner logic" of the transaction or arrangement. At the same time, good faith also requires that there be no dishonesty or unfairness, notions which may even qualify or limit express terms of the contract, at least where any such dishonesty or unfairness is also ruled out by the unspecified inner logic of the contract. Good faith serves other contractual ends as well.

Some of the foregoing rationales may be reformulated in terms of protection of justified expectations of the parties, too. One or more of the above rationales can be deployed to justify applying the general requirement of good faith to each of my six examples, in II above.

Notes

1. Robert S. Summers, *Good Faith in General Contract Law and the Sales Provisions of the Uniform Commercial Code*, (1968) 54 VIRGINIA L. REV. (VLR) 195 ff.

2. E. Allan Farnsworth, *Good Faith Performance and Commercial Reasonableness Under the Uniform Commercial Code*, (1963) 30 CHICAGO L. REV. (UCLR) 666 ff.

3. Steven J. Burton, Eric G. Andersen, CONTRACTUAL GOOD FAITH—FORMATION, PERFORMANCE, BREACH, AND ENFORCEMENT. Little, Brown & Co., Boston 1995, S. 20 ff.

4. Neither UCC § 1-203 nor Restatement § 205 apply the good faith requirement to the negotiation and formation stage.

5. See Farnsworth, (1963) 30 UCLR 674 ff.

6. UCC §§ 2-305(2), 2-306(1), 2-31(1), 2-323(2)(b), 2-328(4), 2-402(2), 2-403(1), 2-506(2), 2-603(3), 2-615(a), 2-703(3), 2-706(1) 2-706(5), and 2-712(1).

7. See Summers, (1968) 54 VLR 214 ff.

8. Uniform Commercial Code Case Digest. Volume 1-201 through 1-203, Clark, Boardman, Callaghan, 1997, S. 708-831 ff.

9. Uniform Commercial Code Reporting Service Findex, PEB Commentary No. 10, 1997.

10. Richard E. Speidel, *The Duty of Good Faith in Contract Performance and Enforcement*, (1996) 46 J. OF LEGAL ED. 537 ff., fn. 19, 540 ff.

11. 1970 *Proceedings of the American Law Institute*, (1970) 47 AMERICAN LAW INSTITUTE PROCEEDINGS 489-91 ff.

12. Robert S. Summers, *The Duty of Good Faith—Its Recognition and Conceptualization*, (1982) 67 CORNELL L. REV. (CLR) 810 ff., 823-24 ff.

13. Steven J. Burton, *Breach of Contract and the Common Law Duty To Perform in Good Faith*, (1980) 94 HARV. L. REV. 369 ff., 373 ff.

14. These remarks are drawn, with some modification, from pages 830-834 of Summers, (1982) 67 CLR 810 ff.

15. See Farnsworth, (1963) 30 UCLR 666 ff.

16. E. Allan Farnsworth, Farnsworth on Contracts, Volume II. Little, Brown & Co., 1990, S. 328 ff.

17. Farnsworth (Fn. 16) 311 ff. See also E. Allan Farnsworth, *Good Faith in Contract Performance*, in Jack Beatson and Daniel Friedmann eds., GOOD FAITH AND FAULT IN CONTRACT LAW. Oxford U. Press, Oxford 1995.

18. E. Allan Farnsworth. *Comment on Michael Bridge's: Does Anglo-Canadian Contract Law Need a Doctrine of Good Faith?*, (1984) 9 CANADIAN BUSINESS LAW JOURNAL 426 ff., 427-28 ff.

CHAPTER 14

SUBSTANTIVE JUSTIFICATION IN CONTRACT CASES — THE PRIMACY OF RIGHTNESS REASONS

I. Introduction

My theses in this essay are:

(1) that the essential content of judicial justifications includes two basic types of reasons which I will call authoritative and substantive. Authoritative reasons are those which appeal primarily to the legal authoritativeness of statutes, cases, contracts, and other antecedent forms of law. (Elsewhere, I have also called these "formal" reasons.) Substantive reasons do not appeal to legal authority. They stand on their own, and consist of moral, political, economic, or other social considerations,

(2) that although authoritative reasons are numerically far more common in judicial justifications, substantive reasons are no less important, especially in the American legal system,

(3) that the types of substantive reasons that figure in judicial justifications may be subdivided into three varieties: goal reasons, rightness reasons, and institutional reasons, concepts I will define,

(4) that rightness reasons and institutional reasons have historically been and continue to be the overwhelmingly dominant varieties of substantive reasons in judicial justification in the general common law of contract in particular, with goal reasons a distant third, despite the fact that goal reasons seem also to be widely available in the cases,

(5) that rightness reasons and institutional reasons have not only been historically dominant, but are also by themselves sufficient for

purposes of judicial justification, and moreover, are normatively superior for such purposes to goal reasons,

(6) that the validity of my historical dominance and normative superiority theses is significant not only in ruling out the historical and normative primacy of a major category of rival reasons, namely goal reasons, but is significant in other ways, too, as I will explain.

II. Main Varieties of Substantive Reasons Figuring in Judicial Justifications

My first thesis is preliminary in nature, and is a thesis about the nature and varieties of substantive reasons to be found in the common law.[1] Substantive reasons consist of moral, political, economic, or other social considerations. Unlike authoritative reasons, which appeal primarily to the authoritativeness of antecedent law, substantive reasons do not appeal to antecedent law. They stand on their own. Substantive reasons are of three basic kinds: goal reasons, rightness reasons and institutional reasons.

A good goal reason derives its justificatory force from the fact that, at the time a judge gives the reason, it supports a decision that may be predicted to have consequences that will serve a good social goal, such as increased health or safety, economic opportunity, child welfare, or increased wealth, as in modern economic analysis, or increased psychic satisfaction, as in some versions of utilitarianism. Goal reasons are essentially predictive, consequentialist, and "instrumentalist" i.e., social goal subservient.

Rightness reasons are different. They presuppose what I call accepted rightness norms. Here are five sketchily stated examples of very general rightness norms addressed to individuals, norms that are widely accepted in Western societies:

(1) "don't knowingly mislead others to their detriment, and make amends if you do"
(2) "give others their just deserts"
(3) "keep your word, and make amends when you don't"
(4) "deal with others in good faith"
(5) "treat similarly situated persons fairly"

The initial acceptance of such norms in a society usually takes many non legal forms, and reveals itself in general social discourse and in corresponding forms of behavior. Thus, in general social discourse, citizens will often state or invoke such norms or fragments of them (however elliptically) as reasons for action, as bases for demands or claims, or as standards of criticism, and so on. Moreover, that citizens accept such norms will be evident in their ordinary non-legal behavior. Thus, citizens regularly act on the reasons generated by such norms in daily life. And more. I might remark here that in a recent book, a fellow contracts scholar, Professor Melvin Eisenberg has advanced our understanding of how lawyers may properly deal with issues as to the existence of particular rightness norms.[2] As Professor Eisenberg stresses, whether a rightness norm exists is not a matter of whether a judge happens to think it ought to exist. The question is whether it represents a community view of right conduct. Here the court can look to prior common law court decisions where such views are often explicitly articulated, or look to unofficial sources such as the values reflected in social structures and institutions. Or the judge may consider how far the norm in question follows from or is consistent with norms that are accepted. The judgment that a norm exists will be subject to checks — the check of discourse with co-judges, the check of discourse with counsel, the check of discourse in legal and other academic realms. I believe I also agree with Professor Eisenberg when he says that: "in short the Court is not obliged to establish empirically that a ... norm has the requisite social support in fact, which it cannot do, but to use [judicially] appropriate methodology to make a judgment on that issue [when the parties raise it]."

Of course, a rightness reason does not come into play merely because citizens generally accept a relevant rightness norm. There must also be facts in the circumstances which bring the norm into play and thereby generate the reason. The kinds of facts which bring a rightness norm into play are either facts about the past interactions of the parties or facts about an existing state of affairs. For example, the facts that Edgar knowingly misled Ben to Ben's detriment would, without more, bring a rightness norm into play thereby generating a rightness reason on the basis of which a judge could justifiably decide that Edgar should make Ben whole.

Rightness reasons may themselves be subdivided into two species, depending on the nature of the essential facts in each. In the first type, the essential facts bringing the rightness norm into play are about the past interactions of the parties. This is true in my reliance example. Moreover, rightness norms requiring the performance of prior agreements and the making of amends for failure to do so generate many such reasons. The past interactions of parties obviously include many instances in which agreements are made so that rightness reasons for such parties to perform arise, and also many instances of breach so that rightness reasons arise for one party to make amends or for courts to require amends. Where the essential facts calling a rightness norm into play consist of past actions of the parties, we may refer to the resulting reason as "antecedentialist" in contrast to consequentialist.[3]

In the second species of rightness reason, the essential facts bringing the rightness norm into play are about an existing state of affairs. The reasons so generated arise under rightness norms applied to existing states of affairs. For example, rightness norms of fair treatment as between similarly situated parties generate many such reasons. Thus, a rightness norm of fair treatment requires for example that a local government authority treat similar bidders on a public works project fairly. The relevant similarities for the purpose at hand may be revealed in present facts entirely without regard to past interactions of the parties. Where the essential facts calling a rightness norm into play consist merely of an existing state of affairs without regard to past interactions as such, we may call the resulting rightness reason present — regarding or "presentialist" rather than "antecedentialist." Of the two basic types, antecedentalist rightness reasons are far more common and will be my main concern.

In rightness reasons, the facts have to be characterized appropriately to determine the applicability of rightness norms. Consider, for example, the general rightness norm which generally calls upon us to honor our agreements. An essential question will be whether the facts of the particular situation involve a genuine agreement and a genuine breach, so that a rightness reason to make amends arises. Thus, the analysis in the construction of a rightness reason is characterizational. We must, for example, appropriately characterize the claimed agreement as a genuine agreement. Depending on whether the facts are appropriately so characterizable, the behavior of a party can be determined to be norm accordant or not. If norm accordant, a rightness reason arises that justifies one decision rather than another. (This is not to say that a rightness reason never conflicts with other reasons. Nor is it to say that the justificatory force of rightness reasons is generally uniform.)

The nature of rightness reasons can be more fully understood if we now compare them in more detail with goal reasons. Before I identify major differences between rightness reasons and goal reasons, I will give several shorthand examples of goal reasons. I have drawn all of these examples from the one branch of the general common law of contract where such reasons are dominant. Consider these examples:

(1) "this contract is unenforceable because the effect of enforcing it and similar contracts would be to restrain trade."

(2) "this contract is unenforceable because the effect of enforcing it and similar contracts would be to encourage divorce."

(3) "this contract is unenforceable because the effect of enforcing it and similar contracts would be to encourage the defamation of individuals."

As I have already indicated, goal reasons are predictive, consequentialist, and instrumentalist, i.e., goal subservient. They are essentially future regarding. Jeremy Bentham was the great inaugurator of goal reasons. Indeed, he viewed all reason as essentially future regarding. He even thought that "thank you" means "more please."

There are several major differences between goal reasons and rightness reasons. First, the usual goal reason presupposes an accepted social goal rather than a rightness norm. The existence of a social goal is not pre-legal or a-legal, whereas the existence of a rightness norm is usually pre-legal or a-legal. To determine whether a social goal exists, we must usually determine whether there is some authoritative policy that authenticates that goal. (Because of this feature of goal reasons, the sharpness of the distinction between many goal reasons and what I have called authoritative reasons is, in this respect, blurred.)

Second, the facts required for the construction of a goal reason always include predictions about the future consequences of a projected decision. Thus in factual terms, goal reasons are predictive whereas rightness reasons are not. Rightness reasons only require inquiry into past facts or present facts.

They are non predictive.

Third, the essential analysis in the construction of a goal reason is instrumental rather than characterizational. The goal reasoner must determine whether and how far predicted decisional consequences may serve instrumentally as means to existing social goals. There is more to this than predicting decisional consequences. Instrumentalist means-end analysis is also required. Now, such analysis differs from the merely characterizational analysis required in the construction of rightness reasons. Determining, for example, whether the past interactions of the parties may be characterized as involving an agreement is a different process from the process of determining whether, for example, the decisional consequences of invalidating an extrinsic oral promise to remove an ice house serve (and serve sufficiently) as a means to the social goal of influencing contracting parties generally to put their agreements in writing. The former is essentially characterizational whereas the latter requires instrumental means-end analysis.

Finally, in overall terms, we may say that goal reasoning is consequentialist and goal subservient in the sources of its justificatory force whereas most rightness reasoning is antecendentialist and norm accordant in this regard. Goal reasons depend for their force on decisional consequences predicted to happen in the future. Thus goal reasons presuppose future, goal subservient, states of affairs, situations that may be brought about through the consequences of decisions. Without such future states of affairs — goals or ends, and without such predicted decisional consequences in the future — means to such goals or ends, it would be impossible for goal "reasons" to have justificatory force. Rightness reasons are very different. They do not depend for their present force on a tomorrow. The justificatory force of a rightness reason (when it has such) derives from the way in which the decision accords with a rightness norm as applied to past or present facts of the case. It follows that a court could have a rightness reason for a projected decision even if there were no tomorrow (or any other future to be predicted). As the philosopher Immanuel Kant once observed, an available rightness reason remains a reason for a decision maker in the present, even though that decision can have no future consequences beyond what is decided (beyond what such a decision entails in terms of immediate implementation if it is to count as a decision at all). Indeed, as Kant pointed out, a rightness reason could be a reason with justificatory force for a decision today even if it were known that the entire society would dissolve tomorrow.[4]

There is here a complication that I wish only to pause and acknowledge. In setting forth my thesis about the nature and variety of substantive reasons in the fashion I have, I do not wish to deny that published court decisions based on rightness reasons have consequences that promote rightness. In the future, obviously, they can have such consequences through general publicity and through the system of precedent. We may conceptualize and refer to this type of phenomenon, if we wish, as a parasitic goal reason -- a reason essentially dependent for any force it has on the force of the rightness reason on which it is parasitic. Of course, that rightness reason itself is in no way dependent for its own justificatory force on the rightness promoting effects that a public decision in its name may have. This is a complication about which I will say no more here.[5]

It is true that both rightness reasons and goal reasons shape and inform the content of antecedent rules and other legal precepts that generate what I classify here as legally authoritative reasons. Rules and other precepts that generate authoritative reasons are not empty husks or shells. Rules and other legal precepts must have material content. Substantive reasons contribute most of this content. But this does not show that there is no meaningful distinction between substantive reasons and authoritative reasons. At the least, it always remains possible to disentangle the formal authoritativeness of a rule or legal precept from the substantive reasoning informing its content.

I now turn to institutional reasons. These are a special class of substantive reasons. Thus, like rightness reasons and goal reasons, institutional reasons consist of social considerations. They may display the structure of either a rightness or a goal reason, yet they remain a special type of social consideration. Institutional reasons arise either: (1) from a requisite, a desideratum, or a limit of the rule of law ideal, or (2) from a requisite, a desideratum or a limit of a legal process or legal structure, or (3) from a requisite, desideratum, or limit of the various assigned roles of parties (official and private) in the division of legal labor within a legal system. Many reasons found in judicial opinions are institutional in at least one of the three foregoing ways. I will now paraphrase a number of illustrative ones.

First, there are those rising from a requisite, desideratum, or limit of the rule of law ideal. Consider, these examples:

(1) "we should adhere to a precise rule here rather than adopt an open-

ended discretionary approach."

(2) "we should not create the proposed exception, for it will swallow up the rule."

Second, there are those institutional reasons arising from a requisite, a desideratum or a limit of a legal process or structure. Consider, these examples:

(3) "it would be impracticable for the court to supervise such a decree of specific performance, and therefore it will not be granted."

(4) "such damages would too difficult for the court to measure, and therefore not recoverable."

Third, there are those arising from a requisite, desideratum, or limit of roles within the division of legal labor. Consider, thes examples:

(5) "an agreement to agree should not be enforced because the court is in no position to make an agreement for the parties."

(6) "it is not appropriate for courts to inquire whether the consideration to be received by one party is adequate."

Institutional reasons are special because they are largely "internal" to the social institution of law. That is, institutional reasons are generated out of features relatively specific and peculiar to the social institution of law — the requisites, desiderata, and limits of the rule of law ideal, of legal processes and structures, and of the essential division of legal labor. On the other hand, rightness reasons and goal reasons are, as I define them here, not generated out of features specific and peculiar to the social institution of law. They are not thus "internal" to law. Indeed, rightness reasons arise regularly in the ordinary activities of life remote from law and its workings. And even though the goal reasons recognized in law presuppose legally authoritative goals, much goal reasoning occurs in daily life entirely independent of legal goals.

Although institutional reasons arise out of the requisites, desiderata, and limits of law as a social institution, this does not make them authoritative reasons. They remain distinct from legally authoritative reasons -- from appeals to stare decisis, to statutes, or to other antecedent legal authority. Thus, the fact that institutional reasons are internal to law and derive from some feature of the social institution of law, such as the limits of judicial remedies, does not make them any the less substantive reasons. Similarly, the fact that institutional reasons also shape and inform the material content of antecedent legal rules and other precepts that do generate authoritative reasons does not make them any the less substantive in nature.

All three varieties of substantive reasons: rightness reasons, goal reasons, and institutional reasons appear in the common law. They shape and inform the content of rules and other precepts that I here classify as legally authoritative reasons. Again, rules and other legal precepts are not empty husks or shells. They have substantive content contributed by substantive reasons, in various complex blends. But apart from contributing to the material content of rules and other legal precepts, substantive reasons have many other roles, too. They are deployed to decide cases of first impression, to choose between conflicting precedent, to over-rule precedent, to formulate new doctrine in its place, and to reinforce available authoritative reasons. They are also deployed to bring substantive standards of criticism to bear.

III.   The Historical Dominance and Justificatory Sufficiency of Rightness and Institutional Reasons

I have now completed my general account of the main varieites of substantive reasons encountered in the common law. I will now take up my second main thesis. This thesis is that, judging from the language of court opinions selected for inclusion in the leading casebooks, rightness and institutional reasons have together been historically far more influential than goal reasons in the general common law of contract, a state of affairs that persists today. This dominance persists despite the fact that goal reasons seem also to be widely available in these same cases. My corollary thesis here is that the rightness reasons and institutional reasons that the judges generally give are also justificatorily sufficient. Thus, judges do not need to resort to goal reasons. I will seek to substantiate my historical dominance thesis and its corollary with reference to the general common law of contract. I will focus on this branch of modern law because I wish to test my theses against the strongest contrary possibility. If any law should reveal the marks of goal-oriented, predictive, instrumental and consequentialist thinking, it would be modern law, for this mode of justificatory thinking rose to prominence in Anglo-American social thought during the 19th century and after. Moreover, the general common law of contract, more than any other branch of private law, invites justificatory analysis in terms of goal reasons, particularly goal reasons of a utilitarian or wealth-maximizing kind such as the promotion of individual and social gains from trade. Thus if the justificatory reasoning that plays by far the largest role in the common law of contract turns out not to be goal reasoning, but rightness and institutional reasoning, it is likely that such reasoning would prove dominant in other branches of private law, too.

It is neither possible nor necessary here to canvass every nook and cranny of the general common law of contract. Instead, I will focus on its major features: freedom of contract, theories of obligation, and remedies. I will not rest merely on evidence that our existing law of contract is consistent with the dictates of rightness and institutional reasons. I will also cite evidence that when writing opinions, judges usually rely upon rightness or institutional reasons rather than goal reasons to justify these doctrines and to apply them in particular cases. I will also point out that many of the leading doctrines of our subject explicitly wear rightness or institutional rationales on their very faces. Throughout, I will indicate how rightness and institutional reasoning are usually justificatorily sufficient, together. Thus, even though judges sometimes also invoke goal reasons, this is usually quite unnecessary.[6]

A. Freedom of Contract

A central feature of our common law of contract is that individuals enjoy broad freedom to enter into agreements. Indeed, despite significant inroads, such freedom is still today the rule rather than the exception. Now, it is possible to justify this freedom on the basis, for example, of goal reasoning to the effect that through contractual exchanges in the present, individuals may maximize utility or wealth, and thus enjoy a more plentiful future. But courts rarely say this. Far more often, they explicitly justify broad freedom to contract on rightness grounds. Thus our society overwhelmingly subscribes to what might be called the rightness norm of autonomous choice: within limits, citizens ought to decide things for themselves -- ought to order their own affairs. At least, they should not be slaves of the state, nor slaves of other citizens, for this degrades individuality and destroys human dignity. And at the most, citizens should enjoy autonomous choice to determine their own ways of life and to govern themselves. Such choice is exercised in large measure through agreements that citizens make with others. Now, such rightness notions as these are not, as such, reducible to the realization of gains from trade or the maximization of mere psychic satisfactions.[7]

Courts commonly invoke the rightness norm of autonomy and similar norms when upholding freedom of contract. Here is a recent representative pronouncement:[8]

[t]he reluctance on the part of the judiciary to nullify contractual arrangements on public policy grounds also serves to protect the public interest in having individuals exercise broad powers to structure their own affairs by making legally enforceable promises, a concept which lies at the heart of the freedom of contract principle.

Within certain limits, our law even allows private individuals wide freedom to enter into enforceable contracts that may in fact bring them less rather than more by way of gains from trade, or wealth, or satisfactions. Of course, this accords with the norm of autonomous self governance.

Furthermore, the rightness rationale here for extensive freedom of contract is sufficient for the purposes of judicial justification. That is, this reasoning requires no further reinforcement. It rests on the norm of autonomous choice, one of the most justificatorily powerful norms accepted in our society. (This does not mean we never over-ride or qualify it.) Of course, goal reasons may play reinforcing roles here. But they are not essential to the justification of this fundamental feature of our law of contract.

When we consider the extent to which institutional reasoning reinforces broad freedom of contract, it becomes all the more clear how dispensable goal reasoning is here. Our courts regularly acknowledge the inappropriateness of substituting the substantive judgment of state organs and officials for those of private contracting parties over a wide range of matters, including choice of education, choice of occupation, choice of marriage partner, choice of lifestyle, choice of leisure pursuits, and much more. The institutional inappropriateness of having state organs decide such matters is itself a major rationale for according private parties broad freedom of contract. Thus it is not merely that the state ought not to decide such matters because this would impair autonomy and offend human dignity. It is also that, in general, the state is not institutionally competent to order the conduct of individual lives — not institutionally competent to prescribe in these ways what the individual should have and do. State officials, including judges, do not and cannot know enough facts.[9] Nor can officials competently substitute their judgment for the judgment of individual citizens where choice calls for the exercise of judgment, which it usually does. For one thing, officials cannot identify and weigh the relevant values at stake on behalf of the affected individual, especially where the relevant values include the preferences and values of the affected individual, as is usually the case. Thus, to substitute state choice for such private choice here is to violate the essential division of legal labor within the social order. It is also for the state to adopt a conception of the individual citizen as a diminished and relatively helpless being whose way of life has to be determined and provided for by the state. Indeed, I find the very conception of the individual implicit in much goal-oriented social theory little short of ignoble.

In sum, the institutional rationale for freedom of contract is institutional in the sense that it derives from inherent limits on the competence of official participants in the general division of legal labor. This general type of institutional reason frequently figures in judicial opinions. For example, we often encounter it in decisions refusing to inquire into the adequacy of consideration, and in decisions refusing to "overpolice" bargains.[10] (I pause here to remark on the extraordinarily rapid return to market economies now underway in Western Europe. Most of my economist friends stress that this will increase wealth. But in stressing this, I think they neglect something much more basic and vital, namely the freedom of choice in economic and other matters that a market economy generally secures.)

B. The Recognized General Theories of Legal Obligation in Contract

The single most prominent structural feature of our law of contract is its multiplicity of general theories of legal obligation. A general theory of legal obligation consists of a comprehensive and systematic structure of concepts, duly organized and specified in legal terms, so to provide for the creation, policing, excuse, defeasance, sanctioning, modification and transfer of a general class of obligations. In the field of contract, we encounter at least the following major theories of obligation:

(1) obligation arising from agreement with consideration,

(2) obligation arising from justified reliance

(3) obligation arising from unjust enrichment

(4) obligation arising from tort (especially negligent misperformance of contract)

(5) obligation arising from promises for benefit received.

It is no accident that we have this multiplicity. Each theory has its own distinct rationale. Moreover, it is my thesis that various forms of rightness and institutional reasoning actually figure in these rationales with goal reasons far behind. Further, such reasoning is justificatorily sufficient.

I turn first to legal obligation arising from a valid agreement with consideration. We can easily think of future-regarding goal reasons which justify legal recognition of obligations arising from valid agreements with consideration. The fulfillment of contract obligations brings gains from trade. It enhances psychic satisfactions; and more.[11]

But official judicial recognition of the general theory of agreement with consideration is, in fact, far more often based on one or more of several overlapping rightness norms and the
reasoning arising under them. I have already introduced the first of these norms, namely the norm of respect for autonomous self determination through free contractual choice.

A second rightness norm of relevance is simply the powerful moral norm that parties who make agreements ought to keep their word. Courts acknowledge this norm through reasons taking a variety of formulations including *pacta sunt servanda*, the "sanctity of contract," and the obligation of "good faith."[12]

A third overlapping rightness norm here is that of mutual trust. According to it, an agreement is a repository of mutual trust in which each side trusts in the other to do as agreed. Often, party A must trust party B to perform after party A has already performed. Simultaneous performance is not possible. Thus, a failure of performance is a kind of abuse of trust.

A fourth overlapping rightness norm widely recognized in the case law is what may be called the norm of reciprocity. The essence of a deal is that each party is to carry out his or her side of it, i.e., provide his or her quid pro quo. This norm is a member of that large family of rightness norms consisting of principles of fairness.

A fifth rightness norm that often comes into play here is simply that the law ought to hold a party responsible when he or she actually induces justified reliance, a norm that applies whenever an agreement with consideration is, as lawyers say, "partially executed."

The foregoing overlapping rightness norms and the reasoning they generate are certainly sufficient to justify judicial recognition of the theory of obligation known as agreement with consideration, without further assistance either from goal reasons or from institutional reasons.

But at this point, a proponent of goal reasoning might wish to argue as follows:

> You have so far said nothing in particular about the doctrine of consideration as such -- the so-called 'bargain' theory of consideration. Yet this doctrine may be the most prominent feature of that theory of obligation known as agreement with consideration. Moreover the frequent judicial articulation of the bargain theory in the opinions indicates that the courts are first and foremost committed to goal reasoning here -- to furthering bargains -- trade and exchange, and thereby to maximizing utility and wealth.

I believe there are at least three answers to this argument. The first is that too much should not be made here of the fact that courts often use the word "bargain" when referring to the doctrine of consideration. The concept of "bargain" should not be equated with the idea of gaining from trade as such. Rather, it is a name for reciprocal conventional inducement, a concept roughly equivalent to the rightness norm of reciprocity. According to this norm, one form of fairness requires that a party honor an undertaking to another where that other has made a reciprocal undertaking.[13] Second, the so-called bargain theory of consideration has now today been reduced very largely to a formality. It requires no type of substantive content. Moreover, a transaction that does not in reality involve a bargain may be enforceable merely if cast in the form of a bargain. There is nothing anomalous about this. A purely formal "bargain" theory of consideration serves all of the main ends of consideration. It induces the parties to exercise caution. It provides evidence of a real transaction. And it provides a channelling facility through which the parties may express legally recognized choices.[14] Third, the courts applying the bargain theory of consideration virtually never require some showing that both parties in some way benefitted from or would benefit from a bargain. Yet if the rationale for the bargain theory of consideration were a maximizing goal reason, one would expect to encounter some such inquiry, at least in difficult cases.

In sum, in judicial opinions, rightness reasons largely account for justified acceptance of the theory of agreement with consideration. Goal reasoning plays a relatively small role. But we may also note the reinforcing influence of one type of institutional reasoning. The very grounding of free contract partly on the institutional inappropriateness of substituting state choice for private choice, implies that the theory of agreement with consideration is similarly grounded. And, in fact, numerous cases so state.[15]

A second basic theory of obligation is that which arises from justified reliance on the defendant's promise. When the reliance is on a promise that is part of an agreement with consideration, such reliance simply reinforces that theory. But when that theory is not applicable, or is legally invalid, or is unenforceable, it is familiar that such justified reliance gives rise to an independently significant obligation under the theory of promissory estoppel. The promise relied on may even be gratuitous.

Again, one can construct goal reasons to justify the theory of promissory estoppel, too. Thus, where the promise is commercial in nature, it can be argued that legal protection of reliance is required to facilitate private planning, productivity, and trade. And in the case of gratuitous promises, it can be argued that reneging donors should generally be held to their promises if the society is to institutionalize a mechanism whereby donors generally can maximize their own satisfactions through donative behavior.

Promissory estoppel as a theory protecting justified reliance on a promise was, however, first authoritatively formulated in section 90 of the Restatement of Contracts (first) in 1932. That formulation is itself a rough legal embodiment of a widely accepted rightness norm having many applications both in and out of the law. This norm is essentially concerned with the just righting of wrongs rather than with bringing about future states of affairs that serve social goals. Thus, section 90 of the first Restatement of

Contracts provided:

> A promise which the promisor should reasonably expect to induce action or forbearance of a definite and substantial character on the part of the promisee and which does induce such action or forbearance is binding if injustice can be avoided only by enforcement of the promise.

Now, this is a doctrinal formulation which, as Llewellyn might have said, wears its rightness character on its face. It is therefore hardly surprising that the case law giving rise to and applying the doctrine includes much rightness reasoning and very little goal reasoning. The following formulation, from the leading case of Goodman v. Dicker[16] is representative:

> Justice and fair dealing require that one who acts to his detriment on the faith of conduct of the kind revealed here should be protected by estopping the party who brought about the situation from alleging anything in opposition to the natural consequences of his own course of conduct.

In another famous case, the court said:[17]

> . . .[A]n estoppel might similarly arise from the making of a promise ... if it was intended that the promise be relied upon and in fact was relied upon, and a refusal to enforce it would be virtually to sanction the perpetration of fraud or other injustice.

Even without reinforcement from institutional rationales, rightness reasoning of this kind is alone sufficient to justify the legal doctrine embodied in section 90, and the now numerous particular decisions in its name. Indeed, the more general "estoppel" norm which section 90 instantiates is, in justificatory terms, one of the most powerful in the whole of American law.[18]

The theory of restitution to prevent unjust enrichment, or "restitutionary theory", as it is sometimes called, is a third theory of obligation widely at work in our law of contract. It often functions independently of the theory of agreement with consideration when that theory is invalid or unenforceable, or is somehow remedially inapposite. Restitutionary theory functions independently of promissory estoppel, too. It is elementary that restitutionary theory generally requires that the claimant have conferred a benefit on the other party, whereas promissory estoppel requires only that the claimant have relied on the promise.

In many cases, after a contractual negotiation or an agreement with consideration goes awry, one party emerges with a benefit received from the other. Often the benefit is part of the very performance that the party benefited sought from the agreement or proposed agreement in the first place, yet the claimant has no contractual basis for recovery of the benefit and no claim, or no sufficient claim, in promissory estoppel.

Nevertheless, to prevent unjust enrichment, courts commonly require the party so benefited to pay the claimant the value of the benefit conferred. As with the other theories, it is also possible to ground this one in predictive and consequentialist goal reasons. For example, it might be argued that if the law did not recognize restitutionary theory, this would make contracting unduly risky, and thus interfere with trade. When things go awry in trading, as they inevitably do in some proportion of cases, the parties should be able to extricate themselves without undue cost. Also, without a remedy to prevent unjust enrichment, aggrieved parties might take matters into their own hands, with consequent friction, disorder, and inefficiency.

But the very nomenclature of the theory of restitution to prevent unjust enrichment reveals its essentially rightness origins, and goal reasoning rarely appears in judicial opinions invoking this theory. Instead, one finds rightness reasoning grounded in notions of what is fair, just, and equitable, as between the parties. As one court recently put it:[19]

> Because ... [such] obligations rest upon equitable considerations, they do not arise when it would not be unfair for the recipient to reap the benefit without having to pay for it.

Although the concept of injustice itself appears on the very face of this theory, the judicial inquiry is not wholly open-ended and discretionary. There are even some well known rules. For example, there is no unjust enrichment if a gift was intended. And there is no unjust enrichment where the benefit was conferred officiously or by a "volunteer". But these rules, too, are grounded in rightness notions of what is fair, equitable and just.

Again, and without reinforcement from institutional reasons, rightness reasoning is alone appropriate and sufficient to justify recognition of the theory of restitution to prevent unjust enrichment.

Fourth, numerous forms of contractual activity or inactivity may generate obligations arising in tort. These include negligent misperformance of a contract, misrepresentation and nondisclosure in contractual negotiations (whether intentional or negligent) and intentional interference with contractual relations.

By far the most common is negligent misperformance of a contract, which may not only constitute breach of an obligation arising from an agreement with consideration but also a tort, at least if there is an applicable public policy such that there would be liability for misperformance if such action were gratuitous. I will here consider only negligent misperformance. The range of liability is very broad. As Prosser and Keeton have said:[20]

> [T]he American courts have extended the tort of liability for misfeasance to virtually every type of contract where defective performance may injure the promisee. An attorney or an abstractor examining a title, a physician treating a patient, a surveyor, an agent collecting a note or lending money or settling a claim, or a liability insurer defending a suit, all have been held liable in tort for their negligence. The same is true of contractors employed to build a structure, to transport people or goods, to install a windmill or a lightning rod, or to shoot an oil well, or a beauty shop giving a permanent wave, or suppliers of chattels and many others.

The importance to a claimant of being able to sue for the tort of negligent misperformance of a contract rather than for breach of an agreement with consideration can be very great. For one thing, the claimant may be able to avoid contract defenses such as exculpatory clauses, lack of privity, and the like.

It is often said that the theory of obligation in tort here is grounded in "public policy" and this has the ring of goal reasoning.[21] But the phrase "public policy" is ambiguous as between norms of rightness on the one hand and social goals on the other. In my view, the tort theory here is usually grounded in the general rightness norm requiring respect and due care for the interests of others. This is one of the most elemental and wide-ranging rightness norms recognized in the whole of the common law. The emphasis in the case law on negligent misperformance of a contract is usually a non-predictive and antecedentialist emphasis on negligent wrongdoing, and on the appropriateness of making amends in the name of reparative justice and equity, not on structuring incentives for the future.[22] Some opinions do speak of deterrence, but in my view this is not really necessary. The rightness rationale is alone justificatorily sufficient.

Of course, the foregoing rightness rationale is reinforced by still other rightness rationales. The negligence that occurs here is negligent misperformance of an agreement, and we have already seen that the obligation to perform pursuant to a valid agreement with consideration is grounded in various overlapping rightness considerations.[23]

My general thesis that rightness and institutional reasoning are historically primary and justificatorily sufficient also holds in regard to the leading legal doctrines governing contract formation. Here, I can only pass in review a selection of these. The actual justifications that courts most commonly give for these doctrines are rooted primarily in rightness reasoning. Indeed, some of these doctrines even wear rightness rationales on their faces quite explicitly.

Consider the so-called objective theory of mutual assent so prominent in the modern law of contract. This theory holds a party to objective manifestations of assent, reasonably interpreted, regardless of lack of actual intent to contract, of uncommunicated mental reservations, of jesting, or the like. Again, we may concede that the objective theory of contract formation facilitates commerce, and judges occasionally so justify it.[24] But rightness norms of honesty and care in communication are by far the most influential here, and are, alone, justificatorily sufficient. One must not deliberately or recklessly, or carelessly mislead the other contracting party. The courts invoke these rightness norms not only in contract cases, but in tort cases, too. But, in addition, a rightness norm already considered, namely, that of protecting the justified reliance of one's contracting partner is also at work.

A related cluster of doctrine governs the effect of mistake or misunderstanding in communication at the formation stage of contracting: section 20 of the Restatement second of contracts encapsulates this doctrine:

§ 20. Effect of Misunderstanding

(1) There is no manifestation of mutual assent to an exchange if the

parties attach materially different meanings to their manifestations and

> (a) neither party knows or has reason to know the meaning attached by the other; or
>
> (b) each party knows or each party has reason to know the meaning attached by the other.

(2) The manifestations of the parties are operative in accordance with the meaning attached to them by one of the parties if

> (a) that party does not know of any different meaning attached by the other, and the other knows the meaning attached by the first party; or
>
> (b) that party has no reason to know of any different meaning attached by the other, and the other has reason to know the meaning attached by the first party.

With its explicit emphasis on knowledge and reason to know, this formulation (which is also faithful to the case law) wears major fragments of its rightness rationales on its face. Here, rightness notions of fault and blame are controlling. Thus, for example, a meaning attached by the first party to an objective manifestation will govern if the first party did not know of a different meaning attached by the other, and the other knew of the meaning attached by the first party. Here we encounter what might be called the equitable equivalent of mutual assent.[25]

Legal doctrines governing the creation and termination of the power to accept an offer are also rooted in rightness rationales. The making of an offer -- the creation of a power to accept -- is an exercise of freedom to contract. The objective theory of contract formation does alter this freedom somewhat. But, as we have already seen, rightness reasoning justifies contractual freedom and the objective theory (if judicial opinions are to be believed).

The legal principles governing termination of the power of acceptance are summarized in section 36 of the Restatement of Contracts (second). These principles too, are very largely implications of contractual freedom. Perhaps the best known limitation on the offeror's power to revoke is now embodied in Restatement section 87(2) which provides:

> An offer which the offeror should reasonably expect to induce action or forbearance of a substantial character on the part of the offeree before acceptance and which does induce such action or forbearance is binding as an option contract to the extent necessary to avoid injustice.

This limitation is grounded largely in the rightness rationale of protecting the offeree from revocation where the offeror knows or has reason to know that the offeree must "undergo substantial expense, or undertake substantial commitments, or forego alternatives, in order to put himself in a position to accept by either promise or performance."[26] As formulated in the Restatement, this doctrine, too, wears its rightness rationale on its face, for it reads explicitly in terms of avoiding the injustice of upsetting justified reliance. The case law here originated largely under section 90 of the first Restatement, and explicitly espouses rightness reasoning. As one leading opinion put it, reasonable "reliance [on the offer] resulting in a foreseeable prejudicial change in position affords a compelling basis" for limiting the power to revoke.[27]

I will now refer only to one other significant cluster of doctrine here, namely that which requires definiteness in the agreement and refuses to sanction agreements to agree. This cluster of doctrine, too, can be readily explained on rightness grounds. An unduly indefinite agreement, or a mere agreement to agree, is not really a full exercise of contractual freedom — not a fully formulated expression of autonomous choice. But beyond this, these doctrines can also be accounted for partly in light of institutional considerations. Indefinite agreements and agreements to agree, if legal effect is to be given to them, require that an organ of the state substitute its judgment in place of the judgment that the parties would have exercised (or very likely have exercised), and thus poses issues of institutional competence. Moreover, the uncertainty of indefinite agreements, and of agreements to agree, limits the extent to which courts can provide an appropriate remedy for breach, another important institutional consideration found in the case law cases) and on the face of statutes in this area.[28]

C. Basic Law Determining the Legal Content of Contracts

A further prominent feature of our contract law consists of the rules and principles for determining the legal content of a binding agreement. Here, the primary legal principle is simply that the terms to which the parties have agreed control. This principle of general contract law, generates a highly important special class of authoritative reasons. This is a class of reasons that the parties may act on, that lawyers may invoke when advising the parties, that judges may rely on when deciding cases, and that independent observers may bring to bear when judging and criticizing the behavior of parties under a contract. The fertility of the terms of a binding agreement as a source of authoritative reasons helps explain why so many contracts are entered and performed without dispute. And when disputes do arise, few of them ever get to court partly because it is possible for the parties to resolve them privately on the basis of the authoritative reasons so generated.

It is natural that the justifications which courts most commonly state for honoring the authoritative reasons generated by the terms of binding contracts consist of rightness reasons and institutional reasons. We have already seen that broad freedom to contract and the theory of obligation known as agreement with consideration are grounded largely in rightness reasons and institutional reasons. What the right hand giveth the left must not taketh away. It would make no sense for a legal system to grant broad freedom of contract and to recognize the theory of agreement with consideration, and then refuse to consider the terms of the resulting agreements binding, i.e., refuse to consider those terms as authoritative reasons. Moreover, courts, as institutions, are, in general, not competent to tell the parties what they ought to want, and all the more so when the parties in their own agreement explicitly spell out what they do want.

But sometimes the binding agreements of the parties are not sufficiently clear or are fragmentary. When so, they are incapable of generating authoritative reasons that are determinative. This gives rise to the well-known need for bodies of law on interpretation and gap filling. In our system, we have parol evidence rules which define the subject matter to be interpreted. We have a generally prescribed methodology of interpretation. We have so-called "implied terms." We also have doctrines giving appropriate effect to course of dealing, usage of trade, and course of performance. And we have suppletive rules for filling certain kinds of gaps. Frequently, we also call on the general obligation of good faith, and on general rightness norms.

Rarely does a court invoke goal reasoning here. Instead, rightness reasons are most often at work. Courts stress that issues of interpretation and gap filling (1) should be resolved so far as possible in a fashion consistently with what the parties did in fact agree on or may reasonably be supposed to have agreed on, and (2) should be resolved so far as possible fairly, for again, in the absence of clear evidence to the contrary, it can be assumed that neither party intended that one should take undue advantage of the other. But institutional reasons are widely at work too. For example, because judges are not institutionally well situated to substitute their own judgment for that of the parties, this inclines them rather strongly to try to identify relatively objective standards of decision in past course of dealing, course of performance, usage of trade, the circumstances of contracting, and general customs of the community. These are all standards which the parties would likely acknowledge in the absence of explicit agreement. To cite one further example, judges (and others) have sometimes grounded the parol evidence rule in significant measure on institutional reasoning to the effect that jurors cannot, in the face of unreliable oral testimony be trusted to give sufficient weight to the fact that the parties have agreed to adopt a written document embodying their agreement.[29]

D. Leading Rules and Principles Governing Performance and Nonperformance

Here I can only consider some of the most important doctrines governing performance and non-performance as they apply to bilateral agreements.

One of the most influential rightness norms in the law of contracts is what I call the norm of *quid pro quo* reciprocity. The law seeks to honor this norm so to secure that each party to an already agreed upon exchange gets his or her *quid pro quo*. Performance, and receipt of the agreed return performance, then, are the essence of a bilateral contractual exchange.

Yet frequently the parties do not spell out explicitly in their agreements all of the steps that they might take to maximize the likelihood that each will receive the agreed *quid pro quo*. Thus the parties may leave gaps as to the order of performance and gaps as to the quality of performance. Here the law has developed "gap fillers" to implement the rightness norm of *quid pro quo* reciprocity. Thus, where an exchange can take place simultaneously, the general law supplies a gap filler - implies "concurrent conditions" requiring that the exchange take place simultaneously, thereby securing, so far as the law can, that each side will get its *quid pro quo*.[30] To the same end, the law generally requires a party to such an exchange who seeks a remedy for breach to allege that he or she tendered performance or was ready to perform at the agreed time, or was excused therefrom.

Similarly, where because of the nature of the deal, the performances have to be sequential rather than simultaneous, the law generally provides gap fillers requiring the party whose risk of nonperformance is the greater to perform first.[31]

Where the gap in the agreement concerns quality of performance rather than timing, the law generally supplies a gap filler to the effect that substantial performance rather than perfect performance is required.[32] This protects the *quid pro quo* expectation of each side. A substantially performing party should be entitled to the *quid pro quo* from the other party, subject to an offset for the shortfall from perfect performance. (Here this right of the substantially performing party also protects against forfeiture.) On the other hand, a non-substantially performing party (one guilty of "material breach") does not give the agreed *quid pro quo* in sufficient measure. Hence the other party should not have to perform, and becomes entitled to suspend or withhold performance, and may, of course, even be discharged entirely after an appropriate period of time.[33] Again, this doctrine helps minimize the risk that one party only will realize the agreed *quid pro quo*.

E. The Law Governing Failure of Basic Assumptions

I now turn very briefly to the law of excuse, including mistake in basic assumption, frustration of purpose, impossibility, and frustration. All such doctrines are regularly justified by the courts on one or more rightness grounds. Thus, with regard to mistake in basic assumptions, in the absence of special circumstances, courts generally excuse the obligation on the ground that the mistake vitiates assent or the like.[34] There was simply no genuine exercise of autonomous choice in the first place. And if it is right to hold a party to an agreement, it is also wrong to hold a party to an agreement not made. With regard to the other excuses, the courts usually stress the unforseeability of the event and thus failure of the parties to address the matter (and thus again a lack of assent) or stress the unfairness of imposing a highly disproportionate cost of performance on one of the parties.

F. Basic Remedial Doctrine

In the general common law of contract, the most prominent measure of damages for breach is lost expectancy. The law normally seeks, within limits, to put the plaintiff in the position the plaintiff would have been in had the agreement been performed. The courts most often justify this measure on the ground that it gives the plaintiff the monetary equivalent of "what was promised."[35] Is a rationale expressed in these or similar terms a rightness reason or is it a goal reason? I would construe it as a rightness reason. It can be readily construed to invoke rightness norms rather than social goals. It requires no predicted facts. Characterizational analysis is sufficient. Instrumentalist reasoning is unnecessary. And, in my view, the structure of the reasoning is antecedentialist rather than consequentialist.

The relevant norms of rightness here are those already considered which require a contracting party to carry out the agreement, or, in the alternative, make amends for failure to do so. These norms, we saw, include the autonomous choice norm, the norm of *pacta sunt servanda*, the mutual trust norm, and the norm of fair reciprocation. Each of these at least requires that what the contract breaker must pay be measured by the terms of the broken promise. The recovery must be compensatory. No more, no less. Thus, to make amends, the contract breaker must pay lost expectancy damages. This is reparative justice.

Occasionally, one finds in judicial opinions a remark to the effect that a lost expectancy measure usually yields the highest damage figure and thus serves best to deter breach of contracts in the future. But even if this rationale were a goal reason, it is one seldom found in the opinions.

At the same time, the courts generally refuse to award punitive damages for breach of contract even though this would deter breach. Most often the courts state that their only province is to award compensation for the loss, i.e., do reparative justice. In addition, the courts also refuse to enforce so-called agreed penalty clauses yielding high recovery although this would deter breach. Usually this refusal is precisely on the ground that these go beyond the terms of the broken promise, and are therefore punitive rather than compensatory. A court may even go on to reject the argument that the enforcement of penalty clauses would have deterrent efficacy.

Not even goal minded economists appear to argue that deterrence is a major rationale for lost expectancy damages. But what they do argue is that the lost expectancy measure as well as other remedial doctrines are justified in terms of goal reasoning to the effect that such doctrines facilitate "efficient breach" and thus maximize social gains.[36] If a contract breaker can gain enough through breach to pay lost expectancy or other damages and have something left over after contracting anew, then it is said that this should not only be allowed but encouraged. On this view, the law discourages so-called efficient breach to the extent that it imposes damages liability that exceeds lost expectancy. Thus, efficient breach theorists rationalize confining damages to lost expectancy or less on the goal oriented reasoning that this will maximize social gains.

This whole issue is complex, but for my purposes, it is only necessary to make three remarks. First, the foregoing economist's goal reason -- efficient breach, almost never appears in court opinions. Second, there is much actual contract doctrine with which it cannot be squared. Third, this goal oriented rationale is, in any case, justificatorily superfluous. The award of lost expectancy damages is already well justified in rightness terms, as I have demonstrated.

There are many other remedial doctrines in general contract law, including those relating to reliance damages, consequential damages, restitutionary recovery, the avoidance of forfeitures, mitigation, and the general denial of specific performance. In court opinions, judges usually justify all of these doctrines on rightness or institutional grounds (or both). Actually, much remedial doctrine is influenced by institutional reasons. For example, because it is difficult to prove total reliance on an agreement, some judges and theorists argue that this supports awarding the most generous of possible measures, namely lost expectancy. Of course, lost expectancy is sometimes itself difficult to prove, whereas out of pocket reliance expenditures are not, and here courts readily grant the latter as an alternative. It is also familiar that specific performance is sometimes denied on the ground that the proposed decree would be difficult for a court to administer.

G. Summary

Perhaps I may summarize in this way. Judges generally ground the leading doctrines of general contract law in justificatorily sufficient rightness or institutional reasons. I think this is a significant finding for reasons I will later explain.

I should, however, stress that my finding is consistent with two further possibilities, namely, that particular goal reasons, too, might as I have indicated throughout, also be available to support these doctrines, and that sticking to rightness reasoning in judicial opinions might even in fact be the best way of serving broad social goals such as the enlargement of the social pie and maximization of satisfactions.

IV. The Justificatory Superiority of Rightness and Institutional Reasons

So far, then, my theses have been that rightness and institutional reasons are the dominant types of substantive reasons in our general case law of contract, and that such reasons are justificatorily sufficient. Now I wish to argue for a further thesis, namely, that rightness and institutional reasons are generally superior to goal reasons for the purposes of justifying judicial decisions in general contract law.

Judges decide most cases in light of already existing common law, that is, in light of authoritative reasons deriving from precedent rather than in light of substantive reasons from scratch, so to speak. Contrary to what some law school casebooks might suggest, even in our highly substantive and anti-formal legal system, judges do not treat every common law case as a case of first impression. Instead, they usually take their justificatory task to be that of demonstrating the applicability of precedent.

If I am right that the justificatory task is most often one of determining the applicability of precedent -- an authoritative reason, two important and interesting questions that immediately arise are these: in our system, how far do judges determine the applicability of doctrine partly by reference to the substantive reasons that figure in its content? Insofar as the applicability of doctrine is so determined, can judges more effectively perform this task when the doctrine is derived from rightness or institutional reasoning than when it is based on goal reasons? I believe the answer to the first question is clear. In the common law, courts often determine the applicability of doctrine by reference to the substantive reasons that shape and inform its content. Indeed, some of our judges even proclaim that such reasons are part of case law holdings.

Assuming then, that determining the scope of precedent in light of its substantive rationale is a legitimate method and widely if not uniformly followed, can judges utilize this method more effectively when the reasons are rightness and institutional reasons than when goal reasons? I believe the answer here, too, is yes. Where the doctrine is based on rightness and institutional reasons, the judge must decide whether facts generating those reasons in the applicable precedent are similarly present in the case being decided. Ordinarily, the adjudicative facts of the case will provide the basis for an answer. If the relevant facts are present, the precedent is in point. If not, it is distinguishable. (Even if in point, there may be still further facts in the present case that render the precedent distinguishable.) This process will be largely characterizational. Of course, some weighing may also be required because the facts in the two cases may implicate the substantive considerations in differing degrees.

On the other hand, when doctrine is based largely on goal reasons, matters are frequently more problematic, at least if such reasons are to be taken seriously on their own terms rather than merely as makeweights. The facts may be rather unclear as to whether the relevant social goal is still authoritative or is sufficiently implicated in the facts of the case. Also, it may not be clear whether the relevant goal serving consequences can be reliably predicted to flow from the decision, even if the goal is authoritative and sufficiently implicated. Similar unclarity of both kinds may also arise with respect to possible countervailing goal serving consequences in the case. The judge may have to go beyond the adjudicative facts of the case, which means the judge must make assumptions, speculate, or predict (on the basis of inadequate facts). Of course, in some cases, this can be done with some certainty. But often this will not be so.

But reasoning from authority in the common law of contract is not confined to reasoning from precedent. A major source of a special class of authoritative reasons here consists simply of the terms of the contract involved. Yet unlike authoritative reasons deriving from precedent, members of this special class of authoritative reasons derive their justificatory force from the rightness rationales on which the theory of agreement with consideration is based. The rightness reasoning is here justificatorily superior to goal reasoning in that it provides the foundation for this major special class of authoriatative reasons for decision -- i.e., terms of contracts.

I now turn to the justificatory task of the judge where a precedent is to be over-ruled, or there is a conflicting line of precedent , or a case of first impression arises. In such cases, the main justificatory purposes of the opinion writer are to demonstrate that the new decision is first, an appropriate one for a court rather than a legislature to make, second, is well grounded in relevant substantive reasoning, and third, is appropriately lawlike. My proposition is that rightness and institutional reasons generally serve these three justificatory purposes of the court better than goal reasons. If the new decision can be based on rightness and institutional reasons, no issue as to the legitimacy of judicial role is likely to arise, given that most of the general common law of contract is so based. Further, the subject-matter of rightness reasons is seldom the kind of subject-matter on which political parties divide, unlike the subject-matter of many goal reasons. Also, courts can be said to be experts at rightness reasons in ways not true with respect to goal reasons. As to rightness reasons, judges have both lay and professional expertise, for not only are these reasons dominant in the case law, they have well understood counterparts in ordinary daily life as well. Indeed, rightness norms are rooted in daily life. As for institutional reasons, judges, too have special professional expertise. They know well what the limits of a judicial remedy are, and the like.

Furthermore, as we have seen, rightness reasons are not predictive and not instrumentalist. This means that the factual foundation at least for rightness reasons will usually appear in the adjudicative facts, and thus be readily accessible to the judges.

The foregoing considerations indicate that rightness and institutional reasons serve better to legitimate judicial action and serve better as substantive justifications in those cases where new ground is broken. Such reasons may aptly serve still another justificatory purpose better than goal reasons. Even in a ground breaking case, it will usually be appropriate for the court to try to formulate its position in a general rule or principle. When this can be done, it demonstrates the law-like character of the decision and serves rule of law values. In my view, rightness reasons and institutional reasons are generally better raw material for the construction of stable rules than are goal reasons. For one thing, the structure of the usual rightness norm generating a rightness reason is itself embryonically rule-like. This is not true of the usual goal figuring in goal reasons. Further, the justificatory force of rightness and of institutional reasons varies far less with social change than does the force of many goal reasons. The force of goal reasons is affected over time by changes in the authoritativeness of goals, changes in levels of goal realization, changes in available social means, changes in the costs of such means, and more. This means that rules, principles, and other legal doctrines based on rightness and institutional reasons promise to be somewhat more stable. In turn, fundamental "rule of law" values are fulfilled. That is, we end up with more law in the form of general rules, a more reliable basis for citizen self-direction and reliance, and better prospects for congruence between judicial decision and antecedent law.

Besides the foregoing, still other considerations are relevant. I will identify only two, one having to do with intelligibility and persuasiveness of the reasons courts give, the other with the efficiency of formulating reasons. The purposes of justification require that the reasons a court gives be readily intelligible and persuasive to all concerned. This requirement is not identical with the requirement that a type of reason have sufficient justificatory force in the circumstances. A type of reason can have sufficient justificatory force, yet not be sufficiently intelligible or persuasive. Whatever the force of goal reasons, especially those generated by contemporary economic analysis, it can hardly be said that such reasons are readily intelligible and persuasive to most of those concerned.

Rightness reasons and institutional reasons on the other hand, are generally intelligible and, if good, then persuasive. Such reasons incorporate familiar concepts from daily life and their applicability to facts can be readily grasped. It also follows that they are explainable to those who lose lawsuits. If it is too much to expect all losers to be persuaded, it remains important for the reasons at least to be intelligible so that they can be contested. Intelligibility and persuasiveness also reduces the need for coercive enforcement (with attendant friction, waste, and loss of liberty).

It is highly desirable for the interested public -- other judges, the bar, affected laity, and law professors to be able to understand how a case has been decided and why. Intelligibility and persuasiveness render the law more understandable to those who must act on it. Intelligibility and persuasiveness also render the law as respectworthy as the merits of the decision allow. Indeed, the more intelligible the reasons, the more the law will be readily appraisable by interested parties and the profession, and thus the more susceptible of rational revision as required over time.

Another basic consideration is this. Other things equal, judges should favor those types of substantive reasons that are efficiently constructable over those less so. In my view, rightness reasons and institutional reasons are, in general, more efficiently constructable than goal reasons. As we have seen, if goal reasons are taken seriously, they will be seen to depend for their force on judicial judgments about the authenticity of goals, which may be problematic. Also, goal reasons depend on reliable predictions of decisional effects, and it may be quite difficult to make those predictions. Further, the precise formulation of relevant goals, and of appropriate levels of goal subservience, may be quite difficult for courts. And, of course, the more "scientific" the goal reason purports to be, the more difficult it will be to construct. Indeed, it is notorious that wealth maximizing reasons advanced by economists are often highly difficult to construct. This is not to mention the fact that in the general common law of contract, anyway, economic analysts often come up with conflicting reasons, on the same facts.

V. Significance of My Theses

One of my main theses has been essentially descriptive. I have sought to show that judges in the general common law of contract have overwhelmingly resorted to rightness and institutional reasons rather than goal reasons, even though reasons of the latter kind may often also be available in the justificatory resources of the cases. Since American judges often resort to substantive reasoning, and since there are very great differences at least between rightness reasons on the one hand and goal reasons on the other, this finding is of scholarly interest in its own right. Although I have confined my sample to cases reported in the leading casebooks, I have no doubt that this finding would withstand the rigors of a more comprehensive and systematic inquiry.

But beyond this, there are further ways in which I think this finding noteworthy. First, it indicates that our judges do not view the general common law of contract essentially as a doctrinal instrumentality for serving the social goals of the American polity. Instead, they view it primarily as a body of doctrine defining and regulating the interactions of contracting parties generally. This strikes me as a response appropriate to the nature and needs of the subject-matter. Secondly, I believe, the almost universal judicial emphasis on rightness reasons rather than goal reasons also signifies that the American judiciary is, at least in this field of law, relatively conscious of the ultimate sources of judicial legitimacy. Certainly the giving of reasons that presuppose and purport to draw upon the social consensus reflected in rightness norms poses few issues of judicial legitimacy. Third, that our judges justify contract decisions mainly on rightness grounds also symbolically reinforces society's rightness norms and thereby nurtures and strengthens the private processes of ordering that depend on those norms -- processes that loom far larger in the overall social institution of contract than do courts and law.

My other main thesis, has been the normative one that rightness reasons and institutional reasons are superior to goal reasons as justificatory resources, at least in the common law of contract. This thesis may be significant in two major respects. First, if I am correct about this thesis, it provides one major explanation for my descriptive finding, namely, that judges are doing what they have found best for their justificatory purposes. This, too, is of scholarly interest in its own right. Second, if I am correct, the judges also ought not to heed contemporary calls to start doing economic analysis or otherwise to "modernize" and make more "scientific" their reasoning. And the judges should also continue to ignore the radical skepticism about rightness reasons that so many of their law clerks have heard in law school classrooms. If it is true that law clerks fresh out of law school write a lot of judicial opinions today, we may note that, judging from those opinions, their professors do not seem to have sold very many of them on goal reasoning. For example, one who searches will find only a tiny handful of contract cases in which the phrase "efficient breach" occurs, yet that is one of the most central ideas in modern, scientific goal reasoning, a style of reasoning now appearing all through the academic literature.

But having said these things, I wish to stress that merely because rightness and institutional reasons are superior for justificatory purposes in contract law, it hardly follows either that the reasons judges actually give in their opinions or the doctrines they evolve based on such justifications are always beyond criticism. Even Pangloss would not say, were he with us, that we are now in the best of all possible contract worlds.

VI. Conclusion

My own academic interests have carried me into jurisprudence as well as the law of contract and I wish to close with some remarks on one aspect of one perennial topic of jurisprudence -- the relation between law and morals.

Oliver Wendell Holmes, Jr., in his famous essay, The Path of the Law,[37] addressed himself to the law student and the lawyer who would, as he put it, "reason aright" on their subject. To that end, Holmes urged the law student and the lawyer to draw a sharp line between the law on the one hand and morals on the other. In this way, he implied that the student and the lawyer will not be so likely erroneously to conclude that the law governing a legal issue is the same as what morality dictates. And he stressed that the law does not always coincide with moral notions. Now, with this I agree. But Holmes went on to suggest that the line between law and morals is rather sharp. Thus, he said that the law has "specific marks", is "a business within well understood limits", and is "a body of dogma enclosed within definite lines."

He urged us to keep this "boundary constantly before our minds," for if we do not, "the mere force of language will invite us" to pass from one domain to the other without perceiving it, especially since "the law is full of phraseology drawn from morals." It cannot be denied that Holmes was including in all this the law of contract. Indeed a number of his examples come from our field.

Holmes is not without followers today, in and out of the academy. Yet his thesis that one can draw a sharp line between law and morals is false. The true content and scope of contract doctrines cannot be satisfactorily determined without reference to the substantive reasons that figure in and lie behind these doctrines, and, as we have seen, these are typically rightness reasons, nearly all of which derive from common moral norms. Lawyers and judges simply cannot work with contract doctrines without adverting to the rightness reasons that figure in and lie behind these doctrines. One can hardly imagine the possibility that this should occur. Thus, if one is to "reason aright" on the meaning and scope of a contract doctrine, one must heed the reasons that figure in and lie behind that doctrine -- and these will usually be rightness reasons. This truth becomes all the more plain when we consider that no hard and fast line can be drawn between cases governed by precedent and cases of first impression, especially in a legal system such as ours in which judges allow substantive reasoning a role in relation to authoritative reasoning much greater than is true in England or on the Continent.

Nor is Holmes correct to hold that there ought to be a sharp line between law and morals here, even if there is not. Holmes is famous for his doctrine that the lawyer will do well to conceive of his task as that of advising the bad man who cares nothing of morals but only wants to know when he will come up against the public force. A former teacher of mine provided a conclusive answer to Holmes here. Professor Fuller's answer is one that students must not miss. To that end, I have even inserted it in the contracts casebook I co-edit. I close with it now:[38]

> It is a very convincing figure which [Holmes] offers us, and it makes a working kind of positivism seem quite plausible. Yet it is apparent that this bad man of Holmes' is himself an abstraction, in two senses. In the first place, it will be noted that it is a peculiar sort of bad man who is worried about judicial decrees and is indifferent to extra-legal penalties, who is concerned about a fine of two dollars but apparently not about the possible loss of friends and customers. To define the law in terms of the viewpoint of one with this attitude is to some extent a begging of the question, and amounts almost to saying that the law is that which concerns one who is concerned only with the law.
>
> In the second place, Holmes assumes that his bad man has already reached a conclusion concerning the legal risks of a particular line of conduct, and he neglects to inquire into the process by which this man would actually arrive at such a conclusion. Let us see for ourselves how this bad man, faced with a specific problem of conduct, would have to reason. He wants to know what it is likely

to cost him to attain a particular objective. Because of the peculiarly juristic orientation of his fears, he will be deterred only by judicial penalties. He must ask himself, then, "What are the chances that my conduct may lead to a detrimental interference in my affairs by the courts?" To answer that, he must ask, "how will my conduct be viewed by judges?" This question he cannot answer merely by consulting the letter of the law, for he will still not know in what direction the letter will be strained in cases of doubt. Nor will it be enough for him "to know his judge." Even if the judge who will decide his case has pronounced and recognizable biases, a bias is, after all, only one factor in a complex equation, and to calculate its effects one must analyze the ethical forces with which it will come in conflict. In the end, our bad man cannot escape having to decide a question of morality. He will have to ask, "how would I myself view my conduct if I were not interested in it? How would it be viewed by a disinterested third party? Would it seem to him to be good or evil?" Only when he has answered this question will he have rounded out the equation on the basis of which he can calculate accurately the chances of judicial intervention in his affairs.

In short, our bad man, if he is effectively to look after his own interests, will have to learn to look at the law through the eyes of a good man. Who, I may add, knows his rightness reasons.

Notes

1. See generally Summers, *Two Types of Substantive Reasons — The Core of a Theory of Common Law Justification,* 63 CORNELL L. REV. 707 (1978).

2. See generally, M. Eisenberg, THE NATURE OF THE COMMON LAW (Harvard, Cambridge Mass., 1987).

3. For a philosophical account of "antecedentalism", see Sher, "Antecedentialism", 94 ETHICS 6 (1983).

4. I. Kant, THE METAPHYSICAL ELEMENTS OF JUSTICE, p. 102 (Macmillan, Library of Liberal Arts ed. trans. by J. Ladd 1965).

5. See n. 1 *supra.*

6. At the outset, it is important to concede that not all doctrines of modern contract law conform closely to what a pure "rightness code of promising" might look like. But from this, it would hardly follow that goal reasoning has been a major rationalizing force in our law of contract. For one thing, it would have to be shown that any nonconformities track goal reasoning in some way. Moreover, to the extent that contract law does not look like what purely rightness reasoning alone would appear to dictate, there is a further possible explanation, consistent with my thesis, namely, the influence of reasons arising from the requisites, desiderata, and limits of the social institution of law, i.e., institutional reasons.

7. Note, the question is not what actually motivates contracting parties. They may well act and talk in terms of increasing satisfaction or wealth. But it does not follow that this is the rationale behind the law.

8. *Maryland National Capital Park and Planning Comm. v. Washington National Arena*, 282 Md. 588, 386 A.2d 1216 (1978).

9. F. Hayek, *The Uses of Knowledge in Society*, 35 AM. ECOM. REV. 519 (1945).

10. See, e.g., *Black Industries, Inc. v. Bush*, 110 F. Supp. 801 (D.C.N.J. 1953).

11. See, e.g., Von Mehren, *Contracts in General*, 7 Int'l. Ency. of Comp. L. Ch. 1 p.20 (1982); and Fuller & Perdue, *The Reliance Interest in Contract Damages*, 46 YALE L. J. 52, 61-62 (1936).

12. See C. Fried, Contract as Promise (Harvard, Cambridge Mass. 1988).

13. See, e.g., *Beck v. Staats*, 80 Neb. 482, 114 N.W. 633, 635 (1908). ("The contract is necessarily reciprocal."); *Tansil v. Horlock*, 204 So. 2d 457, 462 (Miss. 1967). Holmes often stressed reciprocity. See, e.g., O.W. Holmes, Jr., THE COMMON LAW 227-230 (1881) (Howe ed. 1963).

14. See Fuller & Perdue, *supra* n 11.

15. See, e.g., *Hardesty v Smith*, 3 Ind. 39 (1851).

16. 169 F.2d 684, 685 (D.C. Cir. 1948).

17. *Fried v. Fisher* 328 Pa. 497, 196 A. 39, (1938).

18. Professor Neil MacCormick has aptly formulated it in its most general terms:

> If one person acts in a potentially detrimental way in reliance upon beliefs about another's future conduct, and if the latter person has by some act of his intentionally or knowingly induced the former to rely upon him, then the latter has an obligation not to act in a manner which will disappoint the other's reliance.

MacCormick, *Voluntary Obligations and Normative Powers,* 46 PROCEEDINGS ARISTOTELIAN SOCIETY, Supp. Vol. 59 at p. 68 (1972).

19. *Bloomgarden v. Coyer*, 479 F.2d 201, 211 (D.C. Cir. 1973).

20. W. Prosser & W. Keeton, on TORTS 660-661 (5th ed. 1984).

21. Id. at 662.

22. This past-regarding justificatory focus would remain apposite even if we were to hypothesize the absence of any future (as in Kant's hypothetical dissolution of society). That is, even with such dissolution in the offing, a court would still have good reason to require

the negligently performing party to make amends.

23. Also, the fact that goal reasoning in the form of economic analysis may be useful in determining whether due care was exercised -- an appropriate level of precaution -- does not show that the basic duty of due care is itself grounded in goal reasoning.

24. See, e.g., *Kabil Developments Corp. v. Mignot*, 279 Or. 151, 566 P.2d 505, 507 (1977).

25. See, e.g., *Embry v Hargardine, Mckittrick Dry Goods Co.,* 127 Mo. App. 383, 105 S.W. 777, 779 (1907) ("right to rely").

26. Restatement of Contracts, sec. 87, comment e.

27. *Drennan v. Star Paving Co.,* 51 Cal. 2d 409, 333 P. 2d 757, 760 (1958).

28. See UCC 2-204(3).

29. *Masterson v. Sine*, 65 Cal. Rptr. 545, 436 P. 2d 561 (1968).

30. Restatement of Contracts, second, sec. 234 (1).

31. Id. at sec. 227.

32. Id at sec. 237d.

33. Id at secs. 241-2.

34. Id. at sec. 152.

35. *Groves v. John Wunder* 205 Minn. 163, 286 N.W. 235 (1939).

36. R. Posner, ECONOMIC ANALYSIS OF LAW 82 (Little Brown Co., Boston 3rd ed. 1986).

37. O.W. Holmes, Jr. *The Path of the Law*, 10 HARV. L.REV. 457 (1897).

38. L.L. Fuller, THE LAW IN QUEST OF ITSELF 93-95 (Beacon Press, Boston).

Part Five

Critique of Economic Analysis of Law

CHAPTER 15

ECONOMICS AND THE AUTONOMY OF LAW, LEGAL ANALYSIS AND LEGAL THEORY

1. Main Theses of This Paper

The main theses of this paper are:

1. Since about 1960 in the United States there has been an important movement in legal thought applying economic analysis to law (the "law and economics" movement).[1]

2. Some American proponents of economic analysis of law have expressly stated or implied that law, legal analysis, and legal theory have no genuine autonomy of any kind. Instead, law, legal analysis, and even legal theory can all be reduced, without loss, to economics and economic analysis.

3. Although nearly all legal theorists would, I believe, ultimately reject the extreme view that law, legal analysis, and legal theory are all somehow reducible to economics and economic analysis, it can be instructive to take this view seriously and consider how it might be refuted.

II. The Recent American Movement Applying Economic Analysis to Law

Long before 1960, various American laws incorporated economic theories about the proper workings of the American economy. The Sherman Act, adopted by the Congress in 1890 is the leading example. That Act was aimed at monopolistic practices and, as originally adopted, provided in section 1: "Every contract, combination in the form of trust or otherwise, or conspiracy, in *restraint of trade or commerce* among the several states, or with foreign

359

"penalty" clauses, etc. In tort law, there are many articles and books. In property law, there are articles and books. And so on.

Economic analysis of law also provides important contributions that transcend particular fields of law. For example, it reveals starkly how there is no such thing as a "free lunch" (to impose a warranty of habitability on landlords costs money), that parties who ultimately bear the cost of a law may be quite different from those on whom the cost is initially imposed ("incidence analysis"), that those who benefit from the costs of certain activities can often be made by law to bear those costs (when not already doing so), that various costs can be imposed to reduce existing levels of an activity when this is desirable, that the future "incentive effects" of present legal decisions, in addition to "equities", are also of great importance in designing legal rules, that these "incentive effects" extend not only to "primary" out-of-court behavior, but also to such things as decisions to go to court, etc.

III. The Claimed Reducibility of Law, Legal Analysis and Legal Theory to Economics and Economic Analysis

Partly because of the successes, actual and claimed, of the "law and economics" movement since 1960, a few participants in this movement, including some of its most prominent figures, have asserted or implied that law, legal analysis, and legal theory or some combination of these are somehow essentially reducible to economics and economic analysis. Even quite explicit statements have been made to this effect.[5] One might explain these statements merely as the understandable exuberance of those who believe they have something entirely new to say. Or one might explain them as deliberate overstatements intended to attract attention. Such explanations would suggest that the statements ought not to be taken seriously.

But in my view, the general thesis of the alleged ultimate reducibility of law, legal analysis, and legal theory merely to economics and economic analysis ought to be taken seriously. First, such radical reductionist theses in matters of law have been recurrent in American legal thought. For example, in the 1920's and 1930's in the United States there were various thinkers who, under the influence of behavioral social science, held that law is reducible to the behavior patterns of officials and that legal theory is somehow reducible to an empirical science of law.[6] Second, there is evidence that some modern day economic analysts of law do intend to be taken seriously when they advance some version of the reducibility thesis. Important truths are at stake. No doubt the truths varies somewhat, depending on to which subject matter law, legal analysis, or legal theory are said to be reducible: economics, or behavioral science, or philosophy or politics or whatever. Here I will address only the possible reducibility to economics and economic analysis.

Even if truth were not really in dispute, the reducibility thesis is, I suggest, a worthwhile one to refute systematically, for the effort can itself be instructive. Also, the extent to which law, legal analysis, and legal theory are relatively autonomous and thus not reducible to economics and economic analysis (or to any other discipline, for that matter) is an important question in its own right, for law, legal analysis, and legal theory are of immense practical and theoretical significance. If for example, law, legal analysis, and legal theory really are, in the end, little more than economics and economic analysis in disguise (despite what would at least be some excess verbiage), profound reorientations would be required. Many books and articles would have to be revised. Even the existing curriculum of law schools would have to be restructured. Judges might have to be retrained. Many laws might even to be changed! And so on.

Of course, limitations of space impose drastic limits on what can be said here about this large and complex topic. Often I will be able to do little more than cast doubt.

IV. Is Law Reducible to Economics?

The very question whether law is reducible to economics requires clarification. Several different forms of the reducibility thesis may be differentiated. I can take only account of a few of the relevant possibilities.

It might be thought that the essential character of social phenomena such as a legal system is to be found in its primary goal or its "driving force" or the like. Does an economic system have a primary goal or a driving force? Many American economic analysts would say, in rough terms, that the driving force of the American economic system is some form of economic "efficiency" such as wealth maximization. These analysts therefore assert that the primary goal or driving force of the American *legal* system must similarly be such wealth maximization.

But in my view any such description of "the" primary goal or driving force of a legal system must necessarily be inaccurate. No *single primary* goal can characterize anything so complex as a legal system. Lon L. Fuller wrote that a system of law is an "enterprise" for subjecting society to the "governance of rules", i. e., the rule of law, which is itself to be analyzed into a complex cluster of inter-related goals.[7] Beyond such broadly procedural goals, legal systems typically have a number of fundamental substantive ends. For example, the *avowed* ends of the American system include freedom and justice. These ends are not meaningfully reducible to some form of economic "efficiency" such as wealth maximization. The same is true of other basic goals of that system such as fairness and legitimacy in the workings of ongoing legal processes.

The subject matter of those social phenomena traditionally characterized as economic consists essentially of human activities devoted mainly to the *production and consumption of* material goods and services. It is undeniable that some of the subject matter to which law (mainly rules) applies consists of activities that are essentially economic in the foregoing sense. But not all social phenomena are thus essentially economic, and most of the law of American society applies to wholesome private activities of many other kinds not essentially economic: social, familial, religious, educational, aesthetic, recreational, and more. Of course, some of our law applies to numerous unwholesome social activities such as crime and other antisocial behavior most of which is only metaphorically economic.

Also, some wholesome public activities within a society are essentially governmental and legal rather than economic in the sense of being concerned with the production and consumption of material goods and services. These include the recruitment and retention of personnel such as judges and officials, the creation and application of law, the exercise of official discretion, and the execution and enforcement of law. Vast bodies of law apply to such governmental and legal activities, too. Some of this law may be said to *constitute* these very activities. Court actions, for example, are, in a way, *creatures* of law. Such essentially governmental and legal activities must not be equated with "economic" activity in the sense of the production and consumption of material goods and services.

In response, participants in the law and economics movement may argue that even though the subject matters to which much law is addressed are not reducible to essentially economic phenomena, economic analysis nonetheless remains applicable because, as Lord Robbins has suggested, the core of economics is the theory of rational choice and all the social phenomena to which law applies consists of "choosing" activities. But the non-economic activities to which law applies are not all "choosing activities" in the respects required for the ready applicability of economic analysis. Also, once we move away from certain kinds of paradigmatic market activity, the conditions for the ready applicability of economic analysis are frequently much less evident. For example, such "goods and services" as the pleasures of viewing the countryside and the pleasures of family life are not, except metaphorically, divisible into equivalent and measurable units to which economic analysts can readily apply their theory of rational choice. At least, we may say that the reducibility of subject-matter thesis is "not proven", and that the applicability of basic assumptions of the economist's theory of rational choice is thus in doubt. (Economists, of course, are aware of these problems.)

As we have seen, the substance of the laws of a particular society are addressed to social phenomena, non-economic as well as economic. Proponents of economic analysis might urge that, nonetheless, the substantive content of even those laws addressed to non-economic phenomena is determined largely by the teachings of the academic discipline of economics, either directly or indirectly. For example, some economic analysts of law have claimed that the common law of negligence does not derive from a moral injunction requiring elemental due care and respect for others. Rather, these economic analysts say that a defendant is guilty of negligence only if the likely costs imposed by the accident, multiplied by the probability of its occurring, exceed the costs of precautions the defendant might have taken to avert it. This is said to be an economic test. But even if this test may be invoked to help determine instances of negligence, it does not follow that the principle of due care for others is deriveable from this test. The test, insofar as faithful to the principle, is merely a technique for determining the applicability of the principle. The principle is foundational, not economic analysis.

But whether or not the foregoing example truly illustrates a rule the content of which derives from economics (historically or logically), I believe that few legal rules can be said to derive their essential content in any sense from the teachings of any particular academic discipline outside the law. Consider, for example, many of the rules constitutive of various judicial and legislative procedures. If these derive mainly from any discipline, they derive from the form of the law itself, including considerations of due process and of law-like governance. Moreover, insofar as the content of a legal rule can in some sense be said to derive mainly from a discipline external to law, that discipline will often be one other than economics such as political science, psychology, sociology, one of the health sciences or even that branch of philosophy called ethical theory. Even then, it will often be appropriate to say that the law's content derives (historically, logically or otherwise) only partially from one of these so-called "policy sciences", for that content will *almost always* also be partially attributable to the *interaction* between these teachings and available legal means (with all their limitations). For example, the shape of the substantive content of our anti-trust law reflects a concern not only for economic ends but also for the limitations of the law's means of authoritatively finding facts about market behavior (by courts and other bodies).

It should be plainly obvious that the basic form of legal rules is not reducible to that of positive economic "laws" such as the so-called laws of supply and demand. The form of legal rules includes such constitutive features as prescriptiveness, generality, definiteness, completeness, and internal structure, each of which is complex. Legal rules and other such precepts are also *normative* and thus differ in fundamental type from positive economic laws. Most legal rules — civic laws, bind those subject to them, but economic laws do not. Economic "laws" are invoked to *explain* and to *predict*. And despite several decades of American legal theory to the contrary, civic laws are not, essentially, predictions. They are legal *norms*. Of course, it is sometimes wise to try to predict what a judge or an official will do in light of factors other than applicable legal norms. When so, these other factors will typically also include factors that are not economic in character. And the resulting predictions will not, *as such,* qualify as legal norms.

Whether civic laws are reducible in any way to economic "laws" of a *normative* character cannot be decided. This is because within the discipline of economics there is no agreed meaning for the phrase "economic laws of a normative character". Further, the law's five basic techniques of serving social ends cannot be reduced to economic ones, either.[8]

V. Is Legal Analysis Reducible to Economic Analysis?

In my view, there are several varieties of distinctively legal analysis. Similarly, there are several varieties of economic analysis of law. I can take account of only a few of these variations here. Much "positive" legal analysis is devoted to determining what the law is in the first place. It thus deals with the interpretation and application of statutes, of court opinions and of other sources of law. The primary purpose of such analysis (which includes much argumentation) is to establish, for the specific issues at hand, what the law is.

Most positive economic analysis *presupposes* that the analyst knows already what the applicable law is, and goes on to *explain* why that law is the way it is, or to *predict* how particular actors will behave under such a law. Thus the fundamental purposes of much positive legal analysis and much positive economic analysis of law are not at all the same. Admittedly, some economic analysts have also argued for particular interpretations of rules as the ones most consistent with "efficiency", which they assume to be the "real driving force" behind all the legal "verbiage". This mode of positive economic analysis of the "real" content of legal rules has yet to prove itself.

An economic analyst of law might hold that the lawyer, when determining what the law is, engages essentially in a process of prediction, and that the lawyer is therefore doing (albeit less perfectly) what the economic analyst does when he predicts. But the lawyer who interprets and applies authoritative sources is, typically, *not predicting.* He is *presupposing* that the judges will follow the law and is formulating a reasoned judgment about what that law is, in light of the content of the authoritative sources, and in light of generally accepted techniques of interpretation and application.[9] Not every analysis that is future regarding in some way qualifies as predictive.

This also helps explain an obvious difference between positive legal analysis and positive economic analysis. The lawyer's, and judge's, and professor's tools are simply not the same as the economic analyst's tools. The positive economic analyst uses a methodology drawn from positive economics (here, largely the assumptions and techniques of rational choice theory).

In some legal systems (all?) there is a further basic difference signifying the non-reducibility of positive legal analysis to positive economic analysis. Sophisticated legal observers would agree that no sharp line can be drawn between positive legal analysis and normative legal analysis, and many would also agree that it is unhealthy to try to draw such a line. Ideas and principles of what the law *ought to be* do, and should, help shape the determination of what the law is in various ways and respects. Lon L. Fuller was perhaps the most eloquent defender (and proponent) of this view in Anglo-American countries in this century.[10] But it is almost an article of faith with economic analysts that, in the interest of science, a sharp line *must* be drawn between positive and normative economic analysis. Of course, economists recognize that once positive economic analysis is done, the analysis may then supply predictions that figure in normative reasons for decision or standards of criticism. For example, if by positive analysis a lower income group would likely bear a proposed tax, this might generate an argument against the proposal.

Normative analysis in law may be defined as analysis that is concerned not with the construction of reasons that appeal to existing legal authority, but rather with the construction and evaluation of *substantive* reasons that appeal to social, moral, economic, institutional and other considerations of policy or principle. I have elsewhere published a study of substantive reasons that actually appear in American common law cases.[11] The substantive reasons fall into three main categories: "goal reasons" — the justificatory force of which depend on the predicted efficacy of projected decisions to serve good social goals, "rightness reasons" — the justificatory force of which depend not on the predicted effects of decisions but on the accordance of projected decisions with norms of right conduct applicable to past interactions of the parties or the results of those actions, and "institutional reasons" — which are either goal reasons or rightness reasons but relate peculiarly to the institutional roles and machinery of the law.

An example of a rightness reason would be one that says: "We should decide for the plaintiff because the defendant unjustifiably misled the plaintiff to rely to his detriment and must therefore be estopped." An example of an institutional reason would be one that says: "We should decide for the defendant, the plaintiff's father because courts have no means of measuring damages for the social disgrace that the plaintiff claims resulted from being born illegitimate." (Some institutional reasons also have to do with what is required to protect the integrity of the very institutions involved, e. g., proper participation by affected parties in adjudication). The basic types of substantive reasons are invoked by judges most often and most robustly in new cases posing novel issues, in cases overruling past decisions, and in cases of conflicting precedent.

Now, in their own normative analysis, economists often invoke two types of substantive reasons for decisions. I have also published a study of those reasons (jointly with Professor Leigh B. Kelley).[12] The general character of the two main types of "economists' reasons" can also be sketched briefly. The first may be called "Pareto superior" reasons. These derive what justificatory force they may have from the notion that if a change can be made in existing law that makes at least one person better off (by his own lights) and no one worse off (by their own lights) then such a change ought to be made, for it achieves a state that is "Pareto superior" to the status quo. The second type may be called "Kaldor-Hicks superior" reasons. These derive what justificatory force they may have from the notion that if a change can be made in existing law that makes one or more persons better off and some persons worse off but the former gain more than the latter lose, then such a change ought to be made, possibly with compensation to the losers, for it achieves a state that is "Kaldor-Hicks superior" to the status quo. (There are many variations on this.)

Now, the narrow issue I raise here is whether the normative analysis — the goal reasons, rightness reasons, and institutional reasons found in Anglo-American common law (and, if I am correct, in our law generally) — all can be reduced to economists' reasons of one of the two foregoing types. To date, no economic analyst has demonstrated as much, and in my view no such reduction is possible. Rather, if I am right, economists' reasons are merely two subclasses within the general category of *goal reasons,* a general category already recognized in the common law. As such, economists' reasons depend for their force on predicted effects of decisions to serve social goals.

Yet, *rightness reasons* make up the most common type of substantive reason in common law. And again, no economic analyst of law has demonstrated that these reasons collapse into economists' reasons. Unlike economists' reasons and the whole category of goal reasons, rightness reasons do not depend for their justificatory force on predicted effects of decisions. Rightness reasons would have justificatory force even if there were no future and therefore no predicted decisional effects, (as Immanuel Kant once hypothesized). It is true that many reasons *are* consistent in their decisional implications with rightness reasons, but that is another matter.

Finally, institutional reasons arise from what is special to institutional roles and processes inside the law and almost certainly cannot be reduced to economists' reasons.

Frequently there is some unavoidable element of "fiat" in the law. Substantive reasons cannot determine all of the "twists and turns" of the law. Substantive reasons may have no bearing, or they may conflict and be of roughly equal weight so that the matter must be decided by *mere authoritative choice, i. e. fiat.* Note that if an unavoidable element of fiat is involved, there is nothing necessarily pejorative about saying that the matter must be decided by fiat. (The word "arbitrary" is not a good word to use in place of "fiat" here because "arbitrary" does have pejorative connotations.) Although I concede that some unavoidable element of fiat may be involved, I do not imply that this element can be sharply differentiated from all elements of reason. When one encounters an element of fiat, it is usually part of a "mix of reason and fiat", as, for example, in time periods in statutes of limitations.

When a new case arises posing novel issues, or an old case is to be overruled, or a choice made between conflicting precedent or some other creative decision is necessary, the problem for the lawmaker may be one that cannot be resolved in its entirety without resort to some element of fiat. I do not see how normative economic analysis can have anything to say that might be substituted for this element of fiat, yet this element is a significant part of the solution to some important legal problems. If normative economic analysis can have nothing to say here, there is nothing economic to which legal analysis could be "reduced". I concede that normative legal analysis may also have nothing to say here, as well. Still the law has had a good deal of experience with such problems on which to draw. Moreover, some elements of fiat are more readily accommodated within the law than are others. The normative legal analyst, but presumably less so the economic analyst, might have something to say about this (a complex matter I cannot treat here).

When an element of unavoidable fiat is already recognized in the law, the *positive* legal analyst will usually discern this and reason accordingly to determine and apply applicable law. Such "fiat" reasoning will be as near to the "purely authoritative" as is possible. But it is not clear that positive economic analysis has anything at all to say here, either. (Note that such "fiat" oriented reasoning is still not purely authoritative, for it implicitly invokes the ideal of governance according to the rule of law, and this ideal rests to some extent on substantive reasons of fairness and legitimacy.)

VI. Is Legal Theory Reducible to Economics?

Space remains only for the briefest general thoughts on the question: Is legal theory reducible to economics? Legal theory could not possibly be reducible to economics. At the very least, economic analysis of law (1) presupposes the answers to some fundamental questions of legal theory, (2) fails to address certain fundamental questions of legal theory, and (3) addresses, but in an unsatisfactory way, certain other fundamental questions of legal theory.

Economic analysis *presupposes* an answer to the most basic question of legal theory: What social phenomena are to count as legal in character including what kinds of criteria or standards serve to identify valid law within particular societies?

Economic analysis of law does not frontally address *numerous* basic issues of legal theory, including: How far is law formal in nature? In what senses are law, and life under law, normative in character? What items would a reasonably comprehensive inventory of the law's ways, means, and techniques include, and how should the distinctive uses and limits of these be described and characterized? Is any substantive content essential to the existence of law, or can a legal system have just any content? How are basic legal processes to be analyzed? How are fundamental legal concepts such as rule, right, duty, and sanction to be elucidated? What is systematic about a legal system? What are the relations between law and morals? What are the limits of the duty to obey law? And more.

Of the traditional problems of legal theory that economic analysis (in this case, normative) does address, directly or indirectly, perhaps the most important is this: What general theory of value should inform the content of reasons for legal decisions, including decisions adopting rules? This is one of the most significant problems in the entire field of legal theory, and the solution that most American economic analysts today offer to this problem is very largely the solution put forward in the 19th century by Benthamite utilitarians. This solution has always been and continues to this day to be highly controversial. For one thing, it is not evident that utilitarian theory can accommodate the most common general justifying reasons to be found today in Anglo-American common law (and also in many statutory schemes), namely, rightness reasons. It may be that such reasons are, in significant ways, past-regarding and thus quite unlike the future-regarding reasons of consequentialist utilitarianism. Bentham was wrong to believe that "thank you" means "more please".

Notes
1. See, e.g. R. Posner, ECONOMIC ANALYSIS OF LAW, 1977; G. Calabresi, The Costs of Accidents, 1970; M. Polinsky, AN INTRODUCTION TO LAW AND ECONOMICS, 1983.
2. L. Robbins, AN ESSAY ON THE NATURE AND SIGNIFICANCE OF ECONOMIC SCIENCE, 1932.
3. A chosen equilibrium which the participants have no incentive to alter may still be inefficient for a number of reasons. For example, one of the parties may not be required under the law to take into account all the costs attributable to his chosen level of activity, and therefore engage in a higher level of that activity than he would if he had to take all costs into account.
4. Cf. P. Burrows/C. Veljanovski, THE ECONOMIC APPROACH TO LAW, 1981, p. 3-5; R. Cooter, *Law and the Imperialism of Economics*, in: U.C.L.A. L. REV. 29 (1982), p. 1290.
5. Professor, now Judge, Richard Posner is perhaps foremost here.
6. R. Summers, INSTRUMENTALISM AND AMERICAN LEGAL THEORY, 1982, p. 112-115. See also R. Summers, PRAGMATISCHER INSTRUMENTALISMUS UND AMERIKANISCHE RECHTSTHEORIE, Karl Alber, 1983.

7. L. Fuller, THE MORALITY OF LAW, 1969.

8. Compare "the market" as an economist's social technique, with the law's techniques in R. Summers, *The Technique Element in Law*, in: CALIF. L. REV. 59 (1971), p. 733.

9. R. Summers, INSTRUMENTALISM AND AMERICAN LEGAL THEORY, 1982, ch.5. See also R. Summers, PRAGMATISCHER INSTRUMENTALISMUS UND AMERIKANISCHE RECHTSTHEORIE (note 6 above).

10. R. Summers, LON L. FULLER - AN INTRODUCTION TO HIS LIFE AND WORK, Stanford U. Press, 1984.

11. R. Summers, *Two Types of Substantive Reasons*, in: CORNELL L. REV. 63 (1978), p. 707.

12. R. Summers/L. Kelley, *Economists' Reasons,* in: OXFORD J. LEGAL STUDIES 1 (1981), p. 213. See ch. 16 of this collection. See also R. Dworkin, *Is Wealth a Value?*, in: J. LEGAL STUDIES (1980), p. 191.

CHAPTER 16

ECONOMISTS' REASONS FOR COMMON LAW DECISIONS

I. Introduction

When judges write opinions in common law cases they frequently seek to justify their decisions not merely by citing any relevant precedent or other authority but also by setting forth what we will call 'substantive reasons'. Reasons of this kind incorporate moral, political, institutional, or other social considerations.[1] In our view, substantive reasons have primacy over appeals to authority in the common law.[2] Judges must rely on such reasons in cases of first impression, cases posing conflicts of precedent, and in cases involving the overruling or other renovation of precedent. Moreover, judges should and do advert to the substantive reasons behind precedents in order to interpret them and determine their scope.[3]

Two basic kinds of reasons of substance are to be found in common law opinions. First, there are 'goal reasons'. A goal reason derives its justificatory force[4] from the fact that, at the time it is given, the decision it supports can be predicted to have effects that serve a good social goal (in general, or at least in the particular case).[5] Here are three examples of goal reasons:

(i) Because a utility's gas reservoir will adversely affect the health of people living near it, the utility may be ordered to relocate it.[6]

(ii) Because the flow of information about candidates for public office will facilitate democracy, a newspaper that publishes falsehoods may not be held liable unless the newspaper acted in bad faith.[7]

(iii) Because allowing this kind of intrafamily lawsuit will disrupt family harmony generally, the suit will not be allowed.[8]

The second basic type of substantive reason to be found in common law cases we call a 'rightness reason'. A good rightness reason does not derive its justificatory force from predicted goal serving effects of the decision it supports. Rather, it draws its force from the way in which the decision it supports accords with a sociomoral norm of rightness as applied to a party's past actions or to a state of affairs resulting from those actions.[9] This force derives in a special way from how the case *came about*. Here are three examples of rightness reasons:

(i) Since the seller knowingly took advantage of the buyer's illiteracy, ignorance, and limited bargaining capability, the price he charged must be reduced.[10]

(ii) Since the owner of a boat has been unjustly enriched by the plaintiff, who found the boat adrift and, at his own expense, took care of it for the owner, the owner must compensate the plaintiff.[11]

(iii) Since the builder reasonably relied on the owner's untrue representation of fact and thereby suffered a foreseeable loss, the owner must compensate the builder.[12]

Historically, then, goal reasons and rightness reasons are the two basic types of substantive reasons to be found in common law cases. Over the past two decades, an increasing number of academics have advocated that judges *explicitly* introduce economic analysis into the decision of common law cases.[13] To date, few judges have responded.[14] Of course, in fields having to do with monopoly regulation and the like, economic analysis, has traditionally been prominent in judicial opinions. But advocates of economic analysis proclaim its relevance in areas far beyond these traditional ones. Moreover, many contend not only that economic analysis is relevant to determining the most "cost effective" *means* to given goals but that it also generates two important varieties of autonomous substantive reasons that judges may invoke. Such reasons are autonomous in the sense that they purportedly draw upon economic theory — including welfare economics — *for goals as well* as *for prescriptions about means*.[15] In terms of our foregoing division of reasons into goal reasons and rightness reasons, what we will here call 'economists' reasons' consist of two distinct subclasses of goal reasons. The first of these subclasses we will call 'Pareto-superior' reasons. The second we will call 'Kaldor-superior' reasons.

In this essay we will explore the internal structure and the source of the justificatory force of the two kinds of allegedly autonomous economists' reasons and will provide a tentative critique of them.[16] Our primary focus will be on Kaldor-superior reasons, for they have the most wide ranging potential.

We open, however, with Pareto-superior reasons, for to economists they are in a sense primary.[17]

II. 'Pareto-superior' Reasons

Economists have devised criteria for judging whether a reallocation of resources is an 'efficient' means to the goal of 'welfare improvement'. One criterion (and there are many variants) is named for the Italian thinker Vilfredo Pareto, and may be called 'Pareto-superiority'. According to this criterion, a reallocation of resources is 'Pareto-superior' to an antecedent allocation if it makes 'no one worse off and at least one person better off.'[18] Of course, under the circumstances various alternative Pareto-superior reallocations may be possible, and one of these may be preferable on the ground that it makes affected persons the 'most better off'.

Now, who are the 'actors' in the social order who may reallocate resources in ways that are Pareto-superior to alternative allocations? Economists conceive the primary actors to be private parties voluntarily exchanging things in a free, competitive market. The paradigm (but not the only) Pareto-superior reallocation is one in which *both* bargainers gain from their exchange so that both are better off, and no one is worse off.

But private free market bargainers are not the only actors in the social order who may reallocate resources in Pareto-superior ways. Economists have long recognized the possibility that government agencies may also do this. And in recent times some economists and many lawyers trained in economics have come to conceive common law judges as 'resource allocators', too. On their view, a judge in a common law case *may* be in a position to endorse or bring about a reallocation. In turn, such a reallocation may be 'Pareto-superior'. When so, this reallocation generates an argument (according to some economists and some lawyers trained in economics) that the judge may adopt, as a *reason of substance* for a given decision in the case, an 'economist's reason'.

1. Pareto-superior reasons — an example

At least one credible example of a genuine Pareto-superior reason of substance for a common law court decision is required at the outset. The rare availability of such a reason will be apparent from the unusual nature of the case about to be posed. Let us suppose that Adam is a used car dealer in the city of Bodea and has been in business for fifteen years. Assume that fifty years ago the courts in the area occasionally responded to prosecutions of dealers who sold cars on Sunday. Usually these prosecutions were brought as common law misdemeanor proceedings based not on statutes but on court holdings that such activity is 'contrary to good morals'. No prosecution was ever brought unless a local church group filed a complaint with the local district attorney. There had been no prosecutions for twenty-five years, and in recent times Adam had heard only one report (and that ten years previous) that a church might 'start up' a prosecution. (The church ultimately did not.)

Adam regularly did business on Sunday. One day Adam decided to bring a proceeding before Judge Thomas in the local court of general jurisdiction. Adam wanted to secure a declaration that the 'common law misdemeanor' of selling cars on Sunday was no longer valid law since the public no longer viewed such activity as contrary to good morals.[19]

Adam's lawyer filed the relevant papers and served them also on the head of the local association of church groups. The latter did not respond, and did not show up at the court hearing. After the hearing, the judge declared the misdemeanor case law no longer valid. No appeal was taken. (A parallel case from another district did reach the state's highest court and that court in effect upheld Judge Thomas's position.)

Judge Thomas wrote a brief opinion in which he set forth two reasons for his decision:

I hereby declare that the act of selling cars on Sunday is no longer a common law misdemeanor. First, it is evident that such activity is no longer contrary to good morals (if it ever was). Second, I've been reading some economics. This is plainly a case in which I may profitably view myself as an allocator of resources. If I invalidate the common law misdemeanor, I reallocate the legal liberty to the car dealers. This would, under the circumstances, be a Pareto-superior reallocation. That is, it would make some persons better off without making anyone worse off. The car dealers in this case and car dealers in future cases would be better off. So, too, would the future buyers from these dealers. All these parties would have a legal cloud lifted from their activities and certainly Adam values this. At the same time there would be no adverse effects on other parties generally within my jurisdiction.

All possible affected third parties have had due notice of my proposed course of action in this case. No one objects. Furthermore, church groups who might (if anyone would) have sought to initiate proceedings by filing complaints with the district attorney do not, under the law, have a right that they may lawfully sell to car dealers in exchange for not opposing my course of action here. The law simply does not permit such a sale. Order entered.

Judge Jason Thomas
Circuit Court
December 17, 1979

2. The construction of Pareto-superior reasons

The foregoing 'Pareto-superior' reason offered by Judge Thomas is one variety of such reason, namely, that which purports to improve or extend the operation of the market through a reallocation that invalidates a market restriction. There are still other varieties.[20]

For a Pareto-superior reason to be available to a judge in a case, the judge must determine that he has power to reallocate resources through a decision and its implementation. Further, the judge must determine that this reallocation is or would be 'Pareto-superior'; that is, that it would make at least one person better off without making anyone worse off. (Presumably a party might be worse off in the short run yet, better off in the long run, overall, and vice versa.) The judge might need an economist to help him make these determinations. At least three problems arise.

The first problem is that of projecting the subjective responses of affected parties to reallocations that would actually alter their stock of goods. This problem has a subjective and an objective aspect. In our car dealer example, the judge would have to inquire into the likely subjective reactions of Adam and of the church goers to the state of affairs in which the Sunday ban on car sales is lifted. He must determine whether the parties would *view themselves* as better off, worse off, or what. Economic theory, as such, tells us little about how to conduct such an hypothetical and subjective inquiry.

The 'objective' aspect of the first problem is this: There are objective constraints on just what subjective responses of affected parties are to be taken into account. These constraints are partly a matter of law. Thus a 'loser' in the Pareto analysis, for example, is someone who loses something which was 'his' in an objective sense. A person who merely thinks he owns the Brooklyn Bridge and then learns it has been 'taken away' from him is not a loser. The subjective preferences of the parties must be determined in relation to their objective stock of rights. Thus the judge is to ask: Given this stock, would they prefer an alternative stock to it? In our used car dealer case, what exactly was the legal position of the church groups prior to the decision? As projected afterwards? The answer to these questions determines the objective constraints on the subjective responses to be taken into account. Note that economics as such has nothing to say about how the states of affairs *ex ante* and *ex post* are to be defined.[21]

A second problem is that of predicting any likely further effects of the decision beyond those that may have already figured in the characterization of projected reallocations. That is, what will be the *general effects of a rule* based on the decision? For example, how many additional car deals might be made once the restriction is lifted? Might future church members some day take a different view of whether the restriction should have been lifted so that future time additional losses will be registered (retroactively as it were)?[22]

There is a third problem. Once the effects of the reallocation are known and the subjective preferences of the parties ascertained (i.e., whether they view themselves as gaining, or losing, or what), the judge must still consider the conditions under which these preferences are expressed. Is he to count only a well informed preference? If not, then how ill informed can a preference for *ex ante* or *ex post* states of affairs be and still count? Again, economics does not appear to tell us, except perhaps to say that some choices may be 'irrational'.[23]

3. Justificatory force of Pareto-superior reasons

A reason cannot count as a rational basis for a decision unless it has justificatory force. This is true by definition. A reason cannot have justificatory force unless a genuine value figures in it. This, too, is true by virtue of our very conception of what a reason is. Reasons for acting — of which reasons for deciding are but one type — simply have no force unless they bring a value into play. Such reasons are thus quite unlike mere reasons for believing that a proposition is true.

Once a judge's projected reallocation passes muster as genuinely Pareto-superior (and as the best of any possible such reallocations under the circumstances), does it follow that the judge has a reason with justificatory force for a decision? Not without more. So far we only have what economists call an 'efficient' reallocation. We still need to ask why any such reallocation ought to exist or be brought about. We have already said that if an economist's reason is to be constructed, it must be a reason of the means-goal variety — a 'goal reason'. A goal reason is one that derives its force from the fact that at the time it is given the decision it supports will itself serve or will have effects that serve a good social goal. It follows that the immediate goal to be served by means of a Pareto-superior reallocation must, if the reason is to have justificatory force, be good in light of some relevant value or values. As we have seen, this immediate goal may be characterized as a state of affairs in which at least one person is better off by his own lights and no one worse off. Any such goal may possibly be good intrinsically. Or it may be good instrumentally because its realization is itself a means to another good goal (in general or at least in the particular case). The relevant values are, of course, not peculiarly within the economist's field of expertise. In fact, the values that must figure in a goal reason for it to have justificatory force in support of an adjudicative or other public decision are ones that philosophers, social theorists, and jurisprudents have had more to say about than economists.[24]

If one or more persons are made 'better off' and no one 'worse off,' this may mean only that one or more get more of what they want (or something they want more than something they have). That is, want realization increases.[25] Such an increase might serve as our first candidate for status as a goal in our projected economist's reason having justificatory force. We may define want realization simply as that state of affairs in which an individual knowingly has his want met.

Now is want realization intrinsically good? We must not confuse increased want realization with something else that might be intrinsically good, namely increased psychological satisfaction. One may have a want met, and still, because of many factors, not be at all satisfied as a result. In our view, increased want realization (apart from any psychological satisfaction it may bring) is not intrinsically good as such. A world in which one more want is realized would not necessarily be any better than a world in which, all other things being equal, one less want is realized. If this be so, then increased want realization alone cannot be the kind of goal that can, with other required elements of a 'goal reason', generate justificatory force.

Although the goal of want realization *per se is* not intrinsically good, it may be argued that the mere exercise of autonomous free choice often involved in want realization is intrinsically good. We do not know whether this is true. The intuition of one of us is that the mere exercise of autonomous free choice is not, as such, intrinsically good. It may be that the act of freely choosing something can, in this context, be only of instrumental value (perhaps as a means of enhancing one's satisfaction).[26]

Is the goal of increased want realization *instrumentally good?* That is, does it serve as a means to a value that is intrinsically good? Instrumental goodness is contingent. That is, whether a goal is instrumentally good depends on the value served in the particular case. Obviously many particular wants will be good or at least unobjectionable. If the wants realized that figure in the goal of want realization vary enough from case to case in whether they are instrumentally good, it simply could not be said that Pareto-superior reallocations generate a *general* reason with justificatory force. They would only generate *ad hoc* reasons with force. Yet economists' reasons are not intended to be of this merely *ad hoc* character.

It may be that a *general* economist's reason can be generated along the following lines, however. When someone gets what he wants, he will frequently feel more personal satisfaction with his life — more pleasure as Bentham put it. It may be that, in *general,* want realization is instrumentally good because it regularly produces a net increase in *psychological* satisfaction,[27] an intrinsically good goal. But is increased psychological satisfaction an intrinsically good goal? It would appear so (though there are traditions of thought to the contrary).[28] That is, a world in which one person experiences satisfaction would, without more, be better than a world in which no one does. Of course, in a particular case or even in a pattern of instances, increased satisfaction may not be a very weighty intrinsic value. The increased satisfaction might even stem from the realization of an evil desire, for satisfying an evil desire may cause no net decrease in psychological satisfaction (although it generates a rightness reason *contra*). Still, in our view, the goal of increased satisfaction served instrumentally by increased want realization is good, and thus a reason in its name has force that *may* justify a decision. In the absence of countervailing reasons, a decision based on such a reason would be justified. On this, more later.

4. Availability of Pareto-superior reasons

The main types of common law cases of relevance here are four fold. First, there are many cases where the court is not faced with whether to make new law but must determine who has the right in question in light of complex or apparently indeterminate case law. Once the judge hears the case and appropriately deliberates, it will become clear which party had the right all along. This we may call the 'particularizing' case. Since the judge is simply deciding who has the right, not deciding whether to make a change from a status quo, a Pareto-superior reason would be irrelevant, for it is relevant only to justify a change (where at least one person would be better off and no one worse off), or to justify not making a change (where no one would gain or someone would lose).[29]

Second, there are cases where the court is faced with whether to make new law by overruling or modifying an existing right. Here we assume that the case law more or less plainly confers the right on one of the parties, subject to the standing possibility that a future court may overrule or modify the case law from which the right derives. We will call this the 'overruling' case. Our used car dealer example was such a case, and there we saw that a Pareto reason to overrule arose because, on the facts of the case, some would be made better off and no one worse off. That is, the losers (the church goers) did not object to the loss of their right. But this is far from the typical case. Typically, the projected overruling or modification of existing case law deprives the loser of a valued right.[30] When so, the court cannot give a Pareto reason to justify the projected new law for someone will be made worse off. It might be said that a Pareto reason nonetheless arises *against* overruling in the typical case, and that this 'saves' the relevance of such a reason. But if typically in such a case the Pareto criterion opposes overruling (because there would be a loser who would be worse off), then the utility of such a reason is strikingly limited (because of single, rather than double-edged, potential) and is an essentially conservative justificatory resource at that.[31]

Third, there are cases of 'first impression' in which the court must create law. In a 'full fledged' such case, neither party in question has the right. Here, the court might be able to assign the right in a way that makes both parties 'better off' as compared to their antecedent 'zero' positions (or even something better). In that event, the Pareto analysis might generate a reason for decision. But more often, cases of first impression will be matters of degree, depending on the closeness of analogies within existing law. Thus cases of first impression often overlap with 'overruling' cases. When so, there will be losers. Or at least the antecedent legal status quo will not be a well defined state with which to compare projected Pareto reallocations to determine any gains and losses, and thus the outcome of the Pareto analysis will be indeterminate.

Fourth, there are cases where prior case law is in conflict. Usually, no Pareto reason can arise here, for there is either no well defined status with which comparisons can be made (as above), or there will be losers (if either of the parties is assumed to hold the right in question to any degree).[32]

One way to try to resurrect the relevance of Pareto reasons in the second, third, and fourth types of cases, would be to call upon the judge to ask whether, in each such case, there is a *rule* that, in advance of the actual dispute, the parties could have agreed to for the resolution of any such disputes, should they arise. If so, then that rule, as the Pareto-superior rule, should control. This, of course, would call for Pareto analysis, but it would also call for the judge to abandon traditional common law method and decide cases speculatively in accord with hypothetical antecedent agreements of the parties.

5. Pareto-superior reasons — a summary assessment

What we here call Pareto-superior reasons qualify as economists' reasons *par excellence,* if any reasons do. They flow out of standard economic theory. Virtually all economists embrace, in some way, the idea of Pareto-superior reallocations. Yet we have seen that a Pareto-superior reallocation only contingently generates a reason. It generates a reason only if it brings a net increase in psychological satisfaction, and it does this generally (rather than *ad* hoc) only insofar as we assume that want realization generally serves the further goal of increasing psychological satisfaction.

Further, for the justificatory purposes of judges, the key concept of Pareto-superiority is not well defined. The principal indeterminacies are these: nothing in economics specifies what we are to count as the *ex ante* and *ex post* states of affairs to be compared. Also, economics does not specify the conditions of information under which stated preferences qualify.

In addition, economics cannot tell a judge how to determine reliably the likely subjective responses of parties hypothetically affected by projected reallocations.

Finally, Pareto-superior reasons will *rarely* be available to a common law judge anyway.

III. Kaldor-superior Reasons

This kind of reason derives in part from a reallocation of resources that is 'Kaldorsuperior'. Such a reallocation is one in which, unlike in a Pareto-superior reallocation, there is a loser as well as a gainer but the gainer's gains are such that he could compensate the loser and still have some gain left.[33] Economists do not, however, require that actual compensation be paid. Merely because the gainer thus gains more than the loser loses, economists view a Kaldor-superior reallocation as an 'efficient' means to the goal of welfare improvement, and thus recognize a further basic type of economist's reason.

Far fewer economists subscribe to the Kaldor than to the Pareto criterion of efficient resource reallocation. This is largely because many are averse to making 'interpersonal comparisons'.[34] As we shall see, to apply the Kaldor criterion most faithfully, it would be necessary to determine whether the gainer really does gain more than the loser loses, and thus necessary to compare gains and losses of different persons whose preference intensities for the same things almost certainly differ; and economists frequently proclaim that it is not clear how this can be done.

Nonetheless, some economists do go in for Kaldor-superior reasons. And so do some law professors trained in economics, even in fields far outside monopoly regulation and the like.[35] This is not to say common law judges generally resort to such reasons.[36] At least, they rarely give them in explicit terms. Whether they implicitly do so is a matter for debate (beyond the scope of this paper).

In the usual dispute before a common law court, there will be a prospective loser as well as gainer. As we saw, a Pareto-superior reallocation contemplates no losers. Thus the Kaldor criterion (gainer gains more than loser loses) can be satisfied although the Pareto criterion (some one better off and no one worse off) cannot be satisfied.

1. 'Kaldor-superior' reasons — some examples

The following hypothetical examples provide concrete illustrations of purported Kaldor reasons. Although highly simplified, the examples remain generally realistic, except that in each it is assumed the judge decides solely on the basis of the economists' reason arising out of the justificatory resources of the case. Plainly, an economist is not committed by any reason that his discipline may be thought to generate, to recommending that judges decide cases solely in light of that reason. Also, although all the examples involve 'winner take all' results, nothing in economic analysis requires this.

(i) *A simple property case.* Stakeholder has been caring for a semi-wild animal. Edgar claims title to the animal under some old case law, Edgar having coaxed it off Betsy's land. Betsy claims title, too, it having been born on land owned by Betsy. Assume that by the doctrine of relativity of title, Edgar and Betsy's claims are superior to those of all other parties.

Stakeholder turns the animal over to a small claims court and interpleads Edgar and Betsy. The judge determines that Betsy would be willing to pay $150 for it (as it fits into her technological research work), but Edgar would be willing to pay only $100 for it (as he wants it merely for a pet). It is assumed that Edgar and Betsy are not able to bargain with each other successfully.

Judge Wendt awards title to the animal to Betsy and gives the following reason of substance:

> This is a case of first impression. By the Kaldor criterion, Betsy wins. Betsy would be willing to pay more for the animal than Edgar — she would be willing to give up more purchasing power to get it. That is, Betsy would gain more in getting it (by $50) than Edgar would lose in not getting it. Thus awarding the title to Betsy is an allocation that is Kaldor-superior. Betsy therefore prevails. (Of course, Betsy need not in fact pay anything into court for the animal other than Stakeholder's feedbill.)

> I admit that I have applied the Kaldor criterion directly to the facts of this particular case. But I find (on the basis of further evidence in the record) that I would reach the same result if I were to apply it to proposed alternative rules for such cases, too. That is, I find that gains would likely exceed losses more if, *ceteris paribus,* the one who plans to use an animal (born in such circumstances) in his or her own productive activities gets it. Under this possible rule, the Betsys of the world would be the ones who would, as a class, pay more, and thus should win. Now, it will not always be true that we get the same result regardless of whether the Kaldor analysis is applied directly to the particular case or is applied to alternative general rules. It all depends on the facts. But when we can state a rule we should do so. This directly puts the rights into the hands of the class that values them the most and saves transaction costs this class would have to expend to buy the rights from others. It also saves costs of case-by-case inquiry and dispute resolution. [37]

(ii) A simple tort case. Mr. Upland and Mr. Downland owned adjoining

suburban realty. Upland blacktopped some of his realty, and the benefit to him was worth $1000. As a result of the blacktopping, however, water unforeseeably ran off during rainstorms in rather larger quantities than previously and the first significant run off caused $3000 in damages (repeatable). It would cost Downland $500 to prevent these losses. These parties found that they could not bargain and thus settle their differences. Downland then sued for compensation. Assume that no facts were available as to the likely effects of alternative possible rules. Judge Frank decided the particular case in favour of Upland and reasoned as follows:

> There is no governing common law rule in our jurisdiction. I decide for Upland. Downland should have no right to compensation here, and should take precautions to prevent loss in the future. That allocation of resources in which Upland has the right to let water run off freely would be Kaldor-superior. According to the evidence, it would have cost Upland $1000 to prevent loss from such run offs in the first place (before blacktopping, and perhaps even more now). It would cost Downland only $500 to prevent loss. Upland would be willing to pay a sum up to the $1000 it would cost him to avoid the $3000 loss sustained by Downland in order to get the right to let water run off freely, whereas Downland would be willing to pay no more than $500 to have the right to be compensated for future water-caused losses, since he could prevent them for $500. It follows that Downland is the 'cheaper cost avoider'. Hence, Upland would gain more than Downland would lose if Upland were given the right to let water run off freely and Downland were denied a future right to compensation. Thus it will be Kaldor-superior for Upland to win, and I award the right to Upland. The parties have demonstrated their inability to bargain, and in any event, it would save them the costs of bargaining if I award the right as here. (I say nothing of the $3000 loss sustained by Downland in this case of first impression.)[38]

(iii) *A price fixing case.* Two major producers serving an area collude and fix prices of their product. Consumer, who has bought at the higher price, later learns of the fixing and sues to halt it, to collect damages, and to have a fine imposed. Judge Thomas rules as follows:

> Consumer wins on the basis of Kaldor reasoning. We have a flat
> rule against price fixing, even though sometimes price fixing may
> not be anti-competitive. Without price fixing, consumers would
> generally gain more than producers lose, and it is not cost effective
> to inquire into the possibility of pro-competitive effects in every
> case. Now, let me spell out why price fixing is generally not 'Kaldor
> efficient', to use economists' language. Price fixing usually is at
> prices above competitive levels. Where this is so, consumers are led
> to buy alternative goods. Assume these alternatives are of the same
> quality as the price fixed goods but cost more to produce than the
> price fixed goods and thus are priced (even at competitive levels)
> higher than the price fixed goods would be if the latter were sold at
> competitive prices. Here, it is possible to achieve the same benefit
> level at lower resource cost. Consumer demand can be satisfied at
> lower resource cost by making and selling more of the goods the
> price of which has been fixed. The gain to consumers will exceed
> the loss to producers, now and in the future. Consumer prevails, and
> fine to be imposed accordingly.[39]

(iv) *Transaction costs*. Our examples thus far have generally neglected the
bearing of what economists call 'transaction costs'. To remedy this, we now
offer a further example (discursively rather than in the form of a hypothetical
court opinion).

Assume that Foto took Jean's photo without her consent and used it to
advertise his cereal products. Jean sued Foto for invasion of privacy. Assume
an old precedent rather clearly denies a right of privacy in similar
circumstances. The legal issue before the court is whether, in light of Kaldor
analysis, to overrule the precedent and recognize a right of privacy in Jean.

(a) Let us suppose that our judge takes testimony and other direct
evidence on whether a decision overruling the precedent and recognizing a
right of privacy in Jean in this particular case would be Kaldor-superior and
concludes that it would be. That is, on applying Kaldor analysis directly to
the case (rather than to a proposed rule), he concludes that in light of Jean's
willingness to pay, Jean would gain enough so she could compensate Foto

and still have something left. Without more, the judge would decide for Jean.

(b) Our judge should, however, also consider whether the class of Jeans would also be as likely to gain as would Jean and if he so found, the judge would lay down a rule reassigning the right to the Jeans of the world. (Of course, there might be something special about Jean's particular case, and the judge might find that in general the Fotos would lose more than the Jeans would gain, in which event the judge would not overrule the old precedent but would leave the Fotos with the right.)

One economic advantage of adopting a rule rather than merely resting with ad hoc decisions in each particular case is, of course, that this would save costs of such particular inquiries in future cases. Moreover, such a rule would generally put the right in the hands of parties who value it most and thus would save transaction costs they would otherwise have to incur to buy the right were it assigned to the other class of parties. Rules structure incentives — people can act on them to realize gain. But there is still more.

(c) There are further steps the judge should consider which might alter the result so far provisionally reached, and here transaction costs come in again. Let us suppose the Judge makes further inquiry and concludes that whichever way he assigns the right, there will still be some, perhaps much, bargaining over it. In our example, if the Fotos are, on Kaldor analysis, allowed to keep it, some Jeans will still buy out Fotos, for even though Fotos as a class value it more, some particular Jeans will value it more than some particular Fotos. Or, if on Kaldor analysis the right is assigned to Jeans, some Fotos will buy out Jeans, for again, although the Jeans as a class value it more, some particular Fotos may value it more than some particular Jeans.

Moreover, since the judge has decided that the case is one in which such bargaining transactions as the foregoing will occur, he will also want to consider whether whichever way he assigns the right will itself reduce the costs of such bargaining. For if that happens to be the case, he will want to consider these cost savings in the overall picture in deciding what rule to adopt. (Such savings also make more transactions likely, too, and this brings gains.)

To illustrate: Contrary to the assumptions of our example thus far, let us assume that our judge has provisionally decided up through steps (a) and (b) not to overrule but to reaffirm the right of the Fotos of the world to take and use photos without consent of the Jeans; all this, of course, on the ground that if the right were given to the Jeans, they would not gain enough to be able to compensate the Fotos and have something left. Now, on further analysis, however, let us suppose that (1) whichever way the judge assigns the right, there will still be a significant number of buy outs (that is, there will be further trading in the right), and (2) there will be a substantial reduction in transaction costs if the right is assigned to the Jeans. The former kind of determination is easily enough imagined in this context. Thus we may imagine that if the right of privacy is denied to Jeans, some Jeans will care enough to buy back the right in some circumstances. And it is easy to see why, if a right of privacy is recognized, some Fotos would want to buy it. The latter kind of determination is also very easy to grasp on the facts of the foregoing case. We need only to assume that if a right of privacy were assigned to the Jeans, it would be much easier and therefore less costly for the Fotos to identify and interact with any particular Jeans they wish to photograph for they would know what persons these were, than it would be for the Jeans to seek out prospective photographers and make deals with them in advance (assuming the Fotos had the right).

The foregoing saving in transactions costs from recognizing a right of privacy in Jeans could be large enough to offset the margin of gain (including the saving in transactions costs from the Fotos not having to buy out Jeans) that led the judge provisionally to reaffirm the right in the Fotos in this version of our example. This could be true even though with Jeans having the right of privacy, many more Fotos will buy out Jeans (because as a class they value the right more, on our assumptions) than Jeans would buy out Fotos.

Of course, this step (c) could not alter the overall result in any case in which once the right is reaffirmed or reassigned there will be no future transactions in it because it has once and for all reached its most highly valued use. For example, it might be that the Jeans feel so strongly about privacy that very few if any would ever sell their right. Or it could be that they really don't care, in which event the right would remain forever with the Fotos if once so assigned.

(d) Now, let us suppose the judge cannot determine which class, Jean's or Foto's in our example, values the right more under step (b). Would it follow that the judge should simply rest with step (a) and assign the right to the one of the two particular parties who happens in that case to value it the most, and not lay down a rule? No. Again, it might be that the judge would find that there is trading in the right, and although he does not know in general which class values the right the most, he can, under the circumstances, make this trading much less costly by overruling and recognizing the right in the other class. That is, the general savings in transactions costs could offset the projected Kaldor gain from the mere *ad hoc* assignment of the right in this particular case.

Of course, if there is *no* difference in transaction costs from the alternative assignments, this step becomes inconsequential (unless the judge has other means of affecting transaction costs).

2. *The construction of 'Kaldor-superior' reasons*

First, the judge must identify alternative decisions. The *law itself* may constrain the nature and range of these alternatives. For example, traditionally in common law cases there is one winner and one loser and the winner 'takes all'. Also, any rule arising from the decision would operate similarly in the future. For example, in *Jean v Foto* cases, one party would simply get the right of privacy or not get it. In the *Edgar v Betsy* type of case, one of the parties would always get full and exclusive title to the animal. Upland would win all or lose all. The price fixers would either win all or lose all. Again, nothing in economic analysis requires such all or nothing solutions, however.[40]

Second, the judge must determine (so far as is 'cost effective') the allocative effects of each legally permissible alternative decision on *each person affected* by the law suit. Such persons include parties to the suit and, presumably, third parties in the zone of effects. They also include future similarly situated parties to whom any projected *rule* of decision in the case at hand would apply in the future, for as we have demonstrated in several of our examples, it is always possible that special economic gains (in addition to legal ones) may be derived from proceeding by rule rather than *ad hoc*.[41] Again, economics does not itself state who has what *ex ante* or *ex post*. The judge must turn to the law and other sources to determine as much.[42] At the same time, he must decide which parties and other persons gain and which lose on each alternative in order to come up with an *ex post* characterization. This might, as in the price fixing case, call for the application of sophisticated 'price theory'.[43]

Third (or as a part of the second step), the judge must address himself specifically to the 'transaction cost' effects of alternative decisions. As in the *Jean* v *Foto* case, he must consider whether after each alternative decision or rule there is likely to be trading in the right involved, and if so, whether one alternative decision or rule might itself reduce the costs of such bargaining more than others.

Fourth, the judge must measure the allocative effects thus far determined and translate them into a common unit of measurement. The judge can then meaningfully state whether and how much gainers gain and losers lose on each alternative. The judge would want to know not only the measured effects in the particular case but also (if possible) the measured effects of alternative *rules* for such cases. (Statements of transaction cost estimates may already be in appropriately 'measured form', e.g., in legal tender.)

Proponents of Kaldor reasons generally recommend that gains and losses be measured by reference to the *hypothetical willingness of the parties whose interests are antagonistic to pay in legal tender for the right to the resource in issue or to pay to avoid the money costs attendant upon not having the right to that resource.* We will call this the 'willingness to pay' criterion.[44] It is not the only solution to the problem of devising a method for measuring projected gains and losses,[45] but it does *apparently* enable the judge to avoid making interpersonal comparisons in determining such gains and losses (at a price, as we will see).[46]

Thus, for example, in the *Edgar v Betsy* dispute over title to the wild animal, a judge who invokes the willingness to pay criterion to measure gains and losses asks how much each affected party (as individuals and as members of a class to which a rule would apply) would be willing to pay (in money) to have the animal. We assumed Betsy would pay $150 and Edgar $100. That is, Betsy would be willing to give up $150 in other combinations of goods — say a $150 set of phonograph records, or any other things priced at $150. Edgar would only pay $100, and thus would only be willing to give up other real things purchasable at $100. The *Downland v Upland* case illustrates how the willingness to pay criterion works where what is being paid for is the right to avoid incurring a cost. Upland would, as we saw, be willing to pay $1000 to avoid a $3000 loss. Downland would be willing to pay no more than $500 to avoid a $3000 loss, for he could prevent such losses for $500. Hence Upland values the right in question (the right to let water run off freely) more than Downland values the right to preclude the run off.

It should be evident that the foregoing 'willingness to pay' calculus is not carried out in terms of some objective or socially specified standard of valuation. Rather, it is carried out with reference to the subjective valuations of the affected parties or projected classes thereof as expressed in monetary terms, i.e., in relation to other things the parties think they could buy with the same monetarily stated units of purchasing power.

One important theoretical complication concerning the use of willingness to pay in money as the measure and means of valuation should be noted here. Money (or more precisely, individuals' stated or projected valuations of resources in terms of a common monetary standard) is used to determine gains and losses in constructing economists' reasons partly because money can be used in markets to obtain many different goods and services. Thus in a sense, a monetary standard can be used to compare conveniently a person's valuation of a certain quantity of apples and oranges, or of virtually anything else. Thus, when a person says that he values, as in Edgar's case, a certain animal at $100, he is saying that he values that animal the same as he values any other combination of goods that can be acquired (in some market at some prevailing price) for $100. Money thus serves as a standard by which one sort of good can be 'translated' into another at set quantities determined by a market.

However, on careful consideration, a person's *stated* valuation or preference in dollar terms is only an imperfect approximation of his real valuation of resources, which real valuation is at bottom the theoretical target in an economist's reason based on willingness to pay.

How so? The economist's reason is relativized to a certain class of parties (possibly at a certain time, but we shall ignore that complication). Let us simplify things and assume that, as in the case of Edgar and Betsy, we are trying to determine the monetary valuation of a single good or resource by two parties. Each honestly states his valuation of the resource in legal tender (or we evaluate evidence as to what their honest statements of valuation would be). Now, in order for these valuations in legal tender to serve as input to our economist's reason, several assumptions have to be made. For example, we must assume that (i) there is a relevant (prevailing, available) market within which all combinations of goods can be given or have a price, and (ii) that the parties' statements of monetary value of the resource in question sufficiently reflect for *them* the other combinations of goods that they could get for the same amount in the prevailing market. What this really means can be illustrated as follows: If we ask Edgar how much the animal is worth to him, suppose he says $100. But suppose that it has slipped his mind (or he did not know) that at prevailing prices he could buy 20 bottles of his favourite wine (which he really loves) for $100. But Edgar is not indifferent as between that quantity of wine and the animal — he would much rather have the wine. In that case, Edgar's (honest) statement of $100 for the animal is an over valuation. An under valuation might occur if Edgar was not really in touch with what combinations of goods $100 will buy, if, for example, he had been isolated lately and had failed to take account of inflationary changes (dimunitions) in the value of money in terms of combinations of other goods. In either case, if we use Edgar's statement of monetary valuation for the animal as input to a Kaldor reason, we shall thereby be building an inaccurate measure of Edgar's real 'economic' valuations into that reason, i.e., his valuations of the resource in question in terms of other combinations of goods.

Actual market prices for resources will only rarely (if ever) be equivalent to the maximal worth of those resources as defined above. When a court sets out to give a Kaldor reason, then the maximal worth of any affected resources (determined on the basis of the 'willingness to pay' criterion) will be relativized to those parties that might be affected by one or more of the alternative decisions. Where the only persons to be affected by a court's decision are A and B and the only affected resource is R, then even if R has an actual market price, it will still be necessary for the judge to determine or estimate what A and B are willing to pay for R.

Willingness to pay in money, then, is the measure of resource worth to the parties that the judge is to use. Note that this criterion rests on, among other things, *ability to* pay. Also, willingness to pay is most likely to approximate a party's real subjective valuation of a resource when that party is already consuming the good and there are market prices not only for the things to be given up but also for the resource involved. Thus in *Edgar v Betsy,* not only might there be any number of combinations of goods priced in the market at $150, but the animal itself might also have a ready market price, say $150. Let us suppose, however, that while the animal would sell on the market at $150, it is at the same time one for which Edgar has special affection. In principle, there is no reason why *this* 'non-market' private value could not be expressed in monetary terms. In that event Edgar would (if he can afford it) state his willingness to pay at something more than $100. Or to pose a variant of this problem in another context, suppose in the case of *Downland v Upland,* Downland thinks that it would be very *unfair* of Upland not to share part of the $500 cost of putting up a barrier to prevent run off water from causing damage to Downland's property. In principle, this 'non-market' personal value could be monetized and factored into the calculus as a 'demoralization' cost which Downland would be willing to pay something to avoid. Still, to the extent that non-market based monetizations of payments or costs or both figure in the calculus of gains and losses, the real subjective valuations of the parties are likely to be less accurately represented.

We have earlier explored the extent to which the willingness to pay criterion may fail to reveal the true *economic* valuation of the parties. We will now note several other difficulties with this criterion.

The first problem concerns what some theorists call the 'wealth effect'.[47] In trying to determine a party's valuation of a resource on the willingness to pay criterion, there are two seemingly equivalent questions a judge might put to the relevant party: (1) What is the maximum amount you would be willing to pay to get that resource? (2) What is the minimum (the least) amount you would demand in order to give up that resource? The problem is that the answers to these questions may not be the same, even for the same party. Indeed, if the value of the affected resource comprises a relatively large part of a person's net wealth, his answers to the above two questions are likely to differ significantly. To see why this is so, we must distinguish two sorts of case. Suppose that the resource in question is a $200,000,000 yacht, and we put question (1) to Edgar. Unfortunately, Edgar's net wealth is $2000. But suppose we now put question (2) to him. Our question presupposes (perhaps contrary to fact) that Edgar has such a yacht. And Edgar must reach an answer that he would give were that supposition correct. But in that case Edgar is not limited by his actual net wealth, for our very question hypothetically adds the value of the yacht to his wealth. This is the first sort of case. The second sort of case arises when the answer Edgar might give to question (1) is within the limit of his ability to pay. In such cases, his answers to (1) and (2) may still differ significantly. This is because, in general, the marginal utility of wealth or income decreases. If we put question (1) to Edgar this time, we are in effect asking him how much of his first $2000 of wealth he would give up to obtain resource R. Let us say that his answer is $1000, certainly within his ability to pay (if he efficiently liquidates 50% of his assets). But now suppose that he already has R and we ask him how much he would require to give it up. This is our question (2). His answer is likely to be somewhat more than $1000. This is because any sum he would receive to give up R is an added increment to his first $2000 of wealth. In this case, an offer of $1000 might not be sufficient, for this offered $1000 is (or would be) Edgar's third $1000 of wealth, worth somewhat less to him than his second or first $1000 of wealth. It was those first two $1000 increments that we were asking Edgar to 'dip into' when we put question (1) to him.

It might be argued that the wealth effect does not in fact pose an insurmountable problem for economic analysis and for use of the willingess to pay criterion in determining the parties' economic valuations of resources. For there is a more or less natural way for a judge to decide which question, (1) or (2), he should ask each party. Thus, with Richard Posner,[48] the judge must ask question (1) if the resource is not owned by a party, and question (2) if in fact he already owns it. This seems to be the 'natural' choice simply because we want our valuations to be determined with reference to the stock of resources that a party actually has.

However, there may remain a problem in many legal cases. For example, if we recall the *Edgar v Betsy* case, one (perhaps the best) explanation of why Edgar and Betsy are in court in the first place is that each mistakenly believes that he owns the animal outright. But if that were really the case, then it is likely that the court would award the animal to the owner. Why? Because if, for example, Edgar owned the animal (and this was settled in prior law), the uncertainty and consequent costs that would be generated in the market at large in light of the fact that a settled property right had been obliterated would probably cancel any excess gains to Betsy that would accrue simply because she was willing to pay more for the animal. Thus, the court's decision (as set out in the example) may well presuppose that, under existing law, property rights in the animal are indeterminate or at least not settled. But in that case, which of our two questions is our judge to pose to Edgar and Betsy to determine their valuations appropriately? The answer is not clear. If a judge has to choose which to use (because neither party's property rights in the most immediately affected resource are clear or settled), the judge cannot follow the 'natural' routes above, and there may well be differences in the two measures. So, in a sense, the problem remains. How important it may be in practice remains to be seen.[49]

As we have already observed, the willingness to pay criterion is hypothetically applied. That is, in *Edgar v Betsy,* the judge only asks what the parties would *be* willing to pay for the animal. Similarly, in *Downland v Upland* he asks only what the costs to the parties would *be.* The judge does not require that the payments actually be made or costs actually incurred. This, of course, injects evidentiary uncertainties into the calculus of gains and losses---ones which the discipline of economics does not address. Nor does economics specify the conditions of information under which willingness to pay is to be determined.

Fifth, the judge then identifies all gainers, enters their respective gains, and then identifies all losers and enters their respective losses for each decisional alternative. Of course, he takes into account transaction cost effects, too. He thereafter determines whether on any alternative the reallocation involved is Kaldor-superior — that is, whether the gainers would gain more than the losers would lose. He determines this not only for the particular case but (if possible) for alternative rules for such cases as well. If more than one alternative provides a Kaldor-superior result, the judge chooses the one *most* Kaldor-superior. And in general, if a rule can be formulated, he will prefer that to a mere *ad hoc* decision. Of course, it is costly to gather information to construct a rule, and this is a cost that must be counted too.

In the writings of proponents of Kaldor reasons it is sometimes unclear whether a judge is to take into account general third party effects — 'externalities'. These could either increase or decrease satisfactions. If, for example, in the *Jean v Foto* case, the judge only considers the willingness to pay off Jeans as a class and Fotos as a class, this would exclude general third party effects. Thus the Jeans might prefer privacy more than the Fotos prefer having the pictures. Yet millions might derive satisfaction from seeing pictures of Jeans on cereal boxes, and some or all of this might not show up in the gain to Foto, for it alone might not help sell cereal.

But so far we have only identified a number of steps that a judge must confront in determining whether an alternative involves a reallocation of resources that would be Kaldor-superior, where the determination of an excess of gain over loss is made in terms of willingness to pay for the resources (or to avoid a cost), stated in money. Even if a reallocation is thus 'superior', it does not follow that this, as such, would generate a reason with genuine justificatory force.

IV. A Provisional Critique of Kaldor-superior Reasons

Having provided a general account of Kaldor reasons as might be invoked in common law cases, we now turn to our critique. This critique is provisional in the sense that we wish to reserve our final overall assessment until the law acquires more extensive experience with reasons of this kind. It is our view that outside monopoly regulation and a few other areas of the law, judges have seldom explicitly resorted to such reasons. For now, we hope to be asking some of the right questions and will be satisfied if our tentative answers either point in the right general directions or stimulate others to do better.

There is no jurisprudential literature that systematically treats the criteria for judging substantive reasons of any general type, let alone economists' reasons. Beyond introducing the notions that reasons should justify and be 'guidesome', legal theorists have devoted relatively little effort to articulating what we should expect of reasons. Perhaps our own gropings will induce others to address this topic as well.

1. *Does a Kaldor-superior reason have any justificatory force at all?*

Again, for a reason of substance to qualify as a reason, it must have justificatory force, and for it to have such force, a genuine value — either intrinsic or instrumental — must figure in it. In a mere Kaldor-superior reallocation it is true only that there are gainers, that there are losers, and that the gainers gain enough more than the losers lose so that the gainers could *compensate* the losers and still have a 'net gain' (as determined by willingness to pay for a right, or to pay to avoid a cost, stated in money). Again, economists do not generally require, for their reason to have justificatory force, that compensation actually be paid. To them, the important thing is the 'net gain', and this, of course, can occur without the gainer compensating the loser.

Now, a court might also order that the gainers *actually compensate* the losers with the intended result that gainers would still be better off yet *no one would be worse off*.[50] It is sometimes said that we would then have the equivalent of a Pareto-superior reallocation,[51] in which case we could simply return to our earlier analysis in Part II of the force of such a reason. Such court ordered compensation might be appropriate on *non-economic* grounds in any case in which the loser in effect lost what was plainly his prior right (as Downland would if the law had clearly given him a right to compensation). But observe that court ordered payment of compensation to the 'losers' might *not* be appropriate, on noneconomic grounds as well. In the *Edgar v Betsy* case, the court was deciding between two property claimants to the same animal. When the issue is truly one of title, then in the eyes of the law, whoever loses is not the owner and should receive nothing anyway. In the water run off case, we postulated a genuine case of first impression. The loser in such a case at least has much less of a claim to compensation.

We will now consider what, if any, justificatory force a Kaldor *reallocation* generates on its own terms (quite apart from its possible collapsibility into a Pareto reason via the 'compensation' route). Does a Kaldor reallocation *necessarily* generate a reason with justificatory force? For it to do so, at least the 'net gain' goal involved would have to be intrinsically good. That is, an intrinsic value would necessarily have to figure in this goal. Recall that in a Kaldor reallocation it is enough merely that there is a net gain determined by applying the willingness to pay criterion. Let us assume that the 'net gain' figuring in our goal takes the form of a *net increase in want realization*. We have already contended, in relation to Pareto-superior reasons, that this is not intrinsically valuable.[52] If we are correct, then this increase cannot qualify as a goal the realization of which as such generates a Kaldor reason with justificatory force.

But here there is, a still further problem. The Kaldor analysis involves the willingness to pay criterion, and this criterion is applied without actually making 'interpersonal comparisons'. The price paid for this is that willingness to pay may well not track want realization. Tied as it is to ability to pay, willingness to pay simply cannot take account of interpersonal differences in the intensity of wants as such, yet these differences are relevant to whether a Kaldor reallocation truly involves a net increase in want realization. That is, on the willingness to pay criterion, the gainer (e.g., Betsy in our title to the animal dispute) could gain more as thus stated in money than the loser loses, yet there may be no true net gain in want realization (e.g., Edgar might want the animal far more but be without means to bid accordingly). Because of this factor, we cannot even assume that a Kaldor reallocation yields a net increase in want realization, even if that were an intrinsically good goal (which it is not).

Likewise, it is the tentative view of at least one of us that a particular Kaldor reallocation cannot be intrinsically good on the ground that it represents an autonomous exercise of free choice, or enlarges the scope for such choice.[53]

We conceded earlier that a net increase in psychological satisfaction is, however, intrinsically good and thus could serve as a 'net gain' goal that generates a reason with force.[54] Even so, a Kaldor reallocation — as determined by willingness to pay — does not necessarily bring a net increase in psychological satisfaction. We have already seen that willingness to pay does not invariably track net increases in want realization. *A fortiori,* the willingness to pay criterion cannot track net increases in psychological satisfaction. The criterion merely reveals each party's monetary valuations (in relation to their own resources). It is not and could not be a direct measure of satisfaction to each party.[55] Rather, the objects valued are mere means to future satisfaction. Parties do not buy satisfaction as such. Even if we could determine that a reallocation involved a net increase in *want realization,* it still would not follow that this would translate into a net increase in *psychological satisfaction.* People not uncommonly have their wants met and are thereafter disappointed or at least less satisfied than they expected to be.

Thus a specific projected Kaldor *reallocation* is not, on the foregoing grounds anyhow, *necessarily* justified--does not, merely as such, generate a reason with force. Nonetheless, a Kaldor reallocation does not have to be *necessarily* justified in itself in order to generate a reason. But to do so, a Kaldor reallocation must at least serve a genuine value — intrinsic or instrumental. What might this value be?[56] Of course, some of the candidates will overlap with those already considered in deciding whether a Kaldor reallocation is *ipso facto* justified. First, although we saw that a Kaldor reallocation does not always bring a net increase in psychological satisfaction, it may still do so in the circumstances. On our view, this would be a net gain that qualifies as an *intrinsically* good goal. Within a given problem area, however, the means-goal relations between Kaldor reallocations and net increases in psychological satisfaction are not only contingent but may even be highly variable. When so, they would generate a general reason of relatively little force, except when independent judicial investigation also confirmed sufficient efficacy of means for the case at hand (an inquiry that would commonly call for interpersonal comparisons).

On the other hand, the means-goal relations between Kaldor reallocations and net increases in psychological satisfaction might in some contexts lead to net increases in satisfactions with considerable frequency. In that event, a general reason with real force would arise, even without our knowing (through independent investigation) of a net increase in the particular case at hand. For example, if in a case of the *Edgar v Betsy* type, far more often than not an award of title to the highest hypothetical bidder would bring a net increase in psychological satisfaction, the argument would favour such awards, and *ceteris paribus,* the highest bidders should win. Indeed, even if independent judicial investigation in the particular case revealed that for the immediate persons affected there would be no net increase in psychological satisfaction, it would not follow that the putative Kaldor reason would have no force, for it might be that as a *rule* such persons would experience a net increase in satisfaction.

Second, is a Kaldor reallocation a means to an *instrumentally* good goal in the form of enlarged scope for autonomous free choice? This seems not only contingent but highly variable — perhaps so variable that we may be left merely with no general reason. Although the gainers might commonly end up with more free choice in the sense that they would have more resources with which to exercise and implement choice, the losers might commonly end up with what must correspondingly be denominated less free choice and this could regularly be fully offsetting in nature.

Third, are decisions in accord with reallocations that are Kaldor-superior a means to 'maximizing wealth'?[57] The instrumental 'value' or goal to be directly served here is that of maximizing the worth of resources affected by the decision, i.e., that of allocating those resources to parties who value them most. Under the willingness to pay criterion, those parties are the ones who would be willing to pay the most for them.[58] Two issues arise: (1) In what sense, if any, is there a larger pie? (2) What genuine value is served, either intrinsically or instrumentally, in having a bigger pie (in any sense)? Let us suppose that in the name of the gainers gaining more than the losers lose, the court in our dispute over title to the animal awards Betsy the animal (Betsy would pay $150; Edgar only $100), or the court in our price fixing case enjoins the price fixers (for the consumers would gain more), or the court imposes responsibility to take precautions on Downland (the cheaper cost avoider). Now in what sense, if any, is there a bigger pie? It might be thought that there is a bigger pie in the sense that the society's valuations of the resources affected goes up as a result of such court decisions. But this does not appear to be the case. Both before and after each court decision, the valuations by interested parties of the affected resources remain the same (other things being equal). Court decisions as such do not change these valuations (unless, of course, the court orders the resources destroyed or modified in some way). Of course, a court decision can put resources into the hands of those who value the resources most highly. But this is not to increase their value. It is merely to 'actualize' the higher valuation as between the parties.[59] Again, however, this is not necessarily good, and to the extent it turns out to be good it would appear that we have already canvassed the primary value of relevance: increased psychological satisfaction. Is there a bigger pie in the sense that a Kaldor reallocation necessarily increases the total quantity of physical resources either in the particular case, or in the long run (pursuant to rules laid down in the particular case)? No. In our *Edgar v Betsy* example, there is not necessarily a physically larger pie (unless any saving in bargaining costs owing to court resolution is to be so regarded, and court costs must be charged against this). Indeed, this is plainly so if the circumstances leave the judge with no option but to award the animal merely to the highest bidder. Whether or not there is *de facto* a bigger pie depends on the facts of each case. And the predictability of any increase may vary greatly with the circumstances. What values might any actual increase in the physical size of the pie serve? Again, as we have so far contended, there is nothing intrinsically good about having more goods of just any kind. For example, the increase in goods might consist of more alcoholic drink in the hands of our nine million alcoholics! Rather, it is best to say that more goods, or existing goods that will go farther, may be of instrumental value as means to enhanced psychological satisfaction generally. In the end, then, the value to be served through having a bigger pie would appear to be no different from the primary value we have already canvassed: psychological satisfaction.

Fourth, it might be argued on behalf of Kaldor reasons that decisions based thereon will foster social virtues such as productivity, diligence, honesty, altruism, and the like.[60] Of course, it is the courts who are acting in the first instance, not individuals, yet it is only through individuals acting in the social arena that human virtue may improve. We may also imagine decisions based on Kaldor reasons which do not foster these virtues. For example, resources may go to persons who do not *deserve* them. Willingness to pay does not track desert. And further, insofar as any of the foregoing values, e.g., productivity, can be means to psychological satisfaction, this suggests once again that to economists the ultimate Kaldor rationale is increased psychological satisfaction.[61]

Finally, it may be said that decisions in accord with reallocations that are Kaldor-superior have the virtue of being decisions in accord with a manageable, uniform, and predictable decisional technique. But it is questionable how manageable this technique is, a topic to which we will return momentarily. Moreover, it is not at all clear how reliable and predictable the results of the technique would be. We may imagine, for example, that valuations would change with changes in the economy, and this might call for many settled results to be reopened. And it should be recalled that an economist's reason is only one of the possible types of reasons that may be relevant to a judge in a case. These other reasons will prove decisive in some cases and thus limit the claimed uniformity and predictability still more. Further, it has not been shown that alternative types of reasons grounded in such interpersonal considerations as equity and fairness between the parties or grounded in notions of public policy such as health, order, and safety are any the less reliable and predictable as bases for shaping one's conduct.[62] But even if the economist's technique were manageable, uniform, and predictable, this would leave much to be desired. Law must have substantive content, too, and, one hopes, good content. This is but another way of saying that *technique* must be for some goal or goals. Mere technique alone, no matter how manageable, uniform, and predictable, is of highly limited value within most realms of human interaction.

In sum, a reallocation that is Kaldor-superior does not necessarily generate a reason. Such a reallocation will, in conjunction with an independent value, be juistificatory, however. The value most often at work will be a projected net increase in psychological satisfaction. The relative force of a reason in which such a value figures is another matter, as we will see.

2. *Sufficiency of justificatory force*

It is reasonable for common law judges to expect that the types of substantive reasons they are called upon to give will have force sufficient to justify at least some decisions more or less on their own. After all, the main point of substantive reasons is precisely that of justifying decisions (including choices of rules). The sufficiency of their force is important not only to judges and their immediate addressees in actual adjudicated cases. It is also important to other parties who are trying to decide whether to settle their disputes out of court. If the reasons judges give are themselves sufficient to justify actual court decisions at least in some significant proportion of cases, then it is likely such reasons will also influence at least some well-counselled disputants to settle out of court. In such instances, the force of the reason also facilitates dispute settlement.

It follows that a given type of reason of substance would be relatively insignificant as a justificatory resource if it usually served merely as a makeweight or tie breaker and was rarely strong enough to justify any particular decision solely on its own. Certainly the various types of reasons of substance now found in the common law cannot generally be characterized merely as makeweights or tie breakers. Consider, for example, the strikingly strong character of estoppel reasons in certain contract cases and of reasons in the name of public health or safety in certain tort and property cases.

We have already seen that Kaldor reasons are a subclass of 'goal reasons' — reasons of substance which derive whatever justificatory force they have from estimates that the effects of the decisions will serve good social goals. Before inquiring into the sources of the justificatory force of goal reasons in general and Kaldor reasons in particular, we will stop to explain why in our framework of analysis we classify Kaldor reasons as a subclass of what we call substantive goal reasons rather than as a type of reason that itself subsumes or swallows up all other substantive reason types, or at least all other goal reasons. It appears that some economists (and others) contend that a genuine Kaldor reason, properly construed, itself aggregates and nets out any and all relevant forms of value or goal realization.[63] We do not agree that this involves either an appropriate or a faithful conceptualization of non-Kaldor reasons, and because of this we classify a Kaldor reason merely as one among various subclasses of reasons of substance — as, indeed, only one of various subclasses of goal reasons.

We cannot undertake a detailed defence of our view here, however, and will only sketch briefly why we take the view we do. First, all relevant goal reasons in a given context do not collapse into a single all-encompassing Kaldor reason. The 'net gain' goal in a Kaldor reason typically is some form of psychic satisfaction or pleasure. This is simply not the inherent nature of the goals in non-Kaldor reasons. Health, safety, scientific truth, democratic process, etc., comprise possible subject matters of non-Kaldor goals. But in particular cases there may be essential differences between pursuing such goals and pursuing psychic satisfaction or pleasure. Clearly, health, safety, scientific progress, etc., are not simply identical to satisfaction, though in fact they often may be strongly correlated with it. But from this last fact it does not follow that the only basis for judicial resort to reasons in the name of non-Kaldor goals must in turn be pursuit of net increases in satisfaction. It is possible to pursue increased community health, for example, without pursuing an overall, long-term increase in community satisfaction. Thus, if a judge (or a legislator for that matter) wanted a population better fit for war, he might render decisions designed to produce a healthier population. He might pursue community health ultimately in the name of some form of Spencerian triumph of a particular social group or its cultural products, but quite independently of any commitment on his part to increasing the long-term satisfaction of the community. Indeed, achievement of such a goal might result in more pain overall! A judge simply can pursue non-Kaldor goals without pursuing net increases in psychological satisfaction *as such*. The most artistically or scientifically productive community, the most powerful or morally perceptive, the most noble, etc., need not be the happiest. The community which maximizes pleasurable experiences *tout court* is not necessarily the one that seeks to maximize only those pleasurable experiences which independently meet certain qualitative conditions. Further, many non-Kaldor goals can be rationally pursued for their own sakes. We do not see how one can easily argue (or much less just assume) that any goal a judge might rationally pursue must ultimately reduce to net long-term increases in overall psychological satisfaction.

Further, non-Kaldor reasons have a still wider form of independent significance. When judges give these as well as Kaldor reasons and the society acquiesces, this is one of the ways the society shows respect for a plurality of genuine values and therefore 'defines' itself as a society dedicated to health, pleasure, scientific progress, democratic forms, and so on.[64]

Now, what are the features of the strongest possible (or at least very strong) kind of goal reason as such? We may list the principal features as follows:

(1)   The 'facts of the case' — who is in dispute with whom over what — are convincingly established beyond all doubt via reliable testimony or whatever other evidence is required.

(2)   The judge has an unquestionably reliable basis for estimating likely goal serving effects of the decision, and the probability of such effects is itself highly certain.

(3)   The estimated goal serving effects of decision in (2) are not *de minimus,* but, on the contrary, are quantitatively substantial.

(4)   A very strong value (highly prizeable value) 'validates' (either intrinsically or instrumentally) the relevant social goal in (2) and (3).[65]

Now, are there grounds to believe that the usual Kaldor reason given to justify a decision in a typical common law case would not merely fail to measure up to the foregoing features but fall far below them, so that at least in many cases it could only be a makeweight or a tie breaker? Let us consider features (4), (3) and (2), in that order.

Perhaps the most difficult (and important) issue concerns the nature and strength of the value (or values) that is characteristically associated with Kaldor reasons. In general, we have seen that the principal value to be served through Kaldor reallocation is increased psychological satisfaction.[66]

The crucial question therefore is: How valuable or prizeable is increased psychological satisfaction, at least in general? In some areas of the common law, the facilitation of private satisfaction occupies an important (though not exclusive) place. We here have in mind not only the generally consensual field of contracts, but also the law of wills, trusts, and gifts, and a significant portion of real property law. In other fields, such as torts, this is less clear. Of course, the 'psychological satisfaction' element of policies in such fields is hedged in by doctrines reflecting considerations of quite different types, e.g., equitable and other considerations expressed in rightness reasons and in legal norms based on such reasons.[67] Further, many goal reasons[68] often found in the common law invoke values that, as characterized in decisions, have a 'public regarding' flavour as opposed to a merely private want satisfaction flavour. The goals of increased safety and health are good examples. Of course, even with such goals, psychological satisfactions may constitute an important element in their valuableness, though not the only element.[69]

It is difficult to assess in a general way the relative overall strength of a class of reasons which ultimately target increased psychological satisfaction. Let us begin with the simplest case. Imagine that a lawyer for a party in a suit offers the judge the following reason for a decision in his client's favour: 'My client would derive a significant level of psychological satisfaction if he wins'. On the face of it, this seems like an extraordinarily weak reason indeed. It has little intuitive force. Further, it seems somehow inappropriate for a court to give very much weight (or even consideration) to such a reason. What explains the apparent weakness of this reason? There are several factors, but the most obvious is simply this: Only in a rare case would the very same reason be unavailable to the other party! It is no wonder that such a reason is virtually no help in determining which alternative decision is more justified.

Consider the next possibility: 'My client would derive a great deal more from a decision in his favour than would the opposing party from a decision in his favour'. This reason does seem slightly stronger than the first, perhaps because it obviates the limitation noted in connection with our first example. Even so, this reason seems intuitively, rather weak. Why? One obvious factor is that the language in which the reason is couched is, perhaps, relatively unfamiliar and technical. Let us rephrase it slightly: 'My client cares much more about (has a much greater psychological stake in) the subject matter of this lawsuit than does the opposing party'. That seems slightly better, but still relatively weak. What further factors might account for this? One that immediately comes to mind is this: The offered reason takes into account only the comparative levels of psychological satisfaction of the two parties before the court. It is just a fact that often court decisions and precedents affect more than just the immediate parties. But the reason is being offered in the name of satisfaction as such, and affected third parties are also capable of being satisfied or frustrated. Insofar as the court's decision is likely to affect many third parties, their wants must be factored in too. These parties include persons in the zone of immediate decisional effects and future similarly situated parties.

Consider, then, a third possibility: 'A decision for my client will significantly increase the aggregate level of satisfaction or happiness in the community'. Now this does seem to be a much stronger reason than the first two, and it is not too far-fetched to imagine the judge giving such a reason in his opinion (though perhaps in slightly different language, e.g., using phrases like 'public convenience' or 'community harmony').[70] With this third possibility, we have disposed of some of the factors that would weaken the force of satisfaction-based reasons viewed as an independent justificatory resource. However, such a reason may still not strike us as being particularly decisive in a given common law case. Why not? Perhaps it is partly because we know (even without consciously thinking of it) that reasons of other types — sometimes very powerful ones — might frequently support a contrary decision. For example, there may be countervailing goal reasons such that (i) the goals they involve would be disserved by increasing the aggregate level of community satisfaction, or (ii) the values to be realized by serving these alternative goals may not significantly depend on increasing the level of aggregate psychic satisfaction. A particular example would be the following: Many members of a society might prefer to own cars that go very fast and are otherwise of unsafe design (even though this involves some pain, too). Yet courts might hold manufacturers liable for damages for 'design defects' and thus lead manufacturers to build slower and otherwise safer cars, though at the cost of an overall decrease in levels of community satisfaction. Or again, increased satisfaction may be offset by countervailing rightness reasons having to do with the moral or equitable desert of the particular parties before the court or with the fact that increasing aggregate community want satisfaction may be unduly burdensome to (and so unfair to) some members of the community or one of the parties to the case. Many examples might be cited.

Of course, the fact that the goal of increased psychological satisfaction can be (and often is) overridden by other goal reasons and rightness reasons does not show that it is not a significant and valuable goal. For these same other goal reasons and rightness reasons can also be overridden in like fashion. Thus, sometimes fairness in the particular case must give way to concern for community well-being, e.g., in the name of more efficient production.

Now, turning to a further basic factor that figures in the degree of justificatory force of any goal reason, can it be said that the estimated goal serving effects of a Kaldor reallocation — increased psychological satisfaction — is likely to be quantitatively substantial rather than *de minimus?* We cannot see that a general answer is really possible. In many two party disputes which provide relatively little opportunity (on their particular facts) to structure incentives that will have wide application, a Kaldor reallocation might bring relatively little by way of a net increase in satisfaction. In other cases, as in our price fixing example, aimed at large commercial operations or widespread contractual practices, huge social gains might result from a single decision.

In regard to our remaining factor figuring in the justificatory force of goal reasons— predictability of decisional effects — this much can be safely said. Often the generalities and other forms of economic theory used to estimate likely goal serving effects will fail to generate reasonably certain estimates of allocative effects (including increases in net psychological satisfaction).[71] Indeed, many factors may operate even to make these estimates and projections highly speculative. Nonetheless, sometimes the overall decisional effects will be susceptible of accurate prediction.

In general, then, it is very difficult to assess the force of Kaldor reasons *as a class*. But this is also difficult to do with any class of substantive reasons the various members of which differ significantly in justificatory force. On this matter of essential elements of justificatory force, our tentative conclusions are these: specific Kaldor reasons may differ radically in justificatory force, perhaps far more so than rightness reasons, for example. Powerful reasons of other types (reasons involving different kinds of values) are almost always available in decisional contexts and must not be ignored. But for now it appears that economists' reasons of the Kaldor variety may represent a significant justificatory resource in a fair number of cases. Our limited optimism is premised on

> (i) the degree of strength of the general utilitarian principle that *ceteris paribus* human wants ought to be satisfied, and
>
> (ii) the view that sufficiently convincing arguments can be developed to show that Kaldor reallocations (wherein the willingness to pay criterion determines gain and loss) are effective means to significant increases in satisfaction.

3. Extent to which countervailing reasons are readily available

The overall justificatory significance of a general type of reason is affected by the degree to which strongly countervailing reasons concomitantly arise. Thus, even if a relatively strong type of reason ordinarily arises from a given set of justificatory resources, the general justificatory significance of this type of reason is diminished if strongly countervailing reasons concomitantly arise with it. We are not in a position to estimate the frequency of any concomitant countervailing reasons. We will, however, explore in a tentative way the *scope* for such reasons. That scope is considerable. Both countervailing rightness reasons[72] and other subclasses of countervailing goal reasons[73] may regularly arise.

A net gain in psychological satisfaction —the primary value in a Kaldor reason — may in a particular case even be accompanied by the realization of evil or otherwise bad wants. Indeed, the *gainer's* realization of these very wants may even be what it is that actually gives rise to the net increase in psychological satisfaction! As one theorist has put it, the wants of the gainers in a Kaldor reallocation may be 'mercurial, greedy, bigoted, lustful, etc'.[74] (Betsy, for example, may outbid Edgar merely for spite.) Of course this does not diminish the net increase in psychological satisfaction derived from the realization of such wants. The economist's reason as such is left intact. But any morally bad wants thus realized generate countervailing rightness reasons that judges may also quite properly take into account. And these rightness reasons may well override the economists' reason.

At the same time, the want realization that figures in a net increase in psychological satisfaction generating an economist's reason may readily conflict with a social goal such as safety, conservation, health, or the like. The countervailing goal reason that thus arises may also have overriding force.

Now, let us assume that the gainers' wants are not contrary to moral norms and do not conflict with social goals, and thus that no countervailing reason arises from these sources. It might still be that the *losses* of the *losers* in a Kaldor reallocation are not merely personal to the losers but of special social significance. The losers, for example, may be engaged in socially meritorious activities — research, dissemination of information to the public, private charity, etc. — such that after the reallocation these activities would have to cease or diminish. In these circumstances, countervailing goal reasons (in the name of these very meritorious activities) would arise that might well, if combined with the losses to the losers as such, override the gains to the gainers, overall.

At the same time, the losses of the losers in a Kaldor reallocation might also be contrary to applicable rightness norms. Thus they might fly in the face of norms of desert or justified reliance or the like — norms that generate countervailing rightness reasons that alone or together with the psychological losses to the losers and any countervailing goal reasons easily override psychological gains to the gainers (or even such gains combined with the force of any other reasons that parallel these gains).

Even if no countervailing reasons arise in opposition to the gains of gainers (as above), and even if the losses of the losers are not exacerbated by concomitant disservice of goals or by disregard of rightness norms (as above), the reallocation on which the economist's reason rests might still contribute to an existing maldistribution of income. The losers might turn out even with regularity to be poor so that, in effect, the gainers would really be gaining literally at the expense of the poor. Again, this would not diminish the economist's reason as such, but it would give rise to a countervailing reason that judges could be expected to consider.

4. Commensurability with other reasons

In most common law cases not one but several possible reasons for decision come into play. As we have stressed, frequently these reasons will not all be of the same basic type. Some may be other varieties of 'goal reasons' in the name of such values as public health and safety (as in some nuisance cases) or family harmony (as in some intrafamily tort cases). Others may be 'rightness reasons' in the name of norms of right conduct incorporating such values as desert, fairness, dignity, autonomy, and the like.

The common law is filled with goal reasons and rightness reasons. Judges must often resolve conflicts between different goal reasons, different rightness reasons, and different goal and rightness reasons. Judges have accumulated considerable experience weighing such reasons against each other. And, although judges have not always done this well, this does not appear to be because reasons of these types have proven to be insufficiently 'commensurable'. Is the same likely to be true of Kaldor reasons? In our view, most common law judges have had little experience weighing such reasons against each other, against other goal reasons, and against rightness reasons. But even with experience, it may be that judges would have special difficulty determining the force of, and therefore *weighing,* Kaldor reasons against reasons of these other types. We think this may be so partly because there are grounds to believe that such reasons are rather more speculative than many goal reasons. Kaldor reasons call for prediction of cause-effect sequences and for estimates of total resource allocation impact with special reference to changing market conditions. Also such reasons turn on 'appetitive' concepts and experiences the measurement of which in some particular cases seems especially problematic.

To the extent judges find it difficult to cope with the weightings of Kaldor reasons, any of several untoward consequences might ensue. Except where the reasons are quite obviously strong, the judges might simply treat them as makeweights or tie breakers. We have already suggested that if this is all there is to such reasons, then they cannot qualify as a major justificatory resource (at least outside monopoly regulation and like areas). Or the judges might also end up giving such reasons far more than their due. That is, reasons of this kind might become 'over decisive'. Indeed, it appears that if some proponents of economic analysis in the law were to have their way, Kaldor reasons might get more than their due against competing reasons of other basic types.[75]

5. Intelligibility and persuasiveness

Ideally, the reasons judges give should be intelligible and persuasive to the governed. In particular, they should be explainable to losers. If it is too much to expect most losers to be persuaded, it remains important for the reasons to be intelligible to them.

It is therefore not enough for a case to be in fact decided as it should be decided, in light of the true force of all relevant reasons. It should also be possible for the interested public — the bench, the bar, the parties, and related third parties — to see for themselves that the case has been so decided, or at least decided on intelligible grounds. Intelligibility and persuasiveness help make the final decision more acceptable to the parties, thereby reducing the need in the particular case for coercive enforcement (with attendant friction, waste, and loss of liberty). These features also generally render the law more respectworthy and consequently capable of motivating higher levels of conformity. They also render the law more readily appraisable by the public and thus susceptible of rational revision as conditions and values change.

And, as we will see, they make the law more guidesome.

This requirement of intelligibility and persuasiveness differs from the requirement that a type of reason be sufficiently justificatory. The justificatory force of a proferred reason is not identical with its intelligibility or its persuasion potential. A type of reason can have sufficient justificatory force yet not be particularly intelligible or persuasive.

In terms of general intelligibility and persuasiveness, how do Kaldor-superior reasons fare? The answer appears to depend on the particular instance of the reason under consideration. It is possible for a particular reallocation to be Kaldor-superior and to generate a net increase in satisfaction yet the intelligibility and persuasiveness of the specific reason thereby arising be quite limited. Complex economic analysis, including, for example, sophisticated price theory, might have to be brought into play to determine that the reallocation and its effects are truly Kaldor-superior.

Of course, not all instances of the reason will involve complexity beyond the laity. But even when relatively simple economic analysis is required in the construction and formulation of a reason, it may be that relatively few lay persons or even professionals will be able to grasp the reason. (No doubt this helps explain why judges in relatively few common law cases have explicitly resorted to this kind of reason.)

But we must be wary of rejecting economists' reasons on the ground that economic analysis is neither intelligible nor persuasive to the law's various audiences, as matters now stand. For one thing, this would be to cast doubt on any goal reasons in the name of values other than psychological satisfaction but in which economic analysis somehow figures. Indeed, by implication it would be to cast doubt on any reason in which some technical form of analysis is at work. Reasons involving mathematics, the laws of physics, biology, etc., would be in some jeopardy. Furthermore, it might be well that more of the citizenry, the judiciary, and the legal profession should study economics!

At the same time, if the general class of Kaldor reasons would in fact be relatively unintelligible and unpersuasive to the law's audiences in common law cases, this feature would involve costs that would have to be counted.

6. *Transmutability into stable rule*

Reasons of substance are the raw material of rules and related legal norms. At least minimal generality is implicit or explicit in a reason — if essentially the same circumstances recur, then the same reason arises. Of course common law courts, treatise writers, 'restaters', and others go beyond this, and undertake to transmute reasons into explicitly formulated rules and other norms. (Of course, such rules need not be — and are not — absolute and unqualified.)

Why are stable rules and other general legal norms as such important? It is familiar to lawyers that rules serve as vehicles for carrying substantively sound results forward beyond the particular case, secure a measure of equality before the law, and provide predictability with respect to likely official action so that private parties can know their legal positions and thus plan and also decide when and how to settle private disputes.[76] And, as we have seen, there may even be *special* economic gains from rules.[77]

Thus, if economists' reasons should prove inadequate as raw material for the creation of rules, this would ordinarily be a serious deficiency. (It would not, however, follow that economic analysis would be of no use whatsoever to lawyers.) Experience teaches us that the ordinary goal reasons and rightness reasons found in the common law are generally adequate rule 'generators'. What of Kaldor reasons? Such reasons can and do generate rules, as we saw earlier.[78] But one possible ground for skepticism may be noted. Rules originally based on Kaldor reasons would be based in part on such factors as then current market prices, costs of avoidance, etc. It follows that such rules would be subject to change as these factors change. It seems likely that rules so based might even be far more changeable than typical rules we now have in the common law generally. To the extent this is so, many of the values of having rules in the first place would be less well served.

7. *'Guidesomeness'*

Rules and other common law norms are not self-defining. They must be interpreted and applied to concrete particulars. If judges interpret and apply rules mechanically solely in the light of the apparent literal meaning of the words in the rules, then the rules will 'overinclude' or 'underinclude' or both. Many legal theorists have stressed that legal rules and other norms should therefore not be interpreted and applied literally or mechanically but in light of the reasons behind these rules and other norms. To facilitate this 'rationale oriented' mode of interpretation and application, some theorists have advocated that legal rules and other norms be formulated either with their reasons stated 'on their faces' or at least otherwise suitably appended .[79] For example, let us suppose that the stated rationale for a rule requiring that a contract modification be in writing is simply evidentiary, there being skepticism about the reliability of mere oral testimony. If, however, a given seller had actually started to manufacture goods before the buyer repudiated an oral agreement modifying the specifications, *this conduct* should satisfy the evidentiary rationale, too, for it would be corroborative and the court would not have to rely on mere oral testimony.

The foregoing rationale-oriented mode of interpretation and application can be readily defended. Assuming that the rule or other norm is well conceived in the first place, then if and only if it is interpreted and applied in accord with the reasons behind it can the rule or norm satisfactorily serve its ends.

Again, experience tells us that the goal reasons and rightness reasons that judges have traditionally brought to bear in common law cases are appropriately 'guidesome', at least when adequately formulated. What of Kaldor reasons? We have seen that these take the following summary form: 'Decide in favour of alternative X because on that alternative the gainers gain more than the losers lose'.

Can a reason of this general kind sufficiently guide the interpretation and application of any rules into which it transmutes? If we are correct, the law has not yet had sufficient experience with enough Kaldor rules or Kaldor reasons over a wide range of common law contexts to be able to answer this question.

Of course, it may be that the Kaldor analysis generates few stable rules, anyway, besides the rule: 'Always apply the Kaldor analysis'. If that should turn out to be so, the analysis could not survive the requirement, treated in the preceding section, of sufficient transmutability into rules. Moreover, an important parallel issue arises in any event, and we now turn to it.

8. Efficient constructability

If a type of reason is not, in the typical circumstances of its possible availability, efficiently constructable, then it follows that resort to it is not generally worthy of the time and effort required. Again, in our view we do not yet have much experience with explicit judicial construction of economists' reasons in common law cases. Even so, there is some basis for believing that a reason of this nature may prove to be less than efficiently constructable even in the mine-run of cases. We will now explore some of the more obvious difficulties.

First, the judge will often encounter problems in determining whether a projected reallocation is Kaldor-superior. He must cope with indeterminacies in the very methodology itself. For example, in a case like *Edgar v Betsy,* what allowances is he to make for the possible influence of ignorance upon the statements of willingness to pay on the part of the parties? And what is to count as the 'base position' of each party? That is, is each party to be considered a total non-owner or is each to be credited with a valuable chance to become owner? Then how certain do reallocative effects have to be before we are to count them as part of a projected reallocation? Plainly judgment is called for here.

Beyond indeterminacies in the methodology, the judge must gather data and apply economic analysis to it if he is to determine whether a reallocation is superior. Several kinds of serious difficulties may arise all in the same case. And one of these, at least, is sure to arise in almost every case. Sometimes it will be hard to get reliable data. For example, parties (e.g., Edgar and Betsy) are sure to overstate their valuations once they understand that ultimately neither need actually pay anything. It is only a partial answer to say that evidence of their own prior preferences and of related market prices may be used to impeach their credibility and discipline their testimony.

Sometimes sophisticated economic analysis will be called for. Thus, for example, in the price fixing type of case it might be appropriate to bring complex branches of price theory into play. Still other issues of cause and effect will arise, and the bearing of causal generalities in economics may be quite uncertain.

Sometimes there will be insoluble problems of valuation. For example, let us return to the used car dealer example and assume that the churches do object to Sunday sales so that we have losers as well as gainers. How would a price tag — willingness to pay — be placed on the churches' valuations of the right? Here we are at many removes from market analogies, yet surely no court would be content to rest merely with what the churches say their valuations are.

Second, for the putative reason to have justificatory force, the judge must satisfy himself that the reallocation he has found to be Kaldor-superior fulfills an independent value. Here the judge may choose either of two routes. If he rests content solely with the results of applying the willingness to pay criterion, he may, as we have already seen, encounter difficulties in getting reliable evidence of willingness to pay for a resource or to avoid a cost attendant upon not having a resource. But beyond this, and more important, we have also seen that a calculation of net gain based on the willingness to pay criterion is no guarantee of a net increase in psychological satisfaction, the value characteristically associated with Kaldor reasons. If the judges choose to rest content with this, it may be that no independent value will figure in the reason so far as the particular case is concerned. In that event, the judge would have to be prepared to live with a reason having force only because of presumed value realization (net increases) in the mine-run of future similar cases falling under the rule implicit in the decision. (Of course, this state of affairs sometimes obtains with respect to non-Kaldor goal reasons, too.)

On the other hand, if the judge is unwilling to live with a reason that would have force in the case at hand only because of its bearing in future cases, he must engage in interpersonal comparisons of likely psychological satisfaction in the case at hand in order to determine whether in that case there is a net increase in satisfaction in the offing. Economists themselves frequently proclaim that such comparisons are impossible or at least highly difficult on grounds we will illustrate from the case of *Edgar v Betsy*. The issue of any net increase is a factual one. Just because Betsy is willing to pay $150 and Edgar only $100, it does not follow that to award the animal to Betsy would increase net satisfaction. A dollar to Edgar might be worth twice as much as a dollar is worth to Betsy, who is rich. But to determine whether the marginal utility of money to Betsy is much lower than to Edgar would be factually very difficult, for the judge would need to investigate the preference orderings and the psychologies of satisfaction of each party and compare them. To put this another way, the intensity of Edgar's preference for the animal might exceed that of Betsy, yet Betsy might still bid more for it. If Edgar's preference is that intense, his dissatisfaction in not getting it would offset Betsy's satisfactions, and there would be no net gain. One reason it would be very difficult to determine this is that we have no direct or wholly adequate way to measure and compare the magnitudes of preference intensities of different persons.

　　　　Whether the foregoing possibilities really do signal relative or excessive 'unconstructability' is not clear to us. We do note that such reasons have heretofore played a role in the law mainly in monopoly and related fields of *economic* regulation. Moreover, it may be that there are special explanations for the seeming ready availability (and immediate intuitive appeal) of the reasons in those areas. The issue in many of those cases is whether there will be some *fairly large increment* of gain over loss from judicial intervention in the name of removing *market distortions.* Relatedly, the economic analysis of likely effects can proceed in rather more gross or global terms for the segment of the economy involved in the case. This means that close interpersonal comparisons of gains and losses is not required as in a two party tort, property, or contract case. In addition, it may be that we can take it for granted that any sizeable increase in net satisfaction in the offing in such cases will not involve an undue proportion of wants that are objectionable in a suitably strong sense.

9. Possible arbitrariness of boundary conditions

　　　　At least all 'goal reasons' presuppose some 'boundary conditions'. That is, the judge cannot be expected to devote endless energy in each case trying to ascertain all possible future effects of his decision on all possible parties and third parties. But if an analytical scheme for the generation of a reason for decision arbitrarily restricts the range of inquiry relevant to the force of the reason, the force of that reason in the particular case may be problematic. An arbitrary restriction may function either to overstate or to understate the force of the reason. In a Kaldor reason, the restriction would overstate force in any case in which it foreclosed inquiry that would show losses not otherwise registered in the calculus, and would understate force in any case in which it foreclosed inquiry into gains not otherwise registered in the calculus.

Can it be said that the boundary conditions imposed on Kaldor analysis of gains and losses from a reallocation are arbitrary? This question is difficult to answer. As yet no settled or authoritative specifications of those conditions is to be found in the literature. Nor is there an accepted test of arbitrariness. But this much should be clear. Any boundary conditions that confined the gains and losses to be counted merely to those sustained by the immediate parties and future similarly situated parties would be arbitrary. A judicial reallocation would be almost certain to affect still others (who would then be either gainers or losers).

A judge might decide to abandon the willingness to pay criterion and approach the issue of any projected net increase in satisfaction directly. In that event, we might formulate a test of arbitrariness along these lines. The force of a reason increases as its range (in terms of effects radiating from the decision) and its temporal span (into the future along whatever relevant chain of causal effects) increase. Just so its justificatory force decreases (though not necessarily to the same extent) with any additional uncertainty that attends the judge's predictions because of increases in their range or temporal span. And although there is no clear or mechanical way to determine this, in an ideal case the judge would increase the range and span of his predictions just up to the point where increases in uncertainty (or in other costs of acquiring the relevant information) would marginally offset increases in the justificatory force of the reason due to more far ranging predictions. A boundary on the range and span of ingredient predictions that clearly falls short of such an ideal end point would be to that degree arbitrary.

10. General 'range' of reason

It of course counts against the justificatory significance of a type of reason if its range of applicability is quite limited or 'pocketed'.

First, there is what might be called 'conceptual unavailability'. All goal reasons are inherently future regarding. Thus the justificatory scope of Kaldor reasons does not extend to decisions confined largely to the imposition of liability for past losses or harms, i.e., 'sunk costs'.[80] Yet, in a significant proportion of common law cases, the primary issue is not how the future may be fruitfully structured, but only what if anything a court should do about a past 'mess'.

Second, we may also consider the potential range of Kaldor reasons in relation to the main general types of common law cases. There is the 'particularizing' type of case in which the task of the judge is not to justify a change or to justify the status quo but merely to particularize authoritatively what that legal status quo is. Here, the Kaldor analysis is irrelevant, for no possible 'move' is projected.[81] Then there is the 'overruling' (or 'modifying') type of case where the judge considers whether to move away from the existing legal state of affairs and substitute a new one. Here there is, of course, full scope for the Kaldor analysis, subject of course to the various practical limits on the constructability of Kaldor reasons. (Indeed, it may be that Kaldor reasons are *too* powerful — that they would too readily authorize overrulings and thus leave existing rights too much at risk.)

Further, there are full fledged cases of first impression where, for example, the court is asked to award title in novel circumstances, as in our *Edgar v Betsy* case. Here we are projecting alternative legal states of affairs — say, title in one type of claimant or title in another type of claimant. We saw that practical limits and also an important theoretical one may come into play in perhaps a significant proportion of cases. The so-called 'willingness to pay' measure depends on ability to pay, and ability to pay depends on what rights one has, yet in the very nature of the problem, those rights are not specified. At least whenever having the very right in question might affect one's ability to pay and thus one's willingness to pay, the answer to the question: 'How much would that person be willing to pay for the right?' may vary depending on whether it is assumed that the party has or has not the right already. As a result, the calculation of gains and losses may be affected, and the decision be one way, or the other, accordingly. Obviously, a purported justificatory rationale that decides one way and then the other, in the same case, cannot be very helpful to the judge.[82]

11. *Suitability for court use*

Some reasons are not suited for court use. For example, courts ought not to base decisions on straightforwardly 'political' reasons. On the other hand, a legislature may rest with such reasons. It might be argued that the question whether one type of person or group should gain at the expense of another type of person or group mainly in *terms of enhanced psychological satisfaction* (as in a Kaldor reallocation) is essentially a political matter, especially given (i) that decisions based on reasoning to the effect that the gainers gain more than the losers lose may systematically favour the wealthy because calculations of gains and losses are done in terms of the willingness to pay criterion, a criterion tied to ability to pay, and (ii) that judges have little or no control over the nature and size of any 'compensatory' or other transfer payments that the government may make to the less well off.

The limits of institutional competence may also affect the kinds of reasons a court may properly give. As we have seen, Kaldor reasons sometimes call for complex factual inquiries that may be beyond the fact finding machinery of courts. American experience to date with much antitrust litigation is not a basis for optimism.

V. Conclusion

Genuine Pareto-superior reasons will seldom be available to common law judges, mainly because in the usual lawsuit there will be a loser or losers. Kaldor-superior reasons will at least be theoretically available more often, but it seems that they will frequently not be efficiently constructible in particular cases. Moreover, the justificatory force of Kaldor reasons is likely to vary greatly, depending on (among other things) the strength of the connections between the reallocations and the independent values involved (increased satisfaction and the like). Even when this force is considerable, the force of competing goal reasons or rightness reasons (or both) may often override.

In our view, it is still too early to know whether Kaldor reasons have a legitimate future as a *general* justificatory resource. Of course, we may never know this, for judges may decline to experiment with the required explicit resort to such reasons across the common law. In that event, several issues relevant to assessing these reasons would have to be left as we have left them here — largely unresolved. It is certain that any judicial experimentation with Kaldor reasoning that does occur (outside traditional fields) will be the object of keen academic interest. And actual instances of a relatively new and allegedly wide ranging type of substantive reason merit the closest scrutiny, for substantive reasons have primacy within the common law.[83]

Notes

1. Summers, *Two Types of Substantive Reasons: The Core of a Theory of Common Law Justification*, 63 CORNELL L. REV. 707 (1978).

2. Id, 730-34.

3. Id, 730-32.

4. We do not canvass all the reasons why reasons are important in this article. We do assume that objectively sound reasons can be given. We also embrace intrinsic values. We are not unmindful however, that there are those who dissent (a decreasing number these days). See, e.g., Leff, *Economic Analysis of Law: Some Realism About Nominalism*, 60 VA. L. REV 451, 454 (1974).

5. See n. 1 *supra*, 735-52.

6. *Romano v Birmingham Ry, Light and Power Co* 182 Ala. 335, 340-41, 62 So 677, 678-9 (1933).

7. *Coleman v MacLennan*, 78 Kan. 711, 741, 98 P 281, 292 (1908).

8. *Campbell v Gruttemeyer*, 222 Tenn. 133, 137-40, 432 SW 2d 894, 896-97 (1968).

9. See n. 1 *supra*, 752-74. On the relations between the two types of reasons, see n 1 *supra*, 774-82.

10. *Frostifresh Corp v Reynoso*, 52 Misc. 2d 26, 27-28, 274 NYS 2d 757, 758-59 (Dist. Ct. 1966), rev'd on other grounds, 54 Misc. 2d 119, 281 NYS 2d 964 (App. Term, 2d Dep't 1967).

11. *Chase v Corcoran*, 106 Mass. 286, 288 (1871).

12. *Mercanti v Persson*, 160 Conn. 468, 478, 280 A 2d 137, 142 (1971).

13. The literature is growing rapidly. See, for example, G. Calabresi, THE COSTS OF ACCIDENTS (1970); H. Manne ed, THE ECONOMICS OF LEGAL RELATIONSHIPS (1975); Posner, *Utilitarianism, Economics, and Legal Theory*, 8 J. LEGAL STUD. 103 (1978).

14. There is dispute over the extent to which judges *implicitly* use economists' reasons. We cannot go into this here.

15. In this article we do not question the pervasive relevance of economic analysis to questions of means. This kind of relevance does not, however, give rise to autonomous economists' reasons. Further, we would caution against any form of thinking that divorces

goals from means here. See generally, Fuller, *Memorandum*, in ON THE TEACHING OF LAW IN THE LIBERAL ARTS CURRICULUM 37-43 (H. Berman ed 1956).

16. It simply will not do to say that economic analysis is normatively neutral or value neutral. Even the supposedly least controversial economists' criterion includes such words as 'better off' and 'worse off' (though from the point of view of affected individuals).

17. The literature on economists' reasons has become quite rich of late (and there is still more in the pipeline currently). See, for example, Baker, 'The Ideology of the Economic Analysis of Law', 5 *Phil. & Pub. Aff.* 3 (1975); Calabresi and Melamed, 'Property Rules, Liability Rules, and Inalienability: One View of the Cathedral', 85 HARV. L. REV. 1089 (1972); R. Dworkin, *Taking Rights Seriously,* 96-100 (1978); C. Fried, *Right and Wrong, Ch.* 4 (1978); Michelman, 'Norms and Normativity in the Economic Analysis of Law', 62 MINN. L. REV. 1015 (1978); Michelman, 'A Comment on Some Uses and Abuses of Economics in Law', 46 U. CHI. L. REV. 307 (1979); Posner, 'Utilitarianism, Economics, and Legal Theory', 8 J. LEGAL STUD. 103 (1978); Posner, 'Some Uses and Abuses of Economics in Law', *46* U. CHI. L. REV. 281 (1979); Schwartz, 'Economics, Wealth Distribution, and Justice', 1979 WIS. L. REV. 799 (1979); Steiner, 'Economics, Morality and the Law of Torts', 26 U. TOR. L. REV. 227 (1976); Symposium, 'Change in the Common Law: Legal and Economic Perspectives', 9 J. LEGAL STUD. 189-366 (1980). See also forthcoming symposia in the HOFSTRA LAW REVIEW with Professors Michelman, Dworkin, Kronman, Baker and others as contributors.

18. V. Pareto, MANUEL D'ECONOMIE POLITIQUE (2nd ed 1927). Of course a Pareto-superior reallocation may not be what economists call 'Pareto optimal'. It would be so only if no further reallocations could make someone better off without making anyone worse off. There are many variants of Pareto criteria. See, e.g., G. Calabresi and P. Bobbitt, TRAGIC CHOICES (1978).

19. We are not unmindful that this example is unrealistic in several respects. It nonetheless serves our purpose well, including the purpose of stressing the rarity of genuine Pareto-superior reasons (without compensation).

20. It is not even necessary in order for a judicial decision to bring about a Pareto-superior allocation that it do so by facilitating free market exchanges among the parties or others who might be affected by the decision. Indeed, a Pareto superior move is *theoretically* possible even though it involves no voluntary bargains or exchanges whatever. All that is required by the Pareto criterion is that (i) there be a reallocation (or redistribution) of goods and resources, and (ii) that no one affected by this reallocation be worse off and at least one be better off in relation to antecedent preference rankings. All that a judge needs to know is, for example, that the parties would agree to reallocation were it not for some impediment, e.g., that one of them has erroneous beliefs, for example, about what his initial stock of goods and resources is. In such a case, the court can order the relevant reallocation.

21. Perhaps further elaboration is called for. In general, we have an intuitive notion of what is yours and what is mine, but that may not be good enough, for a Pareto reason requires resolving close issues and doing narrow calculations in order to see whether the fundamental constraint on the availability of such a reason is violated, viz., that no one be worse off by

the decision. Consider our car dealer case. We built assumptions into that case designed to avoid these problems. But imagine a slightly different case, one in which there is no settled ban on protected groups such as the churches selling off rights to bring actions for violating the Sunday law against sales of cars. There would then be more voluntary transactions (for the costs of such transactions — risk of legal sanctions — would drop). Even the church groups could get into the bargaining act and offer to pay merchants to stay closed. The merchants would stay closed if the amount offered by church goers exceeded the expected profit to be made from Sunday car sales. There is a catch, however. *Before* the court renders its decision, there were restrictions on Sunday sales of cars. Those who would be willing to pay something to keep those restrictions in place — the churches — benefitted from such laws in a simple way: They were not faced with a situation in which they would have to pay anything to preserve the restriction. The question is: Do we say that the churches, prior to the court's decision, have a right to be free from Sunday car sales (or at least that they were the beneficiaries of the law) so that *this right* is to be included in their 'trading base' for purposes of the initial allocation? Or, are we to say that the churches were merely the beneficiaries of an externality set up by the restrictions and so no better off in relation to their shares before or after the court's decision to remove the restrictions? If the former, the churchgoers would suffer a loss from judicial removal of the ban on Sunday car sales (assuming they cared) and hence no Pareto-superior reason would be available to the court. Nothing in economic theory can determine this matter one way or another. But if the very availability of a Pareto reason depends on such a determination, then in a sense, the Pareto reason cannot have justificatory force unless its presupposition is justified. But such a justification of that presupposition — the criteria we set up for determining allocations — will not come from economic theory nor from any of the values typically implicated by economic theory. This fact calls in serious question the justificatory autonomy of Pareto reasons.

Now, one might think that a simple way around this difficulty would be to let the *existing* laws of property serve to determine who has or gets what under initial and resulting allocations. But of course, that maneuver won't work, as the foregoing example shows. Consider also cases in which property law is to be changed or is indeterminate or consider all those transactions, say in illegal goods, that do represent economic activity but in which the 'owners' of exchanged goods are not, for purposes of property law, considered to be owners or to have rights in those goods. But even if existing property law is taken to determine initial and resulting allocations, the justification for use of this criterion will be no better than the justification for that property law, and such justification will not rest on solely economic analysis, but often on policy-oriented, state-ordered distributions and redistributions.

One might be tempted to think a Kaldor reason — to be discussed later — is immune from such difficulties. But that would be a mistake. Indeed, such reasons could not avoid questions of initial allocations at least insofar as a determination of initial allocations will be relevant to determining (and setting limits on) a person's willingness to pay or what the aggregate gains and losses from the court's decision will be. And depending on our criteria, answers to such questions may be very different.

22. Of course, the churches could not reinstate the restriction later (once lifted) for there would then be losers (the car dealers) and Pareto analysis would not permit this. But the question posed in the text introduces a further fundamental kind of indeterminacy in such economic analysis: Suppose the judge knows now of a possible future change of mind by parties to be affected now. Should he take this into account now in determining whether there will be any losers from a contemplated decision?

23. We suggested earlier that one way in which a court decision could work a Pareto-superior allocation was that the court might order a reallocation that the parties would themselves bargain to but for one market imperfection or another that can't be overcome 'cost-effectively' in such a way that the indicated bargaining will actually occur. But what about the condition, 'would bargain to'? One is inclined to ask, 'would bargain to' under *what conditions* of information? Depending on how much information we assume the parties would have, we will get markedly different results. If we assume that the parties have too much information we may find that they would bargain differently than they would had the market simply taken its natural course, or we may even find that their whole ordering of preferences would have been different. If the parties have too little information, our results will again not track their real, informed preferences, even those that are *de facto*.

24. This may be thought to cast doubt on the very idea of an *economist's* reason. For when it comes to dealing with possible social goals such as net increases in psychological satisfaction, economists are head over heels in value theory, historically a well established branch of philosophy. This remains true even though economists adopt their own names (those of famous economists!) for the relevant value conceptions. More important, it remains true even though the reallocations of resources that their science is concerned with *characteristically* serve some general types of values.

25. The problem of trying to define in a fully satisfactory way a net increase in want realization is not one we can undertake here.

26. To evince respect for the choices of others is something else again, but we cannot go into the complexities of this.

27. The problem of defining a net increase in psychological satisfaction is not identical to the problem of defining a net increase in want realization. At least one can *imagine* computing the intensity and number of units of psychological satisfaction of different persons and multiplying accordingly. How one might do this with respect to wants, however, escapes us.

28. It may be noted that increased psychological satisfaction may derive not only from want realization. Third parties may become satisfied from an occurrence without having antecedently entertained a relevant want.

29. Of course, if the Pareto criterion has *already* been adopted in a relevant common law precedent, then it would become a relevant part of the justificatory analysis, even in a 'no change' case.

30. We should distinguish two senses of 'loser'. A person may be a loser in court without being a loser in relation to what he had initially. These are not, of course, identical. A property claimant, for example, may 'lose' in court, but it may be true that he never really had a good claim, and hence is not a loser in relation to what he had initially.

31. It is sometimes suggested that if courts were to require winners to pay compensation to all losers in, for example, overruling cases, after the compensation is paid, we would have a state of affairs that would be equivalent to a Pareto-superior one (provided costs of exacting and paying the compensation did not wipe out the gain). In this sense, there might be many Pareto-superior reasons. As we will later see, however, economists do not, *qua* economists, even claim that such losers are actually to be compensated. See also n. 50 *infra*.

32. Of course, there are borderline cases and we do not claim that all common law cases fall neatly within our four categories.

33. We name this reason for the economist Lord Kaldor. See Kaldor, *Welfare Propositions of Economics and Interpersonal Comparisons Of Utility,* 49 ECON. J. 549 (1939), in which the 'Kaldor criterion' (gainers gain more than losers lose) is set forth. Today, the criterion is also sometimes called the 'Kaldor-Hicks criterion'. See Hicks, *Foundations of Welfare Economics,* 49 ECON. J. 696 (1939).

34. For a classic statement of this aversion, see L. Robbins, AN ESSAY ON THE NATURE AND SIGNIFICANCE OF ECONOMIC SCIENCE (1935). See also Harsanyi, *Cardinal Welfare, Individualistic Ethics, and Interpersonal Comparisons of Utility,* 63 J. POL. ECON. 309 (1955).

35. See sources cited in n. 13 *supra*.

36. We do not hold that common law courts are not interested in net increases in the satisfaction of individuals! Courts do decide cases on the basis of such notions as 'freedom of contract', 'family harmony', 'public convenience', and 'smooth labour-management relations'.

37. See also *Jean v Foto* in the text.

38. The *Upland v Downland* case introduces what some economists call the 'cheaper cost avoider' principle: Downland is the cheaper cost avoider so Downland must bear the cost. This terminology, however, *is* misleading. It *will* not do merely to impose the cost on the cheaper cost avoider (Downland) without further inquiry into gains. In fact, the imposition of such cost on Downland would not be justified on economic analysis unless the benefit to Upland of blacktopping his driveway exceeded the cost to him of putting in the blacktopping *and* the external harm (or cost of avoiding such harm) to Downland. Otherwise, people like Upland could engage in activities of very low benefit to themselves and at the same time impose huge external costs on other parties merely because those other parties happened to be those who could most cheaply avoid the external harm generated by such activities. That would be the case here if the value to Upland of the blacktopping were only a few dollars more than the cost of its installation, *plus* the costs of most cheaply avoiding resulting harm.

39. Why a 'monopoly' case? Of course, at least in the United States, such a case would qualify in a somewhat extended sense as a 'common law' case. But more pertinently, the case illustrates an economists' reason in its most robust and indisputable form.

40. See Brown, *Toward an Economic Theory of Tort Liability*, 2 J. LEGAL STUD. 279 (1973). See also, Coons, 'Approaches to Court Imposed Compromise', 58 *Nw. L. Rev.* 750 (1964).

41. See our discussion of the *Jean v Foto* case in the text.

42. See n. 21 and accompanying text *supra*.

43. For a tiny sampling of the flavour of such analysis, see the price fixing case in the text.

44. The willingness to pay criterion is deployed over a wide range of contexts in R. Posner, THE ECONOMIC ANALYSIS OF LAW (2nd ed. 1977).

45. An alternative would be to apply the Kaldor analysis *directly* to determine satisfaction, contentment, utility, or whatever. To do this a judge would, of course, have to adopt some uniform unit of measurement (among other things).

46. See text between nn. 52 and 53 *infra*.

47. See, e.g., Baker, *The Ideology of the Economic Analysis of Law*, 5 PHIL. & PUB. AFF. 3 (1975).

48. *Utilitarianism, Economics and Legal Theory*, 8 J. OF LEGAL STUD. 103, 119 (1978).

49. A further problem with the willingness to pay criterion arises because of the 'Kelman effect' which, however, we do not explore here. See Kelman, *Consumption Theory, Production Theory, and Ideology in the Coase Theorem,* 52 SO. CALIF. L. REV. 669 (1979).

50. In most cases there will be additional positive costs of transferring compensation and (sometimes) of enforcing such transfers. Thus, in the *Edgar v Betsy* case, the likely cost would probably be small (if Betsy has $150 of readily disposable cash) — she can simply write Edgar a check. But in the price fixing case, the cost of compensation (and of providing it in such a way that the primary [justifying] gains to consumers aren't nullified) may be enormous. So in general, we cannot say that for every Kaldor transfer ordered without compensation there is a corresponding transfer (in which compensation is required) that is Pareto-superior *and* achieves
the same level of net gain overall.

51. See Kaldor, *Welfare Propositions of Economics and Interpersonal Comparisons of Utility*, 49 ECON J 549 (1939) and I. Little, A CRITIQUE OF WELFARE ECONOMICS (1955).

52. See section II, 3 of text.

53. See further on autonomy, text accompanying n. 26 *supra*.

54. See section II, 3 of text.

55. Note that any such direct measure would have to compare interpersonal satisfactions. Although it may in principle be possible to determine and net the number and intensity of satisfactions (unlike in the case of want realization), factual inquiries of this nature are extraordinarily difficult to make, and it is fairly certain that in many circumstances neither the data nor an appropriately non-arbitrary measure would be available.

56. It is logically possible that independent values of quite different kinds might be served by Kaldor reallocations. We are framing our discussion, however, as a search for values that might be thought of as more or less characteristically associated with such reallocations. But by 'characteristically' we do not envision either logical connection or perfect correlation.
This is not to say that quite different kinds of values cannot be realized in particular

cases by such reallocations, but whether they are and what they will be, will turn on the quite specific facts of the specific cases. If the specific facts of the case indicate that a certain Kaldor reallocation would serve a valuable independent goal, this would favour the reallocation. More importantly, depending on what wants people happen to have, a Kaldor reallocation in a particular case might disserve the goal in question. In that case, we would have a reason (perhaps) to render a decision that precisely was *not* Kaldor efficient. What seems distinctive about Kaldor reasons is that a goal, increasing net social gains generally delimited by the willingness to pay criterion, is invariant across such reasons. If any goal that has a chance of being intrinsically prizeable characteristically, but perhaps not perfectly, tracks the invariant goal of maximizing 'social gains', it is increased satisfaction, happiness, contentment, etc.

57. See Posner, *Utilitarianism, Economics and Legal Theory*, 8 J. LEGAL STUD. 103 (1978).

58. Note, however, that an economists' reason may be available (in certain circumstances) which supports a decision that is *not* the one among the available alternatives which maximizes resource worth the most. For example, suppose that there were three possible decisions, D1, D2, and D3, that a court could render in a particular case. Let the only affected resource be R. It might turn out that D1 maximizes the worth of R relative to D2 and D3, but that D2 maximizes the worth of R relative to D3, i.e., that D2 will result in a greater increase in the worth of R (or less of a diminution in the worth R) than would D3. Finally, suppose D1, the one of three which will increase the worth of R the most, must be rejected because of decisive reasons not derived from economics. D2 might be immune to such attacks. If so, it would still argue in favour of D2 over D3 that the former increased the worth of R more than did D3, i.e., if Kaldor reasons in fact have any independent and objective justificatory significance. Therefore, an economists' reason of this sort can be given to support a decision which does not maximize resource worth relative to all the other possible decisions. Thus, the general decisional criterion which mediates the relevance of Kaldor reasons to all possible decisions is best formulated as follows: *Ceteris paribus,* choose that decision that will increase the worth of affected resources *the most.*

59. Prior to any transfer, the resource or right involved has its maximum worth, i.e., there is some amount more than which no one will pay to obtain the resource, for the value of the resource cannot be affected by transferring it or awarding it to anyone. Prior to any transfer, the resource already had its maximum worth, i.e., there is some amount more than which no one will pay to obtain it. The existence of this amount and thus of its maximal worth remains constant through any transfers, freely bargained or court ordered.

60. See Posner, n. 57 *supra.*

61. Even if the virtues involved are intrinsically valuable, it is not clear that a Kaldor reallocation or pursuit of wealth maximization substantially promotes them or is the best way to promote them.

62. For discussion of these other reasons, see the article in n. 1, *supra.*

63. Professors Kenneth Arrow and Frank Michelman have pointed this out to us. What we offer here addressed to this issue is necessarily abbreviated.

64. Of course in our view Kaldor reasons *a fortiori* do not swallow up 'rightness reasons', even if for some purpose we may 'factor' them into the calculus. But we cannot go into this here.

65. We mean only two things by the words 'social goal': (1) that in general the goal is of a kind that may be pursued within the society on a broad social level and (2) that it is an appropriate goal for judges to try to serve, at least in some contexts. The general efficacy of court decisions as means of serving such goals is a complex matter we cannot go into here.

66. See section IV, 1 of the text, *supra*.

67. See n 1 *supra*, 735-51.

68. See n 1 *supra*, 752-53.

69. See text preceding n. 64 *supra*.

70. It might be thought that a judge simply cannot give a reason with justificatory force without putting it in some such *general* form envisioned in the text. But this is false. If we don't know what the general (aggregate) effects will be, it is still *a* reason for decision that a contemplated decision will increase one persons's satisfaction. It might also be thought that a reason a judge gives must always be in the form of a reason in support of a *rule* for a class of cases. This, too, is false, even with respect to goal reasons, for a judge may sufficiently know likely goal-serving effects of a projected decision to justify so deciding in the particular case yet not be able to identify sufficiently well the combination of general goal serving factors required to formulate a general rule.

71. One issue that we want to raise briefly (but cannot treat here in any detail) concerns the character of the economic generalizations supporting the predictions often ingredient in an economist's reason. Some might object to calling such generalizations 'causal' or 'empirical'; rather, it might still be said that these generalizations are really either tautological or definitional. The plausibility of this claim seems to depend, in the first instance at least, on what one takes the content of the relevant economic generalizations to be. For example, one economic generalization — that if price fixing is removed then, without more, the worth of affected resources will be maximized — could be interpreted as asserting only what is generally or likely to be the case and would not necessarily be interpreted as containing implicitly all of the assumptions, definitions, and boundary conditions that it would have to contain under some relatively formal presentation of micro-economic theory and welfare economics in order for it to assert an unqualified generalization (in the logician's sense). On the other hand, when one states a corresponding generalization in which all such assumptions and definitions are made quite explicit, they do seem to become more like tautologies. This would appear to hold for our pricefixing generalization, especially if we built into it the assumptions that, e.g., all affected parties will be rational (in the game theoretic sense), that there will be no unforeseen transaction or information costs (i.e., that consumers will learn of the lower, competitive prices), etc. From an epistemological point of view, a switch to the more explicit and guarded formulation has its price, for with each new explicit assumption and condition, the less clear it is that the generalization in question actually applies to the particular case at hand (even though on its own, the guarded generalization may be more certain). From a practical point of view, it would probably be

best for the judge to work with generalizations in which all relevant theoretical assumptions were explicit, for in this way he will be aware of precisely what he has to know about actual social conditions in order for his reason and its ingredient causal prediction to be sound.

72. See n. 1 *supra*, 735-51.

73. See n. 1 *supra*, 752-73.

74. Schwartz, *On the Utility of MacKay's Comparisons,* J. OF PHIL. 549 (1975).

75. See, e.g., R. Posner, THE ECONOMIC ANALYSIS OF LAW (2nd ed 1977).

76. For a more extended effort to canvass the 'legal' value of rules, see Summers, *Working Conceptions of the Law* 1 LAW AND PHILOSOPHY 301 (1982).

77. See discussion of *Jean v Foto* in the text.

78. See discussion of *Edgar v Betsy* and of *Jean v Foto* in the text.

79. '[T]he most desirable kind of rule ... is a rule which wears both a right situation reason and a clear scope criterion on its face'. K. N. Llewellyn, 'Grand Style and Formal Style Rules', in W. Twining, KARL LLEWELLYN AND THE REALIST MOVEMENT, 495 (1973).

80. See, e.g., R. Posner, THE ECONOMIC ANALYSIS OF LAW 18 (2nd ed. 1977) and remark in parenthetical text accompanying n. 38 *supra.*

81. Of course, Kaldor may already be 'built in'. Compare n. 29 *supra.*

82. See text *supra.*

83. Finally, we are painfully aware that we have not been able to treat in any kind of detail a number of important issues in value theory. These include the basic questions of whether voluntary choice or psychological satisfaction is intrinsically good and of what it is ultimately for a reason to be objectively sound or have genuine justificatory force. Here, we have only been able to identify those points at which economic analysis in the common law makes contact with value theory proper and to indicate what our intuitions on these issues are.

NAME INDEX

SUBJECT INDEX

Law and Philosophy Library

1. E. Bulygin, J.-L. Gardies and I. Niiniluoto (eds.): *Man, Law and Modern Forms of Life*. With an Introduction by M.D. Bayles. 1985   ISBN 90-277-1869-5

2. W. Sadurski: *Giving Desert Its Due*. Social Justice and Legal Theory. 1985
                                                    ISBN 90-277-1941-1

3. N. MacCormick and O. Weinberger: *An Institutional Theory of Law*. New Approaches to Legal Positivism. 1986   ISBN 90-277-2079-7

4. A. Aarnio: *The Rational as Reasonable*. A Treatise on Legal Justification. 1987
                                                    ISBN 90-277-2276-5

5. M.D. Bayles: *Principles of Law*. A Normative Analysis. 1987
                                    ISBN 90-277-2412-1; Pb: 90-277-2413-X

6. A. Soeteman: *Logic in Law*. Remarks on Logic and Rationality in Normative Reasoning, Especially in Law. 1989   ISBN 0-7923-0042-4

7. C.T. Sistare: *Responsibility and Criminal Liability*. 1989   ISBN 0-7923-0396-2

8. A. Peczenik: *On Law and Reason*. 1989   ISBN 0-7923-0444-6

9. W. Sadurski: *Moral Pluralism and Legal Neutrality*. 1990   ISBN 0-7923-0565-5

10. M.D. Bayles: *Procedural Justice*. Allocating to Individuals. 1990   ISBN 0-7923-0567-1

11. P. Nerhot (ed.): *Law, Interpretation and Reality*. Essays in Epistemology, Hermeneutics and Jurisprudence. 1990   ISBN 0-7923-0593-0

12. A.W. Norrie: *Law, Ideology and Punishment*. Retrieval and Critique of the Liberal Ideal of Criminal Justice. 1991   ISBN 0-7923-1013-6

13. P. Nerhot (ed.): *Legal Knowledge and Analogy*. Fragments of Legal Epistemology, Hermeneutics and Linguistics. 1991   ISBN 0-7923-1065-9

14. O. Weinberger: *Law, Institution and Legal Politics*. Fundamental Problems of Legal Theory and Social Philosophy. 1991   ISBN 0-7923-1143-4

15. J. Wróblewski: *The Judicial Application of Law*. Edited by Z. Bańkowski and N. MacCormick. 1992   ISBN 0-7923-1569-3

16. T. Wilhelmsson: *Critical Studies in Private Law*. A Treatise on Need-Rational Principles in Modern Law. 1992   ISBN 0-7923-1659-2

17. M.D. Bayles: *Hart's Legal Philosophy*. An Examination. 1992   ISBN 0-7923-1981-8

18. D.W.P. Ruiter: *Institutional Legal Facts*. Legal Powers and their Effects. 1993
                                                    ISBN 0-7923-2441-2

19. J. Schonsheck: *On Criminalization*. An Essay in the Philosophy of the Criminal Law. 1994
                                                    ISBN 0-7923-2663-6

20. R.P. Malloy and J. Evensky (eds.): *Adam Smith and the Philosophy of Law and Economics*. 1994   ISBN 0-7923-2796-9

21. Z. Bańkowski, I. White and U. Hahn (eds.): *Informatics and the Foundations of Legal Reasoning*. 1995   ISBN 0-7923-3455-8

Law and Philosophy Library

22. E. Lagerspetz: *The Opposite Mirrors*. An Essay on the Conventionalist Theory of Institutions. 1995 ISBN 0-7923-3325-X

23. M. van Hees: *Rights and Decisions*. Formal Models of Law and Liberalism. 1995 ISBN 0-7923-3754-9

24. B. Anderson: *"Discovery" in Legal Decision-Making*. 1996 ISBN 0-7923-3981-9

25. S. Urbina: *Reason, Democracy, Society*. A Study on the Basis of Legal Thinking. 1996 ISBN 0-7923-4262-3

26. E. Attwooll: *The Tapestry of the Law*. Scotland, Legal Culture and Legal Theory. 1997 ISBN 0-7923-4310-7

27. J.C. Hage: *Reasoning with Rules*. An Essay on Legal Reasoning and Its Underlying Logic. 1997 ISBN 0-7923-4325-5

28. R.A. Hillman: *The Richness of Contract Law*. An Analysis and Critique of Contemporary Theories of Contract Law. 1997 ISBN 0-7923-4336-0; 0-7923-5063-4 (Pb)

29. C. Wellman: *An Approach to Rights*. Studies in the Philosophy of Law and Morals. 1997 ISBN 0-7923-4467-7

30. B. van Roermund: *Law, Narrative and Reality*. An Essay in Intercepting Politics. 1997 ISBN 0-7923-4621-1

31. I. Ward: *Kantianism, Postmodernism and Critical Legal Thought*. 1997 ISBN 0-7923-4745-5

32. H. Prakken: *Logical Tools for Modelling Legal Argument*. A Study of Defeasible Reasoning in Law. 1997 ISBN 0-7923-4776-5

33. T. May: *Autonomy, Authority and Moral Responsibility*. 1998 ISBN 0-7923-4851-6

34. M. Atienza and J.R. Manero: *A Theory of Legal Sentences*. 1998 ISBN 0-7923-4856-7

35. E.A. Christodoulidis: *Law and Reflexive Politics*. 1998 ISBN 0-7923-4954-7

36. L.M.M. Royakkers: *Extending Deontic Logic for the Formalisation of Legal Rules*. 1998 ISBN 0-7923-4982-2

37. J.J. Moreso: *Legal Indeterminacy and Constitutional Interpretation*. 1998 ISBN 0-7923-5156-8

38. W. Sadurski: *Freedom of Speech and Its Limits*. 1999 ISBN 0-7923-5523-7

39. J. Wolenski (ed.): *Kazimierz Opalek Selected Papers in Legal Philosophy*. 1999 ISBN 0-7923-5732-9

40. H.P. Visser 't Hooft: *Justice to Future Generations and the Environment*. 1999 ISBN 0-7923-5756-6

41. L.J. Wintgens (ed.): *The Law in Philosophical Perspectives*. My Philosophy of Law. 1999 ISBN 0-7923-5796-5

42. A.R. Lodder: *DiaLaw*. On Legal Justification and Dialogical Models of Argumentation. 1999 ISBN 0-7923-5830-9

43. C. Redondo: *Reasons for Action and the Law*. 1999 ISBN 0-7923-5912-7

Law and Philosophy Library

44. M. Friedman, L. May, K. Parsons and J. Stiff (eds.): *Rights and Reason.* Essays in Honor of Carl Wellman. 2000   ISBN 0-7923-6198-9

45. G.C. Christie: *The Notion of an Ideal Audience in Legal Argument.* 2000
ISBN 0-7923-6283-7

46. R.S. Summers: *Essays in Legal Theory.* 2000   ISBN 0-7923-6367-1

KLUWER ACADEMIC PUBLISHERS – DORDRECHT / BOSTON / LONDON